BRETT KEBBLE

BRETT KEBBLE
THE INSIDE STORY

BARRY SERGEANT

ZEBRA

Published by Zebra Press
an imprint of Struik Publishers
(a division of New Holland Publishing (South Africa) (Pty) Ltd)
PO Box 1144, Cape Town, 8000
New Holland Publishing is a member of Johnnic Communications Ltd

www.zebrapress.co.za

First published 2006

3 5 7 9 10 8 6 4 2

Publication © Zebra Press 2006
Text © Barry Sergeant 2006

Cover photographs © Robert Botha/*Business Day* (side view of Brett Kebble),
Sunday Times (Kebble giving speech), *Beeld* (car) and AP Photo/Obed Zilwa (funeral)

Lyrics for 'Another One Bites the Dust' on pp. 162–3,
reproduced with permission of EMI Music Publishing

Lyrics for 'Mac the Knife', on p. 261, written by Bertolt Brecht, Kurt Weill
and Marc Blitzstein, reproduced courtesy of Arcadia Music/Sheer Publishing

PUBLISHING MANAGER: Marlene Fryer
MANAGING EDITOR: Robert Plummer
EDITOR: Marlène Burger
PROOFREADER: Ronel Richter-Herbert
COVER AND TEXT DESIGNER: Natascha Adendorff-Olivier
TYPESETTER: Monique van den Berg
INDEXER: Robert Plummer
PRODUCTION MANAGER: Valerie Kömmer

Set in 10.5 pt on 14.5 pt Minion

Reproduction by Hirt & Carter (Cape) (Pty) Ltd
Printed and bound by Paarl Print, Oosterland Street, Paarl, South Africa

ISBN 1-77007-306-X

This is for Cay Petraseni

Contents

Acknowledgements

T HE FIRST WORDS of this book were written on 25 November 2005; the final chapter was done over two days in the last week of March 2006. This apparent spurt of energy on my part belies the great length of time during which the story was writing itself. I first encountered Brett Kebble nearly a decade before he died, but the story had really been going on since 1991.

Across this expanse of time I worked with, and made the acquaintance of, a number of people who contributed, wittingly or otherwise, to this story in both the broad and narrow sense.

Without applying a chronology that a polymath would no doubt insist on, I wish first and foremost to thank all those who contributed to the book but who cannot be named here. They have been acknowledged in other ways. These are the individuals who know too much detail, or who gained knowledge without actively seeking it, or who would be compromised if mentioned by name. There are also individuals who fear for their safety, and specifically asked not to be identified. This book is about Brett Kebble's business career, but in many ways it is a distillation of the stories of so many unnamed individuals. To them, once again, thank you.

The question of relevance always loomed. It was never easy knowing exactly what was relevant to Kebble's business operations. His life was characterised by apparently seamless shifts from business to politics, from mining to fishing, from the arts to property development, from black economic empowerment to ventures – real or imagined – into Angola, and so on. But a line had to be drawn in the sand, and for reasons of irrelevance an entire section of the original manuscript, running to about 27 000 words, was given the chop. Those stories are relevant, but not here.

There are a good number of people who did not contribute to this book as such, but were critically important to my various apprenticeships. It would not have been possible to fully understand Kebble's transactions – real or imagined – without the experience gained, in particular, offshore. Kebble's first really big trick was, of course, one that involved offshore transactions: the acquisition by Randgold & Exploration of BHP Minerals Mali in October 1996.

During the mid-1990s, the offshore partner of BoE Securities, where I was in gainful employment, was the Royal Bank of Canada. The Canadians, like the South

Africans and Australians, suffer a natural bent towards resources, but the Canadians are in a class of their own.

To Robert Lee and Ernie Nutter, Royal Bank of Canada stalwarts who introduced me to their clients on Wall Street, my thanks. Their introductions were generous and enthusiastic, and I was allowed without disturbance to present my analysis of South African and African stocks to clients housed within the electrifying atmosphere of the world's biggest capital market. It was here, more than in London, Toronto or Sydney, and certainly Johannesburg or Cape Town, that I gained the deepest and most enduring understanding of the multifaceted process of investing. Those guys on Wall Street are very good, even if they suffer the ignominy of non-linear events such as Enron. Without being over-defensive, even the very best money managers have to draw a line between belief and suspicion. There are just too many stories around, too many companies and too many opportunities. If suspicion ruled the investment world, there would be no Wall Street. When evil rules over good, there will be no world at all.

Nutter and Lee also introduced me to the more social side of Wall Street, and Greenwich Village, which is a particularly fine place, if you can afford it. Ernie has since moved to the Capital Group of Companies, and can be found, when he is in town, at 181 Bay Street, Toronto, just around the corner from the RBC headquarters. Robert, one of the most professional and knowledgeable sales traders in global resources, is still at RBC, or RBC Capital Markets, to be precise. What would a summer Sunday in Toronto be without Robert Lee, his barbecue and the biggest, juiciest porterhouse steaks in Canada?

Earlier, BoE's offshore partner had been NatWest Markets, and during that era I was a happy apprentice alongside Alan Heap at County NatWest in Sydney. He is still in the same city, but with Citigroup Smith Barney. Like Nutter, Heap is a commodities expert and they are two guys at the top of their profession.

BoE Securities arose from the mid-1990s' acquisition by BoE of Ed Hern, Rudolph, a fantastic firm of stockbrokers in its day, where I had the privilege of working with some outstanding analysts, not least Tom Dale. He is one of a kind, a leading light and a good friend and one of the few people I know who can see through three inches of steel.

On the topic of Ed Hern, Rudolph, there was something of a flashback in the latter days of 2005. While writing this book, when I was sending out flares about the accounts of companies wrecked by Kebble, Johan Blersch, one-time CEO of Ed Hern, Rudolph, appeared out of nowhere on an entirely different matter. Having called me about an article I had written, Blersch – one of the sharpest minds ever known in South African stockbroking and investment banking, too young to now be independently retired – volunteered to untangle the Kebble numbers. It helped enormously that he is a chartered accountant by training, but any oversights or omissions are for my account. Thank you to Johan, not only for the accounts, but also for the many insights and the privilege of working together.

For the period in the early and mid-1990s when I was deeply involved with West Africa, I express appreciation to James Anaman of Ashanti Goldfields for his kindness, courtesy and wise counsel; to Greg Hawkins in Accra for his big heart and willingness to share his enormous expertise; and to Glyn Lewis, a great friend, for his hospitality during my many visits to Tarkwa, especially in the early days when there seemed to be so little hope. Then again, there was always that big, cool clubhouse up on the hill, and the old cooler with lots of iced beer that still had old-fashioned real bottle tops.

Thank you also to John Barker (then *also* with RBC) for the long chats in the deep shade at Obuasi, the Ashanti Goldfields flagship. From those bygone days as well, my thanks to another man from the RBC stable, Simon Catt, who showed all of us that the most complicated investment idea in the world can be lucidly expressed in less than 200 written words. Simon has now settled in London and recently became a father for the second time.

My appreciation also goes to two investment analysts in particular from the BoE Securities days in Johannesburg: Paul Smith (now independent), and Henk de Hoop (now with Barnard Jacobs Mellet), both leading examples of outstanding integrity.

Staying with the professionals, thanks also to Georges Lequime, currently at RBC in London, for his insights into Western Areas and gold stocks in general. One of his colleagues, Mark Smith, has done astounding work researching and identifying mining opportunities north of the Limpopo, and has played a big role, in particular, in opening up the Democratic Republic of the Congo to serious offshore investment. These are the kind of guys who can get this continent ticking the way it should have been decades ago.

Back in Johannesburg, thanks also to Ashwin Mancha, incorrigible fund manager, a friend from law school and again at Ed Hern, Rudolph and BoE Securities. Ashwin is one of those entirely and eternally cheerful people. Early in 2006 he called me from Afrifocus, where he is CEO, to reminisce about my early battles with Brett Kebble. When the chips were down, I know that Ashwin played his cards for me.

For lots of willing and able help in collecting some of the basic research material and data, thank you to Pauline Mawson and to two of my colleagues in particular at *Moneyweb*, Gareth Tredway and Julius Cobbett.

This was always going to be a challenging manuscript, technically not least, and when I was sending out huge flares, Zebra Press, the publishers, were watching over the horizon from Cape Town. Marlene Fryer, a gem, came to the rescue and said that I would be working with *the* best editor. Marlène Burger has been the best editor, a professional with rare qualities and immeasurable insight. Thank you to her, and the team at Zebra, not least another consummate professional, Robert 'the doctor' Plummer.

I have a number of particular reasons for mentioning Alec Hogg, my colleague and, of course, the founder of *Moneyweb*. He has been a constant source of inspiration and encouragement. His devotion to the media is unparalleled and his resolution is as clear as can be found in anyone. When the storm clouds gather and the day is dark, Alec can suddenly turn the world around. We first worked together just over 20 years ago, and this year have been joined by another colleague from that era, David Carte. We also have the wise counsel, in-house, of Jim Jones, editor of *Mineweb*. Jim has been a Kebble critic since Brett first stuck his head above the parapet. To all of those at *Moneyweb*, thank you for enduring my presence, and for your professionalism.

Brian Gibson, who took over the almost impossible communications role at JCI Ltd and Randgold & Exploration after Kebble's ousting, deserves a special word of thanks.

In a broader sense, I would like to acknowledge the influence and inspiration of some favourite writers: Ernest Hemingway, Robert Sabbag and Hunter S Thompson (plus that master lyricist, Warren Zevon). It would be quite the story if Harry Morgan met up with The Duke of Grace in the Confusion. They would have to meet once in Bukavu and once in the Caribbean. Those would be stories for another day.

In a broader sense, thank you to all those with whom I mixed in the mid-90s, in yet another kind of apprenticeship as I travelled to and worked in both of the Americas, Australia, Western Europe, the United Kingdom and various parts of Africa north of the Limpopo River. I was deep in the Amazon, a patron of the strip clubs of Kalgoorlie, manned dealing desks in Toronto and London, deep inside Colombia's narco-economy, in and around the sweatlands of Timbuktu (land of the fabulous Tuareg) and carousing in textbook-perfect Melbourne. I endured the challenge of a Canadian winter, discovered the chaos of a modernising Ghana, navigated the never-ending urban sprawl of São Paulo, visited with hedge funds on Wall Street, tried to charm an exotic gypsy girl on the Left Bank of the Seine, went as a corporate traveller to Sioux City, Iowa, crossed the continental divide to San Antonio, Texas, loved the madness of the Ouagadougou Grand Market in that bicycle-plagued capital of Burkina Faso, floated on the Niger River alongside Bamako, dined in the elegant restaurants of Abidjan, watched the gorgeous girls go by at LeBlonde beach in Rio de Janeiro and tarried a while in that mud-infested little country they call Suriname, known only for producing a few Dutch soccer stars. It's been one hell of a life.

I am especially grateful for one particularly vivid memory of the lonely outback of Ghana, on the Yamfo concession, at the Ntotoroso anomaly and on other properties that today comprise the Ahafo project. In those early days, no one, outside of a few members of the Gencor exploration team, had heard any of those names. I am happy to report that today Newmont, a Tier 1 gold-digger, is developing Ghana into its 'fifth core district'. At Ahafo, Newmont has added 8.9 million ounces of reserves since acquiring the project in 2002, closing 2005 with reserves of 12.2 million ounces. The first gold from Ahafo should be poured later this year. Ahafo has a current mine life of more than 20 years, and at full production should produce 550 000 ounces annually. Exploration at Ahafo remains among Newmont's highest priorities and is focused on 11 existing ore bodies within the project.

Finally, thank you to Craig Stevens, my friend from university days, for listening to me and allowing me to bend his ear so many times. And thank you to the one coded as Honey Bunny. She was the most patient and encouraging of all.

BARRY SERGEANT
7 APRIL 2006
ROSEBANK, JOHANNESBURG

Love or lust makes man sick, and wine much sicker;
Ambition rends, and gaming gains a loss;
But making money, slowly first, then quicker,
And adding still a little through each cross
(Which will come over things), beats love or liquor,
The gamester's counter, or the statesman's dross.
O Gold! I still prefer thee unto paper,
Which makes bank credit like a bark of vapour.

– **George Gordon Byron,** *Don Juan,*
Canto the Twelfth, Stanza IV

Prologue

A S SWIFTLY AND SILENTLY as he had appeared, the mystery man melted into the darkness. Behind him, the silver sedan's powerful motor continued to purr, incongruous testimony to German engineering.

The car's nose was scrunched against the railings that had offered the only bulwark against a headlong plunge onto South Africa's busiest highway, several metres below. The headlights pierced the black void through the metal slats. The unnatural angle at which the crippled vehicle had mounted the kerbstones would instinctively prompt a passer-by to call paramedics, the police, anyone schooled in dealing with what must surely have been an accident.

But the cellphone call made from the overpass by the mystery man was not to summon help. He knew all too well that there was nothing random about the extremely large and lifeless body slumped behind the steering wheel of the car with Cape Town registration plates. As he pressed the number of someone awaiting his call in Pretoria, he alone knew the full and shocking truth. Moments before, in a most deliberate act, a hired gun had spewed seven 9-mm bullets through the open window on the driver's side. A lesser quarry would have died instantly, but in macabre defiance of all natural law, this one had somehow managed to propel the Mercedes S-600 some 500 metres down the deserted, tree-lined street before surrendering to his fate.

As the car drifted across the thankfully empty right-hand lane, rolled onto the kerb and came to a halt, as the lifeblood literally drained from the holes in his upper body, the driver's three assassins got the hell away from their carefully chosen kill zone.

Some of the vagrants sleeping rough at the nearby garden refuse dump might have seen their VW Polo leave. One hobo might even have watched as the mystery man came out of nowhere to review their handiwork. None of them would have understood why it mattered that the man who had just been murdered at the age of 41 was Brett Kebble.

There was a chill in the air, and later that night, it would rain. Weather-wise, the day had been about as perfect as only early spring on the Highveld can be. But for Kebble, as one newspaper would later report, Tuesday 27 September 2005 was the day on which the perfect storm that had been building for months made landfall in his personal domain.

Of the 14 years since Kebble insinuated himself into South Africa's take-no-prisoners mining sector as the 'golden boy', none had been as shitty as what the country's new black elite referred to as twenty-oh-five. He and his father Roger had lost their last chance to get charges of fraud, conspiracy and insider trading dropped and would now have to go to trial. The National Prosecuting Authority had offered a plea bargain, but insisted that Kebble would have to serve jail time, though this might be no more than 90 days, so he had turned them down. He was only marginally more terrified of spending a single hour in one of South Africa's prisons than he was of staying overnight in any African state north of the Limpopo. Besides, a guilty plea would bar him from serving as a company director.

And then there was the bloody tax probe. The SA Revenue Service had been sniffing around since 2000, when some or other snoop discovered that Brett hadn't filed a personal tax return since 1993. His stable of consultants had managed to keep SARS at bay for months, but by April 2006, they would be aggressively going after at least R250 million that Brett and Roger between them owed in back taxes.

There had been unusually high emotional demands, too. Relationships within the family were tense, but it was the black economic empowerment (BEE) brigade that had been neediest of late. Deals that ought to have been closed months before were jammed up, others were stalled somewhere along the pipeline, yet the players still expected their monthly sweeteners, and more. Not long before, Kebble had forked out R600 000 to a Nigerian druglord to settle a cocaine debt run up by one of his 'celebrity' black empowerment patsies.

His own stockbroking account was in the red to the tune of R80 million; a clutch of his favourite toy boy Vaughn's fellow escorts – both male and female – had resorted to blackmail; he'd had to place some of his best-loved properties in both the Cape and Sandton on the market; the Gulfstream and the Learjet were grounded; the fleet of Ferraris and other luxury vehicles was shrinking by the day.

None of this, though, had been as stressful as the bruising showdown from which Kebble had emerged on 30 August not only jobless, but effectively penniless. To be sure, it was deeply humiliating to have been forced out as chief executive of JCI, Randgold & Exploration and Western Areas amid a scramble to locate more than 14 million missing shares and the rest of almost R2 billion that he had siphoned off various company accounts. But the consummate crisis was that he could no longer dip into the corporate piggy bank that had funded not only his personal profligacy for more than a decade, but had also financed the flamboyant lifestyles of those he had made rich and almost famous.

The cash cows had been milked dry. Trading of both Randgold & Exploration and JCI shares was suspended by the Johannesburg Stock Exchange on 1 August, triggering the boardroom end game that culminated in Kebble being booted out. On 21 September, the international ramifications of the nascent scandal had come into sharp focus when the US Nasdaq took the grave step of delisting Randgold & Exploration. For weeks, even as he mustered his considerable charm, charisma and media cheerleaders to spin catastrophe into a *coup de maître*, Kebble had been a truly desperate and frightened man.

It wasn't that he was unduly concerned about the death threats. There had been so many, for so long, that they had almost become routine, and besides, killers with genuine intent rarely warned their victims. Nevertheless, he had hired Clinton Nassif of Central National Security Services in 2004 to ramp up existing precautions, and when the situation warranted, he'd even called on Calla Botha, former rugger-bugger and erstwhile member of the apartheid government's innocuously named hit squad, the Civil Cooperation Bureau.

After all, someone had shot Stephen Mildenhall, chief investment officer at Allan Gray, outside his Cape Town home in August, and Allan Gray was the single biggest institutional shareholder in JCI, Randgold & Exploration and Western Areas. No one had linked the shooting to the firm's involvement in Kebble-led companies, but a little extra protection couldn't hurt. With that in mind, Kebble had recently revisited his life insurance policies and increased them to a whopping R80 million.

The irony was that while his unassuming wife Ingrid and their children, Matthew, Andrew, Hannah and sweet little Lily, stood to inherit a fortune, life as they knew it depended on Kebble finding R5 million, fast. For more than a dozen years, he had cunningly fooled investors, family, friend and foe alike with a slew of bogus transactions involving billions, yet not worth the paper they were written on. But he had never figured out the cash conundrum. There had been assets aplenty and shares by the million, but hard cash was the chimera Kebble never vanquished. No matter how much or how often he stole from the more than 80 companies under his control, regardless of the type and volume of contraband he moved, irrespective of the political patronage he sought and paid for, Brett Kebble's cash anorexia was incurable.

A frugal man might have stashed several hundred krugerrands or a velvet pouch of uncut diamonds somewhere safe for the proverbial rainy day. But Kebble had got away with grand larceny and grotesque looting for so long that rational thought had been subsumed by hubris. Since being sacked, he had called on every business associate and underworld operator still willing to give him the time of day, all but begging them for help to raise the five measly million he needed just to meet his immediate obligations. They were impervious to his pleas; there was nothing left to grift and his doggerel verse was falling on deaf ears. And then, finally, one man tossed out a lifeline.

True, he was a dangerous man, this Mr X, someone no right-thinking individual would dare to double-cross, but Kebble had been doing dirty business with him since 2002. It had started with cigarettes and cannabis, then run the gamut of organised crime on a global scale, involving Asian triads and the Irish mafia, London gangsters and African warlords with blood diamonds to go.

The deal had been slated to go down 24 hours earlier. Kebble had advanced his weekly Tuesday commute from Cape Town to Johannesburg for that very purpose, draining one of his last active bank accounts of R200 000 on arrival. On Monday night, as he drove to their prearranged rendezvous, Kebble spoke to Mr X and learnt that there was a last-minute hitch – not serious enough to abort the transaction, but sufficiently important to warrant a delay. In due course, cellphone records would show that Kebble was at or very near the Melrose Bird Sanctuary, between the Glenhove and Atholl Oaklands off-ramps on the highway from Johannesburg to Pretoria, when that conversation took place.

On Tuesday 27 September, he lunched with financial journalist David Gleason, his friend of 28 years and unchallenged leader of the pro-Kebble media pack. Around 7 p.m., as the polo ponies at the nearby Inanda Club were being bedded down for the night, spin doctor and Washington-trained lobbyist Dominic Ntsele arrived at Kebble's home-away-from-home, the magnificent property set in splendid land-scaped gardens behind sturdy walls at 65 Fifth Avenue, Illovo. They had originally planned to have breakfast together, but despite the fact that Kebble already had a dinner date, had opted for an early supper instead. A cheerful blaze was crackling in the big fireplace in the main reception room, where the two men chatted briefly before sitting down to a simple meal of steak and salad.

The hands on the expensive timepiece that graced the mantelpiece were nudging 8.30 when Ntsele took his leave. Shortly afterwards, his driver Joseph having been given the night off, Kebble eased himself behind the wheel of his Mercedes and gently rolled down the 50-metre driveway, past the manned guardhouse at the electronic gate and turned right into the quiet suburban street. By South African standards, it was late to be setting off for dinner, but his host, Sello Rasethaba, chief executive of Matodzi Resources, Kebble's BEE 'flagship', lived only a ten-minute drive away, traffic permitting.

Oddly, though, when Kebble's butler Andrew Minnaar went off duty around 9 p.m., he was surprised to see his employer's car parked just a little way down Fifth Avenue, the lights and engine both switched off. How long had he been there, and why, have yet to be revealed, but at some point within the next 30 minutes, Kebble was trundling slowly east along Melrose Street Extension, having spoken to Mr X again, the call relayed through the same cellphone mast as their conversations the night before.

Making his way past historic suburbs to Melrose, Kebble might have wondered idly whether Sello's guests would include deceased ANC president Oliver Tambo's film-maker son Dali, former Namibian premier Hage Geingob and the retired MPLA general who were all involved in trying to salvage the lucrative but troublesome Koketso diamond deal in Angola's Lunda Norte province.

But as he approached the pretty little stone bridge over the stream running under Melrose Street, Kebble's mind would have been focused on nothing but the package he would soon hold in his hands.

At the loneliest point of the leafy, fairly well-lit street, with the bird sanctuary on his left, Kebble brought the big Mercedes to a gentle halt and pressed the button to open the window to his right. Two men stepped out from their hiding place under one of the big bluegum trees on the left, close to where the park fence had been cut. They must have been waiting for a while. Police later recovered at least ten Camel cigarette butts from the ground under the tree. A third man held vigil in the VW Polo, out of sight. Two members of the trio had arrived in South Africa very recently, after a circuitous journey that included Mozambique as the last leg. The third was from Pretoria. But would anyone ever know who had paid for this evening's deadly events? Was it, as some have speculated, Kebble himself?

One of the men, holding a small box, sauntered towards Kebble's car. There was nothing menacing about his approach, and even though it was a quiet road and a dark night in the world capital of violent crime, Kebble had no foreboding of danger. Mr X had briefed him well, and in a few minutes he could drive on to keep his dinner date.

Suddenly, with clinical precision and at the speed of lightning, there was a gun, and seven muzzle flashes cleaved the night at such close range that Kebble must have tasted sulphur in the instant before adrenalin flooded his mortally wounded body, allowing him to hit the accelerator.

By 9.30 p.m., it was over. Mr X had made sure of that before placing his call to Pretoria from the overpass.

PART I

Catch me if you can

1

Fifth horseman of the apocalypse

WHEN HE WAS not in fitful sleep, Brett Kebble lived his life like a combine harvester running on an oversized tank of jet fuel. No matter the problem, project or person in his path, the Kebble juggernaut rolled on, chewed it up and spat it out, propelling countless shards of junk skyward, eventually to rain down fretfully on the scorched earth he left behind.

One of his greatest pieces of combine harvester art was unveiled on 9 December 2004, when he announced the Orlyfunt black economic empowerment (BEE) deal. By that juncture, Kebble had cultivated a R5-million-a-month spending habit. He was flying around in some of the smartest private jets in South Africa. The larger of the pair, a Gulfstream II, carried a $16 million price tag. The smaller Bombardier Learjet 45 was a snip at a mere $6 million.

The aircraft were among the toys that Kebble passed off as his own in order to foster his self-made reputation as one of the most powerful businessmen in the land. He had invested countless millions in creating his public image, but woefully little of the story was true. His entourage, which worked tirelessly to promote his profile, was paid partly by him and partly by the listed companies he ran like his own backyard chopshop.

One of the truths was that Kebble was an accomplished pianist; another was that he had powerful political connections. It was also true that he had moulded himself into something of an arts patron by sponsoring a competition that showered cash on starving painters, sculptors and crafters two years in a row, though contrary to popular belief, the money did not come out of any personal Kebble pockets.

This alone might explain why the highly publicised 2006 Kebble Art Awards, already at an advanced stage when the founder died, were cancelled with unseemly haste by his family.

For the most part, the rest of what scriptwriters and actors refer to as 'the back story' had been spun and twisted and contorted so often and so consummately that almost no one questioned any of it. Even mainstream media watchdogs rolled over and became bedazzled, bemused lapdogs, panting about Kebble's self-invented reputation as a mining magnate so faithfully that, while he lived, it remained all but unsullied by the bald truth.

And the truth is that Brett Kebble, gunned down at the age of 41, was one of the sharpest confidence tricksters the South African investment community has ever hosted.

Kebble, apparent man of wealth and taste, was a slick con man with the instincts of a street fighter and an imminent willingness to apply them. He had a black heart and a dark soul and, at some point in his life, he had decided that he would play by his own rules. By the time the Orlyfunt deal came around, Kebble was a truly desperate man. His days were spent frenetically nurturing his BEE connections and the political obligations they carried. He was also involved in numerous attempts to rescue his faltering empire, built from the start on sand – or the powdery dust of the mine dumps that had surrounded Johannesburg before advanced technology and urban sprawl conspired to demolish them.

Kebble was in dire financial straits. Since 1996, when he pulled off some of the most agile acrobatics any stock exchange has ever seen, he had been cash-starved. He had assets and control and wads of paper to prove it, but his pockets, never deep, were empty. After seizing control of a vast array of assets in 1997 – of which only one, Western Areas, was sound – Kebble had embarked on a massive asset-stripping exercise. In immaculately disguised transactions shot through with spin, he sold off assets – or more commonly, bits of assets – and raised hundreds of millions of dollars. But long before he was forced to invent Orlyfunt, the money was all gone.

Fed to media sycophants as a black-owned investment giant run by 'experienced entrepreneurs', Orlyfunt would acquire an extensive portfolio of BEE entities and various mineral right interests for the sum of R1.4 billion from the venerated and long-established JCI.

Nine months later, Kebble would be dead and JCI in disarray, his legacy a convoluted financial travesty that would take months, if not years, to untangle.

After 1996, when he was involved in Randgold & Exploration's acquisition of BHP Minerals Mali and its rotting gold mine at Syama, and 1997, when he hijacked JCI from Mzi Khumalo's African Mining Group consortium, almost none of Kebble's deals stood up. One exception was the Gem Diamonds deal, finalised in 2000, but that was relatively small potatoes for Kebble, and besides, he had hopelessly underestimated the true value of Saxendrift. He had sold out too early on Gem Diamonds, and for too little.

In 1996, Kebble – half nerd, half wolf – had an inalienable confidence in his own abilities. Surrounded by the right people, he was a man in the right place at the right time.

After 1997, he mutated into a parody of his former self, leaving a swathe of destruction in his wake, a wasteland littered with broken promises and damaged people. By the time he announced the Orlyfunt deal, he was less sure of himself. His business model, if he ever had one, was flawed from the outset, because someone had forgotten about cash.

In his scramble to find hard currency, Kebble had acquired a slew of companies, most of them worthless or useless. By the end of 2004, he controlled some 85 entities, but he had no money. From the start, Kebble had perversely specialised in acquiring assets that gobbled cash as eagerly as he swallowed acclaim. The hundreds of millions of dollars he had raised by selling off the family silver from 1998 to 2002 were gone, mostly spent on delusions, on deals that went wrong, on the trappings of a rich-and-famous lifestyle, on luring useful characters from the BEE scene into his web.

His father Roger, who joined Brett in business in 1991, had been of little help, but perhaps that was not entirely his fault. Touted by the Kebble propaganda machine as a seasoned mining engineer, Roger, born on 9 November 1939, was never more than a mine captain, a shift boss with a mine manager's certificate.

Which is not to suggest that Roger was anything but a fine mine captain. Indeed, he might well have been an exceptional one, but a lifelong career in the shadow of a gold mine's headgear does not automatically equip a man to run an empire.

By 2002, however, Roger was a director of more than 90 companies and the keeper of almost as many secrets as his eldest son.

Part of the legerdemain generated by the mighty Kebble publicity machine was that Roger had sold his wine farm and emerged from retirement to join Brett in business in the early 1990s. The less exotic version was that Roger had quit his job with Anglo American to help his son when Brett ran into some kind of trouble dealing foreign exchange.

Brett had come of age as a forex dealer when he quit Mallinicks, a Cape Town law firm, where he was an articled clerk after graduating from the University of Cape Town in 1988. Born in the mining town of Springs, east of Johannesburg, he had a schizophrenic childhood. Home was a series of rough and dusty communities that depended on gold for their very existence, such as Klerksdorp, southwest of the Reef, and Welkom in the northern Free State.

School was the prestigious parochial St Andrew's, in the Free State capital of Bloemfontein, where Brett was a boarder and rubbed shoulders with the sons of wealthy, influential farmers and industrialists. As a teenager, he met David Gleason, who would become a family friend and, as a business journalist, be one of Kebble's most strident media champions.

Brett served his legal apprenticeship with diligence and passed all the exams required for admission as an attorney, but it's doubtful that he ever intended making a career out of practising law.

He did make some useful contacts during his three years at Mallinicks, among them Judy Moon, an attractive blonde who would marry Tokyo Sexwale, a former political prisoner on Robben Island. The charismatic Sexwale went on to become the first premier of South Africa's richest province, Gauteng, and head of the hugely successful Mvelaphanda group.

What Brett did not have at Mallinicks was the largest office, though this would certainly be suggested by his spin doctors. He did, however, buy his own suite of office furniture.

When he quit the firm in 1991, it was to open his own office and move 15 floors upstairs, though exactly what he did from there is somewhat vague. Those who claim to know about such things are adamant, however, that it was not a law office.

The passage of time and the expertise of fudge artists have blurred the details of what happened next, but it is beyond question that Brett Kebble, lawyer, fell foul of the law. While dealing foreign exchange for a diamond firm situated in Franschhoek, a quaint and picturesque town in the heart of the Cape winelands, he got caught with his hands in the cookie jar. His breach of the stringent foreign exchange regulations was so grave that he found himself in serious trouble, and went whimpering to his daddy. Naturally, as any concerned father would, Roger stepped in, but he found himself confronted by Hobson's choice.* It was no small bail out and the consequences were tough. Brett, the dutiful son, was heavily obliged and Roger, the caring sire, would make damn sure he got the payback he deserved. If he was going back into the mining industry, it was not going to be as an employee, but as the boss. Brett was expected to deliver the goods; Brett *owed* him.

Roger Kebble, a man's man, tough and resilient, who would sooner grunt than talk, was a man of the people. At the various gold mines where he had worked, he liked to go to the compound on Sundays and drink beer in the shebeens with the black mineworkers. They would down quarts, the working man's 'juice' in South Africa, a low-cost beer format successfully marketed for decades by SABMiller under brands such as Lion, Castle and Black Label. The mineworkers loved Roger and would sing when they saw him.

By the end of 2004, when Orlyfunt was announced, Roger was a grandfather several times over and, along with his eldest son, in serious financial trouble. The reputed Kebble fortune, apparently held in an entity known as BNC Investments, was a myth. Since their first big deal in 1996, when they had acted in concert with several other people, Brett and Roger cut corners, scorned the accepted rules of corporate governance, skirted the law and generally conducted their business as if they were subject to an entirely different set of standards than everyone else.

---

* From the practice of one Thomas Hobson (1544–1631), who insisted that each customer at his livery stable in Cambridge, England, either take the horse nearest the stable door, or none at all.

There was nothing good or noble about the Kebble code. Early in 2000, Brett and Roger were participating in market transactions designed to boost the stock price of Western Areas, while simultaneously forcing down the value of Randfontein and Harmony shares. Brett wanted to buy Randfontein with Western Areas paper; later, he was forced to fend off a counter-bid from Harmony. He had also made unsecured loans to Durban Roodepoort Deep (DRD), where Roger was the big boss. The Kebbles wanted the stock price of Western Areas to be as high as possible and the prices for Randfontein and Harmony to be as low as possible. They just waded into the market like ravenous carnivores scenting a fresh kill. They attacked their pending criminal indictments relentlessly, with tactics ranging from the odd pistol-whipping to courting political favour. In August 2004, Rivonia trialist and veteran ANC activist Andrew Mlangeni, then aged 81, declared in the parliamentary register of private assets that he had received a house worth R1.6 million and a car valued at R320 000 from his 'friend, Brett Kebble'. Mlangeni also declared that he was the independent, non-executive chairman of a BEE entity, Matodzi Resources, 'of which Kebble is non-executive director'.

By the time Brett announced Orlyfunt in December 2004, he was one of the staunchest and most public supporters of Jacob Zuma, deputy president of both South Africa and the ruling ANC. Zuma, whom spin doctors had ceaselessly toiled to portray as a populist leader, had been implicated in corruption and fraud involving Durban businessman Schabir Shaik, his financial adviser. Zuma, a Zulu, and Shaik, a Muslim, had long been friends and ANC colleagues. In convicting Shaik of criminal activity, Judge Hillary Squires found that his relationship with Zuma had been 'generally corrupt'. Zuma, widely touted as the next head of state, stood accused of accepting more than R1 million in exchange for political favour related to a controversial multi-million-dollar arms deal involving the South African government and a French company.

He was sacked as deputy president and indicted for corruption soon after Shaik's trial ended in 2005. In a separate case towards the end of the year, Zuma was also charged with rape.

Brett Kebble sided with Zuma for purely selfish reasons. On 6 December 2002, he and Roger had been charged with fraud, conspiracy and incitement relating to the manipulation of Randfontein and Harmony stock prices. If he could show that South Africa's judicial system was corrupt, that Zuma was the victim of a malicious, politically based smear campaign rather than a justifiable criminal investigation, Kebble reasoned, he might also be able to discredit the charges he and Roger faced as spurious and part of a power play within the ANC.

What followed was a torrent of accusations and invective directed at no less a personage than South Africa's top prosecutor, Bulelani Ngcuka, and his boss, justice minister Penuell Maduna.

Ngcuka, director of the National Prosecuting Authority (NPA), was already facing a vicious onslaught from within the Zuma camp, including allegations that he had been a spy for the hated apartheid security services. The Scorpions, an elite anti-crime unit that fell under his jurisdiction, spent almost as much time probing the Kebbles as they did on the relationship between Zuma and Shaik, but as 2003 drew to a close, the investigators were forced to defend themselves against accusations that Ngcuka had abused his position while waging personal vendettas.

Ngcuka unwittingly played right into Kebble's hands by holding a media conference to announce that, while the NPA had built a prima facie* case against Zuma, he would not be charged, since the case was not winnable. Two years later, following Shaik's conviction, this decision was reversed, but, at the time, for a predator like Kebble, it was like putting a plump live sheep into a hyena's salivating jaws.

Just when it seemed the situation could get no murkier, Kebble made public letters he had fired off to Maduna, accusing him of nepotism and corruption. It was left to the minister, however, to reveal one of the most bizarre accusations, namely that both Maduna and Ngcuka were 'controlled' by America's spy hawks in the CIA.

Kebble also accused Ngcuka of making 'a shocking series of slanderous and racist statements about me' at an off-the-record media briefing. In one of his most articulate and pontificating moments, Kebble publicly attacked Ngcuka for 'justifying his outrageous behaviour by describing it as routine'. At his vituperative best, this self-righteous, Simon-pure, virtuous pillar of society harangued the country's most powerful lawman for behaviour 'totally unbecoming to his office and also illegal'.

What few people appreciated as the slanging match unfolded was that the attack on Ngcuka was only partly motivated by the fact that he had dared bring criminal charges against Kebble and his father. Ever the opportunist, Kebble intimated that Ngcuka was acting to avenge the humiliation suffered by his old friend Khumalo when Kebble had hijacked JCI, and told the media:

> One of my commercial rivals is a Mr Mzi Khumalo. Mr Khumalo, a close friend of Mr Ngcuka, has declared himself my enemy, in part because I am taking legal action against him, seeking repayment of moneys owed by him to me that are in excess of R50 million. Mr Khumalo has sworn he will bring about my downfall

---

* A legal presumption that arises from a basic showing of 'first blush' facts that would control a decision unless explicitly proved untrue.

and to my face has told me that he will use his friendship with Mr Ngcuka to achieve that. Many people within the political party I support [the African National Congress] heard similar sentiments expressed by Mr Khumalo and tried to explain to Mr Ngcuka that he should not allow his name or that of his office to be used in this way.

It didn't help that Ngcuka's wife, Phumzile Mlambo-Ngcuka, was the Minister of Minerals and Energy at the time and, as such, the cabinet member responsible for the mining industry. She and Khumalo shared a birthday and often hosted a joint celebration, underlining the depth of friendship between the two families.

Kebble also rolled out the fustian against Warren Goldblatt of Associated Intelligence Networks (AIN):

> While I am being dragged through the mud, the illegal acts of those who hound me are ignored. Here of course I refer to, among others, the activities of Mr Warren Goldblatt's AIN, whose bribery and corruption are meticulously documented. In spite of the fact that the authorities have been provided with ample evidence of this wrongdoing, no charges have been brought against Mr Goldblatt, who now openly boasts that he is working for Mr Ngcuka's Scorpions. We have many claims against Mr Goldblatt and his organisation and in an attempt to frighten us, Mr Goldblatt has made many allegations regarding his closeness to Mr Ngcuka and the minister of justice, Dr Penuell Maduna. All of this gives rise to the view that the justice system is in the hands of private groupings. We have notified Minister Maduna of Mr Goldblatt's claims.

AIN had investigated the truly unbelievable events surrounding the so-called Rawas transaction, involving DRD and certain Australian companies under Brett Kebble's control. Lumping this probe with allegations of power abuse was completely out of context, but Kebble was a man with many enemies and he could simply not resist the temptation of throwing AIN into the pot along with some of the others.

In private conversations, Kebble referred incessantly to a cabal that had carefully plotted Zuma's downfall. In his role as chief puppeteer of the Grand Guignol, he placed Sakumzi 'Saki' Macozoma at the centre of the plot. Macozoma was the mastermind, said Brett again and again and again. The chief foot soldiers, he would disclose in earnest conversation, were Ngcuka and Maduna, while their mutual friend Khumalo, protected by Phumzile Mlambo-Ngcuka, controlled the purse strings.

Khumalo certainly had access to a spectacular amount of money – more than R1 billion in cash, in fact – after muscling in on a BEE deal known as Simane in August 2001.

But Macozoma? The slightly built and mild-mannered former political activist was best known at the time for his particularly poor performance in the late 1990s as head of Transnet, South Africa's state-owned transport colossus. Since then, armed with two Bachelor of Arts degrees, including one from Boston University in political science, economics and journalism, Macozoma had fared much better, serving on the boards of the Standard Bank Group, Standard Bank of SA, Andisa Capital (chairman), Business Trust (co-chairman), Hertz Rent-a-Car (chairman), Liberty Group, Liberty Holdings, Lliso Consulting (chairman), Murray & Roberts Holdings, New Africa Investments, Safika Holdings (deputy chairman), Stanlib (chairman), Tutuwa Strategic Holdings 2 and VW South Africa, among others.

Like anyone else, Kebble was entitled to his opinions, and in his opinion, Macozoma wanted to succeed Thabo Mbeki as president of South Africa. In order for this to happen, Kebble argued, Zuma had to be removed from office. Brett Kebble was rewriting the rules of politics.

Interestingly, rumour of Macozoma's ambition resurfaced some three months after Kebble's death amid yet another government scandal, this time involving the National Intelligence Agency's allegedly illegal surveillance of the man Kebble claimed would be king.

A judicial commission of inquiry found no evidence that Ngcuka had ever been an apartheid spy and the allegations against Maduna were never investigated, but both men quit their posts in 2004 to enter the private business sector. Ironically, when President Mbeki finally sacked Zuma, he chose Ngcuka's wife as his new deputy. Her appointment came at a time when Kebble's carefully constructed world was facing collapse, and he was presumably fighting too many fires to comment on the fact that his sworn enemy's spouse was now the second most powerful politician in South Africa, but it must have been a bitter pill for him to swallow.

In addition to crafting more than 85 BEE deals that turned a number of ANC Youth League members into nouveau riche businessmen – at least on paper – Kebble was a voracious property collector. Widely regarded as an investor with impeccable taste and apparently limitless funds, Kebble was the darling of real estate vendors in Cape Town's upmarket suburbs, where he was the apparent owner of some spectacular mansions. They included No. 4 Kirstenbosch Drive, Kirstenberry Lodge, Monterey and a Cape Dutch mansion in Bishopscourt, as well as Fair Seat, his family home where his wife Ingrid and their four children spent most of their time. Vacations were spent at Malgas, a breathtaking property on the Breede River in Swellendam.

From February 2001, Kebble used Melrose House in Johannesburg's northern suburbs as his digs during the working week. It was a fitting abode for a man who commuted between Cape Town and Johannesburg in a Gulfstream or Lear, a truly beautiful architectural masterpiece standing on land of rural proportions in the middle of urban exclusivity. During Kebble's tenure, it was not unusual to find Charles Cornwall, a director of some Kebble companies, wandering around the world-class landscaped gardens, contemplating his navel, whistling to the birds, talking to the trees and muttering things about hedge funds.

In reality, Consolidated Mining Management Services (CMMS), a 98 per cent subsidiary of JCI and one of Kebble's more important slush funds, owned Melrose House.

Kebble used the property for countless business meetings, shuffling from one magnificently decorated room to another as people rotated between the house and the parking lot. Sometimes Roger could be seen, clutching a wad of papers in his hands as he paced around like a giant locust, his beady eyes intent on recognising the instant when his son had finally completed an engagement and was available to talk.

On these occasions, a pair of Mercedes Benz S-600s, used by father and son, would be parked outside, chauffeurs lovingly polishing the beautiful beasts. Each car was fitted with a 500-horsepower, twin-turbocharged V12 engine. The interiors boasted hand-fitted napa leather seats, 12-speaker audio systems, satellite-based DVD navigation systems, and CD and MP3 players. The 14-way adjustable seats circulated temperature-controlled air, the steering wheels were heated and the super-slick chariots had a number of advanced security features, none of which protected Brett against his gun-wielding assassin.

Melrose House underwent extensive renovation while Kebble was in charge. Among its many features was a gigantic dining room, where he would eat a simple and wholesome breakfast after first downing a handful of vitamin and mineral supplements.

But when Kebble realised that the property's value had doubled in just a few years, Melrose House had to go. It was a tough decision, especially since the stately home had once been home to Gavin Relly, erstwhile CEO of Anglo American. Early in 2004, Melrose House was sold for R10 million.

After that, another luxury residence, at 65 Fifth Avenue, near the snotty Inanda Club, where polo ponies are only marginally less cosseted than the members, served as Kebble's Johannesburg base during the working week.

In addition to property, Kebble also accumulated luxury cars, of which he owned at least ten, excluding the Ferraris, which he acquired for the sole purpose of trading. Depending on the time of day, he might have up to ten of the Italian cars, with the distinctive prancing horse badge, on the books.

Physically, Kebble was a big man, and while he wanted to be known as the guy who had the power to influence the luxury car market, he saw no cachet in driving a Ferrari. The car was simply a commodity, to be traded for profit.

Keeping track of the houses and the cars could be seriously confusing at times, and, on at least one occasion, this offered a glimpse of the lighter side of Kebbledom.

Some months after buying a Cape Town property from Brett in the early 1990s, the new owner telephoned one of Kebble's associates.

'What's the problem?' the associate asked.

'I don't know what to do with this car,' the caller said.

'What is it?'

'A Mercedes 500 – you know, the coupé, two doors with the V8 engine. A real little beauty.'

Kebble, it seemed, had forgotten all about the vehicle parked in one of the garages when he sold the house. Arrangements were duly made for the car to be collected.

But if Kebble's memory sometimes lapsed in respect of possessions, it was infallible when it came to music. People who know about such things and heard him play one of his grand or baby grand pianos believe he could have made a living from recitals in the world's great concert halls.

Whether entertaining guests with show tunes by Gershwin or half an hour of a technically challenging Shostakovich opus without sheet music, Kebble was a pianist of note. His ability had been honed since early childhood, when it became apparent to Roger that his eldest son was hopeless at sport but showed exceptional talent in the arts. Brett became 'the piano player', while his younger brother Guy more than met Roger's expectations on the rugby field, playing at both provincial and national level as an adult. Brett's lack of athletic talent did not endear him to Roger, who is said to have sometimes referred to the boy as 'my other daughter'. The shift boss in him found it far easier to relate to Guy, whose academic performance left much to be desired and whose secret youthful ambition was to be a smuggler.

But for all his affinity with the arts, Kebble was a street fighter, with all the ruthless instincts and a black, sneering coldness that a thug with money needs to protect and preserve his interests. When he ran foul of the law in the Randfontein debacle, the first raw strands of paranoia were exposed, but in the grand tradition of street fighters, Kebble simply continued to live by the credo that money could buy anything.

It certainly allowed him to procure the services of David Barritt, a pioneer of low-end tabloid journalism in South Africa and as formidable a spinmeister as they come. As the official Kebble family spokesman and top manager of the Kebble Art Awards, Barritt's annual remuneration was reputed to have been far north of the R600 000 in combined prize money handed out at the inaugural awards in 2004.

'I can't stand him,' Kebble would mutter to anyone he was with after waiting politely for Barritt to move out of earshot.

Also on the image-building payroll for five years was Dominic Ntsele, who fought a daily duel with NPA spokesman Sipho Ngwema outside Durban's High Court to get the best headlines for their respective camps during the Shaik trial. It was never quite clear whether Ntsele spoke for Shaik or Zuma or both, but he was well connected within the media, and his primary role in the Kebble organisation appears to have been to supply selected journalists with information favourable to the Kebbles and detrimental to those they deemed their enemies.

Apart from his assassin(s), Ntsele was the last person known to have seen Kebble alive and face to face on the night he died. Originally scheduled to have breakfast together, their meeting was changed to early evening, when they shared a meal of steak, potato wedges and salad at the Inanda mansion and sang a few verses of Gershwin's 'Summertime'.

When Kebble set off to keep his last, fatal appointment, Ntsele went home, turned off his cellphone and only learnt early the next morning that Kebble had been shot. Some weeks later, he told a *Sunday Times* reporter that he had been so shocked by the news that, after 18 months on the wagon, he had started quaffing double tequilas and Red Bull again.

Kebble once told him, said Ntsele, 'that you cannot conquer fear unless you face death'.

Little did they know when they parted on that fateful Tuesday night that Kebble's words would be put to the test within the hour.

2

Fine wines and fancy cigars

THE BIG ENGINES were making no money for the Kebbles. In December 2004, Brett was chief executive officer of three key companies listed on the JSE, namely Western Areas, JCI and Randgold & Exploration, of which he had seized control in mid-1997. When he announced the Orlyfunt deal, Kebble was surrounded by the directors of all three entities, lending him a veneer of respectability and a patina of validity.

Roger was the non-executive chairman of JCI, in which the Kebble family apparently held its most valuable interests (about 12 per cent of the stock). The financial director was Hennie Buitendag, a chartered accountant and director of various other patches of the Kebble kingdom, including Matodzi Resources, Stilfontein, Rand Leases Properties, Consolidated Mining Management Services (CMMS), Continental Goldfields and Letšeng Diamonds.

John Stratton was an Australian national of sufficient age and experience to have known better than to hang around with Kebble. Charles Cornwall, who had turned partying with the elite polo fraternity into an art form, was too immature to show good judgement. Born on 15 November 1962, he had been appointed CEO of a London and Nasdaq-listed interactive software and technology company, Eidos Plc, in October 1995, but had since resigned.

At Randgold & Exploration, Roger and Buitendag completed the top triumvirate as non-executive chairman and financial overlord respectively. Then there were three black economic empowerment directors, all crony appointments made in July 2003. Brenda Madumise (listed as an independent non-executive) boasted several qualifications, including a law degree and an MBA. Described as a 'non-practising advocate with vast business experience', she was also a director of Khomelela Ltd. Lunga Ncwana's nameplate résumé read:

> He is a former ANC Youth League official where he served until 1999. Since then he has played a key role in various black empowerment transactions, including the acquisition of 70 per cent of a financial services company, Tradek (Pty) Ltd, by Tlotlisa Financial Services, which in turn acquired a 90 per cent stake in PSG Appleton Asset Management and 100 per cent of Lyons Financial Solutions Holdings Ltd. He is currently chief executive officer of Itsuseng Holdings and a

director of Tlotlisa Financial Services (Pty) Ltd, Matodzi Engineering, Equitant Trading (Pty) Ltd and Phikoloso Mining (Pty) Ltd.

Kebble had used a number of these companies, not least among them Lyons and Phikoloso, to buy in his BEE cronies. He had stripped Lyons of its assets, leaving it with just enough business to keep certain black brothers happy. The Phikoloso deal had been truly disgusting, a classic Kebble messy ejaculation where he issued good paper (in this case, Randgold & Exploration shares) at a value far in excess of what was being bought. The profits rendered when the Randgold & Exploration shares were sold in the open market would go to his black brothers and sisters. It was nice work, if you could get it.

Kebble's acolytes had to have the best. It was the multi-million-rand mansion, the sports car, a watch (Rolex being the label of choice) and cigars (Montecristo No. 4, Montecristo A, Hoyo de Monterrey, Partagas, H Upmann, Romeo y Julieta (Cedros Deluxe, Nos. 1, 2 or 3 and Deluxe Turbos) or Cuaba). Then there was the mandatory Moët & Chandon, Dom Pérignon and, for the most devout apostles, single-malt whisky (Aberlour, Edradour, Glenmorangie, Lagavulin, The Macallan, Oban or Talisker).

If one of Kebble's dark disciples *really* counted, an invitation to London would be in the offing. Kebble, a master of consumption, would induct his coterie into the orgiastic rituals of engorge, ingurgitate, overindulge, glut, stuff, gormandise, binge, pig out and satiate. Over a single weekend in London, Kebble blew the equivalent of R460 000, most of it on obscenely expensive bottles of wine (Dom Romanée Conti 1997, Château Valandraud Saint-Emilion 1995, Château Latour Pauillac 1990, Château Le Pin Pomerol 1999, Petrus Pomerol 1998) and wristwatches (Patek Philippe, Vacheron Constantin and Girard-Perregaux).

To be fair, Kebble never forgot the less fortunate, as his publicists were keen to point out: 'The Brett Kebble Charitable Foundation supports a wide gamut of activities in South Africa, including the Brett Kebble Art Awards, the country's largest awards for the visual arts, and the Siphosethu Feeding Scheme, which feeds some 1 500 children a day in poor communities in the Cape peninsula area of Cape Town.'

If there was the sound of music in the background, it was Kebble – again – that one had to thank: 'Mr Kebble, a prominent South African businessman, is a great lover of classical music and … is committed to encouraging the development of classical musicians in South Africa and facilitating a wider appreciation of classical music.'

Kebble never explained exactly who paid for the starving children's meals or, for that matter, who footed the bills for his own groceries and sumptuous dinner parties. Then again, food was only one facet of Kebble's conspicuous consumption.

On one return trip from London, a gluttonous Kebble popped into a shop at Heathrow and bought 50 watches. Two of his fellow executives were with him at the time. Cornwall also picked up 50 watches, while Roger Kebble just observed the spectacle and shook his head, the ostentatious consumerism evidently rather too rich for his mine captain's blood.

In July 2003, Chris Nissen, a former senior ANC politician in the Western Cape, was given a seat on the board of Randgold & Exploration as an 'independent non-executive director'. Now here was a fellow with good-looking qualifications, including a master's degree in the arts and a diploma in theology. In addition, said his pedigree:

> He is currently the chief executive officer of Umoya Fishing (Pty) Ltd and also holds positions as chairman of Sea Harvest Corporation, South African Maritime Safety Authority, Namfish (Pty) Ltd and Boschendal (Pty) Ltd. He is a director of Tigerbrands Ltd, Inkgqubela Fisheries and Marine Development Corporation, Standard Bank SA Ltd, Standard Bank Group Ltd and Golden Arrow Bus Services. He served on various cabinet committees under President Nelson Mandela and President Thabo Mbeki and also acted as deputy speaker of the provincial parliament.

Two of the Randgold & Exploration directors in December 2004, Stephen Tainton and Gordon Miller, would quit soon afterwards. Miller had solid mining qualifications and 22 years of experience in the field. He was a member of the SA Institute of Mining and Metallurgy, and a former vice-president of Placer Dome Incorporated, where he held executive positions in Canada and Western Australia.

When Orlyfunt was announced, the Western Areas board of directors was conspicuously large, given that its sole interest was a passive 50 per cent stake in South Deep, an ultra-deep gold mine west of Johannesburg. The interminable completion of the mine was managed by Toronto-based Placer Dome, which had bought half of South Deep in 1998. The non-executive chairman of Western Areas was listed as Mafika Mkwanazi, with Kebble as CEO. The financial director was Chris Lamprecht, who at the age of 42 had degrees in commerce and an MBA, along with a 17-year track record in the mining industry in corporate and treasury positions.

Gordon Miller was a director until he resigned on 6 May, while Mark Barnes had quit his position on 3 February. Then there were Vaughan Bray, Roger Kebble, Alexander Alan 'Sandy' McGregor (an executive at Allan Gray, an investment house based in Cape Town), Sello Rasethaba (a long-standing Kebble crony) and George Poole, who also resigned on 6 May.

Kebble's much vaunted 'anchor' BEE company, Matodzi, had Andrew Mlangeni, born on 6 June 1925, as its non-executive chairman. Considerably older than most of Kebble's associates, Mlangeni had a couple of arts degrees, was an ANC member of parliament, served on the party's National Executive Committee from 1991 to 1997, and, perhaps most importantly, had impeccable 'struggle' credentials, having spent 26 years on Robben Island as a political prisoner.

Matodzi's CEO was Rasethaba, born on 19 February 1958, and holder of degrees in accounting and German. His interests were listed as transformation of both government and business organisations 'resulting in transformation of relationships and partnerships'. Rasethaba had gained experience in 'the formulation, development and implementation of information technology strategies in South Africa, the US and the UK'.

Also on Matodzi's board was Mafika Mkwanazi, born on 31 January 1954, and holding heavyweight qualifications in the form of two BSc degrees, one of them in electrical engineering. He had worked at Kriel Colliery, ultimately owned by Anglo American, as a junior engineer for two years, and then as unit manager (packaging) at the Isando plant of SABMiller, the giant brewer. Mkwanazi also worked for Bristol Myers Squibb as plant manager and for BMW as corporate quality manager. He was appointed CEO of Metrorail on 1 January 1995, became an executive director of Transnet in April 1996, and was group CEO from February 2001 to December 2003. Mkwanazi was also a director of Nedcor Bank, Autopax, SAA, Letšeng Investment Holdings SA, Freight Logistics International Incorporated and Western Areas.

Matodzi boasted another truly fine director in the form of Thabo Mosololi, financial director of Tsogo Sun Gaming and a director of numerous other entities, including Telkom. Born on 12 September 1969, Mosololi had a BCom degree and was a certified chartered accountant. He initially joined KPMG as an audit manager and senior consultant, then formed TSI Financial & Investment Services, a management consultancy. He was involved in negotiations to form Gobodo Incorporated and rapidly moved into the position of group CEO, with special focus on new business development, strategy, risk management and client relations. Mosololi was listed as a member of the SA Institute of Chartered Accountants, the Public Accountants' and Auditors' Board, the Association for the Advancement of Black Chartered Accountants in SA, and was treasurer of the Johannesburg branch and a member of the Black Management Forum.

Just what he was doing in Kebble's ambit is possibly something only a leprechaun could explain.

Both Kebble and Buitendag were also directors of Matodzi, their key BEE front.

Kebble outsourced certain specialised services, such as those offered by former judge Willem Heath, whose executive consultancy was 'founded on the principles of sound corporate practices'. Heath was an interesting choice, given that he had previously headed the truncated probe of alleged corruption in the Arms Deal that formed the basis of criminal charges against Jacob Zuma and Schabir Shaik.

Heath possessed a certain charming naivety; it was as if there was some part of life, no matter how small, that he had never discovered, and he had absolutely no intention of finding out what it was. His role in the Kebble organisation was vague, but he marketed Heath Executive Consultants as 'a dedicated group of professionals consulting on the variety of complex issues which impede on the prosperity of corporate, private and public entities' and promised to 'promote a risk-free environment in which our clients can prosper'.

As 2004 drew to a close, Kebble's chief security adviser was Clinton Nassif of Johannesburg-based Central National Security Services, registered earlier that year. Nassif was evidently responsible for both the physical security of Kebble interests and confidential investigations.

For the last nine months of his life, Kebble was in a major bind. Notwithstanding the fabulous property portfolio and generous patronage of the arts, the stewardship of apparently great and illustrious companies listed on the JSE, his widely touted reputation as the 'new' Barney Barnato, the Ferraris that he traded like a petulant child playing marbles, the music sponsorships, the Gulfstream and the Lear, the feeding scheme for street kids, the obsession with wristwatches, and the lavish spending on fine wines and splendid cigars, the Kebble empire was technically bankrupt.

Thorough analysis of JCI's annual accounts in particular, along with those of Randgold & Exploration, Western Areas, Matodzi and CMMS for the year ending 31 March 2004, shows that in JCI alone, Kebble was hiding R1.3 billion in debt.

This amount, classified as short-term borrowings, had been buried in CMMS, a 98 per cent indirect JCI subsidiary. After Kebble died, CMMS, a private company not required to make its books public, was exposed as a slush fund.

Apart from the R1.3 billion omitted, apparently irregularly, from JCI's annual accounts, the company published borrowings of R1.6 billion. This amount formed part of the audited financial accounts for the year, signed off by Charles Orbach & Company, but another R1.3 billion in borrowings, though mentioned in the annual report, was not reflected in the financial statements.

In fact, JCI's real borrowings came to a massive R2.9 billion,* nearly twice the figure in the audited report. JCI was technically insolvent. Even the disclosed borrowings of R1.6 billion were sufficiently high for JCI to include the following warning in its 2004 annual report:

---

* See Appendix E, item 17.

24

These financial statements have been prepared on the basis of accounting principles applicable to a going concern. This basis presumes that funds will be available to finance future operations and that the realisation of assets and settlement of liabilities, contingent liabilities and commitments will occur in the ordinary course of business. Accordingly, these financial statements do not include any adjustment relating to the valuation of assets and classification of liabilities that might be necessary were the [JCI group] unable to continue as a going concern.

JCI's directors, led by Kebble, added that 'the majority of the group's BEE investments are now sufficiently mature to provide a core-asset base for a new BEE company float'. This piece of pure nonsense offered the major clue as to how Kebble planned to dodge the insolvency bullet. The 'float' referred to would see the listing of a new entity on the JSE.

History is fraught with planned listings that are only partially successful or fail completely, but JCI's directors insisted that the initiative was 'at an advanced stage and at conclusion will create a vibrant and new BEE entity'. And therein lay the rub:

Some of the shares to be received from this transaction could be realised or utilised to raise funding which, together with cash received, will assist in the de-gearing of the [JCI] balance sheet. The future cash requirements of the group will be satisfied by a combination of facilities raised and in the longer term by income from investments, particularly from mining operations that are coming on stream.

So there it was, in print for all to see: Kebble was going to list some or other big-deal entity on the JSE. This would raise a mountain of cash, much of which would flow into JCI's depleted coffers. Further on down the line, JCI's cash requirements would be funded by 'income from investments' and 'mining operations that are coming on stream'.

None of JCI's investments – of which by far the biggest was its stake in Western Areas – was producing income, let alone dividends. There was nothing new in this. There had been no cash coming in for years. Despite all the fire sales, the nett cash position was negative and counting, as outflows continued and increased.

During Kebble's stellar rise from nowhere man to billionaire, zero to people's hero in less than two years, he had mastered the art of issuing paper. It would be issued to vulnerable investors, mostly professionals who knew no better, while Kebble consumed the incoming cash. The resulting paper storm would send even the toughest junkyard dog running for the horizon with its tail tucked between its legs.

In October 1996, Randgold & Exploration concocted a story on the back of the acquisition of BHP Minerals Mali. The principal asset in the bundle was Syama, a derelict gold mine that the directors of Randgold & Exploration and its subsidiary, Randgold Resources, talked up as if it were El Dorado, Shangri-La and Paradise all rolled into one. The price of Randgold & Exploration shares shot up from R10 in June 1995, when Kebble and his cohorts started hyping the stock price, to just over R41 in February 1997. Syama enabled Randgold Resources to raise tens of millions of dollars from investors when it listed in London in July 1997.

By then, Kebble's reputation was such that he was issuing his personal 'currency' – shares in Consolidated African Mines (CAM), predecessor of JCI. He was using CAM paper to buy all manner of assets, including some good ones, at knockdown prices during a period of poor gold bullion performance. Sellers were accepting CAM paper at 600 cents a share. When JCI was suspended from trading by the JSE on 1 August 2005, it was at just 16 cents a share, 97 per cent less than so many investors had accepted eight years before. There are few better examples of destruction of value.

By suckering various entities and individuals into accepting CAM shares, Kebble gained control of everything from Western Areas to Randgold & Exploration. In the years that followed, he continued to offer paper and succeeded in having it accepted by idiot investors here, there and everywhere. However, when Kebble issued CAM shares in exchange for assets, it was a case of swapping paper for other paper. When he issued CAM shares to raise cash, it was a different story and he had to offer massive discounts.

In 1997, when CAM shares were issued for hard cash, the stock was given out at discounts of up to 77 per cent on the going price of 600 cents a share.

3

The bait

IN DECEMBER 2004, faced with a potentially terminal liquidity crisis, Brett Kebble prepared to stage his most ambitious confidence trick. But for Orlyfunt to succeed, he needed to lay the bait.

First, a black economic empowerment deal had to be done. That's what the law said.* Kebble had sucked blacks from across the business spectrum into the Orlyfunt structure by the time he took it to the market, and institutional investors would be bullied into coughing up hundreds of millions of rand for a junk deal. The names Kebble threw out were impressive enough:

- Lembede Investment Holdings (led by Songezo Mjongile, a member of the ANC Youth League's National Executive Committee).
- Dyambu Holdings (including Baleka Mbete, Speaker of Parliament, but led by Hilda Ndude, a leading ANC Women's League member).
- Itsuseng Investment Holdings (led by two ANC Youth League members, Lunga Ncwana and Andile Nkuhlu).
- Koketso Group (led by Dali Tambo, son of former ANC president Oliver Tambo).
- Masupatsela Group.
- Ikamva Investment Group (led by Sharif Pandor, husband of education minister Naledi Pandor).
- Kovacs Group (led by businessman and ANC provincial executive member Chris Nissen).
- Umoya Group (also led by Nissen).
- Sekunjalo Group (led by Iqbal Survé and including Gilingwe Mayende, former Director-General of Land Affairs).

Orlyfunt, the mother-company-in-waiting, would be directed by Kebble, Mafika Mkwanazi, Sello Rasethaba, Andrew Mlangeni, Lunga Ncwana and Thuthukile

---

*   South Africa's mining charter, which became effective on 1 May 2004, requires companies to achieve a 15 per cent HDSA (historically disadvantaged South Africans) ownership of South African mining assets within five years, and a 26 per cent HDSA ownership within ten years. Under the charter, the mining industry as a whole agrees to assist HDSA companies in securing finance of R100 billion in the first five years to fund participation. Beyond this commitment, HDSA participation will be increased on a willing seller, willing buyer basis, at fair market value, where the mining companies are not at risk.

Skweyiya, the latter listed as chairman and former South African ambassador to France.

Entities that were to be folded into Orlyfunt included JCI Telecommunications, JCI Pharmaceuticals, JCI Property, JCI Engineering, JCI Finance and Equity Holdings, and JCI Mining. Corporate entities slated to fall under Orlyfunt's umbrella included Cueincident, Startrack Communications, DVI Telecoms, SA Bioclones, Advanced Medical Technologies, Nutrx Trading, Mvelaphanda Properties, Boschendal, Rand Leases, Palfinger SA, OD Engineering, African Maritime Logistics, Tlotlisa Financial Services, Ikamva Holdings, Sekunjalo Group, Itsuseng Investments Ltd, and ordinary and preference shares in Matodzi and Witnigel Investments (Pty) Ltd.

Randgold & Exploration would chip into the deal, disposing of its 74 per cent interest in the share capital of Minrico Ltd and its 55.1 per cent interest in the share capital of Free State Development and Investment Corporation (Freddev).

From a transactional viewpoint, the Orlyfunt deal was remarkably simple, especially for Kebble. JCI would sell its portfolio of BEE joint venture investments and various mineral right interests to Orlyfunt for R1.4 billion. Orlyfunt would 'pay' JCI in time-honoured Kebble currency by issuing paper, exactly 80.4 per cent of its issued ordinary share capital.

Orlyfunt would also owe JCI R909.6 million on loan account, secured by a pledge of the JCI assets. The loan would be interest-free and repayable within three years 'from the future cash flows or proceeds of the disposal of the JCI assets'.

JCI would then sell 44.2 per cent of Orlyfunt's issued ordinary share capital for a 'consideration' of R267.4 million to a company owned by the BEE founding partners, NewCo, which in turn would dispose of 30 per cent thereof to 'a broad-base grouping of BEE shareholders'. There would be a similar but far smaller flow-through in the case of Randgold & Exploration.

In the end game, JCI and Randgold & Exploration would hold 40 per cent of Orlyfunt; the BEE founding partners and shareholders would own the remaining 60 per cent via NewCo.

What this meant was that Kebble, along with Mkwanazi, Rasethaba, Mlangeni and Ncwana, would own 42 per cent of Orlyfunt.

It was classic Kebble, with not a cent of cash in sight, and without cash there was no way of financing a deal of any kind, whether BEE or not.

However, Kebble the conjuror still had a few waves of his magic wand to go.

JCI's 2004 annual report devoted several pages to summarising group BEE interests. Page 16 showed that shareholders were given the value of 'empowerment funding', which JCI had derived from BEE, to the tune of R1.6 billion.

Kebble used an annual report containing financial statements signed off by auditors, a document so formal and carefully checked that many serious investors regard it as biblical, as a cradle to house R1.6 billion in imagined value that could not be corroborated elsewhere or traced to financial accounts.

It proved impossible to find details of the R1.6 billion anywhere in the report or statements. Where deals had been financed, such as the ordinary and preference shares in Matodzi and Witnigel, extensive forensic examination was required to set them out.*

In a graphic and tragic illustration of the kind of junk that Kebble was dumping into Orlyfunt, JCI's investments in the Matodzi and Witnigel preference shares were reclassified, according to new accounting rules, as debt rather than investments following the Orlyfunt announcement.

In order to bail out Matodzi, JCI was forced to write off much of this sudden new debt and convert the remainder into equity, taking its stake in Matodzi from zero to 59 per cent. So much for the 'flagship' of Kebble's BEE empire.

The Orlyfunt deal also contained Kebble's capricious poison pills, his daylight robbery clauses. JCI would 'receive a participating preference share in Orlyfunt which will entitle JCI to 60 per cent of any profits realised by Orlyfunt on the realisation of any of the non-mineral right JCI assets; and receive a participating preference share in Orlyfunt which will entitle JCI to 80 per cent of any profits realised by Orlyfunt on the realisation of any of the JCI mineral right interests forming part of the JCI assets'.

Similarly, Randgold & Exploration would receive a participating preference share in Orlyfunt entitling the company to 80 per cent 'of any incremental value realised by Orlyfunt on the realisation of any of the Randgold & Exploration assets'.

---

*   Matodzi Resources changed its name from Witwatersrand Nigel Limited on 2 February 1999. The 'Witnigel preference shares' can be traced to mid-1997, when CAM bought 200 000 000 cumulative redeemable preference shares in Witnigel Investments for 33 333 334 new CAM shares at 600 cents each, giving a putative value of R222 million. After its balance sheet date of 31 March 1998, CAM bought 10 million shares in Saflife from Witnigel for 83 333 333 CAM shares. Here, the value per CAM share was a mere R1.50, giving a putative value of R125 million. The Matodzi preference shares were issued on 1 July 1999, when Matodzi purchased R350 million worth of diamond assets from JCI Gold and CAM. Matodzi (then trading as New Mining) paid by way of issuing 130 million A preference shares at 100 cents each; 200 million B preference shares at 100 cents each and 40 million New Mining ordinary shares at 50 cents each. In its 2005 annual report, Matodzi announced that in order to resolve the company's apparent insolvency, JCI, beneficial owner of the 200 million Matodzi preference shares, had agreed to convert them into ordinary shares on a one-for-one basis. JCI also agreed to acquire for R1 the entire issued share capital of Witnigel Investments, a wholly owned subsidiary of Matodzi. The result was that the Witnigel preference shares were effectively written off, and JCI became the beneficial holder of 57 per cent of Matodzi's issued ordinary share capital. Prior to the conversion, JCI did not own any ordinary shares in the share capital of Matodzi. Matodzi's B preference shares were held by Consolidated Mining Corporation, a subsidiary of CMMS, itself a 98 per cent JCI subsidiary, and JCI Gold, a full subsidiary of JCI.

One of the great ironies of the Kebble affair is that, for all the acclaim heaped on him by publicists, selected journalists and beneficiaries of his largesse within the ANC as a leading proponent of black empowerment, he had no respect for BEE deals.

In the 1999–2000 merger of Gem Diamonds into Trans Hex, Kebble stripped out the profits that Matodzi (then New Mining) was entitled to. On 1 July 1999, Matodzi had purchased R350 million 'worth' of diamond assets from JCI Gold and CAM. A few months later, Trans Hex unexpectedly made a successful bid for Gem Diamonds. Kebble stripped the profits out of the deal for his own account, and it was not until years later that the Gem Diamonds transaction showed up in Matodzi's books.

As early as 1997, Kebble had hijacked JCI's BEE transaction, seizing control of JCI in multiple back room deals that turned him, briefly, into a man worth R1.5 billion.

'I was once a billionaire,' the *soi-disant* mining mogul would tell certain friends and associates.

And then he would tell the truth.

'At least on paper.'

By the time Kebble invented Orlyfunt, there was nothing left to hijack, and unless he could raise hundreds of millions in cash, it would be game over. But the details of the proposed Orlyfunt dumping make it patently clear that Kebble considered this BEE lark as his only legitimate way forward. It was the only possible strong-arm tactic that would work on institutions, the investors that would be expected to cough up the cash. Even so, it was going to be a tough one to sell, given that for years institutional investors had shied away from anything connected to the Kebbles.

There was one major and critically important exception. On 6 November 2002, Western Areas appointed Sandy McGregor to its board of directors. A veteran mining man, born on 13 September 1946, McGregor held degrees in science and arts, and had joined Allan Gray in October 1991, after working for the Gold Fields group for 22 years. He was appointed a director of Allan Gray in 1997.

As early as 2002, Allan Gray, a large Cape Town–based institutional investor with a good name, started buying into Kebble's three key companies. Allan Gray had taken the South Deep bait.

Kebble had already looted much of Western Areas, selling half of South Deep for $235 million to Toronto-based Placer Dome in November 1998. In February 2002, he sold the South Deep derivatives book forward for $104 million. It was one of the worst hedge books ever created in the history of gold mining, but it appeared to have terrified Kebble into leaving South Deep alone.

Mkwanazi, non-executive chairman of Western Areas, said of South Deep that it 'stands like a beacon in the global gold industry', adding:

Most other South African mining companies are now obliged to squeeze the best out of declining mineral reserves, while South Deep is entering its own Shangri-La, the mythical valley in Tibet that represents heaven on earth! With approximately 55.6 million ounces of gold in the proved and probable mineral reserve categories and a life of mine of more than sixty years, South Deep is an enviable asset. As a colleague from a prominent investment company wrote to me recently: 'In valuing mining shares we place great emphases on mine life. The price/earning ratio that one can put on a mine is a direct function of life. The majority of gold mining companies have lives between ten and twenty years. As their lives shorten, the market will continually down-rate them. In order to sustain their ratings the major mining companies have to acquire longer life assets, which are therefore particularly valuable.'

The South Deep twin-shaft complex, under development since 1995 at a cost of more than R4 billion, consists of a single-drop ventilation shaft to a depth of 2 760 metres, and a single-drop main shaft to a depth of 2 993 metres. The sinking of the ventilation shaft was completed in 2001, while the main shaft was commissioned in November 2004.

By 31 December 2003, Allan Gray Funds held 10 per cent of Randgold & Exploration. One year later, Allan Gray held at least 10 per cent of JCI.

By 31 December 2004, Allan Gray Asset Management owned 24.8 per cent of Western Areas directly and indirectly through nominees and custody accounts.

Allan Gray had given Kebble a degree of respectability; there appeared little doubt that Allan Gray would come to the party when Orlyfunt was taken to the market. Kebble could smell cash in the air the way a vulture senses carrion long before the last breath is exhaled:

> From JCI's perspective, the transactions will consolidate in Orlyfunt the majority of its BEE joint venture investments and create an independent capital base that will partner with JCI in future empowerment initiatives. It is intended that Orlyfunt, on its own or in conjunction with other BEE groupings, will list on the JSE in due course, resulting in subsequent substantial cash inflow to JCI, thereby reducing JCI's debt and de-gearing its balance sheet.

There was another critical facet of the Orlyfunt deal that Kebble had not properly explained. JCI's annual report for the year to 31 March 2004, dated 22 October, stated in regard to the Inkwenkwezi Empowerment Group that 'JCI assisted Inkwenkwezi, led by businessman Mafika Mkwanazi, to purchase an 11.6 per cent stake in WAL [Western Areas] from Anglo American'.

Elsewhere, mention was made that 'Inkwenkwezi must pay Anglo by 1 November

2004'. Anglo American's annual report for the year ending 31 December 2004 disclosed that it had 'disposed of a holding of approximately 8.5 per cent of Western Areas in December 2004'.

It was not the first time, nor would it be the last, that Kebble lied in print. By the end of 2004, he had become a dangerous predator, riddled with the deep pestilence of pathological lies.

JCI's annual report for 2004 was a fraud. On 14 December 2005, the company, under control of an entirely new set of directors, issued a media release that admitted:

> The [forensic] investigation has revealed prima facie evidence that there has been misappropriation of company assets, including during prior financial periods. Work is in progress to determine the exact extent of the misappropriation, which could be substantial, as well as to initiate, if necessary, the relevant legal processes ... Shareholders are advised not to rely on prior period financial statements.

Randgold & Exploration made a substantially similar statement. All told, Kebble's Orlyfunt announcement had been based on a carefully conceived and wholly corrupt scheme. But there were other, bigger lies; bigger than even the monstrous falsehoods hidden in JCI's annual report.

Kebble had already started illegally selling millions of shares held by Randgold & Exploration in Randgold Resources, listed in London and on the Nasdaq. He was raising hundreds of millions of rand in cash. Indeed, Kebble was illegally raising more than R1 billion in cash, without telling his fellow directors, without telling investors, without telling regulatory authorities.

Worse, he was telling no one where the cash was going.

And, even worse than that, an important component of Kebble's business affairs had suffered yet another *bouleversement*, aggravating yet another contemporaneous problem growing like a boil on his buttocks. For years, he had harboured a schoolboy fantasy of being a big man in diamonds. The best gem diamonds in the world come out of Angola, and thus, by definition, some of the world's most dangerous people of every ilk can be found lurking in and around the Angolan diamond fields.

Year after year, Brett Kebble had been throwing money around in an effort to get his hands on some of the Angolan action. It was truly irresistible. An Angolan gem diamond of mediocre quality might easily fetch $1 000 a carat. At 5 000 carats to a kilogram, that translates to $5 million. Who the hell wanted to get involved in cocaine, worth a miserly $20 000 a kilogram (uncut) on the streets of New York? Besides, nothing about cocaine was legal, whereas a good proportion of the diamond trade was, or could be made to seem so. That was no big deal, despite the best international efforts to outlaw so-called 'blood diamonds' from Africa's numerous conflict zones.

So Kebble continued to foster his fantasy of becoming a big player in Angolan diamonds. To hell with Russian-born Israeli-diamond tycoon Lev Leviev (of whom Kebble was secretly terrified). To hell with De Beers. Brett Kebble was going to be the self-anointed king of Angola's diamond fields.

The reality was more than a little different.

'Somebody needs to tell Brett Kebble that an Angolan diamond concession needs lots of investment,' said a mining executive recently returned from Luanda.

'Why so?'

'His one concession, the one I saw, consists of a prefabricated hut and a couple of battered pick-up trucks.'

Kebble was deep into a number of rotten Angolan diamond deals when he announced Orlyfunt. He had been ripped off. There was going to be no jewelled crown, no constant flow of flawless gems. But he still needed to account for the big money that he'd lost.

Even as Kebble relentlessly sold off shares in Randgold Resources, he was hunting for one more deal that would furnish him with hundreds of millions of rand in a hurry. He was looking for contraband. He was in contact with key criminal figures who could front a monster illicit deal. Brett Kebble was ratcheting up his smuggling operations.

Brett Kebble was going down.

PART II

Shangri-La

4

Froth in Jakarta, suds on The Street

THERE NEVER IS a good time to die, but Brett Kebble's violent demise at about 9.15 p.m. on 27 September 2005, on a lonely road in the leafy northern Johannesburg suburb of Melrose, was an uncanny reminder that in death, as in business, timing is everything.

If for nothing else, Kebble was known for mining finance. In the arcane world of high finance, most of the action in this particular sector is habitually concealed from the public eye. It is easy enough to go on tours to mines – easier, perhaps, than joining junkets to breweries. As corporate governance, social responsibility and environmental legislation have swamped the global business scene in the modern era, the public face of physical mining has been carefully scrubbed and nurtured.

But behind the scenes, effectively light years away from the pits and tunnels where sweat pours off heaving human bodies, special skills are required. Knowing this, Kebble employed and deployed highly skilled advisers most of the time, though they were sometimes changed as often as his underwear.

Kebble learnt about the inside track of mining finance in just a few years. The roots of his career as a businessman were sunk deeply, and quickly, in and around 1991. His full baptism would be celebrated, certainly by Kebble himself, in mid-1997.

During the mid-1990s, an amalgam of extraordinary events occurred at a number of key locations dotted around the world. As such, the Brett Kebble story literally started on the other side of the globe. It was all about gold. Somehow, it seemed, if it was Kebble, it had to be gold, the most coveted of all minerals and the most controversial, given its multifaceted characterisations. Gold flowed through Kebble's veins across the entire span of his ten-year business career. Kebble changed, but gold stayed the same.

A decade before Kebble succumbed to the business end of a muzzle flash, a large and expanding team of geologists, drillers and all their attendants were working around the clock on an exploration property near the Busang River in East Kalimantan, Indonesia. Sweat-drenched and cursing by day, fighting off swarms of mosquitoes at night, the men were collecting samples on Busang's *Line 59*, a piece of the world that would become truly famous.

Another global gold rush was under way. Moreover, it was spurred on by attractive increases in the price of the precious metal, a process that did not always coincide with a physical treasure hunt. The gold bullion price had moved up from multi-year lows of around $325 an ounce in 1992 to well above $400 an ounce in early 1995. But it was the group pin-cushioning the ground along the Busang River that had caught the imagination of investors around the world. At the Shangri-La Hotel in Jakarta, capital of Indonesia, it seemed that nothing mattered more to patrons than Busang. It was like an epiphany; somehow, everybody who knew – or even talked – about Busang was going to be rich: very rich, and very soon. Busang was magic, and magic was Busang.

John Felderhof, chief geologist at Bre-X, the Canadian-listed company that apparently owned exploration rights over the Busang properties, would later say it was during 1995 on *Line 59* that he realised 'we've got a monster by the tail'.

In an exquisite example of timing, David Walsh had founded Bre-X Minerals in 1989 as a subsidiary of Bresea Resources. During the 1980s, mankind was mining – and buying – ever-increasing amounts of gold, and production in the Western world soared rapidly. A century earlier, global production was about one-tenth of the output achieved in this new era, which saw prospectors flocking to alluvial deposits in such countries as Brazil, Venezuela and the Philippines. Serra Pelada in Brazil, said to be one of the richest placer deposits ever found, yielded 13 tons in 1983 alone. The alluvial workings teemed with desperate *garampieros*, wretched artisanal miners who traded their hard-won gold for alcohol, drugs, women and guns. The rush spread finally to West and East Africa, but wherever it was happening, it was one tough business.

In 1993, on Felderhof's recommendation, Walsh bought the rights over properties in the middle of a jungle near the Busang River. The way Bre-X told the story, some kind of mother lode was hit at Busang. In 1995, Bre-X announced that laboratory work on drilled cores and samples supported an estimate of 30 million ounces of gold *in situ*. The gold had just been sitting there since time immemorial, waiting to be found by some smart operator. If the estimate was even vaguely accurate, Bre-X was a phenomenon. In terms of the universal benchmark, a discovery of one million ounces was regarded as world class, albeit low. At $500 an ounce, mining a deposit of that volume at 100 000 ounces a year for ten years would produce gross annual revenues of $50 million, or $500 million over a decade-long life-of-mine.

Any discovery of more than a million ounces was a phenomenon. Bre-X had already found 30 world-class mines in one location and extraction was still a long way off. The deposit remained open, with considerable exploration work waiting to be completed before a mining plan was even contemplated. Nevertheless, Bre-X was seen as being well on the way to declaring the world's biggest gold strike, possibly even the largest mine in history.

Inevitably, greed and fear entered the equation. The Indonesian president, Suharto,* wanted a chunk of Bre-X, as did the world's major gold mining companies, not least among them Barrick, headquartered in Toronto. The Bre-X story, which had spontaneously combusted into a global wildfire, intensified. Investors everywhere rushed to buy gold stocks, especially gold exploration stocks, known in the trade as 'juniors'.

The Indonesians – the ones who count in stories of this nature – suggested that Bre-X would be unable to run such a huge mine. The helpful alternative was that Barrick top-manage the operation in association with Suharto's daughter, Siti Rukmana. Bre-X, understandably peeved, responded by hiring Suharto's son, Sigit Hardjojudanto, as an adviser. Mohamad Hasan, one of a number of Suharto cronies, came up with a deal that would see Bre-X retaining a 45 per cent stake in the Busang River properties. Freeport-McMoRan Copper & Gold, which had plenty of experience in that part of the world, would be the miners. Naturally, Hasan would take a cut for his pure, unprecedented genius.

As the Bre-X phenomenon drove investors to buy junior gold stocks, exploration companies began sprouting like opium poppies. If some jokers from an upstart Canadian company could hit pay dirt at Busang, why couldn't it happen to anyone else?

There was froth around Bre-X and there was froth around junior gold stocks, but the mid-1990s also whipped up another batch of suds that would develop into the biggest stock market bubble in history.

The world's premier capital market, Wall Street, was quite the place to be at the time. Many investors reckoned that the unsustainable bubble began forming on 9 August 1995. That was the day when Netscape Communications, which had launched the original browser for the World Wide Web, went public. Netscape had planned to offer 3.5 million shares (about 10 per cent of its issue) in its initial public offering (IPO)† at $14 a share. That would raise $49 million in cash and put the company's value at close on $500 million, given that about 36 million shares would be in issue. In the six months before listing, Netscape had recorded sales – not profits – of just $17 million. The idea that the company could suddenly be worth half a billion dollars was a little difficult to grasp.

---

* General Haji Mohamed Soeharto, usually spelt Suharto in the English-speaking world, was a military strongman who reigned as Indonesia's second president from 1967 to 1998.

† An IPO, also known as 'going public', is the first sale of stock (shares) by a private company to the public as a whole. In a typical IPO, the company going public by being listed obtains (and pays dearly for) the assistance of an underwriting firm. The firm, typically a division of an investment bank, helps the company decide on what kind of securities to issue, at what price, and when.

A typical market value (or market capitalisation, based on issued shares multiplied by the share price) would be about ten times a company's annual earnings. If Netscape had earned $1 million in its latest financial year, for example, the stock could expect to achieve a market capitalisation of $10 million. Netscape, however, was in loss. But if investors were convinced that its browser was literally going to take over the world, its market capitalisation would be pushed up as they scrambled to buy shares.

In practice, investors were hysterically certain that Netscape was the best thing since sliced bread. It was going to sell zillions, not millions, of Web browsers. In consultation with Morgan Stanley, Netscape's investment bank and adviser, the decision was made ahead of listing to offer five million shares at $28 apiece. That would raise $140 million in cash. When the stock listed on the Nasdaq, it opened at $71 a share and traded as high as $75 before finally closing at $58.25. Investors had valued Netscape at $2.1 billion.

Over the next few months, the Netscape stock price would rise as high as $171 a share, valuing the company at just over $6 billion. Netscape's revenue soared from $85 million in 1995 to $346 million in 1996, and then to $534 million in 1997. During 1998, Microsoft's browser, Explorer, began to take over, stalling growth at Netscape and pushing the company into loss. From its December 1995 high of $171, Netscape plummeted to $16 a share in January 1998. Later in the year, America Online announced that it would buy Netscape for $4 billion in an all-paper deal.

The apparently sad story of Netscape aside, the demand for Internet stocks, or anything remotely connected to the Internet, had exploded. The so-called boom age of TMT – telecommunications, media and technology – saw 850 companies selling shares for the first time in 1996, notching up an all-time record on Wall Street and raising a total of $52 billion in cash. In April 1996, Yahoo! listed at $13 a share and immediately moved up to $33. For investors, these were wild times, but professional investment analysts were having it rough.

Who could be trusted? In his book *The Number*, Alex Berenson summed up the situation as follows:

> After 1990, only two factors prevented analysts from totally prostituting themselves in the service of investment banking. The first was professional pride, always a thin reed. The second was that an analyst who recommended too many losing stocks could lose the respect of institutional investors. They might punish his firm by sending trades to other banks, by refusing to buy its stock and bond offerings. Securities firms made more money from investment banking than commission, but they still needed big investors to buy stock to make the system work. With the IPO boom, the easiest way for institutional investors to make

money was by getting shares in hot offerings. What happened to the offerings in the long run made little difference; big investors often sold most of their IPO shares in the first few days after a company opened for trading. The old quid pro quo of good research for commissions had turned into a new currency: hot IPOs for commissions. Institutional investors no longer even pretended to care about research.

These were times when the excesses of greed and fear would assume proportions never seen before. It was all about avarice, covetousness and rapacity. The retail investor – the little person, the man in the street – on whom big capital markets ultimately depend, was seen as flea-infested vermin demanding to be chased up a stinking alley and then beaten to death with a blunt object. In honouring competition, investment professionals were just as savage with each other. In his book *FIASCO: Blood in the Water on Wall Street*, Frank Partnoy, who sold derivatives at 'bulge bracket firms' on Wall Street between 1993 and 1995, recalls:

> Following [John] Mack's lead, my ingenious bosses became feral multimillion-aires: half geek, half wolf. When they weren't performing complex computer calculations, they were screaming about how they were going to 'rip someone's face off' or 'blow someone up.' Outside of work they honed their killer instincts at private skeet-shooting clubs, on safaris and dove hunts in Africa and South America … After April 1994, when these [derivative] losses began to increase, John Mack's instructions were clear: 'There's blood in the water. Let's go kill someone.' We were prepared to kill someone, and we did. The battlefields of the derivatives world are littered with our victims. As you may have read in the newspapers, at Orange County and Barings Bank and Daiwa Bank and Sumitomo Corporation and perhaps others no one knows about yet, a *single* person lost more than a billion dollars.

These were savage people, carnivores who demanded heaps of fresh meat on the hour. They had enough people worried. On 5 December 1996, Alan Greenspan, chairman of the Federal Reserve, the US central bank, gave a speech at the annual dinner and Francis Boyer Lecture of the American Enterprise Institute for Public Policy Research in Washington, DC. Apparently concerned about the rate at which stock prices were rising, Greenspan asked: 'But how do we know when irrational exuberance has unduly escalated asset values?'

The phrase 'irrational exuberance' would become one of the best known in the investment world. Later, Greenspan observed:

> We as central bankers need not be concerned if a collapsing financial asset bubble does not threaten to impair the real economy, its production, jobs and

price stability. Indeed, the sharp stock market break of 1987 had few negative consequences for the economy. But we should not underestimate or become complacent about the complexity of the interactions of asset markets and the economy.

In yet another example of serendipitous timing, the stock market boom coincided with one mother of a gold rush. Never before had so many acres around the world been available to exploration for any metal or mineral that mankind chose to seek. Geologists, drillers and everyone else required to find deposits in the first place were able to utilise truly outstanding modern technologies. New processing techniques, including heap leaching and bacterial leaching, meant that even low-grade ores could be mined at substantial profit. Mines that had long been abandoned as uneconomical due to low grades could be brought back to life. By the same token, virgin deposits that had been overlooked for offering once-poor grades could hold the promise of becoming major modern mines. In some cases, it was even profitable to mine discarded waste from previous eras; dumps and the contents of slime dams were being processed all over again.

This was a new age, when mineral economics experts in their various guises would work together on known 'environments for mineralisation'.* They would embark on regional geological surveys with a view to eventually focusing on smaller areas. Remote sensing techniques dominated, and included satellite data, air photo interpretations, outcrop and geological interpretation surveys. The search for new mining deposits also absorbed information from geophysics, the study of the physical properties of the earth.

Geophysical surveys encompass radiometrics (which measures the distribution of three radioactive elements – uranium, thorium and potassium – in the earth's crust), magnetics (aeromagnetic surveys taken from a moving aircraft or helicopter using a magnetometer), and gravity, measured from either airborne (remote) or ground surveys. Further information is gathered from geochemical work by experts who measure the chemistry of rock, soil, stream sediments or plants to determine abnormal chemical patterns that might point to areas of mineralisation. A smaller area identified as holding out good promise would then be drilled, depending on the precise programme. Drilling was expensive, but costs varied among the main techniques employed, namely air-rotary, air-percussion, mud-rotary and diamond core drilling.

For the would-be next Bre-X, the countless acres waiting to be explored and all the devices that could be deployed in the quest were not the only magnets on the

---

* The presence of a target mineral in a mass of host rock.

horizon. Communism, at least as a political system, was dead and buried. Nations everywhere were embracing capitalism and the privatisation of assets that had been seized in paroxysms of nationalisation. Opportunities to strike it rich abounded, but none of the prospects were so run down as those in Africa. A single example from Ghana serves as a useful microcosm.

The Prestea mine, situated on the famous Ashanti gold trend, was commercially commissioned for the first time in 1873, when the slave, ivory and gold trades dominated much of sub-Saharan Africa. Ghana was known as the Gold Coast for good reason. Over more than a century, nearly 10 million ounces of gold had been dug out of Prestea. From 1873 to 1965, the concession comprised a number of different licences operated by independent mining companies. These had all been amalgamated in 1965, eight years after Ghana was granted independence by Britain. The dreaded colonialists and their corporate inventions were given the boot and the vast majority of foreign-owned assets were nationalised. Then, absolutely atypically of post-nationalisation processes, production at Prestea began declining due to lack of sustained investment. Management lost its spark, and the mine was doomed to operate at a loss sooner or later. Eventually, it did. In 1985, Ghana's State Gold Mining Corporation, which had ruined every one of the nationalised gold mines, secured a World Bank loan to rehabilitate them. After three years of continued losses, the decision was taken to privatise. It was one hell of a thing.

Given the fetid swamps of social and economic mayhem that Africa had produced so prodigiously, attracting capital to the continent was no easy task. It helped little that on 6 April 1994, the Rwandan president, Juvénal Habyarimana, and the president of Burundi, Cyprien Ntaryamira, died when a missile brought down their jet near the Rwandan capital of Kigali. Hutu extremists, suspecting that Habyarimana was finally about to implement the Arusha Peace Accords, were believed to have orchestrated the deadly attack. Mass killings started that night and the Rwandan genocide followed. By 21 April, the Red Cross estimated that the death toll already ran into hundreds of thousands. In the months ahead, the total would be put at a minimum of half a million.

But where the potential rewards are great enough, mankind will always take risks beyond the normal. Africa's natural resources remained virtually limitless and heavily under-exploited, despite the spoils harvested by both colonial and national rulers, and so it was that the modern process of privatisation rekindled a pioneering enthusiasm.

5

Free at last

O N T H E B U S I N E S S, social and political fronts, the mid-1990s were a watershed for South Africa. The country had never nationalised its mines, or anything else, and the black majority had never ruled it.

But in 1994, upon the official death of apartheid, the country was handed over to a black government following a peaceful general election, the first based on universal suffrage after almost 350 years of white rule.

When Nelson Mandela was sworn in as South Africa's first black president, the mining or 'resources' sector had five major investment groups. There was the ubiquitous Anglo American Corporation (which also controlled Johannesburg Consolidated Investments, or JCI), Anglovaal, Gencor (formerly General Mining and Finance Corporation, an entity successfully established for the Afrikaners by Anglo American), Gold Fields of South Africa, and Randgold & Exploration (formerly Rand Mines). When the democratically elected government took office in 1994, the South African resources sector plunged into an extensive and unprecedented period of corporate restructuring, which included unbundling.

The process was multipronged, but in essence hinged on simplifying a complex system of interlocking ownerships and directorships, followed by intense refocusing. The idea was to establish separate core commodity focused profit centres, diversify and rationalise non-performing assets to make the newly restructured companies more competitive internationally. Along the way, parts of the original entity would be spun off or 'unbundled'. In simple and extreme terms, a mining house that found itself with interests in, say, ten different areas, might unbundle fully, creating ten independently managed entities.

The mining houses had grown increasingly complex during the apartheid years, as international sanctions took their toll on South Africa. The conglomerates that controlled the bulk of the country's capital were constantly under threat, whether real or perceived, regarding supplies. In generating excess capital, the mining houses were wont to secure supplies of practically everything, ranging from timber to banking services, by buying into entities that supplied such goods and services. Sometimes the support structures were simply taken over, but in either event, when apartheid officially expired, South Africa's mining industry was one of the worst corporate dog's breakfasts the civilised world had ever seen.

A number of shining paths had already been laid out in the international resources arena, not least by Rio Tinto, a diversified miner listed in both London and Australia, and Toronto-based Barrick, a major gold player. It was possible to be either diversified or focused and yet still win the approval of investors. Rio Tinto had shown that, first and foremost, the most successful business model for a diversified miner comprised access to each operation's underlying cash flow. Whenever possible, that access should be at the level of 100 per cent, or as close to it as possible. It was one thing to reflect income from an operation; that might be impressive to some, but what really counted was control over cash flow. This, in turn, meant that underlying operations should remain unlisted, wherever possible. In this case, only the parent company, Rio Tinto, would be listed.

Just as Rio Tinto had earned a solid reputation by focusing on low-cost, long-life, high-quality mining assets, no matter how diversified, Barrick had shown the advantages of being a 'pure play' in gold. Rio Tinto, by contrast, produced everything from gold to iron ore, from coal to copper and diamonds. The modern Rio Tinto was formed in the December 1995 unification of the RTZ Corporation and Conzinc Rio Tinto of Australia through a dual-listed companies structure.

There were some exceedingly bright South Africans who followed foreign developments with great interest. By the mid-1990s, Brian Gilbertson had success-fully launched his CEO career in Johannesburg, and would go on to create one of the world's leading resources exponents, BHP Billiton. Gilbertson all but perfected investor requirements of low-cost, long-life, high-quality mining assets. He also refined and came close to perfecting other critical elements, such as forward growth profiles and the ability of the overall entity to generate significant amounts of cash, almost regardless of the state of the price cycle in any particular period.

By the mid-1990s, South Africa's mining houses had no choice but to kick-start significant and irreversible reorganisation and restructuring. There were lots of pure plays, to be sure, but even in the gold sector, each listed mine was inevitably controlled by a major mining house via an equity stake of 20 to 40 per cent.

The mining houses had created and long maintained a curious structure of management fees. An underlying, typically listed mining operation would pay fees to the 'parent'. The fees would tend to rise gently each year, but would bear no relationship at all to exogenous changes in price – such as gold – to which the mine was exposed. The management fee practice allowed mining houses to control material parts of the cash flow of a mine in which less than 50 per cent was held. Hefty cash management fees paid to the parent mining house deprived the full body of shareholders of what could be a greater return. Immune to prevailing metal or commodity prices, the management fees provided an annuity type income to the mining houses. After deduction of the fees, mines would pay a pro rata dividend to all shareholders. At any given point in time, any serious investigation of the basis – and especially level – of the management fees would raise a number of alarm bells.

Harmony Gold Mining criticised management fees in its filings with the US Securities Exchange Commission (SEC)* in Washington as follows:

> Commercial gold mining in South Africa evolved with the establishment of various mining houses at the beginning of the 1900s by individuals who bought and consolidated blocks of claims until sufficient reserves could be accumulated to sustain underground mining. The mines were then incorporated, but it was not the practice of the founding mining house to retain a majority shareholding. Instead, the mining house would enter into a management agreement with the mine, pursuant to which the mining house would carry out certain managerial, administrative and technical functions pursuant to long-term contracts. Fees were generally charged based on revenues, working costs or capital expenditures, or a combination of all three, without regard to the cost or the level of services provided.

The double milking of underlying mining operations by South African mining houses was unsustainable. It had to be abolished, leaving each operation free to contract for whatever services it did not, or could not, provide in-house.

So it was that, during 1994, Gencor unbundled four divisions: consumer products, energy, forest products and investments. Unbundling quickly became the relatively simple process of freeing up chunks of assets that had become concentrated in the mining houses. Thus, if mining house AAA held, say, a 40 per cent stake in BBB gold mine, a 30 per cent stake in CCC platinum mine and a 20 per cent stake in DDD coal mine, it would simply post the shares (assuming each entity was listed) in each entity to its own shareholders. The separate managements of BBB, CCC and DDD would then be free to focus on their specialised destinies and, all else being equal, AAA would disappear. The original shareholder would then own stakes in three separate companies, rather than one. Shareholder exposure was more specialised, and less diversified, should the original shareholder not retain

---

* A feared US federal regulatory body that requires highly detailed filings from companies listed on any stock exchange in America. A number of South African–based companies are listed in the US and file regularly with the SEC. AngloGold Ashanti, Harmony Gold and Gold Fields, among others, enjoy primary listings in Johannesburg and secondary listings on the New York Stock Exchange, while Durban Roodepoort Deep (or DRDGold), among others, have secondary listings on the Nasdaq Composite. All self-respecting gold stocks should be listed in the US; some of the world's most avid 'gold bugs' are to be found in North America.

shares in each of BBB, CCC and DDD. In due course, each or any of BBB, CCC and DDD could exercise individual choices of merger and acquisition (M&A) activity.

The process was tantamount to a corporate revolution. Even Anglo American was roused by the smelling salts of change, saying it would propose the sale of its 40 per cent controlling stake in JCI pending appropriate and anticipated changes in tax laws. JCI would be split into three entities: one would control non-mining industrial assets; another (JCI Ltd) would control all the mining assets, save platinum and diamonds, which would be retained by Anglo American as the third entity.

The huge energy that beset the South African mining houses in 1994 set in motion processes that would continue for years. The ongoing reorganisation of assets and unbundling (also known as divestment) was only part of the process. Free of the prohibitive shackles of apartheid, the mining houses exploded into frenetic activity beyond South Africa's borders. Gencor, firmly under the watch of Gilbertson, purchased the worldwide mining assets of Billiton, a subsidiary of Royal Dutch/Shell. The latter's process of unbundling was part of a different but simultaneous global dynamic, which saw big companies seeking a return to their core business. Gencor also merged its Trans-Natal coal company with Rand Coal to form Ingwe Coal, from inception the world's largest exporter of steam coal.

In May 1995, as promised, Anglo American unbundled its holdings in JCI into JCI Ltd (gold, ferrochrome, coal and base metals), Anglo American Platinum (a consolidation of interests from both Anglo American and JCI, forming the world's No. 1 platinum group metals producer) and Johnnies Industrial Corporation, which retained JCI's non-mining industrial holdings. It was the beginning of the end for JCI, which had been founded in 1889 by Barney Barnato in the wake of the Kimberley diamond rush and the 1886 discovery of gold on the Witwatersrand.

Barnato had arrived in Kimberley in 1873, aged just 21. With £30 in cash and a box of cigars, he peddled trinkets, juggled for tips, ran a shanty bar, traded in diamonds and even dabbled in prize-fighter boxing. Barnato and his brother Harry would later buy four small diamond claims that the owner had quit as being mined out. Inevitably, there were rumours that the Barnatos were salting their claims with illegal diamonds, but whether this was true or not, the brothers had laid the foundation for a fortune.

Barnato founded JCI as a holding company to administer entities he acquired in Johannesburg in the early years of the biggest gold rush the world has ever seen. Assisted by his nephew, Solly Joel, Barnato reinvested diamond profits from Kimberley in the Johannesburg waterworks and South African Breweries (now SAB Miller), as well as in establishing Johannesburg suburbs such as Yeoville, Berea, Houghton and Doornfontein. His big money, of course, was invested in gold mining via Government Gold Mining Areas, Langlaagte Estates and Gold Mining Company, New State Areas and Randfontein.

Barnato died prematurely in 1897. He had been under extreme stress at the prospect of facing London shareholders displeased with the performance of his mines, and, while travelling to England on the Union steamer *The Scot*, Barnato jumped – or was pushed – overboard near Madeira. The only witness was Solly Joel, who also happened to be the sole heir to Barnato's fortune. By 1939, JCI administered seven major gold mining companies, along with interests in platinum and coal mines.

South Africa's first commercial gold deposits were discovered in the Eastern Transvaal (now Mpumalanga) in 1873, hosted by what the mining community refers to as 'greenstones'. Such deposits can be erratic and gold can be difficult to extract, but on good days, a really rich seam can pay the month's costs. However, South Africa's greenstones were dwarfed by the discovery in 1886 of the gigantic Witwatersrand Basin geological structure, around what was to become Johannesburg. The hosting of the gold was pretty consistent, and the banket that was dug out surrendered gold with relative ease. By 1898, South Africa had overtaken the US as the world's No. 1 gold producer, a position the country has maintained almost continuously ever since. From 1884, the first year of recorded output, South Africa was the source of close on 40 per cent of all the gold production in the world.

Since 1994, a concerted effort has been made to publicise Mapungubwe, an area of open savannah at the confluence of the Limpopo and Shashe rivers abutting South Africa's northern border with Zimbabwe and Botswana. Professional excavation of the settlement at Mapungubwe, first discovered in 1932, indicated that it was a sophisticated trading centre from around 1220 to 1300. A little rhinoceros made from gold plating, dating back 800 years, would seem to debunk the view that gold was first found and mined in South Africa in 1873. Ming pottery and glass beads excavated at Mapungubwe offered apparent proof of trade and diplomatic relations between southern Africa and Asia long before European seafarers rounded the Cape in search of spices. Abandoned in the fourteenth century, Mapungubwe – in what is now the province of Limpopo – was apparently the centre of the largest kingdom on the subcontinent, inhabited by a highly sophisticated people who traded gold and ivory with China, India and Egypt. Whether or not the gold found at the ancient site was mined nearby, or elsewhere in South Africa, or somewhere entirely different, by the mid-1990s, South Africa offered precious little in the way of 'blue sky' to would-be gold barons.

Nonetheless, even the great Johannesburg gold rush seemed to pale by comparison with the fever sparked by Bre-X, king of the global resources jungle in the mid-1990s, which infected a motley collection of players. The Bre-X story found particular resonance within a certain circle, politely described as the bosses at Randgold & Exploration, based at Crown Mines, just south of Johannesburg. Like so many other mere mortals, they were looking for any opportunity that made financial sense, but far from being ordinary human beings, this was the League of Extraordinary Gentlemen made manifest.

Randgold & Exploration had been incorporated on 29 September 1992 and was listed on the JSE, the South African bourse known over the years by several variations on its core name, the Johannesburg Stock Exchange. Randgold & Exploration advertised itself as being engaged in 'the gold mining and exploration business in Africa', and stated that 'substantially all of our profits come from the sale of gold'. Like JCI, Randgold & Exploration boasted a substantial history, with its origins traceable to 1893, when Rand Mines was the first South African mining house – as opposed to operating mine – to issue securities publicly. Randgold & Exploration was established in 1992 to take over the gold and mineral rights (other than coal, platinum and real estate not then being used for mining purposes) of Rand Mines as a result of restructuring (a euphemism for booting out most of the previous directors and management).

The rights included Rand Mines' equity holdings and management agreements with a number of affiliated gold mining companies, such as Transvaal Gold Mining Estates and various exploration sites in Africa. Randgold & Exploration subsequently acquired equity interests in three additional South African gold mining affiliates: Buffelsfontein, Grootvlei and Crown.

However, it was on the back of the heavy-breathing inspiration from Bre-X that Randgold & Exploration separated its exploration activities in 1995 into those carried out in South Africa and Namibia (named the Randblock area), and those conducted in other African states. Randgold & Exploration specifically incorporated Randgold Resources as a 100 per cent subsidiary 'for the purpose of exploring and developing gold deposits from African countries outside the Randblock'. Randgold Resources, the world was told, conducted 'exploration operations on its mineral rights and permits in the countries of Côte d'Ivoire, Senegal, Mali and Tanzania'. Even a cursory investigation would show that the properties concerned were nothing but tracts of dirt. They had been well scrutinised by experienced gold explorers and junked.

But the bosses at Randgold & Exploration were not inclined to let the facts get in the way of a good story, and Bre-X was one hell of a story. In the vast ocean of froth created by the runaway Canadian project, every investor and his dog was looking for the next Busang. Apparently, Randgold Resources was going to provide South African investors with a way to cash in on the Bre-X miracle.

In a sense, Randgold Resources could be 'sold' to a captive audience, given South Africa's draconian foreign exchange or capital control laws, which prohibited residents from investing in any stock not listed on the JSE. Though very much a living relic of the apartheid system, the new democratic government appeared to really fancy the exchange controls. South African residents were obliged to keep as much as possible, if not all of their money, inside the country. Even travel allowances for foreign holidays had strict limits and had to be individually approved.

For Randgold & Exploration, however, a two-tier strategy offered a way to export capital. South African residents could be offered Randgold Resources via its parent company, Randgold & Exploration, which was listed on the JSE. Even if Randgold Resources sought a foreign listing – in London, for example – South African investors could still buy Randgold & Exploration as an indirect, albeit 'impure', entry into Randgold Resources. A foreign listing for Randgold Resources would naturally require permission from the SA Reserve Bank, administrator of the foreign exchange controls, but Randgold Resources stood a chance of gaining such permission, since all its assets would be outside the so-called Randblock. In a foreign jurisdiction such as the United Kingdom, for example, Randgold Resources could raise money from international capital markets on the London Stock Exchange without placing any strain on the South African financial system.

In the global gold equities arena, professional investment analysts were having a tough time estimating the underlying value of listed gold exploration stocks or juniors. A large, active gold stock such as Barrick had operating mines in a number of countries and exploration teams seeking new ones, so investors had a fairly good idea of the company's market value, given the available information on its underground gold reserves, output, cash flows and profits. With Bre-X and other juniors, however, investors had to work with the wonderfully loose concept known as 'blue sky'. A study of market values of gold stocks provided a number of pointers as to how to value the juniors, starting with ignoring South African gold stocks. Investors were looking for magic, but, given that the country had been intensively explored for metal and mineral deposits for more than a century, South Africa in the mid-1990s offered little, if any, 'blue sky'.

In terms of the Bre-X formula, once South Africa had been ruled out of the equation, the investor would seek a stock that was listed in Vancouver, Toronto, New York, London, Sydney or just about anywhere else, as long as it was not Johannesburg. Next, the stock had to be tied to gold exploration, preferably exclusively. These stocks were known as 'pure' gold exploration plays, and naturally included Bre-X.

However, there was no readily available method to value such stocks, which tended to burn cash on exploring, drilling and testing, year after year. Most companies managed to continue operating by undertaking private placements, something of a misnomer, since expert institutional investors rather than small private investors typically provided the funds. Such transactions save the issuing entity a great deal of paperwork. A capital-raising exercise that is made available to all shareholders, known in South Africa as a 'rights issue', and in many other jurisdictions as a 'capital issue', requires the publication of vast amounts of information. By contrast, in private placings, expert or 'qualified' investors avail themselves of all required facts, including confidential ones, before parting with capital. Much of this information is provided by management in verbal form, saving the company the time and expense of producing huge volumes of formal documentation.

By the mid-1990s, there was no shortage of investor capital for junior gold stocks. With Bre-X leading the way, the heat for inventiveness was enormous. Specialist investment analysts would count the acres or hectares within each permit held by a gold exploration stock, add up the total and multiply that by a random number of dollars. When questioned about the basis for this technique, the typical response was that the initial model had been derived from stocks that were, indeed, listed. Thus, if a listed gold exploration junior stock had a market value of $10 million, a 'value per hectare' could be calculated by simply dividing this amount by the number of hectares in the company's name. Once some kind of benchmark had been established, the rush was on for each company to acquire yet more rights, to more hectares. If you want to catch a fish, as the saying goes, you need to have a hook and line in the water.

For a while, this crude methodology seemed to suffice, giving investors a guideline as to which company might find the next Busang. But as the Bre-X story spread like a deadly hurricane, investment analysts refined their work an extra step or two. By comparing the values and activity profiles of all listed gold stocks, it was relatively easy to show that investors awarded a huge premium to a gold exploration stock that had graduated to commissioning its first mine. A gold mine can take several years to commission after discovery, depending on the nature of the under-lying deposit and its geographical location. In South Africa, however, gold mines are the deepest in the world, and on the Witwatersrand a new mine can take up to a decade to commission. In the modern era, as mines reach ever deeper, diggers descend more than three kilometres below the surface, using twin sub-vertical shaft systems. In open-cast gold mines, which are virtually unknown in South Africa and where eventually the mined-out ore body is just a big hole in the ground, some companies have claimed a year from green light to the first pouring of gold.

Beyond the Witwatersrand, most gold mines fall into the open-cast category, including Bre-X.

When the promoters of Randgold Resources opted to separate Randgold & Exploration's activities in 1995 and spin off the so-called Randblock assets, they were led by the first priority of constructing a company that would capture the fancy of professional investors. The patches of dirt that Randgold Resources boasted about were worthless, and Randgold & Exploration knew it. So, while Randgold Resources had been formed as a gold exploration company, first prize would be to acquire an existing operating mine. That was the trick; that was the magic formula; and that was something that simply had to be done. It would just not be good enough to offer the market a piece of barren West African soil. Within the international gold mining equities arena, any specialist investment analyst could show that the high valuations inspired by Bre-X applied to companies that were poking around in weird and wild and wonderful and even dangerous places.

Bre-X fitted the bill perfectly. West Africa was also a hot area, as could be seen from the prices of stocks like Nevsun, domiciled in Canada. West Africa was a particularly good bet compared with most of South America, which remained as dangerous as ever. North America and Australia, like South Africa, were relatively well explored. Western Europe had been mined out of most things, and exploration in Eastern Europe and Russia was incredibly risky, not least from a financial viewpoint. As for greater Asia, while Bre-X had apparently hit one mighty El Dorado, conditions were extreme, and known geological structures were not as promising as in Africa.

At Randgold & Exploration's head office at Crown Mines, the plotting continued. It was one thing to 'materialise' Randgold Resources, but cashing in on the global gold rush was an entirely different matter. Randgold & Exploration had no fewer than 14 directors in 1995, with two additional alternates. This was an inordinately large board, given the nature and scope of Randgold & Exploration's business. There was, however, an extraordinary mixture of skills among the directors, providing the potential to concoct plots varying from the mundane to the mutant.

The full-time executive chairman was listed as Peter Flack, a lawyer by training. He had developed something of a reputation as a turnaround artist, a skill that suited Randgold & Exploration's profile like no other. Flack was also magnificently arrogant; he could, and would, terrify people just by glaring at them.

Frank Abbott was listed as having joined the Rand Mines/Barlow Rand Group in 1981. He was appointed as financial controller of the newly formed Randgold & Exploration in 1992, and promoted to financial director in October 1994. David Ashworth, a British national and a pleasant enough chap, directed new business and exploration. Mark Bristow was listed as director of geology and exploration. Never shy to remind his audience that he held a doctorate in geology and had discovered some or other platinum mine, Bristow had a boyish face and a blind enthusiasm for everything that caught his attention. He wanted to be listened to, and loved talking down to those conniving Canadians and Australians.

Richard Reginald de Villiers was the hapless human resources director, while Lionel Hewitt, a long-time Anglo American man, 'brought with him a level of experience and credibility that went down well among the investment analysts studying the South African mining scene', according to one report. Hewitt was quoted as saying: 'I'm always bumping into good people who have joined Randgold because they are given autonomy at the mines.'

Among the eight non-executive directors, it was perhaps no coincidence that five were foreign. Two – Jean-Antoine Cramer and Ferdinand Lips – were Swiss, while Adam Fleming, Ted Grobicki and David Starling were listed as British.

Fleming, said to be a relative (like so many others of the same name) of James Bond spy-novel author Ian, was educated at Eton College and joined the family business, Robert Fleming Holdings, in 1970. He moved to South Africa in 1991 to open various offices: Fleming Martin in South Africa, Edwards & Company in Zimbabwe and Stockbrokers Botswana.

Cramer was senior partner in Messieurs Cramer & Cie, a Geneva portfolio management company, and president of the Corporate Association of Geneva Investment Managers. He was appointed a director of Randgold & Exploration in 1994.

Lips, a self-confessed gold bug, was punted as a 'well-established and respected authority on gold and the gold market'. His roots were in banking, having been a co-founder and managing director of Rothschild Bank in Zurich before opening his own bank, Lips, in the Swiss financial capital in 1987.

Grobicki was heavily qualified in mining, geology and related fields, and played various roles within mining and exploration companies in South Africa, Namibia and Zimbabwe. In 1979, he was appointed CEO of Texas Gulf Incorporated South Africa, and since then had served at a senior executive level in a wide range of public and private companies in the mining sector.

In 1995, Randgold & Exploration listed three other non-executive directors – Nigel Brunette, David Dods and Fred Stokes – and two alternate directors, Johan Burger and JM Jephson.

There was also a huge wild card in the background, namely Julian Baring of London money manager Mercury Asset Management (MAM). Baring apparently spoke for about 27 per cent of Randgold & Exploration in and around 1995, and had much to say about many things. He had targeted a number of South African mining companies in varying raids of 'vicious commentary'. In particular, Baring ridiculed the management fee system paid in South Africa by operating mines to 'head office'. That system, as widely advertised in the mid-1990s, was, according to one report, 'going out of fashion thanks to the takeover of Randgold & Exploration by a team led by Peter Flack and supported by Julian Baring'.

Baring had started out in then Rhodesia (now Zimbabwe) with Anglo American, before moving to London brokers James Capel, where in due course he became 'the No. 1 mining man'. In 1988, Baring moved to fund management before being swallowed, along with James Capel's £45 million gold and general fund, by MAM. The fund, which also absorbed a number of others, was worth around £1.3 billion in the mid-1990s. MAM was big and was meant to be feared and respected.

It was only natural that the League of Extraordinary Gentlemen wanted to hop onto the gold rush bandwagon. But the plot had to be refined considerably before it could be executed. There were enough obstacles in the way, including fairly serious competition, which included some of the best mining men Africa had ever known. As for entrepreneurial skill, there were few as nimble and fleet-footed as the Canadians, in particular, and the Australians.

Fortunately, Flack had focused on drawing the right people into Randgold, not least among them the father-and-son team of Roger Kebble, listed simply as a director, and Brett, who held the rather strange position of commercial director in a company that had a clutch of managed investments, but not a single hands-on operation.

Roger had 'emerged from retirement' to take over Rand Leases, which lay adjacent to the grand old lady of the West Rand, Durban Roodepoort Deep. Negotiations to merge the two were proposed in December 1994 and concluded by July 1995.

Brett had jettisoned his original career choice, the law, to embark on one of the wildest rides in the annals of South Africa's mining industry. Randgold would serve as the launch pad for some of the most audacious – if not downright illegal – get-rich-quick schemes since the bygone era of Barnato, Cecil John Rhodes and the Randlords, who wrested fortunes from the blue gravel and yellow rock that put Africa's southernmost tip among the most coveted scrubland on earth.

6

From Tarkwa to Timbuktu

I F RANDGOLD & EXPLORATION was going to buy an operating mine in order to climb onto the Bre-X bandwagon, it would probably be found in West Africa, where Randgold Resources already held a number of exploration permits. West Africa was, at the very least, a corner of the world known to host gold deposits. The Birimian belt, a super-group of geological units formed about 2.1 billion years ago, hosted the legendary Obuasi gold mine in Ghana, operated by Ashanti Goldfields.

Obuasi had been in commercial production for more than a century, and experts who visited this monster during the early 1990s invariably described it as the most complex gold mine in the world. It operated several different processing units, cooking up various types of ore ranging from greenstones and quartzes to sulphides and oxides. However, the real challenge for the operator lay in the manner in which Obuasi, a village-city with a winning soccer team, had become almost indivisible from the mine. Gold theft of one kind or another was rife and almost impossible to eradicate. The mine had always been regarded as a national asset, but to some, it also represented a source of sustained support for those who had lived in the tradition of the great Ashanti tribes for centuries.

In 1994, Ashanti Goldfields went public by way of an IPO, listing its stock on the London Stock Exchange, as well as in Ghana. There was a measure of déjà vu about the move. Ashanti Goldfields had first been listed on the London Stock Exchange in 1897. In 1968, Lonrho, listed in London and Johannesburg, acquired Ashanti Goldfields and took the entity private. The government of Ghana held a 55 per cent stake in Obuasi from 1972, when a coup d'état led by Colonel Ignatius Acheampong toppled KA Busia's democratically elected regime. The state actually seized 55 per cent of all mining companies, but Lonrho retained an equity stake in Obuasi and remained, by and large, in control of day-to-day operations.

At the time of the 1994 re-listing in London, the government privatised Ashanti Goldfields by selling 25 per cent of its holding, reducing its equity stake to 30 per cent. However, it continued to hold a 'golden share' – a single 'poison pill' share that could block any attempted takeover.

Everyone had a go at Obuasi. Artisanal miners, known as *galamsey* or *garampieros* (in South America), had worked the famous quartz veins in and around the deposit for as long as anyone could remember. The mine's commercial history could be traced back to March 1890, when two Fante merchants from Cape Coast, Joseph E Ellis and Chief Joseph E Biney, and their accountant, Joseph P Brown, secured mining concessions of over 25 900 hectares in and around Obuasi. The partners crossed the River Pra into the kingdom of Adansi and studied *galamsey* working the outcrops for the King of Bekwai. Their concession in the Obuasi district, in the foothills of the Moinsi and Kwisa ranges between the Oda and Offin rivers, was thought to be the 'neglected El Dorado' that explorer Richard Burton had described. The new owners of the Obuasi concessions were intrepid, or mad, or both. Few Europeans were unaware of how the omnipotent Ashanti dynasty had terrorised intruders and dominated neighbours for centuries. On the flip side, British soldiers who returned home from the Ashanti wars often carried nuggets of ore bearing glittering streaks of the precious metal.

Elsewhere in Ghana, miners continued to dig pay ore out of the ground. In 1993, a quantum change was about to take place at Tarkwa, close to Obuasi and about 300 kilometres from the capital of Accra. Large-scale gold mining had started at Tarkwa in the last quarter of the nineteenth century, and continued through nationalisation and even after acquisition by Ghana's State Gold Mining Corporation from private companies owned by European investors. In 1993, Gold Fields, one of the world's major gold-diggers, became the new Tarkwa operator. For a relative pittance – less than $10 million – the Johannesburg-based company acquired 71 per cent of the equity in Tarkwa. The Ghanaian government held its 10 per cent so-called 'free carry', with the balance of the equity held by another private sector investor. By some measures, the Tarkwa mine was a bit of a plum, with access to the national electricity grid, road infrastructure and an ample water supply. Most consumables were trucked in from either the nearest seaport, about 140 kilometres away at Takoradi, or from Tema near Accra.

Tarkwa had come into the hands of Gold Fields thanks not least to Bernard van Rooyen, a director of a number of companies and unquestionably one of the most knowledgeable and well-connected mining men on the African continent. When it came to mining in Africa, there was no fooling with the 'Silver Fox', as some knew Van Rooyen. He had waited years, if not decades, to get back into African gold mining. It was no fluke that he kept his eye on Tarkwa – Obuasi was simply not available; its major outside shareholder, Lonrho, was not going to sell its stake in such a prize.

Van Rooyen was keenly aware that Tarkwa needed a singular individual, somebody who could live in a jungle, a remote area with unpleasant weather, far from modern amenities. More importantly, it would have to be someone who could endure the scourge of the Harmattan, that bastard of a wind that blows southwest and west off the Sahara and consumes the skies, horizon to horizon, from November to March with its evil orange haze; the wind that travels, when it really blows, across the Gulf of Guinea and the Atlantic, all the way to South America; the wind that can drive man and beast to distraction and irritation, yet is called 'The Doctor' by some for its cooling effect.

Van Rooyen needed somebody who could manage and control Tarkwa, a mine that had become a beast, while at the same time appreciating that this was potentially one of the finest gold mines in the world. Famous for his ability to select the best for a particular job, Van Rooyen chose Glyn Lewis.

Lewis was an engineer who turned out to be one of the best mining men to ever work in Africa. He had enrolled at the University of the Witwatersrand's renowned mining school for an engineering degree in 1976 and was a brilliant student. A man's man to the core, Lewis chose his friends carefully. If you had to go to war and you could take only one person with you, Lewis was the man you'd want. He blossomed in his chosen profession, and his achievements at various Gold Fields mines in South Africa were carefully noted.

Van Rooyen gave Lewis one month to pack up his life and get to Tarkwa. South Africa was still a year away from its first democratic elections, but Van Rooyen had sensed, ahead of any other mining man, that the last rites were being administered to apartheid. He had started negotiating on Tarkwa with the Ghanaian authorities as early as 1988, and when Lewis hit the ground running in 1993, Gold Fields became the first South African mining company to set up camp not only in Ghana, but in the whole of West Africa.

Just 18 members of the Gold Fields SA staff, led by Lewis, were seconded to Tarkwa. When they arrived, they found a totally run-down tropical beast. The offices and the residential compound for senior management, situated on a hill, were in an advanced state of disrepair, though there was evidence of a glorious past in the size, scope and design of the houses, and the mining property as a whole. The clubhouse, also built atop a hill, was a splendid monument to the past, with a washed-out, tropical appearance and deep verandas that gave it a cool and peaceful feel. After Lewis arrived, cold beers were always available deep inside the building, across a large expanse of floor with a beautiful inlay of coloured glass chips.

The mine itself was a wreck. Lewis sensed that he could squeeze about 50 000 ounces a year from the residual underground reserves, but the costs would be high, and in just a few years, after more than a century, the mine would be worked out. Gold Fields had contracted to run the underground mine for six years, and Lewis knew this would demand special attention. So good was he at his job that he doubled production from the old workings in both 1994 and 1995, but, like Van Rooyen,

Lewis sensed that something much bigger was lurking just below the surface at Tarkwa, and before long, Van Rooyen despatched exploration teams to the mine.

One day in 1995, Lewis took a familiar drive to a small sandy hill overlooking the area where the surface gold was being proved up. He looked over Akontansi East; he looked over Mantraim; he looked over Pepe; he looked over Akontansi Ridge and Kottraverchy. Lewis was excited by the prospect of building a really big, perhaps huge, world-class mine. While Akontansi was the king of this prospect, there was gold in all the areas. That year, Tarkwa announced results of further exploration drilling on the mine's surface deposits, citing an indicated resource of 7.5 million ounces of gold, with further potential. A feasibility study to start a major new mine was also announced.

It was going to be one hell of a thing.

By the end of 1995, gold was looking very good for Ghana. Ashanti's expansion at Obuasi had borne fruit, and Cluff Resources Plc turned on the lights at the Ayanfuri mine. From 1988 to 1995, seven major open-cast gold mines had been opened in Ghana; of the 12 formal mines operating in 1995, six accounted for a total of 89 per cent of recorded country gold output, starting with Obuasi (56 per cent) and followed by Teberebie (14 per cent), which was adjacent to Tarkwa, Iduapriem (7 per cent), Bogosu (6 per cent), Ayanfuri (3 per cent) and Tarkwa (3 per cent). The Ashanti Goldfields mining complex at Obuasi increased production by 13 per cent in 1995 to 29 138 kilograms, somewhat less than the 31 103 kilogram-target that had been loudly proclaimed ahead of the London listing in 1994. The million-ounce target for the year had been missed, and investors would never forget it.

*   *   *

On the other side of the continent, and in line with many other African states, Tanzania had done a great deal since the 1990s to become more attractive to the international investment community. The National Investment Promotion Act, introduced in 1990, offered a bunch of cherries that sparked a gold rush in and around the greenstone belts south of Lake Victoria, one of the world's biggest expanses of fresh water and the largest of Africa's Great Lakes.

Exploration companies rolled in from Australia, Canada, South Africa, Sweden and the United Kingdom. At Mwanza, situated on the southern reaches of Lake Victoria, gold was much more than a rumour. During the mid-1990s, the Bulyanhulu prospect, discovered by *galamsey* some 15 years earlier, astonished investors as it materialised commercially under the hands of geologists working for Sutton Resources of Canada. The deposit was rich and extensive, and, like so many other goldfields in Africa, it was crawling with artisanal miners. Close on 200 000 people living in the immediate area had to be told, tactfully and gently, that their mining activities were illegal.

Companies of all kinds and sizes were running around the goldfields. During 1995, Resolute Samantha of Australia, renamed Resolute, paid $25 million for a 50 per cent stake in the Golden Pride prospect held by Samax Resources of the United Kingdom. Randgold Resources Tanzania (a joint venture between Randgold Resources of South Africa and Canada's Pangea Goldfields) was formed in September 1995 to explore the Golden Ridge project. Pangea also held rights to a number of other prospective gold properties, including joint ventures with Anglo American on the Kahama and Chocolate Reef properties. Ashanti Goldfields was keenly at work on the Bulyanhulu South and Rubondo properties.

In early 1996, Ashanti acquired an 85 per cent interest in the old Geita mine and adjacent exploration properties in the Lake Victoria gold belt, via acquisition of Cluff. Ashanti Goldfields also focused attention on a four-kilometre-long northwest extension of the Lone Cone-Geita banded ironstone ridge. Other companies noted in the area included East African Gold Corporation, Princess Resources, Patrician Gold Mines, JCI, Tan Range, Serengeti Diamonds and International Gold Exploration. East African Gold reported a hit on its Kitongo property.

Since this was Africa, gold was hardly a novel story. In ancient times, the ferociously powerful Monomotapa kingdom, centred on what became the ruins of Great Zimbabwe, had dominated the area. The kingdom's influence stretched across modern-day Zimbabwe, the northern regions of South Africa, Mozambique, Zambia, Malawi and Tanzania. On the continent's eastern flank, it extended into the Land of Zanj, where Swahili traders took gold from Great Zimbabwe up the coast past Kilwa and Mogadishu, as far as the Gulf of Aden and on to Asia. By the fourth century, Great Zimbabwe was exchanging ivory, copper and gold for seashells, china, cloth and glass beads. When the Europeans arrived, Great Zimbabwe was at its peak. Like the Arabs, the Portuguese first and foremost wanted gold, which became inextricably intermingled with the Swahili coastal culture, stretching from Somalia in the north to Mozambique in the south. Centuries later, many of the ancient coastal cities still dot the landscape, among them Mogadishu, Brava, Pate, Lamu, Malindi, Mombasa, Zanzibar, Mafia, Kilwa and Sofala.

Zanzibar, perhaps the least changed among them, was one of the major ports from which slaves were shipped out of Africa. Slavery had developed into a serious business when Arab raiders began arriving in the ninth century to ferry their human booty to markets in Mesopotamia, India, Persia and Arabia. By the nineteenth century, the slave trade was large and lucrative, with regular and massive forced exits. The most notorious and biggest slave trader was Hemedi bin Muhammad el-Marjebi, an Afro-Arabian also known as Tippu Tip, for the chattering sound of gunfire associated with his presence.

Born in Zanzibar, Tippu Tip launched his career in the early 1860s south of Lake Tanganyika. Financed by sultans, and by applying a careful blend of force and diplomacy, he soon won a near monopoly in the ivory trade. He then moved northwest, into what is now the Democratic Republic of the Congo, establishing a new headquarters at Kasongo in 1875. By 1880, Tippu Tip had built a large commercial empire between the upper Congo, Lake Tanganyika and Bagamoyo on the coast, where the slaves were shipped to Zanzibar for sale and transport to foreign shores. Tippu Tip met and helped several famous Western explorers of the African continent, not least among them Henry Morton Stanley. On a single foray to capture slaves, history records, Tippu Tip raided 118 villages and killed 4 000 people. When Stanley reached his camp, the slaver had 2 300 captives, mostly young women and children, chained and ready to transport halfway across the continent to the markets of Zanzibar.

In 1887, Tippu Tip was named governor of the Stanley Falls District in the Congo Free State. He died in 1905 at his home in Stone Town, the main settlement on the island of Zanzibar.

Africa survived Tippu Tip, just as it has survived looters of every hue and nationality over the centuries. The present-day Swahili are an exotic mixture of indigenous Africans, Arabs, Shiraz Persians, Indians, Indonesians, Portuguese and other Europeans, but they remain forever linked to the ancient Zanj. Their language is an amalgam of the original Zanj tongue and a dozen other cultures. It is a complicated, sophisticated language with poetry in the sound and a pedigree going back more than a millennium. The official language of Tanzania, Swahili is widely used as a lingua franca in eastern and east-central Africa. Also known as Kiswahili, it is the most widely used language on the African continent. It is one of the many languages of gold.

*   *   *

In the African context, Ghana had long run a poor second to South Africa as a gold-digger. Tanzania and Mali, in turn, were traditionally the strongest contenders for Ghana's position, and, during the new gold rush, Mali rated as one of the top five prospects around the globe.

Mali's capital, Bamako, served as a kind of headquarters for the explorers that flooded into the country, led by Canada's Nevsun, but Kayes, unofficial centre of the Kéniéba gold district to the west of Bamako near the border with Senegal, was the centre of the physical gold rush. There is also highly prospective ground south of the capital, where the Société des Mines d'Or de Syama, SA (Somisy) had operated a gold mine for several years at Syama, 75 kilometres southwest of Sikasso.

In the Kéniéba district, La Société d'Exploitation des Mines d'Or de Sadiola, SA (Semos) was well on the way to being a major gold mine in 1995. It poured its first gold at Sadiola Hill, about 80 kilometres southwest of Kayes, on 20 December 1996. The ownership of Semos was typical of alliances formed in the mid-1990s. Anmercosa Mining (West Africa), a subsidiary of Anglo American, held 38 per cent, as did Agem of Barbados, a subsidiary of International African Mining Gold (or IAMGOLD) of Canada, with the government of Mali holding 18 per cent and the balance being in the name of the International Finance Corporation, a member of the World Bank group.

Reports of gold strikes galvanised the close-knit exploration community at Kayes and quickly spread. It was a busy time, as a US Geological Survey report for 1995 showed. Afko International, a subsidiary of Afko Korea, continued a feasibility study on its permit within the Kéniéba district. US-based Azco Mining, and West African Gold and Exploration of the British Virgin Islands, a joint venture of Eagle River International of Vanuatu and Lion Mining Finance of the United Kingdom, organised the Sanou Mining Corporation in 1996. Sanou held a 100 per cent working interest in the Médinandi and the Dandoko concessions, acquired from the Russian consortium, Guefest.

Emerging Africa Gold of Canada was evaluating the Kolomba-Mancouke, Koulo and Narena permits. Etlin of Australia drilled its Yatela gold permit, north of Sadiola. International Tournigan Corporation of Canada was exploring the Diangounte West property; Nevsun was drilling on the Tabakoto East concession north of Tabakoto, and Oliver Gold of Canada was funding the feasibility study of the Segala concession to earn a 50 per cent interest in the property from Mali's Consolidated Mining Corporation West Africa (CMCWA).

Trillion Resources of Canada acquired 51 per cent of CMCWA, with a 29 per cent interest being retained by Consolidated Mining Corporation of South Africa and 20 per cent by the Malian managing director. Oxford Resources of Canada was evaluating the Sélou, Dialafara-Rhama and Kéniéba group exploration permits. Pan African Resources of Canada conducted a reverse circulation-drilling programme on the four-permit Dioulafoundou property, and was also evaluating the Melgué and the Ouaiaga permits. Meanwhile, Pangea sampled the Fodie property north of Sadiola. Raymor Resources of Canada acquired an 85 per cent interest in the Yeremounde gold property from Comifa of Mali. Ressources Robex of Canada acquired a 51 per cent interest in the Diangounte and Kata concessions from N'Gary

Transport. Ressources Robex and Alpine Exploration of Canada were evaluating the Baroya concession with Somex of Mali. Reunion Mining of the United Kingdom was exploring Sonarem's optioned Sanoukou exploration permit. Sadiola Exploration of the British Virgin Islands, the 50:50 joint venture of Anmercosa and Agem, was drilling the Dinnguilou and the Farabakouta prospects, and evaluating the Alamoutala concession in the Sadiola I permit area adjacent to Sadiola Hill.

Companies with exploration permits for the Kangaba, Kalana and Syama regions south of Bamako included Alagona Trading, Anmercosa and Barrick. Mink Mineral Resources of Canada, along with Viceroy Resources of Canada, was evaluating the Niaouleni gold concession. Oxford was studying its permit area in the Kangaba region. Pacific Galleon Mining of Canada acquired an interest in the Finkolo concession and an option on the Niena concession north of Syama. Pangea was evaluating its Foulaboula property. Sahelian Goldfields of Canada, formerly McNickel, assembled the Kourémalé-Salémalé property from six non-renewable local prospecting authorisations. Sodinaf of Mali was evaluating its Kodieran prospect, and Young Poong Mining and Construction of Korea completed its initial reconnaissance programme at the Gouenso gold project. Following a study of the Kalana underground gold mine, partners Ashanti Goldfields and JCI announced a no-go.

Despite the frenzy of activity in western and southern Mali, gold mining was nothing new to the area. For millennia the yellow metal, along with ivory, copper, salt and slaves, formed the lifeblood of ancient African kingdoms. Gold played a prominent ceremonial role, as illustrated most ostentatiously by the Ashanti kings, who both hoarded and wore it in abundance. There were gold sandals and chains, gold anklets and staffs, gold tunics and swords, gold bracelets, amulets and headdresses. It seemed that everything was made from gold, including the Ashanti Golden Stool, the ultimate symbol of royal power. But Africa was less attached to gold than such displays suggested.

As far back as 500 BC, Herodotus recorded how horse-drawn chariots crossed the Sahara via routes that were followed for millennia. There were two major routes, from Morocco and Egypt, which converged on the upper Niger River before branching into the goldfields of Senegal and Ghana. Egypt and Middle Asia had serious appetites for gold; it was gold that had built and sustained the magnificent ancient kingdoms of both Ghana and Mali. The powers of the ancient African kings depended on controlling the traffic of gold from Senegal and Ghana to the north.

Countless texts show that the ancient kingdom of Ghana, which was far bigger than the present-day country, was centuries old when the first Muslim traders arrived in West Africa in the ninth century. At that time, the capital was situated at Koumbi Saleh, north of Bamako and about 50 kilometres inside what is now Mauritania. The basis of trade in and out of Koumbi Saleh was gold. Following the Arab conquests, Berber nomads had been drifting south from Morocco, and by the ninth century they controlled many of the Atlantic Saharan caravan routes, launching regular attacks on the more settled inhabitants of the kingdom of Ghana. Gold was one of the main targets. The threat from the Berbers proved to be relatively short-lived after they started fighting one another, but Ghana eventually fell to an Islamic uprising, supported by Almoravid tribes.

In 1235, the first Malé, Ruler of Mali, emerged. The Mali kings opened up new goldfields along the Black Volta and further south, in modern-day Ghana. They extended their power to the thriving centres of Timbuktu and Gao, terminuses of the shortest routes across the Sahara, and shipped gold with gusto, mainly to Egypt. The capital of the ancient Malian empire was at Niani on the Sankarani River in Guinea, a small and unimportant tributary of the Niger, but close to alluvial goldfields. The Malians controlled the greatest African trade routes from the Niger River cities of Djenne, Mopti, Timbuktu and Gao. From the desert terminus of Agadez, Tuareg camel trains came and went via the oases of the Sahara, carrying gold to Tripoli and Alexandra, and returning with salt from the desert. Venetian traders struck their coins from Ghanaian gold that had been transported by pirogue down the Niger River. Timbuktu, which had originally been a nomad camel-trading centre, became a centre of great importance for Islamic learning in the fourteenth century.

Musa, sometimes called Kanku Musa, made his hajj to Mecca in 1324, taking with him, it is said, at least 8 000 soldiers, courtiers and servants, driving 15 000 camels laden with gold, perfume, salt and stores of food. Musa showered so much gold on the economy that the value of the currency in the region remained debased for more than a decade. In time, another kingdom, Songhai, replaced Mali. The Sultan of Morocco wanted West African gold, so he sent an army across the desert in 1590. It took many years, but the Songhai would eventually fall.

This was gold country, to be sure, but in 1996, an ominous warning emerged from Mali. Timbuktu Gold Corporation of Canada, formerly Choice Software Systems, had acquired and then worked the Sitakili gold property. Drill results – indicating values of up to 200 grams of gold per ton of ore – triggered spectacular runs in the stock price. A modern open-cast mine could make good money with yields of a few grams a ton; a yield of 200 grams (or more than six ounces of gold) per ton was very, very rich.

Subsequent investigation by the Alberta Stock Exchange determined that there was 'compelling evidence of deliberate sample enrichment'. This practice, known as 'salting' (as in sprinkling salt over food), was hardly new, and was almost to be expected in the heady atmosphere of a gold rush.

Then there was Glen Harvey Harper. This corporate sharpshooter was president and chairman of the board of directors of Golden Rule, a Canadian company. Harper occupied the same positions with Hixon Gold Resources, a public company controlled by Golden Rule, which owned 46 per cent of Hixon's shares as of 30 September 1996. Hixon, which was listed on the Vancouver Stock Exchange, issued a press release on 3 June 1996, announcing that it had acquired an interest in the Stenpad concession in Ghana. Golden Rule, which had bought an option to acquire a 50 per cent interest in the property, said that initial prospecting, geological mapping and sampling had identified 'several gold mineralisation anomalies'.

On 3 October, Golden Rule reported that 'significant' gold values had been identified as a result of exploration at Stenpad during the summer. That morning, Golden Rule's stock opened at $2.15 a share, compared to a range of $1.05 and $3.35 over the previous 12 months. Until 27 March 1997, Golden Rule continued to release updated exploration results from Stenpad, including 'extremely positive' assay results from both trench and soil sampling. As early as 25 October 1996, Golden Rule advised the public that 'the gold zone has the potential to host a multi-million-ounce deposit'.

Over the ensuing six-month period, the price of Golden Rule shares rose to peaks of $13.80 on 27 January, and $12.40 on 14 March. With some 24.3 million shares outstanding as of 30 September 1996, Golden Rule's market capitalisation rose from about $52 million on 3 October 1996 to a high of $335 million on 27 January 1997.

On 15 May 1997, Golden Rule issued a press release about Stenpad results obtained separately by the Ghana Minerals Commission and by CME Consulting, an independent consultancy sponsored by the commission. The statement indicated that the CME and Ghana Minerals Commission results were 'significantly different' from results previously obtained.

Harper served a prison term in Canada for insider trading, but the perpetrators of the underlying fraud remained at large. The new gold rush would be marked by as much cheating and chicanery, fraud and felony as any stampede in history, and, thanks to technology, the impact would be both global and immediate.

PART III

The sting

7

Value is what you get

O N 20 JANUARY 1966, Warren Buffett, a resident of Omaha, Nebraska, and one of the world's best-known investors, wrote a letter to his partners containing one of his greatest and most important observations:

Price is what you pay. Value is what you get.

This gem of wisdom, along with its wide-ranging implications, lies at the heart of any examination of the company-founding acquisition made by Randgold & Exploration in 1996. It also represents the metaphorical holy water used to baptise Brett Kebble as an apparent financial wizard.

For months before the 1996 acquisition of BHP Minerals Mali Incorporated, the Randgold & Exploration team in Johannesburg, led by executive chairman Peter Flack, had been getting its ducks in a straight enough row. The League of Extraordinary Gentlemen was seriously at work.

The ducks were fairly rough decoys, but the quintessential formula appeared surprisingly simple. Randgold & Exploration was going to acquire an operating, non–South African gold mine to add to the extensive list of exploration properties that Randgold Resources had acquired elsewhere in Africa. At the time, Randgold Resources was an 89 per cent subsidiary of Randgold & Exploration.

Randgold & Exploration was going to give South African investors their own version of Bre-X. It would be an opportunity to buy into a global gold rush that, by its own definition, excluded South African gold stocks. In effect, South African investors, hamstrung by exchange controls, would be buying into a Johannesburg-listed stock that represented the controlling stake in a 'foreign' gold exploration and production company.

The formula had been carefully crafted by Randgold & Exploration, and advisers to and friends of the company, not least among them Julian Baring at Mercury Asset Management in London. He had indicated that MAM would provide a healthy degree of necessary institutional support. Randgold Resources had, of course, been 'materialised' in August 1995, when Randgold & Exploration 'bought' eight million shares (at $0.63 each) for $5 million in the company of which it already owned 100 per cent. The amount just happened to be the exact figure at which Randgold & Exploration valued Randgold Resources immediately after the transaction.

In order to further fund development of Randgold Resources, and its exploration activities in particular, Randgold Resources issued 0.95 million shares in February 1996, apparently to North, an Australian company, raising $9.1 million in US currency. The shares were effectively sold for $9.63 each. Just how the overall value of Randgold Resources ballooned from $5 million to $86 million in six months could be debated at some length, but the figure was arrived at by merely multiplying 8.95 million shares by $9.63 per share.

Regardless of exactly how and why this monstrous revaluation took place, it foreshadowed a recurring pattern in the months ahead. Simply put, Randgold & Exploration wanted investors to believe that Randgold Resources was worth lots and lots and *lots* of money, and then some. The greater the value that could be attributed to Randgold Resources, the greater the nett asset value (NAV)* that could be attributed to Randgold & Exploration. In the meanwhile, it was Randgold & Exploration, not Randgold Resources, that was listed. After the private placing in February 1996, Randgold & Exploration still owned 89 per cent or eight million of the shares that had been issued by Randgold Resources. A majority holding of that magnitude allowed Randgold & Exploration to do whatever it liked with Randgold Resources Ltd (RRL).

What happened next was as nifty a sleight of hand as any cardsharp might perpetrate. On 28 October, Randgold & Exploration issued a public circular to shareholders containing details of its purchase of BHP Minerals Mali, a 100 per cent subsidiary of Broken Hill Proprietary Company Ltd, a large Melbourne-based mining and resources company long known as 'The Big Australian'.

The circular provided a neat summary of what Randgold & Exploration was up to, or at least what it thought it was up to:

> The acquisition of BHP Mali is in line with RRL's strategy of combining continuing exploration programmes, at various stages of development, with advanced projects and operating mines. The acquisition adds a major gold producer to RRL's existing portfolio of prime exploration properties in West, East and Central Africa and increases RRL's resource base to some five million ounces of gold. This is in line with RRL's strategy of transforming itself from a pure exploration operation into a substantial mining and resource company.

At the time, Randgold Resources had no advanced projects and certainly owned no operating mines, but apparently no one noticed.

---

* The nett asset value of a company is typically computed by subtracting its liabilities from its assets. The NAV per share can then be calculated by dividing the total NAV by the number of shares issued. Given that companies only publish detailed financial statements once a year, calculation of an accurate 'market-related' NAV for a company can present various challenges.

The explanation of just what was to be paid to BHP for the Mali acquisition was as clear as sludge. The official circular issued by Randgold & Exploration said that debentures to the value of $48 million had been 'issued by the issuer'. In fact, a $48 million convertible bond had been issued just ahead of the acquisition being announced. The issue had been made by a Randgold & Exploration subsidiary, Randgold Finance (British Virgin Islands) to unidentified investors, apparently in Europe. The securities were listed on the Luxembourg Stock Exchange.

However, the part of the circular that attempted to explain just what BHP was to be paid read like gibberish conjured up for mongrels: 'The purchase consideration payable to BHP Holdings amounts to $53 million and will be financed in part by the issue.'

The issue referred to was the convertible bonds issued by Randgold Finance to the value of $48 million, which flowed through to Randgold & Exploration as cash. To complicate matters, Randgold & Exploration inserted another company, Randgold Resources Holdings (RRH) between itself and Randgold Resources. Randgold & Exploration held 100 per cent of RRH, which in turn held 89 per cent of Randgold Resources. There was no need for the existence of either Randgold Finance or RRH. The announcement continued:

> In addition, BHP Holdings has retained a loan against BHP Mali to the value of $31 million, which amount is deemed by the JSE to also form part of the consideration. $30 million of the proceeds of the issue have been used by RRH to acquire 1 176 470 new shares in RRL at a subscription price of $25.50 per RRL share. RRH has ceded its rights under the agreement to RRL in consideration for the issue by RRL to RRH of 2 036 337 new shares in RRL at a subscription price of $25.50 per share and the payment by RRL to RRH of $30 million, which funds have been used by RRH to satisfy the cash portion of the purchase consideration.

Something that was infinitely simple in concept and practice had been rendered virtually incomprehensible. Randgold & Exploration had raised $48 million ahead of the acquisition of BHP Minerals Mali. The only element of the deal that was clear from the official document was that BHP would be paid $30 million in cash.

All Randgold & Exploration had to do was explain the payment to BHP. Instead, the company was clearly on a mission to make the transaction as complicated as possible. The steps announced and applied in practice appeared to go something like this:

1. Upon issue of the convertible bonds, $48 million in cash flowed into Randgold Finance, a 100 per cent subsidiary of Randgold & Exploration. In reality, $48 million in cash flowed into Randgold & Exploration.

2. The intention was for Randgold Resources to purchase BHP Minerals Mali. Given that Randgold Resources had little cash to speak of, it would have to be a paper transaction. Randgold Resources was going to have to issue shares. According to the Randgold & Exploration circular, RRH applied $30 million of the new money to buy 1 176 470 new shares in Randgold Resources. In reality, the new shares were issued to Randgold & Exploration. *No cash changed hands.*
3. Randgold Resources then bought BHP Minerals Mali from RRH by issuing 2 036 337 further shares to RRH and also 'paying' $30 million in cash to RRH. In reality, the $30 million in cash that had flowed into Randgold & Exploration as part of the $48 million issued had not moved. All that had happened was that Randgold Resources had issued 3.2 million new shares (2 036 337 plus 1 176 470). *No cash changed hands.*
4. Randgold Resources had now issued a grand total of 12.2 million shares. The apparent reality was that, in little over a year, the 'value' of Randgold Resources had increased from $5 million to $310 million. How so? In August 1995, the value of Randgold Resources computed at $5 million (the initial eight million shares multiplied by $0.63 a share). This increased in February 1996 to $86 million (8.95 million shares multiplied by $9.63 a share). The fresh issue of 3.21 million shares took the grand total of shares issued in Randgold Resources to 12.2 million. Multiply the latter by $25.50 a share, and the total value of Randgold Resources had suddenly rocketed to $310 million in little more than a year. Even more perplexing was the fact that, in the last transaction, not a cent of cash had found its way to Randgold Resources.
5. The $30 million cash to be paid for BHP Minerals Mali bought an entity with debt of $31 million attached. The Randgold & Exploration circular clearly stated that the debt was 'deemed by the JSE to also form part of the consideration'. When an entity is regarded as a going concern, it's normal for debt 'bought' to be seen as part of the investment cost of the transaction. Here, the $30 million cash would be added to the $31 million debt, which would then be paid off from future profits made by the entity acquired. However, there were strong indications that far from the Mali acquisition being a going concern, it was technically insolvent. The $30 million cash payment was for an entity with an NAV of just below zero for the buyer ($30 million paid in cash, minus $31 million in liabilities).
6. A $23 million loan (quite separate from the $31 million debt) suddenly appeared from nowhere. Randgold & Exploration compounded the legerdemain by stating in its official circular that: 'The purchase consideration for the acquisition, payable by RRH to BHP Holdings, amounts to $53 million which, assuming an

exchange rate of R4.48 per US dollar, equates to approximately R237.5 million, made up of $30 million in cash and a $23 million loan against RRH, which may be converted by BHP Holdings into a maximum of 2 036 337 of the RRL shares held by RRH. In addition, BHP Holdings will retain a loan against BHP Mali to the value of approximately $31 million, which has been guaranteed by Randgold and which amount is deemed by the JSE to also form part of the consideration.'

It thus appeared that a $23 million 'loan' (which BHP apparently held against RRH) could be converted into more than two million Randgold Resources shares. That would put the price at $11.30 per share, yet the same circular stated that 2 036 337 Randgold Resources shares were issued to RRH at $25.50 each. The Mali acquisition was becoming truly unbelievable. Any super-slick salesman would notice that 2 036 337 Randgold Resources shares multiplied by $25.50 per share computed to $52 million. By adding the $30 million cash payment, the total came to $82 million.

7. Randgold & Exploration wrestled with the three figures mentioned in its official circular: $30 million (cash), $23 million (a loan) and $31 million (a serious loan). Added together, the total was $84 million. In reality, for a cash outlay of $30 million, BHP Minerals Mali had a negative NAV (for the buyer) of $24 million.

8. Randgold & Exploration chose to use the total of $84 million to illustrate the 'value' it had added to its own business interests via the purchase of BHP Minerals Mali.

This was the kind of message that was being drummed out to investors by, among others, Julie Walker of the *Sunday Times Business Times*, who wrote a fairly influential and widely read weekly column on stocks. For months, Walker had been recommending Randgold & Exploration as a stock to buy.

In early November 1996, she wrote: 'Flack says that among the highlights were [*sic*] the takeover by 90 per cent-held Randgold Resources of BHP Minerals Mali for $82 million settled in cash and through the issue of Randgold Resources shares.'

The $82 million cited by Walker could be traced back to the calculations in Step 6, or seen as a slight variant of the $84 million described in Steps 7 and 8. She made no mention of either of the two loans for which Randgold & Exploration was ultimately answerable. Instead, it appeared that the cash payment of $30 million had been added to the loans to arrive at the total of $82 million. This was extraordinary, but no more so than the evidentiary material showing that the valuation of Randgold Resources had shot up from $0.63 to $25.50 a share in 14 months.

It cannot be emphasised strongly enough that the Randgold Resources shares were 100 per cent under the control of Flack; he could have issued them at any price. The value was irrelevant, since Randgold Resources was unlisted. For all intents and purposes, Randgold & Exploration was issuing shares *in* itself, *to* itself. In the absence of a wider context and understanding of the intentions of Flack and certain others, the transactions were completely unorthodox and bizarre.

In the years ahead, Randgold & Exploration would become more circumspect about describing the Mali acquisition. In its 2004 filing with the Securities Exchange Commission (SEC) in Washington, the company stated:

> In October 1996, we acquired from BHP International Incorporated, or BHP, through an intermediate holding company, Randgold Resources (Holdings) Limited, or RRHL, the entire issued share capital of BHP Minerals Mali Incorporated (which was later renamed Randgold Resources Mali Incorporated, or RRML) and the benefit of $78 million in shareholder loans. The main asset of RRML was a 65 per cent interest in Société des Mines de Syama SA, or Somisy, whose assets included the Syama mine. RRL then acquired the investment in RRML in exchange for the issuance of 3 212 812 new shares at $25.50 per share. As part of that transaction, we guaranteed a $32.2 million loan, including interest, which remained owing to BHP from RRML.

No mention was made of the $30 million in cash that was paid to BHP. By all accounts, it was paid, but by Randgold & Exploration. In the company's annual report for the 12 months to 31 March 1998, which also contained figures for the previous financial year, an entry in the 1997 cash flow statement read: 'Cash paid for BHP Minerals Mali Incorporated – R135 million.'

Given the average exchange rate at the time, the R135 million was equal to almost $27 million. In the Randgold & Exploration filing with the SEC, the loan owing to BHP was stipulated as $32.2 million, rather than the $30 million found in earlier texts. It was also made clear that Randgold & Exploration guaranteed the loan. However, there is no easy way of knowing what was meant by the reference to 'the benefit of $78 million in shareholder loans'. There was also the appearance of a new entity, Randgold Resources Mali Limited (RRML). In addition, BHP Holdings was changed to BHP International.

Thus, years down the line, the transaction can be crystallised as follows:
- Randgold & Exploration agreed to buy the Mali entity (BHP Minerals Mali Incorporated) from BHP.
- Randgold & Exploration paid cash of R135 million (about $27 million) to BHP.
- Randgold & Exploration guaranteed to BHP a $32.2 million loan owing by the Mali entity to BHP.

- Randgold Resources, an unlisted entity, issued stock to its parent company, Randgold & Exploration, thus acquiring the Mali entity in a paper transaction. In this deal, no cash changed hands.

The opacity of the transaction raised leading questions about price and value, bearing in mind Buffett's observation about both. The four points that summarised the Mali deal were all that needed to be said, except for one other thing. What counted – and it was truly the only thing that counted – was the value, if any, at which BHP Minerals Mali would have changed hands between a willing seller and buyer, in an open market, at arm's length and in a transparent transaction.

It seemed clear that in agreeing to buy the Mali entity, Randgold & Exploration was to pay $30 million in cash for an operating mine, which included $32.2 million of debt that Randgold & Exploration would be liable for and that had to be settled. On this basis, the NAV of the Mali entity appeared to be just below zero.

In examining the value of BHP Minerals Mali, there was no question that BHP was as keen as a razor to be rid of the asset. In its 1998 annual report, BHP stated:

> While developing its activities around core assets in its principal areas of business, BHP is reviewing its assets as part of a portfolio restructuring process. As a consequence of this review, a number of assets were sold during 1997–98. The restructuring process is continuing on the basis of assessments of the future competitiveness of such assets and their prospects for adding value for shareholders. Portfolio restructuring may entail sale of assets, changed ownership arrangements or financial restructuring. Assets which are likely to come into consideration in the portfolio restructuring process are non-core, under performing, small scale and/or high cost assets, and those that do not fit BHP's strategic direction.

In the year to 31 May 1997, BHP Minerals Mali was the only asset that BHP sold. The company's 1998 annual report stated that the loss 'attributable to members of the BHP entity arising on disposal' of BHP Minerals Mali was A$24 million. The report made it clear that BHP was exiting neither gold nor Africa:

> Gold and zinc remain the primary targets but major exploration programs are in place for a range of other minerals including nickel, platinum, coal, diamonds and titanium. BHP conducts extensive mineral exploration programs in Australia, North and South America, Africa, Asia and other parts of the world.

However, as far as Flack and the Randgold & Exploration directors were concerned, the Mali transaction had instantly converted Randgold Resources into an entity worth hundreds of millions of dollars. Flack, who was by now conducting himself as a Master of the Universe, was not one to mess with. If he said Randgold Resources was worth $25.50 a share, that was as good as law, and in a lucid moment, he reinforced this claim in writing.

In a document titled *Annual Review 1996*, he waxed lyrical about Randgold Resources and its apparent accomplishments. Randgold & Exploration was changing its financial year-end from September to March, but the year to 30 September 1996 had been such a busy period that it warranted special attention, said Flack. The financial statements were neither audited nor reviewed by Randgold & Exploration's auditors, Deloitte & Touche. The first page of the document gave some indication of what would follow: 'The dinosaur grew an enormous body while its brain remained small, thus evolving itself into extinction. The elephant, on the other hand, developed mind and muscle at the same rate, and survives happily to this day.'

Flack was having fun, it seemed. The Randgold & Exploration share price was flying high as a kite; in just a few years, it had risen by 1 000 per cent, in round figures. With that kind of power, Flack could all but write the law. On page 11 of Randgold & Exploration's 1996 annual review, the market value of Randgold Resources was given as $244 million, despite the fact that the company was not listed and thus did not have a market value in the sense that the term is generally understood. A stock needs to be listed to earn the acclaim of market value. Had Flack ventured a little closer to the facts, he would have admitted signing off on a value that was the result of a horribly complicated formula concocted by the Randgold & Exploration directors.

On page 10 of the same document, Flack did explain that the value of Randgold Resources, including BHP Minerals Mali Incorporated, had been calculated at $25.50 per share, 'being the directors' value'.

The division of $244 million by $25.50 meant that Randgold Resources had 9.6 million shares in issue, somewhat more than the 8.95 million that could be accounted for at that stage.

The $244 million comprised by far the single biggest component of the overall NAV calculated for Randgold & Exploration as a whole. Trailing far behind was Randgold & Exploration's stake in Harmony, which of course was listed and, as such, did indeed possess a market value, set at $51 million on 6 September 1996. The total NAV for Randgold & Exploration was given as $439 million, which just happened to translate to exactly $10 (or R45) per Randgold & Exploration share. The round figures were just too convenient to be credible.

Flack appeared to include or exclude figures at will. While Randgold & Exploration's annual review for 1996 offered the market value of Randgold Resources as at 6 September and included BHP Minerals Mali, the effective date of the acquisition was not until 7 October. This technicality aside, Flack should have included the total of issued Randgold Resources shares at the time the transaction was completed, namely 12.2 million. At $25.50 a share, that would have 'valued' Randgold Resources at $310 million, a great deal more than the $244 million Flack used in the review. It was unlikely that he would short-change his shareholders by more than $70 million (more than the true value of Randgold & Exploration's stake in Harmony), so this was a serious oversight.

Peccadillos aside, what was Syama really worth? The global gold mining fraternity, and indeed the mining fraternity as a whole, comprises a surprisingly tight-knit group. One of the many idiosyncratic rules is that nobody *sells* a mine; mines are *bought*. Put another way, when a mining company has proved its worth, it may become a target for takeover. This kind of activity, which is rarely hostile, usually pans out as an agreed merger and acquisition. Syama, however, was being sold. It was not being bought.

When Syama was put on the block by BHP early in 1996, 'everyone' had gone to look at it. Some experts, such as Greg Hawkins, had been commissioned to examine the mine in great professional detail. He had been based for some years in Accra, Ghana, as director and founder of CME & Company, and consulted for a number of companies on their African mining projects, including Anglo American, Barrick, Nevsun, Banro, Cypress Amax, Gold Fields and JCI. Armed with a BSc in geology from the University of Alberta and an MSc in mineral economics from McGill University, Hawkins was ideally qualified for this work, and he diligently went to size Syama up.

'Offer them $1,' he jokingly suggested.

In other words, Syama was a piece of junk.[*]

For Flack and the entire Randgold & Exploration board, Syama was El Dorado, the property that would somehow, for reasons still unknown, become the mother of all gold mines. The directors had done a magnificent piece of work in the so-called unlocking of value. From just above zero, they had created more than $300 million worth of value in Randgold Resources in little more than a year. Flack put it thus in the annual review:

> When the new team took over two years ago, the Randgold share price stood at R8.50. By early September this year it had risen to R37.50 and our market capitalisation had increased by 487 per cent to R1 486 million. Investors have

---

[*] BHP should have closed Syama down or, technically speaking, placed the mine on care-and-maintenance before putting it on the market. That much was clear when prospective buyers began checking out Syama, and the picture became even clearer in hindsight.

clearly supported not just our basic strategy but also the results of its continued implementation.

Further down in the document, Flack again patted himself on the back: 'If the surging [share] price still lags the NAV, it is only because we ourselves have moved the goalposts so far through the acquisition of substantial assets.'

In mid-1995, the Randgold & Exploration stock price was trading at around R10 a share; at the start of 1996, it was nudging R15. As noted by Flack, the stock traded close to R40 a share in the latter part of 1996, by which time Randgold & Exploration had published information that attributed to the company an NAV per share of R45, of which more than half was contributed by the holding in Randgold Resources. Measured from 1993, the Randgold & Exploration stock price had increased from roughly R4 to R40 a share, an increase of 1 000 per cent, giving it the status of 'ten bagger', a term first heard on Wall Street.

Stock price movements of such magnitude do not occur without certain investors cashing in. Among a number of innovations that Randgold & Exploration apparently brought to the South African scene, it was no surprise to find stock options. As early as 1 September 1993, Randgold & Exploration had set aside seven million of them, more than 10 per cent of the 43.9 million shares it had in issue when the BHP Minerals Mali transaction went through.

The majority of these shares, 4.8 million, had been granted during 1994 at R11.76 each. No details were given previously about which individuals held these options, but some interesting figures emerged in the circular about the Mali acquisition. As of 23 October 1996, it was clear that the two Kebbles, along with Adam Fleming, were by far the biggest beneficiaries of the stock option scheme. Each of them held more than one million shares. Curiously, Flack held none at all.

It was also of interest that in the 12-month period to 30 September 1996, the eight executive directors of Randgold & Exploration were paid an aggregate sum of R5.6 million, an exceptionally good package, for the time, of about R700 000 each. Even more striking was the fact that, during the same period, they benefited to the tune of R8.2 million in terms of the nett value of stock options exercised.

It was at least of equal interest that Randgold & Exploration had entered into three-year employment contracts with Flack and Brett Kebble in their respective capacities as executive chairman and commercial director. A key term of the contracts, which would terminate on 31 August 1997, was 'a restraint of trade, which precludes the divulging or disclosure of information, the enticement, solicitation or canvassing of the services of any person, company or entity with which Randgold & Exploration or its associated companies have a written agreement, or interest in any business which competes with the business conducted by Randgold &

Randgold & Exploration: interest of directors, 23 October 1996		
	Beneficial	
Director	Direct	Indirect
PH Flack	–	–
F Abbott	–	–
D Ashworth	36 941	–
DM Bristow	1 066	–
NRG Brunette	2 000	–
JP Burger	–	–
JA Cramer	–	–
RR de Villiers	–	–
AR Fleming	–	1 024 603
TSA Grobicki	–	–
L Hewitt	48 622	50 000
RB Kebble	1 051 800	–
RAR Kebble	1 051 800	–
F Lips	–	–
DH Starling	–	–
ZB Swanepoel	–	–
Total	2 192 169	1 074 603

Exploration or its associated companies. The restraint of trade is effective for a period of one year from the date of termination of employment.'

The implication was that Flack and Kebble had likely promised to deliver something that the others could or would not. However, with the Mali acquisition under their belts, the Randgold & Exploration crowd could move on to the next big step in the plan to take over the world. That, of course, was the listing of Randgold Resources in London. Ahead of that, it was all about driving up the value of Randgold & Exploration and Randgold Resources. As Walker boldly stated in the *Sunday Times Business Times* in November 1996:

> In five weeks flat, Randgold raised $48 million through the issue of seven per cent debentures convertible into Randgold ordinaries at R39.01 in 2001. Flack notes that the calibre of the underwriters – Capels, Rothschilds, Morgan Grenfell and Société Générale – was a vote of confidence in Randgold's credibility overseas. No SA company has issued paper on more favourable terms, and it was pleasing that the issue was four times subscribed. Flack says the value of the issue exceeds the entire market capitalisation of Randgold two years ago when the former management was outvoted.

With Christmas and South Africa's annual silly season over, 1997 opened with confidence at a high pitch among the Masters of the Universe at Randgold & Exploration and Randgold Resources. Investors were now being force-fed. Expansion into Africa had been fast and effective. Randgold Resources had identified 217 targets in West and Central Africa; a resource base of nine million ounces in four countries had been defined over 18 000 square kilometres. Another $39 million had been earmarked for exploration over the next two years. Randgold Resources had geologists working in 22 permit areas in seven countries.

The gold price continued to tank, steadily and surely.

8

A likely tale or two

O N 19 MARCH 1997, some kind of shit hit some kind of fan. Word spread rapidly to global markets that, for reasons unknown, Michael de Guzman, chief geologist at Bre-X's Busang prospect, had exited a helicopter over a remote part of the Indonesian rainforest. His remains were found four days later in the jungle, mostly eaten by animals and identifiable only from molars and a thumbprint. There had already been some fairly stinky rumours about Busang, where De Guzman was the boss on the ground.

Bre-X's parent company, based and listed in Canada, had first said in 1995 that the gold deposit at Busang could be as much as 30 million ounces. The estimate increased in 1996 to 60 million ounces and, early in 1997, to 200 million ounces. The Bre-X stock price had rocketed to a high of C$280 a share early in 1997, equal to a market capitalisation of $4.4 billion in US currency.

On 26 March, Freeport-McMoRan, an established mining outfit and possible partner in Bre-X's gigantic Indonesian 'find', announced that its own due diligence core samples showed 'insignificant amounts of gold' at Busang. Hysteria overwhelmed Bre-X's stock and a mild contagion hit listed gold equities in general, but the fallout had only just begun. The Toronto Stock Exchange had added Bre-X to its premium TSE 300 index; there had even been talk of adding the stock to the most prestigious barometer in the world, Wall Street's Dow Jones Industrial Average.

David Walsh, founder of Bre-X, dismissed all the criticism, claiming that ghostwriters on the Internet had sparked the panic. Various professional investment analysts, notably Canadian Egizio Bianchini, dismissed the negative rumours around Bre-X as preposterous. It was no surprise that another independent entity, Strathcona Minerals, was employed for further analysis. The results, published on 4 May, went so far as to find that the Busang ore samples had been salted with gold dust shaved off jewellery.

As it turned out, the apparently deceased De Guzman had controlled access to the Busang site; he and his most senior aide, Cesar Puspos, had handled the original samples during transfer from the drill site to the assay laboratory. Everybody was suddenly suing everyone else, but the Canadian financial sector suffered most. The biggest fraud in the history of gold also proved a major embarrassment for Peter Munk, the boss at Barrick. The head of the Toronto stock exchange was booted out, triggering a tumultuous realignment of the various Canadian stock exchanges. The story had international implications; specific new securities regulations were put in place to cover anything to do with mining.

The sudden and unwanted scrutiny would make it far more difficult for Randgold & Exploration to sweep the problems at Syama under the carpet. There was no question about gold being in the ground at Syama. That was never the issue. The problem was that Syama was a piece of junk. Once upon a time, it had been a fairly decent mine, but those days were long gone.

As an open-cast operation, Syama had produced 125 000 ounces of gold in the 1996 financial year to 30 September. The mine had switched from oxide to sulphide ores in 1994, according to Randgold & Exploration: 'Syama was originally commissioned in 1990 as an open-cast oxide mine. In September 1994, facilities to exploit the sulphide body were completed as part of an $89 million expansion programme.'

Syama faced several challenges. The ore body was typical of surface gold deposits. Down to a certain depth, where countless years of weathering had separated gold particles from their host, it hosted oxide ores. This kind of ore was easy and inexpensive to treat, with the free milling gold literally streaming out of the plant. But this kind of ore body typically changes, at depth, from oxide to sulphide. The deeper ore, which has not been weathered, requires pre-treatment, allowing, in crude terms, for a man-made oxidised ore to be produced. In extreme cases of bad luck, however, some gold deposits prove to have sulphides that are classified as 'refractory'. In such cases, a stubborn host rock really does not want to let go of the gold. There are two main choices in tackling refractory sulphides: lots and lots of roasting, or biological oxidisation. BHP had not fully recognised just how stubborn the sulphides at Syama would prove to be, leading in turn to design problems in its sulphide plant.

In the nett result, while Syama as a whole reported an operating profit of $9 million in the year to 31 December 1993 and a healthy $10 million profit in 1994, the mine crashed to a $1 million loss in 1995 as the oxides were replaced by sulphides.

Syama faced an additional special challenge in that the entire mining facility ran off diesel generators; the new sulphide plant demanded significantly higher power input. Over three consecutive financial years, the mine's working costs increased from $13 million to $17 million, before exploding to $37 million in 1995, the first full year in which the sulphide plant was in operation. Seen in the context of economic substance rather than gold mining, Syama was being destroyed by its sulphide plant. The mine was ruined.

The financial position had deteriorated to the point where the balance sheet of

BHP Minerals Mali showed on 30 June 1996 that Somisy itself was in debt to BHP Minerals Mali to the tune of $93 million for loans, $20 million in accumulated interest and $9 million for sundries. Read together with the published Somisy balance sheet, this pointed to Syama being technically bankrupt. It owed more than $100 million, and was incurring ongoing profit and cash flow losses at the operating level.

Long-time Randgold Resources CEO Mark Bristow spelt out the position in an August 2005 interview with *Mining Weekly*: 'Randgold Resources bought BHP Mali at a $400/oz market value, having to borrow money, issue shares and even write out an IOU in order to do so.'

By definition, Bristow would never concede that Syama was a piece of junk. In March 1996, when Randgold Resources started taking a close look at the mine, gold bullion was trading around $400 an ounce. Since then, it had fallen steadily and surely to around $370 an ounce in the closing days of 1996, but the show had to go on. It was clear that nothing was going to stand in the way of listing Randgold Resources in London. Flack, bellowing like a bull during the rut, was advertising prices of up to $30 a share for Randgold Resources. If seven million new shares were issued at that price, $200 million in cash would come rolling in. The London listing of Randgold Resources was 'intended to provide exploration capital to fund an aggressive strategy to start a new gold venture every 18–24 months'.

In the end, just ahead of the London listing in July 1997, only five million shares could be placed, and only at $15.50 each. Gold traded as low as $318 an ounce during July. The Randgold Resources IPO raised nett proceeds of $77.5 million. Bristow recast events in August 2005, telling *Mining Weekly*: 'But with a $40 gold price fall during the prelisting roadshow, the issue had to be repriced, the prospectus rewritten and only $83 million was raised, culminating in the creation of what really amounted to a public company with a strategy.'

It was certainly an interesting strategy, and one that appeared to be based on taking wild gambles that the gold price would simply continue rising, allowing the Masters of the Universe to convert pieces of junk into real gold mines. The strategy also relied on the notion that anything anyone else could do, Randgold & Exploration and Randgold Resources could do better. The true cynic might observe that the world would have been a better place if all the gold mines on earth had surrendered to this tribe of superior beings, these self-styled Masters of the Universe.

But to some investors, price represents all they know about a particular stock. When Randgold Resources listed in London, the price of Randgold & Exploration in Johannesburg was down to R15 a share from all-time highs of around R41 earlier in the year. While the falling gold price exacerbated fallout from the Bre-X fraud, there was no question that a number of serious investors had devoted time to examining the sharp realities becoming apparent at Randgold & Exploration and Randgold Resources.

Immediately after the London listing, Randgold & Exploration cracked down on Randgold Resources with heavy cash calls. The London issue proceeds of $77.5 million were partly used to retire the retained loan from BHP of some $32.2 million. Randgold Resources also converted an $18 million loan owed to a subsidiary of Randgold & Exploration into 1 090 909 ordinary shares in Randgold Resources (equal to $16.50 each).

Within weeks of its London IPO, Randgold Resources was once again heading for cash starvation and Syama was on the way to oblivion.

When Randgold & Exploration and Randgold Resources executed the Mali acquisition in October 1996, more than just Syama was purchased. There were also three exploration properties in the package, namely Loulo, Yanfolila and Morila. On numerous occasions, Randgold Resources made statements to the effect that the Morila deposit had been discovered during December 1996. Above all others, Bristow had to know that this claim was nonsense. In its circular issued on 28 October 1996, Randgold & Exploration stated:

> The main assets of BHP Mali are gold mining operations located in Mali, the most significant of which are a 65 per cent shareholding in the Syama gold mine, a 20 per cent shareholding in Loulo, an advanced gold mining exploration project, together with the right to acquire a further 31 per cent shareholding, as well as the Yanfolila and Morila exploration permits.

It seemed clear from this official statement that Morila was regarded as the least important element of the package. Later in the circular, investors were informed that the Morila exploration permit was granted to BHP Minerals Mali on 3 June 1993. This should not, however, be read as implying that Morila was discovered by BHP. The Morila anomaly was found long before 1993, by Bureau de Recherches Géologiques et Minières, or BRGM, an entity owned by the French government that conducted enormous and detailed mining surveys in former French colonies. The Morila deposit, as such, was first identified by BHP.

The Randgold & Exploration circular also stated in respect of Morila:

> Exploration expenditure to date of $700 000 has been applied in carrying out regional soil sampling and detailed programmes involving geological mapping, ground geophysical surveys, pitting and auguring, followed by 2 000 m of diamond drilling.

Diamond drilling is serious stuff and invariably indicates a high degree of confidence that a property will prove to be economic, in a mining sense. In the case of Morila, however, the odds on a potential mine appeared to lean towards the 'highly likely' category. The 'scout' 1 927 metres of diamond drilling indicated 'the presence of significant mineralisation'. Bristow had signed the circular as the competent person required by regulations. In regulatory documents, a 'competent person' who signs off on the mining data is akin to an auditor, who signs off on financial matters. In the modern era, Bristow would not have qualified as such, due to potential conflict of interest.

Bristow proved human enough to rewrite the history of Morila after signing the report. As *Mining Weekly* told the story:

> The Australians had written Morila off as a 300 000 oz surface expression, but as Bristow paged through the BHP due diligence on a flight from London to Mali, he was intrigued by boreholes that had patchy but significant grades in the 10 g/t range.

Bristow's selective memory, or positive amnesia, became manifest on many occasions, probably far too many to count. For all his boyish charm and insistence on being called 'doctor' – at least in print – it seems fair to say that some of Brett Kebble's larcenous marketing and commercial skills had rubbed off on Bristow.

If the true potential sitting below the ground at Morila really only struck him on that flight from London to Mali some time after October 1996, he was somewhat slow on the uptake. Experts familiar with the situation in West Africa at the time knew that serious attempts were made to split Morila from the BHP package. Canada's Nevsun, for one, had a profound idea of what was sitting within the Morila concession. Nevsun looked at all the BHP assets that had been put on the block and made out a strong case for its willingness to buy the Morila prospect separately.

BHP, however, refused to buckle, insisting that Morila be included in the same package as Syama. Not even the most serious contenders were prepared to bid for Morila with Syama and its debilitating debt attached. It became ever clearer that BHP had wanted a 'clean' exit from Mali in order to maintain a favourable relationship with that country's government. The key priority was to find a buyer who would continue to run Syama; job losses connected with a large transnational resources corporation would stink up the joint for a long time. From a corporate viewpoint, it was far easier for BHP to lump its Mali assets together in a single deal, and that was how things ended up. Nevsun bought nothing but the Kubi Village prospect in Ghana from BHP, though the directors were enormously disappointed that Morila had slipped through the cracks.

Randgold & Exploration Structure, October 1996

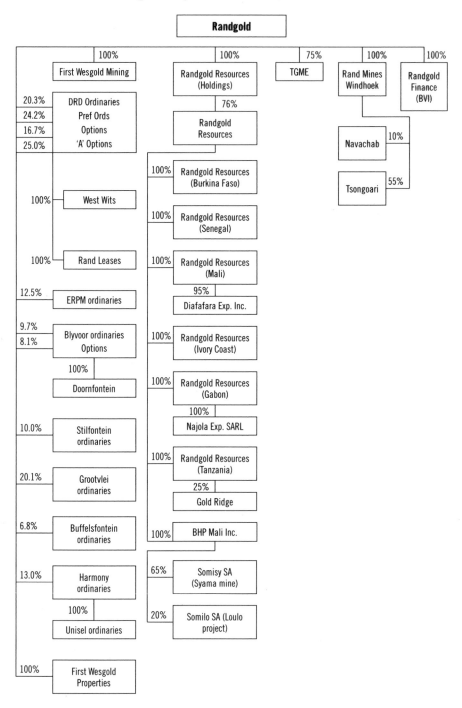

Bristow continued to display a gracious blind spot. In a document filed as recently as 27 October 2005 with the Securities Exchange Commission in Washington, Randgold Resources stated: 'We discovered the Morila deposit during December 1996 and we subsequently financed, built and commissioned the Morila mine.'

A major problem with this statement is that it failed to explain that Randgold Resources did not operate Morila, at least not in the accepted sense of the word. That was explained more candidly in the 2004 Randgold Resources annual report:

The mine is controlled by a 50:50 joint venture management committee with day-to-day operations being the responsibility of AngloGold Services Mali SA (Anser), a Malian subsidiary of AngloGold Ashanti, under an operating agreement.

PART IV

Days of thunder

9

A swine among swine

WHILE BRETT KEBBLE was cashing in the many, many millions he had made from the Randgold Resources escapade in 1996, he was planning an audacious raid on a new set of gold mining assets. It was to be a deadly attack, recognised as such by only a few.

They were the chosen few: individuals whom Kebble needed to bankroll his ambitions. They were also the kind of people who expected to be paid back, and definitely not the kind you would knowingly renege on.

It was in 1996 that Kebble first went into combine harvester mode. It appeared to be of no importance that, whether he liked it or not, the period was dominated by a steadily ailing dollar-gold price. Kebble had toasted stardom with gold-specked water during 1994 and 1995, when the price oscillated broadly between $375 and $400 an ounce. This relative stability in gold bullion markets had allowed Kebble and his mentors – Julian Baring, Adam Fleming and Peter Flack – to focus their minds on other interesting facets of life, not least of which was making tons of money.

The dollar-gold price started its southward trajectory in early 1996 after peaking at around $410 an ounce. No self-proclaimed gold bull would believe that the price was truly in trouble, but, early in 1997, reality began to bite, all the way down to the marrow. To be in the gold business was like working and sleeping in a tropical sweatshop.

The phenomenon had less to do with the broad fundamentals of gold bullion than with developments surrounding the dollar. At some point in 1995, the greenback entered a protracted multi-year bull market. The price of gold bullion has relationships with any number of components in financial and monetary markets, as well as with metals, minerals and commodities, and not least with crude oil. But it is possible that of all gold's liaisons, none is so intimate as that with the dollar. From 1995, the gold–dollar relationship worked almost like clockwork. If the dollar strengthened, the gold bullion price would move in the opposite direction. This inverse correlation would prove to have a confidence factor greater than 90 per cent.

There were many reasons for the dollar–gold link to manifest in this fashion, not least among them gold bullion's status as 'anti-money'. For a number of investors, gold is the anti-dollar, the antithesis of the almighty greenback, which represents the ultimate form of fiat (paper) money. The anti-money scenario virtually dictates that, when the greenback does well, gold bullion suffers, and vice versa. As 1997 wore on, the gold price moved ever closer to $275 an ounce and slowly continued to fade, touching multi-year lows of around $250 an ounce by the end of 1999.

Kebble was a gold bull, period, and just about everything he did as a businessman was based on the assumption that the dollar-gold price would rise, and continue to do so. This kind of blind faith is an endearing feature, possibly the only one, of a human subculture known as 'gold bugs'. These characters tend to be tough, and may even acknowledge an alternative description of themselves as 'gold swine'. Swine, at least, are bigger than bugs, and live much longer in normal circumstances.

Bug or swine, Kebble was far from alone in holding steadfastly to his one-way bet on the dollar-gold price. Besides this self-inflicted blindness, which had no charitable intent and could not be traced to any kind of divine inspiration, Kebble was also vulnerable to the realities of his spin being unwound. That, no doubt, is why he was working on raiding another set of gold assets long before the Randgold & Exploration stock price began descending into a ditch.

It would be an understatement to say that Kebble cooked up a truly astonishing plan. It was premised on the issuance of over-valued paper. For a predator such as Kebble, nothing could beat the issuance of over-valued shares for undervalued shares. In its refined form, this technique of investing can yield results nothing short of miraculous and amazing. For Kebble, the lessons learnt at Randgold & Exploration in 1996 were the foundation of almost everything he would do thereafter.

First, he had to do whatever was required to talk up the price of the stock in which he stood to gain. In 1996, that meant Randgold & Exploration subsidiary Randgold Resources (which was only listed in London in mid-1997). Randgold Resources, according to the directors of Randgold & Exploration, had increased in value over 14 months from $5 million to more than $310 million. The only material change in the underlying business model over the period was that Randgold & Exploration and Randgold Resources had bought Syama, a wreck of a gold mine in Mali attached to tens of millions of dollars in debt.

Second, Kebble needed to know when to cash out. That appeared to be simple enough. By the time investors had reason to be suspicious of the Randgold & Exploration story, Kebble had long since banked his fortune. Now, with the many millions that he (and a number of others) had made from Randgold & Exploration and Randgold Resources, Kebble was on the prowl for a much bigger kill. He was looking to apply the tricks he had learnt to something monumental. For a serial murderer, the thrilling anticipation of the next strike always exceeds the satisfaction of the last, and Kebble was the new killer in town.

His next raid was rooted in May 1995, when Anglo American moved into top gear both in its unbundling and black economic empowerment initiatives. South Africa's best-known corporation had separated one of its many associates, Johannesburg Consolidated Investments (JCI) into three separate components:
- JCI Ltd (holding interests in coal, ferrochrome, gold and base metals);
- Anglo American Platinum (platinum mining, processing and refining), which Anglo American would retain; and
- Johnnies Industrial Corporation (Johnnic), JCI's non-mining industrial holdings.

Not even the long-deceased Barney Barnato, JCI's founder more than a century before, could have thought so far ahead. JCI had served well, and would now be chopped up in the name of progress and advancement. South Africa was mesmerised by the huge deals awaiting consummation.

In 1996, Anglo American placed Johnnies and JCI on the block, insisting that the buyers should be black. In due course, a black business group, National Empowerment Consortium, bought 20 per cent of Johnnic, but that is another story. For Kebble, the only tale of interest was JCI, or, to be precise, the remnant of the JCI group that boasted four core mining investment areas:
- Gold (Randfontein, 31 per cent; Western Areas, 35 per cent; HJ Joel, 57 per cent and Lindum Reefs, 84 per cent).
- Coal and base metals (coal miner Tavistock, 100 per cent; a 58 per cent stake in United Carbon Producers and 33 per cent in Consolidated Murchison (which produced gold and antimony), plus a 56 per cent stake in chrome producer Consolidated Metallurgical Industries).
- A mineral rights and exploration division, represented via a 41 per cent stake in Freddev (Free State Development Corporation), and a 45 per cent stake in Barnex (Barnato Exploration), both listed in Johannesburg.
- Numerous sundry interests collected over decades, including valuable financial investments headed by a 7 per cent stake in Anglo American Platinum and 9 per cent in Johnson Matthey, various mineral and exploration rights and properties.

Kebble, however, had numerous hurdles to cross before he could even contemplate a raid on the JCI assets. Even then, he was interested only in the gold. His immediate problem was cash. The raid on JCI as a whole was going to cost at least R2 billion. The fact that Kebble was not black was a mere technicality that could easily be overcome.

There was a great deal of action and interest around the sale of JCI, but of the many suitors, Mzi Khumalo, chairman of Capital Alliance, emerged as not only being in control of the African Mining Group (AMG), but also the person most likely to win the bid for JCI.

Capital Alliance, formed in 1994, was controlled by the Khumalo consortium, with McCarthy Retail and Rand Merchant Bank (RMB) holding minority stakes. Early in 1996, RMB's stake was bought out, raising the consortium's interest to almost 76 per cent. Just ahead of the bid formation for JCI, Amalgamated General Assurance Holdings (AGA) acquired Capital Alliance in a reverse takeover. Controlled by JSE-listed Saflife, AGA was later renamed Capital Alliance Holdings, which, it was said, had built up assets of R3.8 billion. Khumalo's consortium was also the majority shareholder in Saflife, along with Investec and Saflife Holdings.

Khumalo's consortium attracted great human talent. During 1996, Mark Barnes, former deputy managing director at Standard Corporate and Merchant Bank, and Arnold Shapiro, previously senior portfolio manager at Old Mutual, joined Capital Alliance under Khumalo in order to bid for JCI. According to Barnes, 'Mzi had quietly built up the group and I could not let up on the opportunities that presented themselves at Capital.' Other names associated with Saflife included Gary Burg, Larry Nestadt, Stephen Koseff, Marcel Golding and Johnny Copelyn. A number of prominent empowerment names were associated with AMG, not least Bobby Makwetla, Reuel Khoza, Don Ncube, Max Maisela, Don Mkhwanazi, Eric Molefe, Audrey Mokhobo, future president Thabo Mbeki's wife Zanele, Tiego Moseneke and Phineas Mojapelo.

In November 1996, the AMG consortium won a neck-and-neck bidding war for 34.9 per cent of JCI, held by Anglo American and its main associate, De Beers. The deal was closed at a very rich R54.50 per JCI share, but it was hardly unusual to pay a premium for control. In terms of how big the cheque would be, the broader AMG group had tendered a winning bid of R2.5 billion (the equivalent of about $610 million). Khumalo had also apparently secured the right for the AMG consortium to buy the Anglo American group's remaining 12.7 per cent stake in JCI. This option, which would give AMG unfettered control of JCI, was available as a right of first refusal for a period of five years. The deal was officially recorded by Anglo American as a sale, in 1996, by itself and De Beers, of 'an initial 30 per cent' out of the two entities' 47.5 per cent interest in JCI. Forty-six million shares in JCI were sold to AMG and Saflife Ltd.

Winning the auction was one thing. Paying up was another. While Capital Alliance Holdings was the main vehicle for the deal, its parent company, Saflife, would raise R1.4 billion of the cash required. Further funds had apparently been secured from institutions believed to include Investec, SBC Warburg and Standard

Corporate and Merchant Bank. The deal had to be financed within months and the cash put on the table by the end of February 1997. Due in no small measure to the falling gold price, the JCI stock price had already dropped heavily from levels seen when the bids closed. Saflife and Capital Alliance announced various desperate measures to keep the deal alive, including a Saflife rights issue. Anglo American and De Beers relaxed their stances; the offer was now that 30 per cent of JCI would be sold. AMG was given a one-year option to buy the remaining 4.9 per cent on offer. The Saflife rights issue, underwritten by SBC Warburg, was a magnificent flop, but one way or another, the deal was settled, at least for the moment.

In March 1997, the JCI board of directors was reconstituted, with Khumalo as executive chairman. In early May, JCI chief executive Bill Nairn quit after 33 years with the group. Khumalo announced that the new JCI board had yet to be reconstituted, and offered assurances that shareholders would have a say in the process. Upon Nairn's departure, Khumalo told the *Sunday Times Business Times* that Kebble 'will definitely not play an executive role at JCI and will not accept a non-executive advisory role at JCI – as rumoured by the press – either, because I haven't offered him one'.

In July, Kebble joined JCI, cutting all ties with Randgold & Exploration. As far as the outside world was concerned, Kebble was appointed to head JCI's gold division. The departure of Nairn (who later resurfaced at Anglo American) aggravated negative sentiment around the JCI stock. From R50.50 a share in February, it spiralled treacherously and relentlessly downwards to around R16 by November. In between, several kinds of hell broke loose.

At any particular point in time, no one really knew what was going on. As winter set in, Khumalo's world collapsed. The big investors that had backed AMG were baying for blood and money. They wanted JCI's assets systematically liquidated and cashed in.

In early August, JCI, described as South Africa's first black mining house, announced that it would fundamentally restructure over the next few months and split into three entities: a corporate parent unit, a gold company and a multi-commodity firm. There was also talk, as the saga continued to develop at breakneck speed, that JCI wanted to acquire the 26 per cent stake held in Lonrho by Anglo American and De Beers.

During 1996, Anglo American had led a group bid for Lonrho, a conglomerate listed in London and Johannesburg. Under the indomitable Tiny Rowland, who had been ousted from the top executive position in 1993, Lonrho had collected a great showcase of assets that happily coughed out cash. One of the most prized, Lonrho Platinum, held all its South African operations in the Eastern and Western Platinum mines. Lonmin, as it was to be known, was highly desired by its competitors, but continued to evade their grasp. The Anglo American and De Beers stakes in Lonrho were soon rendered academic by competition authorities in Europe. In 1995, the European Union had blocked a possible full merger of Lonrho with Gencor's Impala Platinum, citing an anti-competitive outcome. The EU then objected to the Anglo American group holding in Lonrho, given that Anglo American was the controlling shareholder in Anglo American Platinum, the world's No. 1 player in platinum-group metals (PGMs). The commission ordered Anglo American to reduce its holding in Lonrho to 10 per cent over two years in order to allay a number of concerns, not least the possible concentration of control in the production and pricing of PGMs, key ingredients in vehicle and other exhaust catalysers. At the time, Impala, long a 26 per cent direct shareholder in Lonrho Platinum, was itself awaiting the outcome of an appeal against the EU's finding.

From around mid-1997, Khumalo had been plotting to acquire the Anglo American-De Beers stakes in Lonrho at 155 pence a share. As Lonrho's price fell towards 100 pence, Khumalo spun out the wisdom that the stock was actually worth between 180 and 200 pence a share. Lonrho offered JCI 'an attractive opportunity to internationalise its operations, provide it with access to foreign capital and operational synergies on complementary assets'.

Khumalo directed an equal level of passion towards dealing with JCI's gold division. In September 1997, he told investors that he had no doubt Kebble and his team would 'implement a strategy which will have a significant impact on the group's profits'. In the same month, JCI announced agreements to sell Tavistock, the South African coal miner, for R1.7 billion to Lonrho subsidiary Duiker.

In October, Kebble announced that the 'new' Western Areas would be the vehicle for JCI's emerging gold interests in Africa, Australia and Southeast Asia. He and the Randgold crowd had long impressed investors by addressing the notion of shareholder destruction arising from management contracts owned by mining houses with underlying operating mines. On this score, Kebble said there were nett cost savings to be had of $25 per ounce of gold at Western Areas and $16 per ounce at Randfontein, provided the management contracts were killed off. Randfontein, already more than a century old, would now, for no particular reason and despite an apparently moribund gold price, miraculously have another 23 years of life. Kebble spun out the honey, declaring Western Areas 'one of the world's great gold assets'. Toronto-based Barrick, Kebble complained, enjoyed a rating ten times higher than Western Areas, but he failed to volunteer any reasons for the discrepancy between the two. In the absence of freak or abnormal factors, markets ascribe different stocks different valuations for what appear to be, particularly in hindsight, remarkably sound and logical reasons.

Kebble's arrival at JCI had sparked wild speculation by wild people. There had been talk that JCI's three gold mines would go their separate ways: Randfontein to Durban Roodepoort Deep (where Roger Kebble was overlord); Western Areas to Kloof, one of the big Gold Fields mines; and HJ Joel to Beatrix, in the Gencor stable. But the plans for JCI's gold division moved as regularly as a whore's knickers. The next story (more or less) was that the gold assets, including HJ Joel, Randfontein and Western Areas, were to be collapsed into JCI Gold. For terrified investors watching the saga unfold, the gold story continued to mutate. JCI announced that it would merge Western Areas and HJ Joel into a 'quality' gold mining group fit for global expansion. Khumalo, however, tried to sing a neutral tune, telling investors that JCI was exploring for gold, copper, cobalt and iron in eight African countries, while associate Barnex continued gold prospecting at Ghana's Prestea concession area. JCI had bought 67 per cent of Kimberley Resources, a multi-commodity resources group operating out of Perth, Australia, boasting gold interests in Indonesia and Tanzania and diamond concessions in Australia.

The warbling grew soft and the Fat Lady was nowhere in sight.

In late 1997, as confirmation of rising tension between Khumalo and Kebble, JCI said it would sell to Anglo American its interests in HJ Joel and Western Areas, along with remaining interests in Anglo American Platinum, plus management contracts and specified mineral rights. There it was: gold bullion had slipped below $300 an ounce on 25 November, and Khumalo took the decision to sell what many regarded as JCI's prize gold assets. According to JCI's version of events, the group was unable to 'attain a critical mass and a strategic position in the current restructuring in the South African gold industry'. Following the new proposals from Khumalo, Anglo American would hold 70 per cent of HJ Joel and 56.4 per cent of Western Areas, stakes that would be earmarked for vending into its subsidiary, AngloGold. The creation of AngloGold saw nothing less than the world's largest gold company, with an annual production of six million ounces.

For Kebble, it appeared to have all ended in tears. JCI would be left with 34 per cent of Randfontein and some rat-and-mice residual gold assets, plus Tavistock (if the sale to Lonrho's Duiker fell through), the stakes in Consolidated Metallurgical Industries, Freddev and Barnex, and a number of exploration and development projects, such as Sukhoi Log in Siberia, the Bothaville heavy mineral sands project and a Congolese copper–cobalt venture. Khumalo, apparently oblivious to what was happening in the war-torn Democratic Republic of Congo, enthused about JCI teams 'drilling in Lubumbashi'. The group was also evaluating a hot-briquette iron project at Beira, Mozambique.

In the background, the broader resources sector in South Africa continued its deep involvement with significant, if not unprecedented, upheaval and restructuring. Kebble was massively frustrated at being moved to the fringes of the process, where he was engaged in a fierce and deadly personality clash with Khumalo. Just as Kebble wanted to be king, so Khumalo wanted to show that he could run a major corporation. When the two were not fighting, they were leaving investors increasingly confused and frustrated. Even as the company was falling apart, JCI – for which read Kebble – bought 15 per cent of Gencor's Beatrix in an attempt to participate in or influence the creation of a giant called Goldco, an event that was being carefully orchestrated by Gencor and Gold Fields.

JCI commenced the sale of assets; its 9 per cent stake in London-listed Johnson Matthey raised a princely £105 million. Khumalo continued to chase liquidations to finance the purchase of the Lonrho stake, and met EU competition officials in Brussels to discuss the issue. However, even if JCI and Lonrho somehow got it together, there was a huge potential bitter pill for Kebble. Lonrho owned a significant minority stake in Ashanti Goldfields in Ghana, and Khumalo had made no bones about the fact that it was already up for sale.

If Khumalo's plots and plans regarding the Lonrho stake materialised as planned, JCI would have to cough up £326 million (in cash, kind, or a mixture of the two) in December 1997 to become Lonrho's biggest shareholder. Khumalo's idea was to increase the JCI stake in Lonrho to 29.9 per cent (just below the level that would force a compulsory offer to all shareholders) and then persuade Lonrho to merge with JCI. An earlier attempted merger had failed when the proposal was rejected in June by Lonrho chairman John Craven, against the wishes of some of the group's executives.

The authorities in Brussels, meanwhile, remained concerned that Anglo American continued to hold a 13 per cent stake in JCI and was still represented on the JCI board. Pressure from the financiers of the sale of 30 per cent of JCI to AMG remained locked in place. They wanted out, and they wanted cash. It was anticipated that, in a full merger, Lonrho would pay between £450 million and £500 million for JCI, with funding coming, at least in part, from sales of its key hotel and motor vehicle assets.

However, the JCI train was by now well and truly derailed, and by mid-December groups of infuriated stakeholders were brandishing swords over Khumalo's head. Only one thing was clear and unambiguous: the JCI stock price had totally collapsed since Khumalo and his consortium had bought in. Beyond the objective and extraneous fact of a diseased dollar-gold price, JCI was seen as having been trashed. Trade unions were infuriated by the way Khumalo was selling off JCI's stakes in Western Areas and HJ Joel. Even so, in typically rebellious fashion, Khumalo had rubbed salt in the wounds by calling for yet a further sell-off of JCI's gold assets. Kebble, never one to miss a mess if one was brewing, faced the loss of more than R100 million (on JCI's account, of course), given JCI's purchase of the minority stake in Beatrix. The scales tipped in Khumalo's favour when the EU gave the green light for JCI to merge with Lonrho.

Then, on Friday 19 December, Khumalo resigned as chairman of JCI. Just a week before, the consortium – AMG, Saflife, Anglo American, etc. – had mandated Khumalo to proceed with the plan to merge JCI with Lonrho. Khumalo's resignation followed specific concerns in and around Southern Mining Corporation (SMC), a JSE-listed stock that was prospecting for heavy mineral sands that produce a variety of output, including titanium, rutile, ilmenite and zircon. Khumalo had apparently agreed that JCI would buy 20 per cent of SMC for R252 million. There were a number of problems, not least that SMC owned what were generally regarded as dodgy projects and prospects. To compound the lack of demonstrable fundamental value, Khumalo had not asked for, nor been given, JCI board approval to buy the stake in SMC. Worse still, Khumalo served as a director of SMC and owned stock options in the company. He conceded that the JCI board 'decided the level of entry could not be justified in terms of the limited information on the viability of the [Bothaville] project, which had been tested only at laboratory level', but maintained that there was 'no cost at all to JCI', since SMC had not been paid. Inevitably, SMC threatened to sue Khumalo via JCI.

Johnnic CEO Vaughan Bray emerged as JCI's new chief executive. He had been an executive director of JCI from 1984 until it was put on the block in 1994, and a director since. After Khumalo quit, there were endless negotiations on what would happen next. It was more of a circus than ever. What did happen rates among the messiest and meanest stuff ever concocted within corporate South Africa.

The sale of 30 per cent of JCI had turned into a full-blown nightmare for the sellers. Just as Khumalo had argued that Lonrho was worth closer to 200 than 100 pence a share, it took no rocket science to realise that a dismembered JCI was worth considerably more than the stock price reflected. It made sense, as such, to conduct an organised asset strip. The parties needed to agree which assets – if any – to keep within JCI and which to sell. Those that were jettisoned had to be sold for cash, wherever possible, and the loot returned to JCI's shareholders in the form of a cash dividend. These shareholders, the backers of AMG, would then be left with an interest in the residual JCI, if any, plus cash received from the dividend. While some were still pondering the merits of this proposal, JCI was unbundled into non-gold and gold interests, which were to be injected into JCI Gold. Somehow, Kebble was getting his way. Every voice that could be heard was calling for maximum cash extraction, yet Kebble had managed to allow JCI Gold to fall through the cracks. Those cracks were significant, given the assets to be housed within JCI Gold. For reasons that would only become apparent many months later, it was Kebble's script that was being followed.

JCI's stake in Western Areas, along with its stake in Randfontein Estates, would be at the heart of the new company, JCI Gold. But, in practice, much more than gold would be injected into JCI Gold, namely:

- the 26 per cent stake in Randfontein, which incorporated the delisted Lindum Reefs;
- the 45 per cent stake in Western Areas, which also held 48 per cent of Barnex; and
- JCI Projects (packed with a vast array of interests that dated back decades).

As such, and critically, Anglo American did not, as originally expected, acquire the JCI stake in Western Areas. According to Kebble, each of JCI Gold's three arms would have a 'clearly defined profile and separate but compatible strategies that will share synergy benefits, cost savings and management'. Naturally, JCI Gold removed the management contracts with Western Areas. The Randfontein Estates management contract was next in line.

Western Areas was positioning itself as a 'global mining business with growth potential based around its wide ore body'. Western Areas, explained Kebble, was 'JCI Gold's designated growth company holding all the quality gold assets and could well list offshore'. The revised strategy, management structure and style, and independent business focus were reflected in the proposed name change from Western Areas Gold Mining Company to Western Areas Ltd. To the extent that JCI Gold would hold gold assets such as Randgold Resources and others, they would be offered to Western Areas, and those that didn't fit with either Western Areas or Randfontein Estates would be disposed of.

JCI Gold exchanged its stake in Barnex, the portfolio of South African and African mineral rights and the Western Areas management contract, for new Western Areas shares. The assets in Indonesia and Sukhoi Log were excluded for the moment. Reading between the lines, Kebble had sold the story, and done so successfully, on the basis that he was going to turn Western Areas into the Mother Ship.

In March 1998, JCI Gold was officially launched, with Wiseman Nkuhlu as chairman and Kebble in the executive deputy chairman slot. Other board nominees included Marcel Golding, chairman of Hosken Consolidated Investments, Gibson Njenje (described as a businessman), Eric Molefe, another businessman, and Tiego

Moseneke, a lawyer. In one of his masterstrokes of understatement, Kebble said he would focus on strategic and commercial issues, while day-to-day running would be in the hands of a management team drawn from the ranks of the current executive. John Fox Brownrigg was appointed managing director.

Ghosts of the Lonrho deal, which never materialised, rose in March 1998. In the all-out bid to extract cash from JCI to be returned to the beleaguered backers of AMG, Tavistock and UCP were sold to Lonrho-controlled Duiker; Consolidated Murchison was bought by listed Metorex; and CMI was sold to Sudelektra, of which 40 per cent was owned by Swiss-based minerals and metals trader, Glencore. JCI's stakes in HJ Joel and Anglo American Platinum were swapped out with the Anglo American and De Beers interests in Lonrho, leaving Anglo American and De Beers with 5 per cent of Lonrho.

In corporate action so complicated that it left investors dazed and confused, Investec brokered the climactic end game by taking over the 21 per cent Lonrho stake from JCI. It was sold back to Lonrho for cash, which was returned to the original backers of AMG via material special dividend payments. Shareholders who had not completely jumped ship, such as Anglo American and De Beers, ended up not only with cash, but also with stakes in JCI Gold. By now, JCI Gold was being described, once again, as 'JCI'. In fact, the 'new' JCI was really just the 'old' JCI, stripped of the assets that had been sold to raise cash. AMG's interest in JCI was now, or so it was explained, via a 70 per cent holding in JSE-listed Witnigel, previously a virtual shell with rat-and-mice mining interests, but now punted as a mining investment house with a 'major asset' amounting to 13 per cent of JCI.

What the hell was Witnigel? What was it suddenly doing in the middle of things? Investors were reassured that AMG had joint control of JCI via a voting pool agreement with BNC Investments, which, it was said at the time, also held 13 per cent of JCI. BNC apparently represented the interests of the Kebble family, but it was just another new name that suddenly popped up. When it was pointed out that the nine-person JCI board had five AMG appointees, Kebble insisted that 'there are no circumstances under which any party in the pool agreement can cast a veto vote – it is true joint control via consensus agreements'. The other major shareholders in JCI, said Kebble, were North American financial institutions, passive investors who apparently held as much as 42 per cent of JCI. Kebble, along with the AMG, had a pre-emptive right to a further 30 per cent of JCI and, through BNC, Kebble also held pre-emptive rights over Witnigel, should AMG decide to sell its stake. It then emerged that in the Khumalo days, JCI's major shareholders had included not only Saflife, AMG, Anglo American and De Beers, but also Consolidated African Mines (CAM).

What the hell was CAM? How did BNC fit into the picture?

On 26 June 1998, investors were told that JCI Gold would focus on managing its operational assets plus JCI Projects, of which it owned 100 per cent. JCI Gold's principal assets now comprised 45 per cent each of Western Areas and Freddev, the Randfontein service agreement, offshore development assets and about R150 million in cash. In September, JCI Ltd, that venerable mining house, was delisted from the JSE and the ghost of Barney Barnato vanquished. As for Khumalo, he cut all ties with JCI and transferred his interest to JSE-listed Gold Fields Properties (later renamed Mawenzi, whose stock price plunged from R2.40 to 35 cents a share in 1998).

On 15 July 1998, when CAM published its results for the year to 31 March, one amazing and shocking truth emerged. It required many skills and extensive knowledge of the context to figure it out, but eventually the clear and simple fact was that Brett Kebble had been in control of JCI for months.

10

A bit of a billionaire

IT WAS A STUNNING COUP D'ÉTAT. There had been no single event, but Brett Kebble had turned high finance into an art form that owed no homage at all to individual taste. He had fooled everyone, possibly even himself.

Kebble's secret weapon had been Consolidated African Mines (CAM). More than anything else, this entity would shadow the life and times of the allegedly intrepid would-be mining magnate.

CAM was at the centre of some of the most complex deals ever seen in South African corporate history. It was the antithesis of the kind of company that Warren Buffett would have invested in. He has said repeatedly, over many years, that he would invest only in companies that he understood. It is unlikely that many investors ever understood CAM, and that suited Kebble down to the ground. He ran the company, but he needed a small army of external experts to support and publicise his oversized ego, masquerading as genius and greatness. With CAM, Kebble was a man among men, his place in the sun an island in a sea of coconut milk generated by serious professional players. The names were to be seen in 'tombstone' announcements, jargon for the list of professionals who sign off on regulatory information published by listed stocks for shareholders. CAM issued one such announcement in July 1998. At the bottom, there was an impressive-looking tombstone:

Consolidated African Mines
Johannesburg
3 July 1998

....

Merchant Bankers
Société Générale
Nedcor Investment Bank Ltd
Joint Sponsoring Brokers
Frankel Pollak Securities (Pty) Ltd
Members of the Johannesburg Stock Exchange
HSBC Simpson McKie (Pty) Ltd
Member HSBC Group
Members of the Johannesburg Stock Exchange

Legal Advisers
Bowman Gilfillan Hayman Godfrey Attorneys
Established 1902

Reporting accountants
Coopers & Lybrand

Auditors and accountants
Charles Orbach & Company

These are people presumed to have the very highest standards of corporate governance; people who preach and practise and display true and proper fear of death for not being 100 per cent straight; people who silently demand to be respected as pillars of society; people who only positively affect the stature and status of our life and times; people who are truly special.

The princes within this coterie of professionals were the investment bankers. Wall Street had always been home to the greatest of them, the original Masters of the Universe, the eaters of raw flesh. Wall Street's Big Swinging Dicks inspired investment bankers everywhere. Investment banking is one big game, but it can be a pretty serious one, given the vast sums of money that players stand to earn. In practice, as long as investment bankers are making good money out of any particular client, they are prepared to do almost anything, within reason, along with the lawyers, accountants, auditors and other professionals. These are the motley crews of professional millionaires who make the world go round. Some of them are both spineless and gutless, and it is doubtful if there is a good one among them.

Buffett has a folksy take on everything in investing, including bankers. On 2 October 1987, the *Washington Post* quoted him as saying: 'Wall Street likes to characterise the proliferation of frenzied financial games as a sophisticated, prosocial activity, facilitating the fine-tuning of a complex economy. But the truth is otherwise; short-term transactions frequently act as an invisible foot, kicking society in the shins.'

Kebble was no businessman with a vision. He was, first and foremost, a trader. To him, the short-term transaction was everything. He loved to trade clandestinely in the market, pushing stocks around. There was even jargon for this kind of behaviour: 'jobbing'. By now, Kebble's game was big, and growing by the minute. He was riding the market and he had become a master of paper.

On 31 March 1997, CAM had 17.4 million shares in issue. Exactly a year later, the number was 527.3 million. As a rule, companies agonise before issuing any new shares, no matter how few, and almost regardless of the reason. Even then, it is normal, if not compulsory, to put the proposed issue of fresh shares to the vote at a company's annual general meeting. Where permission from shareholders is required in a hurry, an extraordinary meeting can be convened. This is unusual in itself, but, when it happens, the company in question is invariably involved in making an acquisition and needs permission in a hurry. Acquisitions often pop up out of nowhere, pushing companies into emergency mode.

Companies also issue shares in order to cater for stock options that have been offered and accepted by executives and employees. Such proposed share issues must be discussed and pre-approved at the AGM. All in all, companies that experience a doubling in issued shares in a year or so are as rare as rocking horse shit, though this can occur when a company acquires a similar-sized entity, with a similar value, in an all-share acquisition.

The point can be laboured, but under normal operating circumstances, companies resist the issuance of shares for the simple reason that it dilutes the interests of existing shareholders. For example, if a company with 100 shareholders and 100 shares declares a dividend of R100 in total, each shareholder is paid R1 in cash. Double the number of shares in issue to 200, and the same dividend declaration halves to 50 cents per share. So unpopular is the issuing of shares that great numbers of companies buy back their own shares. In the example used, if the company bought 50 of its shares back, the dividend declaration would translate to R2 per share, 100 per cent more than the R1 dividend. Share buy-backs are one of the main components of what is generally known as capital management, which also includes dividend payments. Optimum capital management is aimed at increasing the wealth of shareholders on a sustainable basis and at a superior rate.

For Kebble, rules and acceptable practices were things to be tested, pushed to the limit, stretched, strained and, if required, broken. With CAM, he had done something that was probably unprecedented on any stock exchange, anywhere. In a single year, he took the number of issued shares in a listed stock from 17.4 million to 527.3 million. It was a thirtyfold increase.

In the fallout from the disastrous JCI black economic empowerment transaction, Kebble had mopped up the mess by issuing paper in the form of CAM shares. He had convinced all and sundry that he could, and no doubt would, add value. In the 1997/8 financial year, there had been nine key transactions.

The first set the scene for those that would follow. CAM purchased the entire issued share capital of Khumalo Alliance (Pty) Ltd by issuing 23 550 000 new CAM shares at 600 cents each. In other words, CAM bought Khumalo Alliance for 23.6 million shares. When the two figures are multiplied, a putative value of R141 million is arrived at. The value is putative because Khumalo accepted that the

CAM shares were worth 600 cents each, but this does not mean that Khumalo believed the shares were worth that much. Price is what you pay. Value is what you get. *No cash changed hands.*

CAM then bought the entire issued share capital of Chendini Investments for 22 916 667 new CAM shares at 600 cents each (putative value: R138 million), and the entire issued share capital of Craftwise Investments for 81 216 667 new CAM shares at the same price (putative value: R487 million). Both entities held interests in JCI. *No cash changed hands.*

Next, CAM bought 3 110 570 shares in JCI Ltd for 23 847 703 CAM shares at 600 cents a share (putative value: R143 million), followed by one million shares in Randgold & Exploration for 6 433 333 new CAM shares at 600 cents each (putative value: R39 million). *No cash changed hands.*

CAM then bought the issued share capital of Consolidated Mining Corporation (CMC) for 244 455 365 new CAM shares at 600 cents each. The putative value was R1.5 billion. *No cash changed hands.*

However, since the Kebble family controlled CMC, this transaction allowed Brett to look around with some satisfaction and reflect on the fact that he was now a billionaire. The Kebbles now controlled CAM and, on paper, their stake was worth R1.5 billion. Just a few years after going into business, Brett Kebble was a billionaire, and he had plenty of paper to prove it.

CAM then bought 200 million cumulative redeemable preference shares in Witnigel Investments for 33 333 334 new CAM shares at 600 cents each (putative value: R222 million), and another 1 072 349 shares in JCI Ltd for 21.9 million new CAM shares at 315 cents each (putative value: R69 million). *No cash changed hands.*

At that point, Kebble had doled out CAM paper with a combined 'value' of R2.2 billion. CAM also raised a little cash through four sales of shares, though buyers were utterly unconvinced that they were worth anything like 600 cents each. Nevertheless, a cash total of R73 million was raised as follows:

- 348 338 new CAM shares sold at 306 cents a share (cash value: R1 million);
- 12 989 096 new CAM shares sold at 215 cents a share (cash value: R28 million);
- 20 000 000 new CAM shares sold at 136 cents a share (cash value: R27 million);
- 18 862 810 new CAM shares sold at 145 cents a share (cash value: R17 million).

On 31 March 1998 there were 527 285 706 CAM shares in issue, of which just over 46 per cent were under the control of Kebble or his family. In addition, 79 359 907 CAM options were in issue.

After the balance sheet date of 31 March, CAM bought 10 million shares in Saflife from Witnigel Investments for 83 333 333 CAM shares. The value was a mere R1.50

per share, giving a putative value of R125 million. Apparently, someone was not convinced that CAM was worth R6 a share. *No cash changed hands.*

While the paper transactions totalled R2.3 billion, when it came to hard cash, Kebble had raised a mere R73 million. The combined transactions left 610.6 million CAM shares issued, of which Kebble controlled 244.5 million, or 40 per cent.

What had CAM paid for? What value did it get? How did the buyers benefit? According to the nett asset value calculation published with the 1998 annual results, CAM comprised:

CAM: Market valuation NAV	
31 March 1998	**Rm**
JCI Ltd	525
Mawenzi	197
Randgold & Exploration	48
Randgold Resources	31
Saflife	514
Other	56
Total NAV	**1 371**
Issued shares (m)	619
NAV per share (cents)	221

It was pure Kebble alchemy, and just about no one had the vaguest idea what was going on, except that there seemed to be some correlation with the June 1997 announcement about one of the many JCI shareholder agreements. Kebble was broadcasting his apparent genius in a manner that bamboozled all and sundry. He let it be known that NK Properties (NKP) would wholly own CMC, which he would manage and which would be the vehicle through which the Kebble family maintained its investments in Randgold and other mines. The records show that when Kebble took control of CMC, it was a near worthless little mining house with interests in gold, diamond and asbestos exploration, management and finance. It had a 75 per cent interest in Egoli Consolidated Mines, which was engaged in gold and diamond mining, a 14.4 per cent interest in Carrig Diamonds, a 57.3 per cent interest in South East Rand Gold Holdings and a 34 per cent interest in HVL Asbestos (Swaziland).

CMC was delisted from the JSE on 29 August 1997 after it was bought out by NKP, which morphed into CAM. Just months earlier, CAM had issued hundreds of millions of shares to CMC, making it a 100 per cent subsidiary. Kebble had inserted his own and his family's interests into CMC during 1996 in the simplest possible manner. After he took control of CMC, it issued shares to BNC Investments, buying the Kebble family interests and effectively listing them on the JSE. In the deal that had turned Kebble into a bit of a billionaire, CAM issued hundreds of millions of shares to CMC, giving his family effective control of CAM. Kebble thus controlled JCI Gold.

In June 1997, Kebble had informed investors that should the JCI–Lonrho merger succeed, NKP would lift its stake in the new group. Once again, apart from making tons of money – and it really was tons, measured in paper terms – gold was at the forefront of Kebble's plans and NKP would focus on the precious metal.

'We think,' Kebble said, 'that many gold assets are undervalued and we would be prepared to swap our other assets for gold assets.'

The June 1997 JCI shareholders agreement saw the NKP stake in Capital Alliance grow to 47 per cent and its stake in Saflife increase to 34.9 per cent. All that had happened, as would eventually emerge many months later, was that NKP was mopping up the JCI mess by issuing paper, paper and still more paper to disillusioned investors. In June 1997, the hype was that, as part of the shareholder agreement, NKP 'bought Khumalo Alliance, which has 16.4 per cent of Saflife, from BNC – a company controlled by the Kebble and Khumalo families – in exchange for NKP (CAM) shares. Saflife has 30 per cent of JCI and NKP (CAM) a direct 6 per cent stake in JCI.'

Saflife's rights issue, the *Sunday Times Business Times* reported, had been 'only 46 per cent taken up, leaving underwriter SBC Warburg with R600 million worth of scrip. This has been sold to NKP for NKP scrip.'

In translation, this meant sold to CAM for CAM scrip, market jargon for paper shares.

One disillusioned shareholder after another had accepted NKP (CAM) shares at 600 cents each. Kebble had mastered the technique that worked so well for Randgold in 1996, when the company's 'value' increased from $5 million to $310 million in 14 months. With CAM, Kebble made everyone punch-drunk with the promise that it was, and would be, worth 600 cents a share, come hell or high water.

He was not alone, of course, in broadcasting the story. He had a small army of investment bankers on retainer, and they were expected to preach the 600 cents myth as vigorously and savagely as was required.

For Kebble, it must all have been too beautiful for words. However, the NAV shown for CAM on 31 March 1998 was still messy, given that multiple distributions (unbundlings) still had to be made by various parties. While further transactions were also conducted, the NAV published by CAM one year later offered a far clearer glimpse of what was sitting in CAM. By then, JCI had been fully unbundled into JCI Gold and cash, much of which exited to the original AMG backers. Saflife had also made its distributions (including JCI Gold) and had disappeared from the list of CAM's interests. Apart from a new acquisition, Gem Diamonds, CAM looked much like a gold mining holding company. Sitting inside JCI Gold was the all-important stake in Western Areas, but, even at that stage, the extent of CAM's debt was as noticeable as its lack of cash.

The nett asset value per share was shown by CAM itself to be 143 cents on 31 March 1999. This was a far cry from the 600 cents a share that Kebble and his strongmen had so remorselessly proclaimed from the rooftops in 1997, but he had any number of explanations for the disappointingly low NAV. To reassure investors, he even published his own version of CAM's NAV on the same date.

In the world according to Brett Kebble, CAM's NAV was 257 cents a share, 80 per cent more than the value derived from market prices. The stock prices for JCI Gold, Randfontein and so on were just plain wrong. If investors listened to Kebble, they would understand the truth. The market was wrong and Kebble, that bit of a billionaire, was right.

The number of CAM shares in issue increased to 661 million as at 31 March 1999, compared to 619 million a year earlier. Although the figures did not always add up – a recurring theme in Kebble's chaotic world – CAM said that, during its 1999 financial year, it had acquired another 400 000 shares in JCI by issuing 8 650 407 CAM shares at 123 cents each (putative value: R11 million). *No cash changed hands.*

CAM: Market valuation NAV	
31 March 1999	**Rm**
Gem Diamonds	23
JCI Gold	1 046
Randfontein	74
Randgold & Exploration	71
Randgold Resources	16
Other	41
Unlisted	
Pref shares	130
Other	27
Mineral rights	74
Other	8
Loans	75
Loans payable	–96
Current liabilities	–546
Total NAV	**943**
Issued shares (m)	661
NAV per share (cents)	143

CAM: Kebble's NAV valuation	
31 March 1999	**Rm**
Gem Diamonds	27
JCI Gold	1427
Randfontein	127
Randgold & Exploration	308
Randgold Resources	67
Other	68
Unlisted	
Pref shares	130
Other	27
Mineral rights	74
Other	8
Loans	75
Loans payable	–96
Current liabilities	–546
Total NAV	**1 697**
Issued shares (m)	661
NAV per share (cents)	257

CAM also bought 9 423 000 shares in Simmer and Jack Mines by issuing 3 140 000 CAM shares at 120 cents each (putative value: R4 million). *No cash changed hands.*

During the 1999 financial year, cash of R32 million was raised in three tranches: 20 350 000 CAM shares at 70 cents each (R14 million); 8 650 000 at 75 cents a share (R7 million) and 9 200 000 at 120 cents a share (R11 million). While Kebble preached lofty figures for CAM's 'true' NAV, he was selling CAM shares for as little as 70 cents each in order to raise cash. At that price, the valuation for CAM was nearly 90 per cent less than the mid-1997 valuation of 600 cents a share.

Heaven is a glorious place to be when you are a billionaire for a bit. The investment bankers, along with the lawyers, accountants and other professional advisers, had laughed all the way to the bank. Someone really ought to have been reading Warren Buffett at bedtime. On 20 June 1994, a *US News & World* report quoted him as follows: 'Full-time professionals in other fields, let's say a dentist, bring a lot to the layman. But in aggregate, people get nothing for their money from professional money managers.'

11

Payday for one shady character

ANGLO AMERICAN'S BID to sell off a controlling stake in earmarked JCI assets to black economic empowerment partners had ended in floods of tears. Anglo American and its associate, De Beers, had received mostly cash for selling 30 per cent of the original JCI, but, in less than a year, JCI had been disembowelled.

Mzi Khumalo was out of the picture, apparently disgraced. A material number of JCI's most valuable assets had been liquidated for cash to partially settle the rabid demands of finance houses and investment banks that had so greedily backed the original deal. The remaining assets, most importantly a controlling stake in Western Areas, had ended up in JCI Gold. That entity, in turn, was under the control of Brett Kebble and the extended, undefined Kebble family, which included at its core Roger, the father.

If CAM's nett asset value as calculated by Kebble was indeed R1.7 billion on 31 March 1999, the family's stake was worth about R600 million. There was no question that the Kebbles had made many millions during 1996 and in the early part of 1997, when the Randgold & Exploration stock price was running up to its record high of around R41 a share. Those tens of millions had apparently been converted into hundreds of millions through a rapid-fire set of transactions executed by Brett in mid-1997.

That was just about the time when Randgold Resources was listing in London and when the dollar-gold price fell $40 an ounce in a very short time indeed. There was a modicum of panic in physical gold markets; gold stocks were being pounded. The heavy downdraft turned into violent headwinds as the realities of the Bre-X fraud continued to bite into gold equity markets. Kebble, however, had maintained his unshakeable belief in the yellow metal. In the mid-1997 JCI shareholder agreements, he had been able to talk all and sundry into accepting CAM paper. So desperate were the sellers that CAM went like hot cakes at 600 cents a share.

There was, however, a monumental twist. When Kebble prevailed upon terrified JCI shareholders, he had very little cash and, given that he had control of JCI's gold assets firmly in mind, he needed a great deal of hard currency just to get into the game. Even at this relatively early stage, before his name became synonymous with questionable deals, Kebble had little creditworthiness beyond the cash he could stump up as surety for debt. He could not raise serious financing in Johannesburg or anywhere else in South Africa, let alone abroad. But not all was lost. By this stage, Kebble had lunched and supped with and bumped into any number of deal-makers, and some of the shadier ones were drawn to him just as strongly as he gravitated towards them. They could use one another.

One of these shady characters, in particular, bankrolled Kebble to the tune of tens of millions of rand. Sharp as he was – and he was very sharp indeed – even he bought into some aspects of Kebble's portrait of the universe.

Despite having managed to seize control of JCI Gold in mid-1997 and simultaneously turn himself into a paper billionaire, Kebble's stewardship of the company via CAM hit stormy waters from the outset. Barring an absolute miracle, there was no way that CAM's stock price was going to see 600 cents a share again. What little cash Kebble had raised by selling CAM shares for as little as 70 cents each was as good as it was going to get. CAM's cash haemorrhage intensified.

It was never clear how many millions Kebble borrowed from the shady character. What Kebble did with the money was even more obscure. The only certainty was that Kebble had run up an astronomical debt, and the shady character started calling for payback at a fairly early stage. The shady one was only human, according to some who knew him, and his nervous system was fully functional. The Kebble imbroglio had made the shady one skittish from the moment he became moneylender in chief.

Kebble needed a life raft, and he would be thrown one – albeit punctured and not fully inflated – but it would not come from the gold sector. It came from diamonds.

Renowned from 1996 among those who knew no better as a deal-maker, Kebble had been introduced to a diamond prospect in the Northern Cape that counted among its assets a farm called Saxendrift.

On 18 September 1998, a JSE-listed stock, Consolidated Diamond Corporation (CDC), changed its name to Gem Diamond Mining Corporation and became the vehicle for Kebble's next adventure. Gem, the records show, prospected for and mined diamonds on the farms Saxendrift, Geduld and Whitewaters between Douglas and Prieska. Gem also owned the Samada diamond mine in the Ventersburg district and the Perdevlei kimberlite mine north of Barkly West.

The emergence of Gem Diamonds on the JSE was mired in drama. The shady character had been the majority shareholder in CDC, which had become a major liability for all kinds of reasons. One of the biggest mistakes had been made at the Samada mine, which had been improperly designed and completely overcapitalised relative to what could and should have been done. Tens of millions of rand had been wasted, and the shady character needed an exit.

Opportunity appeared to have come knocking in the form of John Bristow, brother of Mark, of Randgold Resources fame. John Bristow was trying to create enthusiasm for Saxendrift, which was housed in a corporate entity known as Northern Cape Diamond Mines. A Johannesburg financial services boutique, The Corner House, run by Dennis Tucker, took an interest. The Corner House was closely linked to Kebble in a number of ways; indeed, it was widely assumed that he had financed the facility. Be that as it may, Kebble learnt about Saxendrift at a time when the shady one was becoming increasingly concerned about the foreign debt owed by CDC and was seeking payback from Kebble. A deal was structured that in many ways was a clone of the irregular corporate finance techniques used for the Randgold & Exploration and Randgold Resources acquisition of BHP Minerals Mali in 1996.

It was the shady one who came up with the money to set the diamond deal in motion. He paid the owners of Northern Cape Diamond Mines, Vic and Eddie Pienaar, R33 million in cash. Very few individuals knew about this transaction. The shady one then took a 'flick' by flipping the entity into CDC for R100 million. In practice, CDC issued fresh shares to the shady one to the value of R100 million. It was the familiar story of using over-valued paper to pay for real assets. The effect was that the shady one increased his stake in CDC, diluting that of other shareholders. It was naughty, oh yes indeed.

In the next stage of the deal, newly created Gem Diamonds would go to the market with a rights issue to raise a large sum of cash in order to properly capitalise the recently acquired assets, particularly Saxendrift. Well, that was the official story, anyway.

Tucker packed his Corner House credentials and obligingly set off on a roadshow with a heavily hyped presentation. CDC had just paid R100 million for Saxendrift, a great asset, blah, blah, blah. Behind the scenes, CAM had agreed to participate in the issue of fresh shares that would see CAM end up with a 34.9 per cent stake in Gem Diamonds. The trick, of course, was that the shady one would be by far the biggest shareholder in Gem Diamonds and the cash from the rights issue would be under his control. Kebble was trying to honour the payday that the shady one was due, but, in reality, CAM would be the entity that obliged, using its own cash.

The Gem Diamonds capital-raising exercise was as successful as the plotters had anticipated, and about R85 million in cash rolled in. Institutional fund managers, who would have had little or no knowledge of what was really going on, pledged most of the money. The shady one had seen his R33 million used as potent leverage to raise R85 million. Given his stake in Gem Diamonds, he had roughly doubled his cash outlay for Saxendrift. It was a very cool deal.

While CDC changed its name to Gem Diamonds only on 18 September, news of the underlying larceny had been fed to the 'right' network of people as early as

10 June, when CDC was quoted at 99 cents a share. In the next ten trading days, the share price increased to 480 cents a share, an appreciation of 385 per cent.

For Kebble, the Gem Diamonds deal was fundamentally rare in many senses. Despite cloning the paper-hype technique that had worked with devastating effect in the Mali deal, the Gem Diamonds deal involved an asset that was producing nett positive cash flow. Saxendrift was no Syama, though it did present certain challenges. The mine on the farm was processing ore from alluvial deposits, a nightmare for geologists and mine owners. The majority of ore bodies, whether gold, iron ore, copper or diamonds, can be slowly and scientifically 'virtually' reproduced, for the convenience of the human eye, by impressive computer programs. On the ground, the techniques of advanced mineral economics rely ultimately on closely spaced diamond drillings that extract neat cores from the potential ore body. In the case of alluvial diamonds, it is all but impossible for geologists and mineral economics experts to offer confidence as to the extent and grade of the ore body. Alluvial diamond deposits are the creation of countless years of river action, disturbed by invariably disruptive events such as non-linear occurrences, like floods. In practice, commercial mining on alluvial diamond deposits tends to focus on blocks, where ore from a promising or known zone is processed. Geologists can contribute some knowledge to interpretation of what may happen next, but this kind of mining is very much a hit-and-miss affair. Blocks are mined for as long as the diamonds are coughed out and the mine can pay its bills. On some days, although they are rare, a real beauty emerges from the dreadfully noisy separation plants. At Saxendrift, exceptional quality gem diamonds were found on a fairly regular basis, some exceeding 50 and even 100 carats.

For Kebble, however, the Saxendrift deal had served its immediate purpose: the shady character had bagged tens of millions. The CAM stake in Gem Diamonds now looked like the kind of investment that could be conveniently dumped into Kebble's anchor BEE company. On 1 July 1999, New Mining Corporation (formerly Witwatersrand Nigel or Witnigel, and later to become Matodzi Resources), announced that it had purchased a package of diamond assets from CAM for R350 million. New Mining, already known as the 'rubbish bin' for assets Kebble considered spent, would serve as the prototype for his many future BEE deals.

Topping the list of assets was a 50 per cent interest in Guild Hall No. 22 Investment Holding Company (Pty) Ltd, which held a 35 per cent stake in Gem Diamonds. New Mining thus acquired 35 per cent of Diamonds. By this stage, however, Tokyo Sexwale's Mvelaphanda group held half of the stake in Guild Hall, giving Mvelaphanda an effective 17.5 per cent stake in Gem Diamonds.

Sexwale would later recall that Gem Diamonds was the deal that established

Mvelaphanda as a genuine BEE entity with a sustainable future. He entered the deal when news spread that Kebble was vending a bunch of diamond assets into New Mining. Before the deal went through, Kebble had been heavily persuaded that Mvelaphanda should receive Gem Diamonds shares at 250 cents each. Mvelaphanda would then finance the deal by future dividends from its stake in Gem Diamonds, a structure common to many BEE deals.

When it was pointed out that, given cash flow projections for Gem Diamonds, it would take Mvelaphanda 27 years to come up with the funding at 250 cents per share, the deal appeared dead. Kebble was told that if the shares were vended to Mvelaphanda at 150 cents each, the payback period would be reduced from 27 to five years. He agreed, and the deal was done.

At New Mining, among other assets being acquired from CAM for R350 million were mineral rights adjacent to the Saxendrift mine, a 50 per cent stake in the holding company of the Letšeng La-Terae diamond project in Lesotho and a stake in Mawenzi Resources. New Mining was also acquiring 100 per cent of Ekuseni Resources, which had a 29 per cent interest in DiamondWorks, a Toronto-listed company with prospects in Angola and Sierra Leone.

Kebble's abiding affair with weird and complicated financial transactions grew by the month. In its report for the financial year to 31 March 2000, CAM said it had disposed of certain assets not forming part of its 'core gold mining assets' to New Mining. The consideration, CAM said, was worth R350 million and was 'discharged in full' by New Mining, which issued to CAM:

- 40 million ordinary shares in New Mining at 50 cents a share;
- 50.5 million 'participating cumulative variable rate convertible redeemable A preference shares' at 100 cents each; and
- 200 million 'cumulative variable rate convertible redeemable B preference shares' at 100 cents each.

Once again, it was paper, paper and more paper. Assets were being injected by CAM into New Mining. New Mining, in turn, was discharging its side of the deal by issuing paper to CAM.

Mvelaphanda's involvement in Saxendrift turned up a number of surprises. It took only a cursory inspection for Sexwale and his management team to realise that the mine was being run appallingly. The entire operation on the farm was under the control of just one man, Hennie de Jager, and he was clearly out of his depth. Sexwale initiated a complete revamp of the mine, starting with a comprehensive change in management. In no time at all, Saxendrift was going places and, with hard-core management specialists having replaced De Jager, the really big gem diamonds that Saxendrift was famous for started reappearing.

In mid-December 1999, less than six months after CAM's announcement of its injection of diamond assets into New Mining, Trans Hex, a serious diamond miner listed on the JSE, announced that it had agreed to a merger with Gem Diamonds. The deal was subject to a normal list of preconditions, but the parties hoped to complete it by the end of April 2000.

It was difficult to put an exact figure on the value of the deal, since Gem Diamonds shareholders were to receive an agreed number of Trans Hex shares for every 100 shares held in Gem, plus a cash dividend. The value of the Trans Hex shares would depend on the date of sale, a decision that rested with each individual shareholder.

To all intents and purposes, however, the deal could probably be valued at about R125 million, including a R25 million cash dividend. It was favourable to all sellers, who made substantial profits. Exactly who these parties were remains a matter of some conjecture, but bear in mind that, on 1 July 1999, New Mining announced that it would be buying a set of specified diamond assets from CAM. In future New Mining annual reports, purchases were dutifully reported as of 1 July 1999 of 100 per cent of Ekuseni Resources, Brakfontein Diamante, Consolidated Resources and Exploration, IEN Investments, Newlands Minerals and Tavlands.

According to the annual reports, the acquisition of Guild Hall No. 22 was only put through on 27 March 2002. Kebble had taken the Gem Diamonds deal out of the rubbish bin, reshuffled the shareholding structure and 'rewritten' the deal in such a way that he could milk profits for his personal benefit.

Such disgraceful misappropriation of profits had already become a regular feature of his business dealings.

Even so, Gem Diamonds was packed with ironies. Kebble had bought into the company via CAM in order to overinflate the price of Gem Diamonds on the back of the Saxendrift transaction. In a mutant version of the Mali deal, R85 million in cash had been raised by Gem Diamonds, partly settling some of Kebble's debts with the shady character. Kebble, however, appeared ignorant of the fact that Saxendrift was generating positive cash flows. Even worse, he appeared completely ignorant of the fact that Saxendrift was mismanaged; it took Sexwale to recognise and realise its full value. In the four financial years after Trans Hex absorbed Gem Diamonds, Saxendrift generated around R275 million in cash. Given that Trans Hex had paid some R125 million for Gem Diamonds, it was a healthy enough return. For once, Kebble had sold something for far less than it was really worth.

The shady character stood to gain substantially from completion of the merger. He sent one of his runners, Paul Main, to pick up the cheques. Main pocketed about R5 million for himself, apparently for 'finding' Saxendrift in the first place, but, even so, there was no denying that Monty Koppel, shady character and resident of London, harvested a double payday from the Gem Diamonds saga.

PART V

Killing a billion

12

The calm before the storm

I N 49 BC, when Caesar and his army crossed the Rubicon, a river boundary between Italy and Gaul, it was interpreted as meaning that the Roman Emperor had made an irrevocable decision. Having found its way into the English language, this useful reference to irreversible commitment is as good a benchmark as any by which to measure the Roman candle that was Brett Kebble's business career.

Kebble spent much of 1996 and 1997 executing enormously successful paper transactions through which he acquired tangible assets by issuing over-valued shares of companies he controlled. These shares were his own personal currency, his own paper money, and, for a brief time, Kebble's currency enjoyed a modicum of respect. However, investors grew wary of the endless unfulfilled promises and garishly complicated corporate structures he created. For his part, Kebble had acquired a motley collection of assets that were nett absorbers of cash.

Brett Kebble, maverick, had overlooked or ignored the basic business model that investors demand of mining companies. The model was hardly complicated, with its focus on low-cost, long-life, high-quality mining assets, with the parent company holding as close as possible to 100 per cent of the underlying asset. In one concept, the focus was on control of sustainable cash flows. Kebble offered investors none of these characteristics in the companies he controlled and, as early as 1998, it was clear that he should have unbundled them.

However, stubborn and tinted by malice given the mega-deals flooding the broad South African mining sector, the maverick had decided to develop a business model that was pure Brett Kebble. It was, by definition, starved of cash. Instead of unbundling and finding a new *raison d'être*, Kebble started raising cash from the assets he controlled. Each exercise was carefully and immaculately marketed to investors in a cunning and beguiling manner. On each occasion, professional investors in particular should have been calling for Kebble's head. Instead, they either went along for the ride or ignored him to the extent that it was possible to do so.

If one could pinpoint the date on which Kebble forded his personal Rubicon, it would probably be 30 November 1998. That was the day on which he announced that Placer Dome, a respected Canadian gold mining outfit, had signed a 50:50 joint venture (JV) with Western Areas. It was a step – just one step – towards Kebble's Next Big Thing. The foreigners had effectively bought 50 per cent of the Western

Areas ore body. In days to come, the distinction between Western Areas and its ore body would become rather important: Placer Dome was buying 50 per cent of the *ore body*, not of the mine.

The announcement, however, stated that Placer Dome *was* buying half of the mine, including all the assets and liabilities: mining authorisations, mineral rights, surface rights and rights to conduct mining activities, as well as all geological, operating and technical data relative thereto; fixed and development assets; stocks, accounts receivable and payable; contracts, goodwill and intellectual property but excluding the financial assets (cash and hedging contracts), shares in other companies and mineral rights outside of the mining authorisation area.

The tombstone for the announcement looked impressive enough:

November 30 1998

....

Joint financial advisers in South Africa
The Corner House
In the United Kingdom
CIBC World Markets

Joint sponsoring brokers
Merrill Lynch
Smith Borkum Hare

Merrill Lynch South Africa
Member of the Johannesburg Stock Exchange
SG Frankel Pollack Securities
Member of the Johannesburg Stock Exchange
HSBC Simpson McKie
Member of the Johannesburg Stock Exchange

Legal Advisers
Deneys Reitz Attorneys
Moseneke & Partners

Most of the names on the tombstone were big, or big enough, with the possible exception of The Corner House, though the name of Dennis Tucker was familiar in the public domain as being from or representing this entity. Tucker had been a freshman, living in the same hall of residence at the University of the Witwatersrand as Glyn Lewis in 1976. Both had graduated as mining engineers. At the time that Kebble announced the sale of half the heart of Western Areas, Lewis was well into the build-up of production from the Tarkwa open-cast gold mine in Ghana. After a period of drilling, feasibility studies and project development – including the removal of overburden and the resettlement of some 22 000 people – mining had started at Tarkwa in 1997. Ore processing commenced at the Tarkwa North Plant in March 1998, and Lewis moved on to the build-up at Tarkwa South Plant. Gold Fields was looking great when Tarkwa rapidly grew into a legend as one of the biggest open-cast gold mines in the world.

Lewis was riding the crest of an enormous wave, with Tarkwa yet to be fully appreciated in South Africa, though he had suffered some severe personal setbacks, such as the loss of one of his beloved Staffordshire bull terriers to a Gaboon viper. There were also the tropical diseases. Lewis himself had been the victim, more than once, of incessant assaults by malarial mosquitoes and had underestimated the damage that something so small could inflict.

Tucker, on the other hand, suffered nothing in the way of personal discomfort as he cavorted between Johannesburg and Cape Town, singing songs of junk to institutional fund managers. It was unimaginable that the lives of the two mining engineers, who had eaten, studied and drunk together, could have grown so far apart.

Tucker had worked in the mining environment, but found that it was not to his liking. There was big money to be made elsewhere – really big money. He moved into stockbroking and made something of a name as a gold analyst at one of Johannesburg's better-known brokerages, where he quickly learnt of the Kebble family's quest for riches. Despite his lack of qualifications in finance, Tucker was acutely aware of the liquidity problems that Brett aggravated with every new move that he made, and developed something of an affinity for the Kebble family's financial structure. His shortcomings in the financial sphere were completely outweighed by his enthusiasm for putting up a good fight as a professional salesman. Like a lawyer defending a client on a socially unpopular rap such as indecent assault, Tucker punted the Kebble stories that he sold on a purely professional basis.

Ahead of the Placer Dome announcement, Tucker had been preaching the benefits of holding Consolidated African Mining (CAM) paper, the vehicle that since mid-1997 had housed the Kebble family's financial interests in the mining sector. He championed Kebble's personal paper currency, CAM shares, and had one of the loudest voices in mid-1997 when Kebble was convincing all and sundry that CAM was truly worth 600 cents a share. The opportunities had been so enticing that Tucker quit his respected employer and established The Corner House, a name that more fairly belonged to the long-departed Barney Barnato.

The original Corner House had remained standing at the intersection of Commissioner and Simmonds Streets in central Johannesburg. More than a century ago it had been Barnato's head office and, at one stage, housed a king's ransom in gold in dozens of bank-like vaults behind the innocuous facade. Tucker's exploitation of the name was not inappropriate, given the number of fawning journalists and a good many professional investment analysts who described and regarded Kebble as the 'new' Barnato. The comparison had also been bandied about at the time of Kebble's audacious mid-1997 hijacking of the 'new' JCI, which comprised the earlier company's residual mining assets, from its intended BEE partners. Barnato's Johannesburg Consolidated Investments, chopped up into three, including the residual assets, by Anglo American in 1995, had finally disappeared from the JSE in 1998.

By the time Kebble announced the sale to Placer Dome of half of the Western Areas ore body, known as South Deep, he had all but abandoned the previously remorseless game of selling 'nett asset value', or NAV. As even a half-baked gold equities investment analyst would know, gold stocks are rarely a play on NAV. Almost universally, they trade at a premium to NAV.

However, there was something of a kink in the rules that CAM readily exploited. Despite its various exposures to the metal, CAM was not a gold stock. It was new and fell immediately into the trap of adopting the structure of a holding company or mining house. These were the very structures that were being creatively destroyed with huge energy all around Kebble, mainly by unbundling. The new entities, such as Gold Fields, were exposed to a number of gold mines, but ownership of the underlying assets was as close to 100 per cent as possible. The global investor in the resources sector was prepared to pay a premium for the type of structure that possessed a high degree of control over underlying cash flows. The precedents, established by the likes of Rio Tinto and Barrick, had existed for sufficient time. All told, investors were wary of buying CAM's discount-to-NAV story. In due course, it became dead meat, a redundant value argument that had no place in the modern resources sector.

After trading at close to 700 cents a share in mid-1997, when Kebble issued hundreds of millions of CAM shares to seize control of what would become JCI Gold, CAM was a heavy, then steady loser. By the end of 1997, the stock was trading below 200 cents a share. It was at less than 100 cents a share when the Placer Dome deal was announced. The NAV discount story, which had worked with deadly effectiveness during 1996, when the Randgold & Exploration stock price had been driven relentlessly upwards, was history. Kebble needed to reinvent himself; he had to *find* a Rubicon.

The Placer Dome deal allowed Kebble to weave his latest unseemly tapestry of guile, assisted by his incumbent professional advisers and salesmen, including Tucker. According to the official pre-Christmas party notice, the deal introduced 'a highly experienced international operational partner to the Western Areas mine'. The introduction of Placer Dome 'should have the effect of maximising the value of Western Areas' remaining 50 per cent holding' in South Deep. Besides that, the announcement crowed, the deal would reduce operational risk and 'immediately release shareholder value'.

Placer Dome had agreed to pay Western Areas $235 million in cash, plus an annual payment in gold of 1.75 per cent of the Canadian company's share of the joint venture's production for the life of the mine, as well as an additional 1.75 per cent on Placer Dome's share, should the combined output exceed one million ounces of gold a year.

It can safely be assumed that the Western Areas directors were told about, knew about and accepted the Placer Dome deal. At the time, the Western Areas board had enough members to field a rugby team, with three players on the bench. On the executive side there were no fewer than eight directors: Brett Kebble (deputy chairman), John Fox Brownrigg (MD), Sydney Caddy (chief operating officer offshore), David Kovarsky (finance director), Gordon Miller (chief operating officer local), Trevor Raymond (investor relations), Craig Lawrence (human resources) and Derek Webbstock (general manager). There were also an astonishing 11 non-executive directors: Wiseman Nkuhlu (chairman), Vaughan Bray, Paul Ferguson, Marcel Golding, Roger Kebble, Eric Molefe, Tiego Moseneke, Gibson Njenje, Graham Wanblad, Timothy Wadeson and Christopher Yates.

The Placer Dome announcement was deliberately decked in tinsel by a Kebble facing mounting pressure. Apart from the failure of the discount-to-NAV story, the dollar-gold price remained in a rut. Gold mining in South Africa was about as tough as it had ever been. In 1998, country gold production amounted to 464 tons, less than half the historical peak production of 989 tons dug out in 1970. As the average age of South African mines increased, so the quality of the pay ore deteriorated. The average grade recorded during 1998 was 5.09 grams of gold per milled ton, compared to a figure of nearly three times as much, 13.28, in 1970. South Africa retained its No. 1 gold-digger position in the world in 1998, but its contribution to world output had dropped to 19 per cent from 68 per cent in 1970. Dollar-gold prices, at 20-year lows, continued to force restructuring, realignment and streamlining of the domestic gold industry.

Seen as a whole, the industry was sharply focused on cutting operating costs to the bone and improving productivity. Strategically, the various gold mining blocs worked around the clock to optimise development of reserves by swapping assets between neighbouring mines. Pride was swallowed and egos put on hold as farm fences were taken down. The efforts saw the number of South African gold mines in a marginal position decline to five in 1998 (producing 50 tons of gold a year and employing 28 000 people) from nine the year before.

A marginal mine of any kind is one that remains vulnerable to closure or severe rationalisation over long periods of time. Even once highly profitable, efficient and productive mines become marginal as they dig deeper and grades deteriorate. Eventually, the mine passes into post-marginal territory as it is finally mined out. Other kinds of marginal mines include those with insufficient reserves or hampered by low grades of metal or mineral, and those with difficult working conditions. As long as a marginal mine remains in business, its stock price offers the greatest relative upside, or leverage, to a sustained increase in output prices. This is especially so when a marginal mine has somehow managed to stay in business through a trough in product prices.

Despite the maturity of the South African gold mining sector and the enormous depth of new projects, groups with big balance sheets held the faith through 1998. Four significant projects continued apace, namely Avgold's Target, AngloGold's Moab, Gold Fields's Oryx and, of course, Western Areas' South Deep, absorbing much of the domestic gold sector's $380 million capital outlay for the year. Hope burnt bright as AngloGold considered plans to develop its experimental Western Ultra Deep Levels project, which would run a single shaft down to 5 000 metres to access resources containing 1 500 tons of gold at a hefty grade of 10 grams a ton.

Big deals in the resources sector remained in the headlines during 1998 and the gold sector was as busy as ever. The mega-merger of the gold assets of Gold Fields of South Africa – now the 'old' GFSA – and Gencor, announced in October 1997, was finalised on 2 February, creating a sleek-looking Gold Fields. The new boy on the block rated as one of the world's top five diggers, with annual output of three million ounces of gold. The Gold Fields SA operations had been consolidated under Driefontein, Beatrix, Kloof, Oryx and St Helena. The Gold Fields offshore stable was dominated by Tarkwa in Ghana.

Gold Fields retained technical rights to the BIOX gold biological leach process, which uses bugs to free gold from stubborn ores. GFSA itself continued to disgorge its non-gold interests, liquidating the copper-lead-zinc operations of Tsumeb Corporation in Namibia. In South Africa, GFSA sold the O'Kiep copper mine to Metorex; its Gamsberg zinc deposit interests and coal assets were sold to Anglo American; Zinc Corporation of South Africa was sold to Iscor; and group chromite reserves were bought by Associated Manganese Mines of SA. After a full and value-added restructuring and unbundling, GFSA was flagged for delisting from the JSE in 1999. Meanwhile Gencor, which had previously consolidated all its non-precious metal holdings into Billiton, which listed in London in 1997, was left with Impala, the No. 2 platinum-group-metal (PGM) player.

AngloGold, already the world's No. 1 gold-digger, continued to restructure. In July, the company subdivided its Vaal Reefs, Free State, Western Holdings, HJ Joel and West Wits gold mining complexes on a production shaft basis into 16 separate business centres, most of which were given new names. The 16 gold mines or profit centres, of which 14 were in South Africa, included Great Noligwa, Kopanang, Tau Lekoa, Moab Khotsong (formerly Vaal Reefs shafts 8, 9, 10 and 11 respectively), Bambanani, Tsepong, Masimong (formerly Freegold shafts 1, 2 and 3), Matjhabeng (formerly Western Holdings), Joel, Western Deeps East, West and South, Deelkraal and Elandsrand.

On 15 October, Anglo American made headlines by announcing that it would merge with Minorco, its international associate, to form a new company, Anglo American Plc, which would shift its headquarters and primary stock listing from Johannesburg to London. De Beers, which had earlier severed its management ties with Anglo American, swapped its 38.2 per cent interest in Anglo, its 22.5 per cent interest in Minorco and a minority interest in several other non-diamond companies jointly held with Anglo American for shares equal to a 40 per cent equity interest in the new entity. Anglo American transferred its interest in the diamond industry's Central Selling Organisation to De Beers while retaining a 33 per cent interest in De Beers/Centenary, the broader De Beers group, via its 58 per cent holding in Anglo American Investment Trust, known as Anamint.

In addition to diamond interests held through De Beers, the new Anglo American had restructured its assets into a number of separate operating companies. As part of the latest package, AngloGold paid $550 million to acquire Minorco's gold holdings in Argentina, Brazil and the US. Anglo American Platinum Corporation, formerly Rustenburg Platinum Holdings and the world's leading PGM producer, was established to run the combined PGM assets of Anglo American and the previous JCI.

On 6 August 1998, Roger Kebble added fat to the fire by announcing a project predicated on digging up most of Johannesburg, or at least rendering it unfit for human habitation. Durban Roodepoort Deep (DRD) proclaimed that a 40 million ounce gold deposit lay beneath the streets of South Africa's financial and economic hub. There was no news in that, but, according to Roger, the Argonaut Project was nearing the climax of a pre-feasibility study, due for completion in September. It would take at least R100 million to properly investigate ways of getting the gold out of the ground without razing Johannesburg's sophisticated infrastructure, but the payoff would be enormous, Roger crooned.

Needless to say, Argonaut was a hilarious fantasy that vanished into thin air.

In September, Harmony Gold Mining, independent from Randgold & Exploration since 1997, acquired Masimong Mine (formerly Freegold Shaft 3) from AngloGold and Anglo American for $15 million, along with the 86 per cent Gold Fields stake in the so-called Evander group of gold mines (Kinross, Winkelhaak, Leslie and Bracken) for $93 million. Harmony also bought the Bisset gold mine in Manitoba, Canada, and sold its Consolidated Modderfontein and Grootvlei mines to Petra Mining for close on $16 million. Harmony won permission from the SA Reserve Bank to refine its own gold production, using a new solvent extraction hydrometallurgical process developed by Mintek in Johannesburg.

Surrounded by these momentous deals, Kebble might have felt a loneliness, an isolation from the powerhouse of the gold mining sector. That would be understandable, but not the fact that he appeared to have learnt nothing from the 1997 collapse of Randgold & Exploration's stock price, triggered in turn by the meltdown of the Randgold Resources stock price. By selling half of South Deep, Kebble ignored one of the most basic rules of the industry: gold mines of quality are not *sold*, they are *bought*.

Kebble sold half of South Deep for far too little. The Placer Dome deal was hailed by the media as the first that had attracted a foreign investor to take a bet on a South African gold mine. Behind the excitement, however, Kebble continued to face a liquidity crisis. Placer Dome offered a temporary get-out-of-jail pass, but it moved Kebble and his dubious vision one step further away from the model demanded by global investors in resources, namely a listed mining stock that enjoyed control over underlying cash flows generated by long-life, high-quality, world-class assets. Western Areas, or South Deep to be exact, offered a great ore body that had every chance of attracting some very serious investors. However, the CAM stake in Western Areas via JCI Gold was equal only to about one third of the issued shares. That exposure had now effectively been halved by the Placer Dome deal. It was also apparent that Kebble was not really going to be involved in the operational control of Western Areas.

He told shareholders that a committee 'equally represented by Western Areas and Placer Dome', but chaired by Placer Dome, would manage JCI Gold. In February 2000, the committee's powers became apparent when Western Areas announced that it would be retrenching most of its corporate staff since, 'with the mine in any event being managed by Placer Dome ... Western Areas no longer has any significant operating assets to manage'.

Ahead of the original Placer Dome announcement, Kebble needed to blow as much hot air as he possibly could. There were already some blots on the landscape. The story about Randgold & Exploration and Randgold Resources and all those unlimited ounces of African gold to be found outside South Africa had become a bad joke. On 3 March 1998, Peter Flack had stepped down, or been forced out (the details seemed irrelevant) as executive chairman of the two companies. Naturally enough, Roger Kebble replaced him. Flack's departure was a soupçon of things to come from the African side.

Under the bright auspices of CEO Mark Bristow, Randgold Resources continued pouring millions of dollars into Syama, the piece of junk that had been the nodding cat on the mantelpiece among the Mali gold assets bought from BHP. Randgold Resources had, of course, raised a nett amount of $77.5 million from its London IPO, but most of that was gone. Thanks to promises (and signatures) from the Randgold & Exploration crowd, Randgold Resources had to pay more than $32 million of the London proceeds to BHP to retire debt acquired as part of the deal. Randgold Resources, starved for cash, concluded a very, very quiet offer during 1998, when it placed 13 254 612 fresh ordinary shares, raising $13.2 million before expenses. That computed to roughly $1 per share and compared poorly with the $15.50 a share that investors had paid during the mid-1997 London IPO. The $1 a share was a fraction, in turn, of the $30 a share that Flack had crowed from the rooftops ahead of the London listing and a lot closer to the $0.63 valuation that Randgold & Exploration had placed on the share when it materialised Randgold Resources in August 1995. In the space of just three years, the 'value' of Randgold Resources had gone from $1 to $30 and back to $1 a share. What kind of a skunk story was this?

By 1998, investors had suffered more than enough damage, but there were still some relics prepared to stump up a little more cash for Randgold Resources. Flack refrained from explaining why the 1998 placement was made at $1 a share, opting instead to mumble about other opportunities that he wished to follow, such as game farming. As if to underscore his disgrace, Randgold Resources was allowed to convert a $20 million loan owed to Randgold & Exploration by issuing new shares to its parent company. This kind of conversion, which rarely happens between two entities operating at arm's length or independently, is generally a sign that the debtor (in this case, Randgold Resources) is headed for the junkyard, but has effectively won a stay of execution from its parent company. The technique used, the conversion of debt into a Kebble-controlled company's paper, was completely atypical within the family's increasingly Augean stables.

Could Kebble and his consorts do anything right at all? Few were even asking the question. Late in 1997, the *Sunday Times* awarded Barnato Exploration, or Barnex, eighth place in the *Business Times Top 100 Companies*, a survey that rated stock price performance over five years. Barnex was one of three JCI or 'Kebble' companies in the Top 10 that year. The others, Lindum Reefs and Western Areas, could both be traced back to spin-outs from Randfontein a decade before.

Barnex, like so many Kebble-related companies, lacked any infrastructure of its own; it had engaged JCI to provide it with secretarial, financial, administrative, technical, engineering and procurement services. As might be expected, the spectacular rise in the Barnex stock price had nothing to do with its structure. Barnex had inherited a number of minerals rights and, most prominently at the time, held 90 per cent of Prestea, one of the great historic gold mines in Ghana, just up the road from Tarkwa.

Barnex, which was listed only in Johannesburg, had signed the Prestea deal in 1995. When Randgold & Exploration started whipping up the froth around Randgold Resources, sharp-eyed investors took a ride on the Barnex stock price. The company had much the same characteristics as Randgold Resources. If a gold mining story from West Africa via Randgold Resources could pump up the stock price of its parent company, Randgold & Exploration, why should Barnex not partake in a stock price expansion? Indeed, the facts show that Barnex was a far better bet, in terms of Prestea's potential quality. Furthermore, just as Gold Fields had acquired its majority stake in Tarkwa for a song, so Barnex had bought a majority of Prestea for next to nothing. All Prestea needed was sufficient funding and the right management team. The problem was that a Glyn Lewis cannot be found on every street corner. Late in 1997, Barnex director Peter McKenna told *Business Times*:

> Underground mining at Prestea is not really the target. It has been mined for more than 80 years and has yielded 200 tons of gold. We will continue to mine 50 000 ounces a year, more or less at break-even under current market conditions. The real carrot at Prestea is the presence of perhaps 12 million ounces of gold in surface reserves that are mineable through open-cast methods. Once these reserves are proven, we will be looking at a mine with a 20-year life, producing some 150 000 ounces of gold a year at a cost of less than $200 an ounce.

For his part, Kebble, who had been in control of Barnex since mid-1997, said JCI would probably sell its 46 per cent stake in Barnex to Western Areas, the vehicle 'through which JCI has elected to undertake international expansion in search of good-quality gold-mining assets'. McKenna's mention of the potential millions upon millions of ounces of gold waiting to be mined economically at Prestea was no doubt inspired, at least in part, by the continued stream of great news coming out of Tarkwa. Besides Obuasi, the big Ashanti Goldfields mine, Tarkwa and Prestea were the two most prospective properties in Ghana. Strangely, however, there was no mention of Randgold Resources when Prestea arose for discussion. When the Kebble family made its grand move in mid-1997 and hijacked JCI's gold assets, it would have made impeccable sense to consolidate Prestea into Randgold Resources. This made even more sense given the complete absence of Randgold Resources from Ghana, which continued to rank as the most prospective country in West Africa, if not the entire continent, for new or renewed gold projects.

It was entirely correct that Barnex had made improvements to the productivities and efficiencies of the underground operation at Prestea. It was equally true that Barnex conducted exploration programmes and feasibility studies at Prestea on the near surface resources amenable to open-cast mining. But, according to the record, JCI and Barnex closed down the Prestea underground mine in September 1998. The decision would have been influenced by the patent knowledge that Syama was sucking down millions of dollars like a hungry vacuum cleaner and not generating a cent of profit.

JCI and Barnex put Prestea on the market. In one of life's innumerable nods to the proverbial sour grapes, Barnex announced that closure of the underground section of Prestea had been 'imminent' when it took over the mine in 1995.

Barnex and Prestea were yet another example of Kebble being involved in the sale rather than purchase of a gold mine. For all the claims made by McKenna and Kebble, it took absolutely ages to sell Prestea. On 28 January 2000, Barnex announced that an agreement to sell the mine had been delayed due to certain factors relating to decisions awaited from the government of Ghana. The tombstone looked impressive enough:

28 January 2000
Merchant Bank and Corporate Adviser
Standard Corporate and Merchant Bank

Reporting accountants
PricewaterhouseCoopers Inc
Chartered Accountants (SA)

Sponsoring brokers
Merrill Lynch South Africa (Pty) Ltd
Member of the Johannesburg Stock Exchange
BoE Securities
Member of the Johannesburg Stock Exchange

Attorneys
Deneys Reitz Inc

Independent Technical Adviser
Venmyn Rand (Pty) Ltd
Mining and Minerals Management Advisers

On 15 November, Barnex announced that the Ghanaian government had advised 'that it is seeking to abrogate the company's rights'. Finally, on 12 September 2001, Barnex announced that it had sold its 90 per cent shareholding in and all claims against Barnex (Prestea) to Golden Star Resources Ltd. The buyers paid $13 million 'plus a nett smelter royalty'. The cost was dear; Barnex wrote off R154 million on the transaction.

As the Randgold crowd continued to make variegated fools of themselves in West Africa, the South African gold mining sector remained as hot as a glowing iron. In February 1999, Driefontein, Gold Fields, AngloGold and Anglo American announced a complex set of transactions aimed at further rationalisation and restructuring. First, Gold Fields would acquire AngloGold's entire interest of 21.5 per cent in Driefontein, one of the world's greatest gold mines, for $230 million. The deal also gave Gold Fields a controlling interest in the Western Ultra Deep Levels ore body. Second, there would be a parallel stock swap between Gold Fields and Anglo American, increasing the latter's equity interest in AngloGold to 53.7 per cent. Third, the new Gold Fields would acquire all the outstanding minorities in Driefontein and would also wholly own, as its core assets, Beatrix and Kloof, along with 100 per cent of Leeudoorn, Libanon and Oryx, plus 70 per cent of Tarkwa and 54 per cent of St Helena. The new Gold Fields would boast annual output of some four million ounces. Gold Fields was sticking as closely as it could to the model of acquiring underlying assets and controlling as close to 100 per cent as possible of underlying cash flows.

In the background, metal and commodity prices remained depressed. Despite the hardship this inflicted on the global resources sector, where most dollar metal and mineral prices were at or near multi-decade lows, it was business as usual. In 1999, according to the Minerals Bureau, the total value of sales of primary metals and minerals by South Africa amounted to $12.5 billion for the year, of which $9.5 billion was exported. The total value of all processed mineral materials was $3 billion, of which $2.4 billion was exported. The major exports by value in 1999 were gold ($4.1 billion), PGMs ($2.9 billion), coal ($2.4 billion), ferro alloys ($1.1 billion), aluminium ($894 million), steel ($802 million), iron ore ($360 million), copper ($227 million), and nickel, chromite, manganese and vanadium at between $149 million and $190 million each. Other significant exports for which individual value data were not provided included diamonds, titanium and zirconium.

13

Showdown at Randfontein

S HORTLY BEFORE CHRISTMAS 1999, Brett Kebble and his band of merry sorcerers let rip with an announcement that included almost all the listed stocks in the broader Kebble group. This time, the tombstone was graced by the names of Chase Manhattan, Standard Corporate and Merchant Bank, and Standard Bank London, which were 'authorised' to announce that the JCI-Randgold group would be restructured and simplified. The big deal was billed as a 'R7 billion restructuring'.

---

7 December 1999
Proposed Restructuring of the JCI-Randgold Group under Western Areas

···

Western Areas Ltd
Randfontein Estates Ltd
JCI Gold Ltd
Randgold & Exploration Company Ltd
Randgold Resources Ltd
Free State Development and Investment Corporation Ltd
Barnato Exploration Ltd

Consolidated African Mines (CAM), the chief weapon of the Kebble family investments, was conspicuous by its absence.

The gist of the proposed transaction was thankfully simple in that Western Areas was looking to acquire all the minorities in the other named companies and change its name to JCI Ltd. In other words, or so it seemed, Kebble was finally moving to consolidate related operating mines and companies under one umbrella. He appeared at last to have cottoned on to the business model that had been so enthusiastically followed by the likes of AngloGold and Gold Fields.

If the restructuring worked out, Randfontein, Randgold & Exploration, Barnex and Freddev would end up as wholly owned subsidiaries of JCI Ltd. The company's main operating asset would be a 50 per cent joint venture interest in Western Areas and a 100 per cent interest in Randfontein.

JCI Ltd would own at least 61 per cent of Randgold Resources, interests in two 'substantial' gold projects under development, a 50 per cent stake in the joint venture at South Deep (within Western Areas) and an interest in Mali's Morila, 80 per cent held by Randgold Resources. The tombstone for the announcement was packed with titbits. At prevailing gold prices, JCI Ltd's operating results would be enhanced by the Randfontein mine and the anticipated growth in Randgold Resources as a result of development of the Morila project and an expected increase in Syama's 'profitability'. In addition, JCI Ltd would:

- hold interests in a diverse portfolio of gold exploration projects primarily in Africa, with a focus on West Africa;
- own an extensive portfolio of South African mineral and participation rights;
- own the technical expertise and resources of JCI Projects; and
- have a portfolio of investments in various South African mining companies, including an 11.3 per cent interest in Durban Roodepoort Deep.

Brett Kebble hoped also to own all of Randgold Resources; the new JCI Ltd would look to list on an international stock exchange. If it all worked out, the combined group would boast gold reserves of 36 million ounces, gold resources of 67 million ounces and annual production of 'more than' 1.3 million ounces. All told, JCI Ltd would be the world's No. 9 gold-digger and No. 6 in terms of reserves. Kebble scoffed at estimates that, prior to the proposed transactions, the seven mentioned companies were carrying R1.2 billion in debt.

'The group has R2 billion nett cash,' he blustered. 'There is a measure of debt, but the new company will be debt-free and R800 million cash positive.'

In theory, the deal, if successfully executed, would give Kebble full control of multiple underlying cash flows. However, with or without the deal, very little nett cash was being generated and a great portion of it was being absorbed. South Deep, the only real asset within Western Areas, was now 50 per cent owned and operated by Placer Dome and was years away from full production. South Deep was eating cash, as was Syama in the Randgold Resources stable, but Randfontein was doing surprisingly well, given the gold price at the time. The other assets proposed for the new group required big balance sheets, as shown by the Barnex decision to exit the Prestea project in Ghana.

The tombstone for the announcement could have launched a thousand ships clad in gold with sails of silk:

7 December 1999

....

Joint financial advisers to the restructuring and to Western Areas
Chase
Standard Bank Resource Banking

Attorneys
Bowman Gilfillan Inc

Reporting accountants
PricewaterhouseCoopers Corporate Finance (Pty) Ltd

Independent financial adviser to Barnex, Freddev, Randfontein and Randgold
RMB Resources
A division of FirstRand Bank Ltd

Joint sponsoring brokers to Barnex, Freddev, JCI Gold, Randfontein and Western Areas
BoE Securities Ltd
Members of the Johannesburg Stock Exchange
Merrill Lynch South Africa (Pty) Ltd
Members of the Johannesburg Stock Exchange

Independent technical adviser
Steffen Robertson and Kirsten (South Africa) (Pty) Ltd

Sponsoring broker to Randgold Resources
HBSC Investment Bank Plc
Members of the London Stock Exchange

Sponsoring broker to Randgold
HSBC Securities (South Africa) (Pty) Ltd
Members of the Johannesburg Stock Exchange

While the new JCI Ltd might be challenged by cash demands, no such thing could be said of its proposed board of directors. Kebble had assembled the consummate League of Extraordinary Gentlemen, starring Henry 'Hank' Slack, former CEO of Minorco, lately the offshore arm of Anglo American, and a former director of Anglo American. Once married to South African mining mogul Harry Oppenheimer's only daughter Mary, Slack was tapped by Kebble to be JCI's new non-executive chairman.

Wiseman Nkuhlu, director of companies, former non-executive chairman of Western Areas, Randfontein and JCI Gold, was proposed as Slack's deputy. Roger Kebble, chairman of DRD, Randgold & Exploration, Randgold Resources and

CAM, non-executive director of Western Areas, JCI Gold and Randfontein, was proposed as chief operating officer. David Kovarsky, director of Western Areas and Randfontein, former finance director of Avgold and CEO of Times Media Ltd, was proposed as finance director. John Fox Brownrigg, MD of Western Areas, director of Barnex and Randfontein, former CEO of the gold and uranium division of the original JCI Ltd, was proposed as technical director.

Brett, of course, would be the CEO, while maintaining his standing as executive deputy chairman of Western Areas, Randfontein and JCI Gold, CEO of CAM and JCI Gold, chairman of Barnex, director of Freddev, non-executive director of Randgold Resources and chairman of CAM.

The list of suggested non-executive directors for the new JCI opened with Vaughan Bray, non-executive chairman of Freddev, former CEO of Johnnic Industrial Corporation and former finance director of JCI. He was followed by Mark Bristow (CEO of Randgold Resources), John Hick (former business development director of Dome Resources and Placer Dome), Frank McKenna (a partner at McCarthy Tétrault, a Canadian law firm, and former premier of the province of New Brunswick, Canada), Bill Nairn (non-executive director of AngloGold and former MD of the original JCI), Rupert Pennant-Rea (former deputy governor of the Bank of England and a director of Sherritt Gordon, a Canadian mining company), Royden Richardson (consultant to Royal Bank of Canada and former owner and managing partner of Richardson Greenshields, a Canadian securities firm), Tokyo Sexwale (chairman of Gem Diamonds and former premier of Gauteng) and Mark Wellesley-Wood (consultant and former head of mining corporate finance with Dresdner Kleinwort Benson).

The restructuring announcement came as resorts all across South Africa braced for the annual influx of December visitors and the country shifted into summer holiday mode. But a funny thing happened on the way to paradise, and exactly three years later, Brett and Roger Kebble, their financial wizard Hennie Buitendag and Western Areas were indicted for fraud, conspiracy and insider trading.

The 12 charges against them were extremely grave and had been formulated on the basis of an extensive forensic probe by some of South Africa's most experienced investigators and prosecutors.

The state alleged that, from January to October 1999, Western Areas, Buitendag and the Kebbles had broken a slew of laws by attempting to implement a restructuring of the companies in the JCI-Randgold group. For most of 1999, Brett Kebble was:

- deputy chairman and CEO of Western Areas;
- deputy chairman and a director of JCI Gold;
- CEO and a director of CAM; and
- deputy chairman and a director of Randfontein.

During the same period, Buitendag was a director of CAM and JCI Gold and acted effectively as financial director of both.

Roger Kebble was:

- executive chairman and a director of DRD;
- chairman and a director of CAM;
- a director of Randfontein;
- chairman and a director of Randgold & Exploration;
- chairman and a director of Randgold Resources;
- a director of Western Areas; and
- a director of JCI Gold.

The plan, as outlined, was for Western Areas to acquire the entire issued share capital of Western Areas, Freddev, Barnex and Randfontein and be renamed JCI Ltd. However, between the lines it was apparent that the chief obstacle facing the Kebbles was acquisition of Randfontein's issued share capital. When the overall stratagem was first conceived, the JCI-Randgold group and DRD collectively held less than 35 per cent of Randfontein's entire issued share capital.

According to the announcement made on 7 December 1999, Anglo American, BNC Investments (the entity holding the Kebble family interests), Debhold (representing the interests of De Beers), JCI Gold, New Mining, Randfontein and Randgold & Exploration 'collectively holding 42.7 per cent of the issued share capital of CAM, have undertaken to vote in favour of the ordinary resolution authorising CAM to vote in favour of the Randfontein share scheme'.

Anglo American, Debhold, JCI Gold and Randgold & Exploration held a further combined stake of 8.3 per cent directly in Randfontein. JCI Gold and Randgold & Exploration also directly held 46.8 per cent of the options issued by Randfontein.

The master plan was that Western Areas would use a 'scheme of arrangement' and offer 60 of its own shares for every 100 shares in Randfontein, without a cash offer as an alternative. It was classic Kebble: all paper and no cash.

Section 311 of South Africa's Companies Act (No. 61 of 1973) requires a 'minimum approval threshold' for a proposed scheme of arrangement, namely approval by at least 75 per cent of the voting shareholders present at the relevant meeting. The outcome of the vote at the required meetings was preordained, given existing stakes by the Kebbles, except in the case of Randfontein. Some serious conniving would be required to secure that vote.

Implicit in the Randfontein offer was that movements in the Western Areas stock price would almost certainly play a role in deciding whether or not shareholders accepted the offer. For Kebble, the most favourable outcome would have seen the Western Areas stock price continuing to rise and the Randfontein price falling.

The problem was that if investors generally, or even just a few beyond the Kebbles and Buitendag, became aware of a clandestine plan to buy Randfontein shares, the stock price would likely increase. This was precisely the opposite effect required by the master plan, but the Kebbles, along with Western Areas and DRD, had allegedly devised a stratagem to surreptitiously acquire sufficient Randfontein shares by means of nominee companies that were not part of the JCI-Randgold group, to exercise as many votes as possible at the shareholders' meeting. Since the proposal legally qualified as an 'affected' transaction, the Kebbles had to be very, very careful. This was going to be quite different from exceeding the speed limit.

In South African law, an affected transaction includes any deal that has the effect of vesting 35 per cent or more of the voting rights at meetings of a company 'in any person, or two or more persons acting in concert, in whom that extent of exercisable votes did not vest prior to the transaction'.

The 'offer period' for the Randfontein shares commenced on 6 December 1999 and ended on 17 January 2000. The state alleged that, in the three months leading up to 6 December, the Kebbles, Western Areas and DRD had secretly bought Randfontein shares without making an offer to shareholders on terms similar to the *most favourable* of such purchases. According to the indictment against them, the purchases included:

- 500 000 shares in the name of Argonaut between 11 and 21 October;
- 3 957 200 shares in the name of Hencetrade 170 (Pty) Ltd between 22 October and 23 November;
- 143 155 shares in the name of Australia's Continental Goldfields Ltd on or about 16 November.

The indictment also listed the following Randfontein shares bought during the offer period at prices above the offer price:

- 374 300 in the name of Millennium between 17 and 29 December;
- 591 200 in the name of Hencetrade between 29 December and 8 January;
- 409 600 in the name of Argonaut on 6 and 7 January;
- 387 000 in the name of Roc Investments between 8 December and 11 January;
- 422 700 in the name of DRD between 6 and 10 January.

If the allegations against them were proved in a court of law, the Kebbles, along with the other accused, would be in big, big trouble. The deals were toxic to the extent that shares in Randfontein had been bought for cash during the offer period and within the three months prior to 6 December 1999. The shares that had allegedly been acquired in this way carried 10 per cent or more of the voting rights exercisable at a class meeting, yet there had been no offer to Randfontein shareholders in cash, or accompanied by a cash alternative, at not less than the highest price paid by the Kebbles, Western Areas and DRD.

In making their case against the Kebbles, investigators had the benefit of a substantial paper trail. It was further alleged that, between 7 December 1999 and 6 January 2000, the Western Areas Share Incentive Scheme, also known as the Western Areas Share Trust (WAST), bought 2 391 100 Western Areas shares. From 22 to 29 December, Brett Kebble was accused of buying 66 600 Western Areas shares. Both transactions made sense to the extent that the demand for Western Areas stock would exert upward pressure on the stock price as part of the alleged conspiracy.

Brett and Roger were also accused of instructing Buitendag to issue the following cheques against the Western Areas account, No. 92452, at the Standard Bank, Johannesburg, and payable to DRD:

- 3831 for R14 690 501.85 on 14 December 1999;
- 3886 for R28 013 039.62 on 22 December 1999;
- 3908 for R32 180 608.33 on 24 December 1999;
- 3921 for R12 965 185.31 on 4 January 2000; and
- 3924 for R23 453 118.34 on 11 January 2000.

Buitendag allegedly conveyed instructions on JCI Gold letterheads to officials and/ or employees at Western Areas to issue the cheques as short-term loans to DRD. Roger Kebble then allegedly caused cheques drawn on DRD's bank account to be issued to stockbrokers EW Balderson and Consilium as follows:

- 1957 for R6 237 459.58 in favour of EW Balderson, 1958 for R10 845 253.77 in favour of Consilium on 14 December;
- 2015 for R6 889 629.26 in favour of Consilium, 2016 for R18 721 198.90 in favour of EW Balderson, 2017 for R2 392 211.45 in favour of Consolidated Mining Management Services (CMMS) on 24 December;
- 2019 for R22 108 534.53 in favour of Consilium, 2020 for R10 072 274.80 in favour of EW Balderson on 28 December;
- 2021 for R12 238 306.28 in favour of Consilium, 2022 for R726 879.03 in favour of EW Balderson on 4 January; and
- 2037 for R22 218 859.65 in favour of Consilium, 2038 for R1 234 258.69 in favour of EW Balderson on 11 January.

And then along came Bernard Swanepoel.

On 5 January, Harmony made an 'unsolicited' bid for Randfontein, one of the companies for which Western Areas had made an offer that formed part of the conditions to its own shareholders. Harmony's offer for the entire issued share capital of Randfontein consisted of 31 ordinary shares for every 100 Randfontein shares, or a cash alternative of R11 for every Randfontein share held, or a combination of shares and cash.

Harmony's offer was officially announced at 8.37 a.m. on 6 January 2000. Brett Kebble was aware of the pending offer at least 24 hours earlier, and instructed Consilium stockbroker Mark Sonik to borrow between two and five million Harmony shares for the purpose of launching a 'bear sale'.* The borrowing of listed shares, or scrip, forms a perfectly normal part of modern fund management. Here, the intention was to suppress the stock price of Harmony on the JSE so as to prevent the company's offer being perceived by Randfontein shareholders as more favourable than that made by Western Areas.

Consilium duly borrowed 140 000 Harmony shares from Absa Securities, and later another 23 800 from EW Balderson, but that was it. Before the JSE opened for trade on the morning of 6 January, Brett instructed Sonik to aggressively sell 'as many Harmony shares as the market can bear'. At 8.58 a.m., two minutes before the opening bell, Consilium entered an order on the JSE's electronic JET system to sell 5 000 Harmony shares at R32.50 each. Because the selling order was greater than the buying orders, the algorithm used in the JET system calculated an opening price of R32.50.

Consilium sold 174 800 Harmony shares by way of bear sales that day. By the close of trading, the price of Harmony shares had increased again, closing at R36, despite the aggressive interventions by Consilium.

There was in the Harmony offer that evil word, twice: cash.

For a Kebble, it was as a wooden stake is to a vampire, as salt is to a slug.

The JSE Surveillance Division received a complaint about unusual trading activity in Harmony shares on 6 January and launched an investigation, requesting information from both Consilium and the financial advisers to Western Areas. On 12 January, Western Areas issued a Stock Exchange News Service announcement, disclosing that:

- 1 197 500 Western Areas shares were purchased on the account of WAST on 7 December 1999;

---

* The origin of terms applied to falling (bear) and rising (bull) markets remains uncertain. Many years ago, 'bear skin jobbers' in the US would sell bear skins they did not yet own. This is most likely the origin of the term 'short sellers', still applied today to speculators who sell securities they do not own. Such parties are betting that prices will fall, allowing them to profit from buying later at lower prices, and selling higher at earlier prices. Bull and bear baiting were once popular sports; bulls tend to sweep their horns in an upward motion, while bears tend to rake downwards with their paws. Either way, the Wall Street adage is: Bulls make money, bears make money, pigs get slaughtered. Apparently, the enemy is greed.

- Brett Kebble purchased 86 600 Western Areas shares between 22 and 29 December;
- WAST purchased 2 391 199 Western Areas shares between 7 and 22 December.

Prior to 12 January, neither Brett nor Roger, Western Areas nor DRD had disclosed any purchases or sales of Randfontein shares directly in their own names, or indirectly through nominee or other entities.

Who ratted on Brett Kebble and his band of knaves? No one more sinister than a clutch of professional investors who could not help but notice a frantic scavenger in the markets.

Prosecutors, however, found a great deal more, such as that Western Areas had allegedly failed to provide Randfontein shareholders with all the data necessary to make a properly informed decision. The shareholding of a number of Kebble-related companies in Randfontein was simply not disclosed. The state alleged that CAM had an additional holding of 1.4 per cent; that Consolidated Mining Corporation, a wholly owned CAM subsidiary, held 8.35 per cent; that DRD held 0.65 per cent; that Millennium held 0.57 per cent; that Argonaut held 1.40 per cent; that Roc Investments (Pty) Ltd held 4.22 per cent; that Hencetrade 170 (Pty) Ltd held 3.04 per cent; that First Wesgold Mining (Pty) Ltd, a subsidiary of Randgold & Exploration, held 2.65 per cent, and that Continental Goldfields Ltd, a company incorporated in Australia of which Brett and Roger had been directors, of which Buitendag still was a director and of which CAM owned 30 per cent, held 0.22 per cent.

On 13 January, the joint financial advisers to the Western Areas scheme of arrangement told the directors that they were prepared to continue acting in this capacity only on certain conditions. First, they demanded the immediate resignation of Brett Kebble from the Western Areas board and all other companies in the JCI-Randgold group that they advised. Second, they demanded an investigation by an independent committee that would make public its findings. The scope of the investigation had to include the circumstances surrounding the acquisition by DRD of Randfontein shares, the provision of finance to DRD by Western Areas, and the acquisition of shares in Western Areas by Brett and WAST. Third, the advisers demanded an announcement by Brett outlining the events surrounding the purchase by DRD of Randfontein shares in order to confirm that the joint financial advisers had no knowledge of, nor had offered any advice regarding the deal.

On 14 January, trade in Western Areas shares, as well as shares and listed options in other companies in the JCI-Randgold group, were suspended from trading on the JSE following a request by the Western Areas board of directors. The only exception was Randgold Resources, which was listed in London.

The situation was growing uglier by the day. On Tuesday 11 January, the Securities Regulation Panel (SRP) had contacted various individuals in connection with certain trades in Western Areas and Randfontein shares. The next day, the JSE contacted various individuals regarding certain trades in Western Areas shares. That evening, Western Areas' financial advisers, Chase and Standard Bank, as well as its legal and other advisers, learnt for the first time that direct or indirect financial assistance had been provided to DRD to cover recent purchases of Randfontein shares in part or entirely. The Western Areas board of directors was informed by Chase and Standard Bank that such assistance had been provided on the sole authority of Brett Kebble. The board had neither approved, nor was it consulted in respect of, such financial assistance.

In terms of the SRP rules, the acquisition of Randfontein shares by DRD, coupled with the financial assistance to DRD by Western Areas to facilitate such acquisition, made DRD a 'concert party' to Western Areas in respect of the Randfontein 'schemes'. As soon as was practically possible on being informed of the financial assistance provided to DRD, Western Areas, together with Chase and Standard Bank, contacted the SRP and the JSE to furnish them with all known details relating to the story, and to notify them that negotiations with Harmony regarding its acquisition of Randfontein were at an advanced stage.

On 13 January, Brett Kebble resigned his position at Western Areas with immediate effect. The tombstone that appeared a few days later included more lawyers than usual.

---

17 January 2000

....

Joint financial advisers to the restructuring and to Western Areas
Chase
Standard Bank Resource Banking
Attorneys to the restructuring and to Western Areas
Bowman Gilfillan Inc

Legal advisers to Chase and Standard Bank in terms of the restructuring
Edward Nathan & Friedland (Pty) Ltd

Joint sponsoring brokers to Western Areas
BoE Securities (Pty) Ltd
Member of the Johannesburg Stock Exchange
Merrill Lynch South Africa (Pty) Ltd
Member of the Johannesburg Stock Exchange

On the same day that Kebble quit, the Western Areas board appointed a subcommittee in terms of the conditions set by the joint financial advisers, which issued its report on 1 February. During the course of its investigation, Kebble told the subcommittee that he had had no authority to bind Western Areas to make loans to DRD aggregating R111 million, and that although he knew he had to consult the board of directors of Western Areas and obtain their approval, he had not done so. Buitendag told the subcommittee that although he had used JCI Gold letterheads to facilitate the payment of money to DRD, he was acting in his personal capacity and not as a director or executive of JCI Gold.

Harmony increased its offer on 14 January to either 34 Harmony shares for every 100 Randfontein shares, or R12.25 cash per Randfontein share, or a combination of shares and cash. Paper, cash, or a mixture of the two, and now more shares were being offered and more cash had been put on the table.

The game was surely up for what would have been *the* League of Extraordinary Gentlemen at the new JCI Ltd.

On 18 January, DRD's board of directors appointed a subcommittee to investigate the alleged use of funds received from Western Areas to finance certain share trades, as well as alleged irregularities and related contraventions. This subcommittee issued its report on 23 February.

In its filings with the Securities Exchange Commission in Washington, Randgold & Exploration did its damnedest to sugar-coat the Randfontein debacle. As if relating a campfire anecdote, Randgold & Exploration reported that in July 1999, Western Areas, together with its subsidiaries and related companies, entered into discussions with a view to simplifying the various shareholding structures, focusing on the group's core gold businesses. On 6 December 1999, Western Areas made an offer by way of a scheme of arrangement to its shareholders. This transaction was contingent on the successful conclusion of various simultaneously announced schemes of arrangement.

Late in January, Western Areas concluded an agreement with Harmony to sell all of its shares and options in Randfontein for R21 million. Separately, Harmony and the so-called Randfontein shareholder group agreed that Harmony would acquire all shares and options held by the group. In total, this amounted to some 11 per cent of the issued shares in Randfontein and 46.4 per cent of the options. As a result, with effect from 1 January 2000, Harmony acquired 6 328 855 Randfontein shares held by CAM, 30 900 Randfontein shares held by JCI Gold and 693 900 Randfontein shares held by Brett Kebble for a cash payment of R12.25 per share. Brett always was as quick to accept a cash offer as he was shy to make one. Harmony also bought 5 571 773 Randfontein options held by JCI Gold for cash at R2.76 each.

On 3 February, the shattered Western Areas board announced the withdrawal of offers to various companies, including JCI Gold, Randfontein, Barnex, Freddev and Randgold & Exploration. Harmony took control of Randfontein's management immediately, and by 30 June had acquired 100 per cent of the company's outstanding ordinary share capital and 96.5 per cent of the options. Swanepoel, the Harmony CEO, famously vowed: 'We will get our hands dirty until we live, eat and breathe Randfontein.'

In Washington, Randgold & Exploration duly informed the SEC that fraud charges were pending in South Africa against Western Areas, Brett, Roger and Buitendag, arising from the proposed acquisition by Western Areas of JCI Gold Ltd, CAM, Free State Development and Investment Corporation Ltd, Barnex 'and ourselves'.

There was at least one remarkable twist to the Randfontein imbroglio, and it came from the other side of Johannesburg. DRD readily conceded that it owed R111 million to Western Areas for advances made between December 1999 and January 2000, when the Western Areas offer was open and in the public domain. However, as it turned out, the loan was used to buy 7 187 000 ordinary shares of Randgold & Exploration, 6 268 000 ordinary shares of JCI and 15 128 500 shares of CAM for a total of R98.2 million.

Just 812 100 ordinary shares in Randfontein were bought at a cost of R8.6 million, along with 2 349 000 Randfontein options at a cost of R4.4 million. During this period, the architects of the conspiracy would have wanted Randfontein share values to decrease; they would have been *sellers*. By the same token, they would have been *buyers* of Western Areas.

However, they would never have been so dumb as to use the funds diverted to DRD to buy Western Areas shares; that would have been a more brazen criminal offence than any of the other allegations. As to Randfontein, the intentions were schizophrenic; the alleged conspirators wanted the stock price to be as low as possible in order to enhance the attractiveness of the Western Areas offer. At the same time, they wanted to control as much of Randfontein's issued shares and options as possible. The latter would have translated into buying Randfontein securities; the former implied the sale of such securities. Apparently, the conspirators lost much of the plot, using most of the cash diverted to DRD to buy stock in other entities in the JCI-Randgold group. The entire exercise looked horribly futile and rather amateurish.

Brett Kebble had dabbled previously in Randfontein's affairs, dazzled as he was by the amount of cash that the mine could generate, even at low gold prices. During the December 1998 quarter, Randfontein was seen to spend R170 million buying

7.7 million Western Areas shares. Randfontein also lent JCI Gold a cool R100 million in hard cash. Despite JCI Gold's minority stake in Randfontein, JCI Gold, in the form of Kebble, held the Randfontein management contract and controlled underlying cash flows at the mine.

It was convenient enough to force Randfontein to buy shares in Western Areas, given Kebble's secret plan to acquire control of all of Randfontein. However, there was also a view that Randfontein had bought the Western Areas shares in order to settle its management contract with JCI Gold. In other words, Randfontein would 'pay' JCI Gold to cancel its management contract with shares Randfontein had bought in Western Areas.

If nothing else, it was a convenient moment to revisit the thorny management contract controversy that had been instrumental in favourably thrusting the Rand-gold crowd into the investment limelight in and around 1995. They had gained significant support among investors by calling for the cancellation of management contracts with mines, given that the parent mining houses held only minority stakes in the underlying mines. In practice, this call for cancellation had translated into something very, very different. In the Randfontein case, as late as 1999 the underlying mine was expected to pay massive amounts before the management contract would be cancelled.

The full benefit of the cancellation fee – around R170 million, in Randfontein's case – would accrue to a party (in this instance JCI Gold) that held only a minority stake. The amount required to settle a management contract was typically calculated by using nett present value (NPV) methodology, where a stream of future cash flows are discounted, using an accepted rate, to a single present lump sum of cash.

Kebble's earlier popularity in calling for the cancellation of management contracts had translated in practice to a malodorous falsehood. Even worse, once the management contract had been cancelled at huge cost, the previous 'parent' entity – in this case JCI Gold – would often simply continue to supply managerial and other services to the underlying mine, but now at market-related prices.

It was no joke that, as part of Harmony's acquisition of Randfontein, Harmony agreed to acquire the management contract from JCI Gold for R140 million. In practice, this was settled by the offset of R101 million owing by JCI Gold to Randfontein, and the balance by the transfer of 1 879 518 Western Areas shares to JCI Gold.

∗　∗　∗

It was like a nuclear fallout zone. It was ground zero. Brett Kebble had utterly destroyed his chances with Randfontein and the wider JCI-Randgold restructuring.

And then, like the mythical phoenix rising from the ashes, he was back.

On 26 October 2000, Vaughan Bray, acting CEO of Western Areas, announced that his board of directors had reappointed Kebble as a director of the company. He would also become CEO of Western Areas with immediate effect.

Bray said the process of identifying opportunities for enhancing shareholder value at Western Areas was reaching 'a critical stage', and it was the board's view that Kebble was best equipped to lead the company during this time, when 'major strategic decisions' would have to be made about its future. Kebble, Bray pointed out, had elected to resign from the Western Areas board earlier to clear the way for internal and external investigations into alleged irregularities in defence of the hostile bid for Randfontein. While these investigations found that Kebble had committed 'a breach of corporate governance', he had done so 'with the best interests of the company and its shareholders at heart'. Bray explained that it was the understanding of Western Areas that the SRP had completed its investigation and that an investigation by the Financial Services Board was still under way.

All things considered, however, the board was of the opinion that the time was right for Kebble to return and make what was regarded as 'an indispensable contribution to the future of the company'.

Given what would materialise in the years ahead, the Western Areas directors who voted to reinstate Kebble might have experienced one or two sleepless nights. Apart from Bray, those who could have attended that fateful board meeting were Wiseman Nkuhlu (as non-executive chairman), John Fox Brownrigg (MD), Paul Ferguson, Roger Kebble, David Kovarsky, Eric Molefe, Bill Nairn and Christopher Yates. There were also two alternate directors: Graham Shuttleworth and Vincent Uren.

14

Past imperfect, future tense

LONG BEFORE BRETT KEBBLE was reappointed CEO of Western Areas in October 2000, his business life had become obsessively focused on hunting for cash. It was a desperate quest that often bore no fruit. The creation of a giant new JCI Ltd had been primarily driven by Kebble's need to find new ways of milking cash out of the system. Instead, he had been disgraced.

The directors at Western Areas who reappointed him to the top job can have had no inkling that a major criminal indictment against Brett and Roger, Hennie Buitendag and the company itself was in the pipeline. The one great irony was that the alleged fraud had failed to deliver Randfontein, particularly since the conspirators could have resorted to a number of other, fully legitimate options towards this end.

After all, some cash had been available, even if it had come at the high cost of increased debt levels within the Kebble-controlled companies. But Brett had never even contemplated offering any kind of cash option to Randfontein shareholders. He had become just too accustomed to selling paper to investors. It had worked with devastating effect in 1996, when the Randgold Resources story powered the Randgold & Exploration stock prices to levels that allowed Kebble and the chosen few to make millions. The paper trick worked again in mid-1997, when Kebble cleaned up the JCI mess by offering millions of CAM shares to disgruntled stakeholders and shareholders who had backed the sale of a 30 per cent controlling stake in JCI to a black consortium.

But the offer of Western Areas paper to Randfontein shareholders had failed and restructuring of the so-called Kebble companies, headed by Western Areas, had collapsed in a heap. Had the plan succeeded, Kebble had some fairly dramatic and imaginative, albeit unsustainable, ideas about how to improve liquidity. Instead, he had been reduced to a desperate cash hunter. His socks were frayed.

By now, it was clear that Kebble had little, if any, entrepreneurial talents. But his ego, which had assumed monstrous proportions during 1996 and 1997, had not diminished a single iota. The stark reality was that Kebble had only ever orchestrated one really decent deal, and even that carried all kinds of qualifications.

The merger of Gem Diamonds into Trans Hex had established Tokyo Sexwale's Mvelaphanda as a viable black empowerment company. Saxendrift had made that deal work, but it was not Kebble who had bought the property or replaced the management. Mvelaphanda had added the value that enabled shareholders to cash in, while Kebble delayed transfer of the interest he held in Gem Diamonds to New Mining, his version of a BEE concern. Most of the rifled profits had been used to pay Kebble's personal debt to the shady character in London and to finance his egregiously flamboyant lifestyle.

Cocooned in a paper world of his own making, Kebble had become the Grand Panjandrum.* His demeanour swung from cunning fox to silver-tongued con artist, but the interminable search for ready cash brought out the very worst in him. Kebble had become as nasty and horrible a man as it was possible to be.

In the battle for Randfontein, he had been nothing short of savage. Now West Africa was back on the agenda. Randgold Resources was sweating blood, and the Syama mine in Mali had returned to haunt those who had sung its praises in 1996 and 1997.

The mine had turned out to be an even bigger dung heap than the most cynical observer could have imagined. It just sucked down money, millions and millions of dollars, but Randgold's CEO, Mark Bristow, had become as stubborn and endearing as a donkey. He marched immutably on, bearing the cross on a back lashed and bloodied by increasingly horrific figures. Not for the first time, Randgold Resources changed its year-end to December during 1999. For the nine months ending 31 December, the company posted a nett loss of $78 million. Accumulated losses stood at $175 million. But there was still Morila, the only possible means of staving off complete destruction of Randgold Resources and its majority shareholder, Randgold & Exploration.

Just ahead of the infamous deal in October 1996, when BHP sold Syama and the rights to the Loulo, Yanfolila and Morila permits, Randgold & Exploration had issued $48 million in convertible bonds via one of its subsidiaries, Randgold Finance. The bonds had been fully guaranteed by Randgold & Exploration and payday was at hand. Randgold & Exploration was controlled by its chairman, Roger Kebble, presiding over a board of tame directors who towed the line: David Ashworth, Bristow, Grant Fisher, Graham Shuttleworth and the ubiquitous Buitendag.

The Kebbles tackled the Randgold Resources problem in a devious and unsavoury

---

* A panjandrum is defined by *Merriam-Webster* as 'a powerful personage or pretentious official'. It is a nonsense word, coined by British actor and playwright Samuel Foote around 1755. According to the *Oxford English Dictionary*, Foote made up a line of gibberish to 'test the memory of his fellow actor Charles Macklin, who had asserted that he could repeat anything after hearing it once'. Foote's made-up line was, 'And there were present the Picninnies, and the Joblillies, and the Garyulies and the Grand Panjandrum himself, with the little round button at the top.' Some 75 years later, Foote's passage appeared in a book of children's stories by Anglo-Irish writer Maria Edgeworth. It took another 25 years before English-speakers actually incorporated 'panjandrum' into their general vocabulary.

manner. Under Brett's direct influence, Barnex, part of the broader JCI-Randgold group, launched a rights issue in December 1998 that raised R222 million in cash. However, only 48 per cent of the issue was taken up, with Western Areas, having underwritten the issue, absorbing the rest.

In September 1999, Randgold Resources obtained a short-term loan of $50 million from Barnex. The loan, which was rand denominated, bore interest at the SA Reserve Bank's prime rate plus 1 per cent, and was negotiated at a juncture when the dollar-gold price sank to multi-decade lows of just over $250 an ounce. Randgold Resources, which had absolutely no creditworthiness, had agreed that the loan would be convertible into Morila equity if not repaid by 31 March 2000.

Bristow somehow managed to extend the conversion date to 15 August, but in return for this accommodation, Kebble punished Randgold Resources to within an inch of financial death. The company would have to pay an additional $3 million plus a fee of $32 787 for *every day* that the loan was outstanding after 1 July.

Poor, poor Randgold Resources. As the deadline loomed, the company sold half of its 40 per cent stake in the Morila joint venture to AngloGold for $132 million in cash. On 3 July, the loan from Barnex was paid in full.

In September 2001, Randgold Resources completed a mandatory share re-purchase programme, buying 6 882 423 shares from its parent company, Randgold & Exploration, for $48 million. The Kebbles had orchestrated a magnificent cash asset strip of Randgold Resources. Of the $132 million raised by selling half of Morila to AngloGold, $52 million had gone to Barnex (Brett) and $48 million to Randgold & Exploration (Roger).

Within days of the share buy-back, Randgold & Exploration redeemed the $48 million convertible bonds issued in 1996 by its full subsidiary, Randgold Finance (BVI). The figure was exactly equal to the amount Randgold & Exploration received from Randgold Resources. The coincidence was striking, but Randgold & Exploration avoided the chopping block, at least for the moment.

Randgold & Exploration was forced into redeeming the convertible bonds by using $48 million cash, since the alternative option of converting the bonds into Randgold & Exploration stock was utterly unattractive at prevailing share price levels. Had the bonds not been repaid in cash, Randgold & Exploration would no doubt have been forced into liquidation, since it had guaranteed the bonds. Randgold Resources would then have been swallowed alive by the creditors.

On 18 February 2002, Western Areas announced that South Deep had been refinanced, 'using a long-dated derivative structure, based upon the selling of options on a portion of Western Areas' 50 per cent share of South Deep's gold production over 12.5 years. This arrangement raised cash of $104 million. Work is ongoing to increase the facility and thereby raise approximately $21 million to increase the total to $125 million.'

The idea, apparently, was to 'release value for shareholders'. At the time, Brett said that, while the derivative structure was conservative, it would not only provide for the Western Areas portion of South Deep's ongoing capital expenditure, but also allow for the payment of 'special dividends' to Western Areas shareholders.

As ever, the devil lurked in the detail. JCI Gold had 43 per cent of Western Areas, while CAM held 64 per cent of JCI Gold. The Kebble family interests were represented by an ever-declining stake in CAM, held via BNC Investments.

Juicy special dividend payouts from Western Areas would help cut debt at JCI Gold and CAM, where auditors Charles Orbach & Company had just issued warnings over debt levels. The JSE similarly published a warning to investors over debt concerns at the two companies. By forcing Western Areas to raise $104 million and then pushing this up to $125 million, Kebble was borrowing cash on the strength of a good asset in order to set up a milk cow for his family interests.

That was the bottom line.

No matter how fleet Kebble's verbal tap dance in describing the issue, the cash was being borrowed by mortgaging parts of South Deep's future gold production to finance houses. In typical Kebble mode, the cash was raised in a most complicated manner by use of derivatives.* Even given the arcane language of derivatives deals, Kebble's description was as legible as Incan hieroglyphics:

> Western Areas has implemented a derivative structure, based upon the selling of options on a portion of Western Areas' 50 per cent share of South Deep's gold production. Option premiums have been received upfront and payment of premiums for the bought options has been deferred. The accounting treatment has resulted in the raising of a deferred expense asset and a deferred income liability in respect of premiums payable and received on the options. Premium income and expenses are amortised to the Income statement over the period of the structure (12.5 years).

---

* There are probably thousands of definitions for 'derivatives'. According to Warren Buffett, derivatives essentially 'call for money to change hands at some future date, with the amount to be determined by one or more reference items such as interest rates, stock prices or currency values. The range of derivatives contracts is limited only by the imagination of man (or sometimes, so it seems, madmen).' PTI Securities and Futures of Chicago, Illinois, define a derivative as a financial instrument, traded on or off an exchange, the price of which is directly dependent upon the value of one or more underlying securities, equity indices, debt instruments, commodities, other derivative instruments or any agreed-upon pricing index or arrangement. Derivatives involve the trading of rights or obligations based on the underlying product but do not directly transfer property. They are used to hedge risk or to exchange a floating rate of return for a fixed rate of return.

On the subject of derivatives, Warren Buffett, that canny and unimaginably rich investor from America's heartland, had the following to say in his 2000 annual report to shareholders of Berkshire Hathaway, of which he was both chairman and CEO:

We [Berkshire Hathaway] try to be alert to any sort of mega-catastrophe risk, and that posture may make us unduly apprehensive about the burgeoning quantities of long-term derivatives contracts and the massive amount of uncollateralized receivables that are growing alongside. In our view, however, derivatives are financial weapons of mass destruction, carrying dangers that, while now latent, are potentially lethal.

Quite simply, Buffett viewed derivatives as 'time bombs, both for the parties that deal in them and the economic system'.

Brett Kebble was in love with derivatives.

He put three types of derivatives in place: put options bought, call options sold and call options bought. The prices ranged between $260 an ounce of gold in the early years of the structure and $333 an ounce in 2014. However, the bottom line was fairly easy to express on 29 November 2005, when spot dollar-gold prices topped $500 an ounce. If gold bullion remained at $500 an ounce until 2014, the Western Areas hedge book was 'under the water' by roughly $500 million on 29 November 2005. In other words, Western Areas was technically insolvent.

However, various financial institutions, not least Investec, which carried an exposure to the Western Areas hedge book, had every reason to arrange a bail out, announced on 30 August 2005.

The magnitude of the error Kebble had made in restructuring the Western Areas hedge book during 2002 (there was already one in place) can hardly be over-emphasised. The board of directors that would have voted on the CEO's new hedge book included Roger Kebble (non-executive chairman), John Fox Brownrigg, Vaughan Bray, Bill Nairn and Vincent Uren, along with four new board members that some investors would categorise as Kebble cronies, namely Chris Lamprecht, Sello Rasethaba, Gibson Njenje and Charles Cornwall. Investors might be forgiven for wondering if any of these learned stewards of their money ever read an article published in the *Washington Post* on 20 January 1987, where Buffett wrote:

It has always been a fantasy of mine that a boatload of twenty-five brokers would be shipwrecked and struggle to an island from which there could be no rescue. Faced with developing an economy that would maximize their consumption and pleasure, would they, I wonder, assign twenty of their number to produce food, clothing, shelter, etc., while setting five to trading options endlessly on the future output of the twenty?

15

The first whiff of death

G OLD MINES ARE NEVER *SOLD.*
A gold mine or a gold stock with several operating mines can, of course, be *bought,* but, even then, the principle of supply and demand does not apply. Within the industry, when a gold mine is offered for sale, the first question is likely to be why? If a gold mine was so damn good, why would anyone want to sell it? Surely it would be a priceless asset? Is the seller hiding something?

On the other hand, directors of listed companies in particular have an obligation to negotiate the best possible deals for shareholders, so it is possible that a great gold mine could, in fact, be sold, but only for an exceptionally good price.

When a gold stock or gold mine is indeed *bought,* the predator, whether friendly or aggressive, successfully executes a merger and acquisition plan. If the deal is friendly, the result is a merger; where the deal is hostile, the result is a takeover or acquisition. Some mergers and/or acquisitions are never completed, most commonly because the would-be buyer offers too little (as determined by the collective body of potential sellers) and refuses to budge beyond a certain limit, or where the sellers want more and refuse to reconsider (which amounts to pretty much the same thing).

Despite the great volume of mergers and acquisitions that characterised the global gold sector from about 1990, it remained one of the least consolidated among the broader resources sector. Iron ore, for instance, has long been dominated by only three really big producers: Rio Tinto, BHP Billiton and Brazil's Companhia Vale do Rio Doce, with South Africa's Kumba in a distant fourth or possibly fifth position. The gold sector has a long way to go before it looks anything like the iron ore production industry.

Years of substantial momentum in corporate activity have seen barely a month go by without some or other drama in the global gold sector. By December 2005, it was home to eight so-called Tier One members: Newmont (the biggest in terms of market capitalisation at $20 billion), Barrick, Placer Dome, Kinross, AngloGold Ashanti, Gold Fields, Harmony Gold and Newcrest.

Tier Two members included the likes of Lihir Gold, Oxiana, Oxus Gold, Randgold Resources, IAMGOLD, Bema Gold, Eldorado Gold, Meridian Gold, DRDGold (formerly Durban Roodepoort Deep), Glamis Gold, Agnico-Eagle and Goldcorp-

Wheaton. The next category, 'emerging producers', included Ballarat Goldfields, Gabriel Resources and Alamos Gold.

In November 2005, at least one big play, an unsolicited bid by Barrick (market capitalisation $14 billion) to buy Placer Dome ($10 billion) was under way. On 23 November, in the time-honoured manner of the big egos that inevitably seem to set up camp in the upper echelons of gold companies, Placer Dome unanimously recommended that shareholders reject Barrick's hostile takeover bid. Placer Dome had naturally consulted its financial advisers, who just happened to be among the meanest names on Wall Street: CIBC World Markets, Goldman Sachs & Co, Morgan Stanley & Co. Each adviser found – of course – that Barrick's offer was inadequate from a financial point of view. Said Robert Franklin, chairman of Placer Dome: 'We believe Barrick's offer is financially inadequate, opportunistic and fails to recognise the value of Placer Dome's assets and long-term growth profile.' In the horse-trading so typical of this kind of corporate activity, Peter Tomsett, president and CEO of Placer Dome, riposted: 'It's easy to see why Barrick needs Placer Dome, but it's difficult to understand why Placer Dome should want Barrick.'

Barrick's offer was seen as rotten and not reflective of 'an adequate premium for control of Placer Dome'. Amid the thousands of words generated by merger and acquisition battles, the bottom line is price satisfaction on both sides. It would have been spectacularly unusual if Barrick had played an opening gambit that over-valued Placer Dome. Indeed, Placer Dome's directors would almost certainly have required immediate medical attention!

Barrick president and CEO Greg Wilkins told a gold conference on 30 November that Barrick's offer was 'full and fair, and nothing that Placer Dome has said in response was new or unexpected. We see no reason to amend our bid one iota. Barrick is already offering a substantial 27 per cent premium.'

The thing was, however, that Placer Dome was not for sale; it was not being *sold*, but could be *bought* by Barrick if the price was right. Besides, the Placer Dome directors were bound, in more ways than one, to obtain the best possible deal for shareholders. By the same token, Barrick was under an obligation to get the best possible deal for its shareholders. Tactics and behaviour can become fairly wild during mergers and acquisitions, and it is not at all uncommon for 'good news' announcements to be brought forward as part of the game plan. On 30 November 2005, for example, Placer Dome made a splash by releasing fresh details of its Bald Mountain project. Predictably, Barrick reacted by saying that it was fully aware of such details and had factored them into its offer package for Placer Dome.

Suddenly the invective and fireworks were over. On 22 December, Barrick and Placer Dome jointly announced agreement on 'a friendly transaction' under which

Barrick increased its offer to acquire Placer Dome. The revised offer was some $10.4 billion, compared to the original offer of $9.5 billion.

Because gold mining is not an exact science, it has to be said that in specific unsolicited instances, part of a gold mine may, indeed, be sold. In a deal that came to light at the end of November 2005, Rio Tinto entered into contracts to sell its 14.5 per cent stake in Lihir Gold for some $295 million. CEO Leigh Clifford reeled out a classic company line in explaining the transaction: 'Rio Tinto generally does not hold long-term minority positions in other listed companies. Following our relinquishment of management rights announced on 16 September 2005, we have taken advantage of the current favourable market conditions to sell our holding in Lihir.'

Rio Tinto was staying true to its long-term business model by remaining focused on low-cost, long-life, high-quality mining assets, no matter how diversified, and securing as close to 100 per cent as possible of each mining operation's underlying cash flows. After Rio Tinto let go the management contract at Lihir, there was simply no point in hanging on to a minority 15 per cent stake in the company. A stake of that size, with nothing attached, fell outside Rio Tinto's business model.

Special situations aside, however, Tier One gold producers are involved in never-ending assessments of up-and-coming junior players. As such, the most vulnerable gold stocks are juniors that can be easily swallowed by the balance sheets of the giant Tier One diggers. There is no shortage of juniors, many of which are run and part-owned by personalities who embrace entrepreneurship. If their ventures attract offers that cannot be refused, they tend to sell out and move on to new areas of exploration.

The global gold sector is riddled with spies and spotters, each striving to be first to identify the next sexy deposit. During 2005 alone, various significant decisions were made about a number of gold projects dotted around the world, not least by Bema (Cerro Casale, Chile), Coeur d'Alene (Kensington, Alaska), Pan American (Alamo Dorado, Mexico), Bema (Kupol, Russia), Agnico-Eagle (Goldex, Quebec), Eldorado (Efemcukuru, Turkey and Tanjianshan, China), Northgate (Kemess North, British Columbia) and Goldcorp (Los Filos/Bermejal, Mexico).

But Tier One and Tier Two producers always take the biggest heat, given that internal company efforts cannot generally replace reserves in the ground at the same rate that gold is being dug out and depleted. Beyond the efforts of internal exploration teams, which may be strung out across the globe, the bigger gold-diggers really have only one option: they need to buy mines, which is a tough job, given that gold mines are not *sold*. However, the modern investor insists that all companies, including gold-diggers, continue to grow ever bigger.

Deals involving Tier One predators going for juniors crop up with a fair degree of regularity. On 21 November 2005, for instance, Gold Fields announced that it had entered into an agreement to buy the part of Bolivar Gold that it did not already own. The offer was for $330 million in cash, equal to a premium of 40.9 per cent over the volume-weighted average trading price of Bolivar during the 30 trading days prior to the announcement. Such a 30-day price calculation is typical, if not standard, in merger and acquisition activity.

Some investors might have seen the premium price offered by Gold Fields as being on the high side. Bolivar, listed in Toronto, operates the Choco 10 open-cast gold mine in the El Callao district of Venezuela's Bolivar state. Choco 10 went into commercial production on 1 August 2005 and, according to Gold Fields, total production was expected to be around 190 000 ounces during 2006. As of 31 December 2004, Choco 10 had 1.3 million ounces of proven and probable reserves* from 21.4 million tons of ore at an average grade of 1.9 grams per ton, contained within a measured and indicated resource of 1.8 million ounces and a further 1.7 million ounces of inferred resource.

Gold Fields, active in exploration in Venezuela since 1992, already had a joint venture agreement with Bolivar, covering some 25 000 hectares surrounding Choco 10. The region is 'highly prospective and significant potential exists to increase reserves and production', according to Gold Fields. 'El Callao is part of a well-established gold mining region, with historic production dating back more than 200 years. There are several other gold mines in the region including the Colombia mine owned by CVG-Minerven; the Tomi and La Victoria mines owned by Crystallex; the La Camorra mine and Mina Isidora development project owned by Hecla and the privately owned San Raphael mine.'

Curiously, the ebb and flow of the global gold mining sector apparently meant little or nothing to Brett Kebble. He seemed to delight in doing exactly the opposite of what investors demanded, no matter how flexibly, in wealth-creating gold mining activities. His bloody-mindedness cost investors untold millions.

Kebble had been involved in the 1996 acquisition of Syama, a gold mine that was sold rather than bought. Conventional wisdom dictates that when a gold mine is put up for sale, prospective buyers know that something is likely to be seriously awry.

---

* Proven and probable reserves are classified as those for which quantity is computed from dimensions revealed in outcrops, trenches, workings or drill holes; grade and/or quality are computed from the results of detailed sampling, and the sites for inspection, sampling and measurement are spaced so closely and the geologic character is so well defined that size, shape, depth and mineral content of reserves are well established. The definition of 'probable' reserves is similar; the degree of assurance, although lower than that for proven reserves, is high enough to assume continuity between points of observation. After proven and probable reserves, the next step down the ladder of certainty is 'measured and indicated resources' and, after that, 'inferred sources'.

From acquisition in October 1996 to the middle of 1997, Randgold & Exploration and its subsidiary Randgold Resources coughed up $62 million in cash for Syama. The vast majority of the money came from institutional investors, who trusted what they were being told.

But no matter how many millions were thrown at attempts to bring the mine to profitability, Syama remained a dust hole. In January 2001, after more than $100 million in cash had been funnelled to Syama, mining operations were suspended, ostensibly due to 'continued losses caused by falling gold prices and power problems'. Syama was placed on a care-and-maintenance programme, as should have been the case when BHP had put it on the market during the first half of 1996. Syama was back up for grabs, and, on 15 June 2004, Resolute Mining bought the 80 per cent share held by Randgold Resources, paying $6 million in cash and assuming liabilities of $7 million.

Before making its offer, Resolute had made an extensive study of Syama. In addition to its own staff, outside expertise was commissioned for sample preparation (Analabs, situated at Morila), sample analysis (Analabs, Morila and Perth), metallurgical test work (AMMTEC Limited, Perth), process plant options (Geoff Motteram, Geomett), roasting test work (AMMTEC under supervision of Ken Kellet), plant engineering (Lycopodium), power and electrical (Geoff Bailey, BEC and John Shackleton, electrical consultant), plant capital costs and operating cost review (Lycopodium), resource modelling (Hellman & Schofield), geotechnical (Chris Orr, George Orr and Associates), pit design and mining schedule (James Pearson, consultant mining engineer), mine scheduling, equipment and tender documentation (David Cooper, Mining Resource Solutions), review of underground options (Peter Hepburn-Brown, Resource & Capital Management, and Rapallo), review of in wall ramp and underground (Guy Simpson, Rapallo), environmental audit and data compilation (Earth Systems, Digby Wells and Associates), air pollution modelling (Environ), and weather station and data management (Sentinel).

In its report, Resolute dealt with the refractory sulphides that had apparently caused all the heartache. 'In October 1995, after 12 months of operation, BHP identified major problems with the whole ore roast.' After that, Syama was for *sale*. In June 1996, as Resolute put it, Randgold Resources made an assessment of upgrade potential as part of its purchase and proposed two stages. After buying the mine, Randgold Resources proceeded with the proposed expansion, then found that 'the resultant plant had numerous operating problems'. It was pretty rough stuff. Randgold Resources found that it 'could not operate continuously due to the power plant overloading and reliability problems'. Recoveries did not improve.

The upgrades, which had cost tens of millions of dollars, had as much effect as peeing into a hurricane. Randgold Resources 'determined to shut down the sulphide circuit and revert to treatment of low grade oxide stockpile before placing the mine on care and maintenance'. The oxides had, of course, been the sweet surface material that Syama mined before hitting the deeper, hard, stubborn sulphides. It is normal procedure in open-cast mines to stockpile a good portion of the initial oxides, which can be processed to 'sweeten' returns should the mine experience some or other unforeseen difficulty.

The Resolute report contained at least one piece of truly shocking information. In order to mine Syama with any hope of making profits, Resolute would have to build a new processing plant. Yes, a *new* processing plant. BHP had built a plant that was improperly designed and Randgold Resources, in full apparent knowledge of the problem, had built another, of equally inadequate design. It was a cock-up of monumental proportions, and it would cost Resolute $82 million to build a new plant.

Randgold Resources had created one, and only one, sweet thing at Syama: retained tax losses in excess of $123 million, though these could only be offset against future profits. Randgold Resources, the swaggering braggart, had created one of Africa's biggest tax shelters.

But there was always Morila ...

In a near-farcical account, Randgold Resources told the Securities Exchange Commission in Washington: 'By the end of 1996 we had discovered the gold deposit at Morila and we successfully proved up the reserve to five million ounces by the end of 1999. We commenced construction in 1999 and commissioned Morila in October 2000.'

Actually, Randgold Resources had been forced to sell half of its 80 per cent stake in Morila to AngloGold in July 2000 for $132 million in cash. But for this, there was no doubt that Randgold & Exploration would have defaulted in September 2001 on the $48 million convertible bonds issued in 1996 by Randgold Finance (BVI).

Of all the deals that Kebble concocted, the sale of half of the Morila interest might well have been the dumbest. In its 2000 financial year, Morila coughed up bottom-line profits of $20 million as it built up to full production. In 2001, the profits exploded to $80 million, of which just 40 per cent went to Randgold Resources.

In 2002, Morila's profits were a staggering $227 million, and again Randgold Resources received only 40 per cent. Kebble paid a high price for ignoring the rule that gold mines, or parts of them, are never *sold*. Apart from the forward 'losses' suffered after the sale, control over the cash flow from this potential golden goose had also been forfeited.

Albeit by default, the JCI-Randgold group had finally found the cash cow it so desperately needed, but they blew it.

By the end of February 2002, after Kebble had forward-sold a hefty chunk of gold production from Western Areas for the next 12½ years, he had run out of ideas. Within the broad JCI-Randgold group, there was little left for him to sell in terms of serious numbers. His attentions shifted to CAM, in which most of the Kebble family interests remained vested. Once again, paper started flying out of CAM. On 16 July, CAM issued a monster 474 337 213 new ordinary shares at 45 cents each to buy out the minorities in JCI Gold. CAM had changed its name to JCI Ltd little more than a week before and, on 16 July, following a scheme of arrangement with CAM, JCI Gold delisted. The CAM paper that had become Kebble's personal currency was replaced by new specie: JCI paper.

On 26 June, JCI had issued 220 million new ordinary shares at 45 cents each as part consideration for the acquisition of a 40 per cent interest in Letšeng Investment Holdings SA. CAM shareholders had previously approved the acquisition of an interest in Letšeng, a dormant diamond mine in Lesotho, for a total consideration of some R166 million. Payment would take the form of the 220 million JCI shares and $6.5 million in cash.

On 2 September, JCI issued yet another 344 488 942 ordinary shares at 45 cents each in terms of a rights offer, raising R155 million in cash before costs. The issue had been underwritten by BNC Investment (Pty) Ltd, representing the Kebble family interests, and Investage 170 (Pty) Ltd, which was under the control of JCI's directors.

JCI also issued 202 300 024 'convertible redeemable 50 per cent secured debentures of R1.25 each, bearing interest at prime', which were listed on the JSE on 15 July. The debentures could be converted into JCI ordinary shares on 15 January 2006 on a one-for-one basis or, at the election of the holders, redeemed at the issue price.

By the financial year-end on 31 March 2003, JCI had 1.75 billion shares in issue, in excess of a billion more than the 712 million in issue a year earlier. In one of its previous manifestations, CAM, there had been just 17.4 million shares in issue on 31 March 1996. In the space of seven years, issued shares in the entity had increased one hundredfold, a manoeuvre that was surely unprecedented on any stock exchange in the world.

During the 2003 financial year, JCI granted 83 million fresh stock options, mainly to its directors: Brett and Roger Kebble, Hennie Buitendag, Charles Cornwall and John Stratton. Whereas 29 million shares had previously been optioned to directors, by 31 March there were 112 million JCI shares under option.

Kebble was trying desperately to consolidate his personal and family interests. All told, he held 230 million JCI shares on 31 March, or 13 per cent of the total, plus a further 14 million options. Roger held a mere 15 million shares, plus 14 million options.

On the last day of the financial year, JCI stock was quoted at 58 cents a share, 92 per cent down on the high of 680 cents seen during the *belle époque* of 1997, when Brett was mopping up fallout from the sale of the 'old' JCI to Mzi Khumalo and the AMG consortium. Those were the days, all right, the excessive, glittering, gaudy, extravagant, tumultuous days.

In mid-1997, the Kebble family's interest in JCI was worth R1.5 billion, at least on paper. By 31 March 2003, the value had plummeted to R142 million, and falling. Had Brett posted a truthful personal résumé in JCI's annual report, it would have looked something like this:

JCI Limited
(formerly Consolidated African Mines Ltd)
(Reg No. 1894/000854/06)
(Incorporated in the Republic of South Africa)

....

Roger Brett Kebble (39)
BA (Political Science) (UCT), BA LLB (UCT)
Born on 19 February 1964
Brett is a director of Barnato Exploration, Matodzi Resources, Rand Leases Properties, Randgold & Exploration, Western Areas and Stilfontein Gold Mining
October 1996
Bought Syama – blew more than $100 million in cash
November 1998
Sold half of South Deep for $235 million in cash
September 1999
Sold Prestea, a whole gold mine, for $13 million
January 2000
Forced to sell stake in Randfontein to Harmony
July 2000
Sold half of Morila for $132 million in cash
September 2001
Redeemed Randgold Finance BVI convertible bonds; blew $48 million in cash[*]
February 2002
Sold South Deep derivatives book forward for $104 million[†] in cash
December 2002
Charged with fraud, conspiracy, incitement and insider trading
31 March 2003
The Kebble family fortune, worth R1.5 billion six years ago, is down to R100 million, and fading

<u>This is one tough business</u>

Brett Kebble's business career, launched on the froth of the BHP Minerals Mali acquisition in 1996, had foundered. With no control over cash flows and no nett cash coming in anyway, Kebble had been on the cannibal run for years. The assets that had effectively been acquired by issuing CAM paper had been gutted in order to raise cash. The gold price had bottomed out in August 1999 and would not reverse a multi-year bear market until April 2001. By then, there was precious little left for Kebble to carve up. Brett Kebble was slowly self-destructing. The air was pregnant with the first faint whiff of death.

*   The bonds were convertible on 31 September 2001 to cash or Randgold & Exploration shares at R39.01 each. The stock was quoted at R9.40 a share on conversion date. Had the Randgold & Exploration stock price been sufficiently attractive, bonds would have been converted, leaving Randgold & Exploration with an effective $48 million in cash.

†   In November 2005, the book was $500 million under water.

16

The British mud wrestler

L ONDON INVESTMENT fund manager Mercury Asset Management (MAM) was said to have been primarily responsible for a major change in executive control at Durban Roodepoort Deep (DRD) in 2000. It was MAM, of course (and specifically Julian Baring, who had retired in 1996), that had played an instrumental role around the early 1990s in calling for radical reform of South Africa's resources sector.

Roger Kebble joined DRD in August 1994, when it formed part of the Randgold & Exploration structure. DRD* had been set free to pursue its own destiny, if such a thing was possible under the senior Kebble.

In the wake of the Randfontein debacle and under pressure from MAM, Roger stepped down as executive chairman of DRD on 3 May 2000 to become a non-executive director. Mark Wellesley-Wood, who hailed from London's financial district, the City, became non-executive chairman on the same date.

MAM had been a willing institutional backer of the initial Randgold & Exploration story, not least when Randgold Resources was created in 1995. Since then, a torrent of water had flowed under the bridge, and MAM's pressure for reform focused on the activities of Brett and Roger Kebble, who had become so dangerous that they ought to have carried surgeon general's warnings.

---

* DRD was first registered on 16 February 1895. During 1996, DRD bought the entire share capital of West Witwatersrand Gold Holdings, parent company of West Witwatersrand Gold Mines, or West Wits, by issuing, in classic Kebble style, paper – in this case, 1 846 087 ordinary shares. At the same time, DRD bought Consolidated Mining Corporation's loan to West Witwatersrand Gold Holdings, and the entire issued capital and shareholders' claim and loan account of East Champ D'Or Gold Mine, a gold mining company with mining title in the West Rand, west of Johannesburg. Also in 1996, DRD was listed on the Nasdaq exchange in the US. In August 1997, DRD bought the mineral rights represented by the Argonaut Project from Randgold & Exploration. On 15 September 1997, DRD bought the entire share capital of Blyvoor-uitzicht Gold Mining Company, or Blyvoor, in exchange for 12 693 279 ordinary DRD shares. On the same day, DRD bought Buffels in exchange for 14 300 396 ordinary DRD shares. On 14 September 1998, DRD bought Crown in exchange for 5 925 139 ordinary DRD shares. On 16 August 1999, Buffels acquired the majority of the assets and liabilities of the Harties mining operation from Avgold Limited, a South African mining company, for R45 million. During September 1999, DRD bought 28 693 002 (19.9 per cent) ordinary shares in Dome Resources, or Dome, for R34.9 million (about $3.3 million). On 13 March 2000, DRD made an unconditional offer to the shareholders of Dome to acquire all the shares in Dome which DRD did not already own. DRD completed this acquisition in June 2001. During August 2000, DRD decided to cease all operations at the Durban Deep Section and both underground and open-cast operations at the West Wits Section after the South African government withdrew its water-pumping subsidy.

Wellesley-Wood and Roger were the proverbial chalk and cheese. The former was a qualified mining engineer and had spent more than two decades in London as a stockbroker and specialist in raising finance for mining companies. Wellesley-Wood was also a chartered engineer (UK).

Roger, hard-boiled and as rough as a honey badger's backside, was a mine captain and graduate of the University of South Africa's executive and management development programmes. These correspondence courses are designed to teach business and financial skills, including strategy implementation, operations and supply chain management, marketing and information management, accounting and economics. On paper, Roger was completely outclassed by Wellesley-Wood, a man with quaint British manners and a polished etiquette, who had married into a moneyed family.

Wellesley-Wood had been diplomatic when Roger stepped down, saying the move would mitigate any conflict of interest that might arise from Roger's position as executive chairman of Randgold & Exploration and other directorships.

Wellesley-Wood was not shy to speak his mind. Wellesley-Wood was one hell of a chap. Wellesley-Wood was intrinsically British when he paid tribute to Roger in the DRD annual report for the 12 months to 30 June 2000:

> I would like to add my support to all those who have acknowledged the tireless contribution made by Roger Kebble to the inception and formation of the company. He is a relentless mining enthusiast whose grasp of problems, wit and intelligence are the stuff of legends. History will recognise his transformation of a 60 000 ounce per year, almost bankrupt, high-cost gold producer into a new mining house as a visionary move. I am pleased that the board will continue to have access to his experience.

Within a relatively short time, Wellesley-Wood did a very un-British thing by morphing into the financial version of a serious and resolute mud wrestler, a tall one with long arms and a shiny head and bespectacled face. Given the time and place, the transformation was fortuitous.

On 3 November 2000, Wellesley-Wood announced that Mike Prinsloo, chief executive officer at DRD, had taken 'indefinite leave'. Wellesley-Wood carefully picked his way through the explanation, saying that Prinsloo's departure from DRD was 'in no way related to the company's investigations into certain financial irregularities'. As an interim measure, Wellesley-Wood assumed the role of CEO and asked Roger to assist in an executive capacity. Roger duly agreed to become deputy chairman of DRD.

The fact of the matter was that DRD had received notice from its auditors,

Deloitte & Touche, on 14 August outlining 'material irregularities' in the company's affairs. A special committee was established to investigate 'unauthorised payments' and breaches of corporate governance associated with them. The committee consisted of Wellesley-Wood, Ian Murray (a DRD director), Charles Valkin (a partner with Bowman Gilfillan, DRD's independent legal advisers) and Mark Pinnington (a director of Deloitte & Touche Forensic Services). Mandated by DRD's audit committee to investigate the relevant matters and assisted by Control Risks Incorporated, the committee was instructed to institute legal proceedings in respect of potential recoveries.

Wellesley-Wood was already investigating Roger when he placed him in an executive position. The mud wrestler and the honey badger were about to get up close and personal and all bets were off.

There was no question that some interesting deals had gone down in the past few years. Transactions under the forensic microscope included the invalid issuance and allotment of 8 282 056 ordinary shares in DRD during July and October 1999 to various creditors of Laverton Gold, a listed Australian company, and its subsidiary, PT Barisan Tropical Mining, in respect of the acquisition of the Rawas gold mine in Indonesia.

Rawas was a piece of junk that ceased operations in March 2000.

DRD's eight million or so 'Rawas shares' were issued to Rothschild Nominees, Maxidrill, PT Petrosea TBK, Repadre International Corporation, Minproc Engineering, Rio Tinto Rawas Holdings, and five companies directly under the control of Brett, or, more specifically, the Kebble family, namely Continental Goldfields, Consolidated African Mines, JCI (Isle of Man), Weston Investments and CAM Australia. No fewer than 3.4 million of the Rawas shares issued by DRD had gone the way of these five companies.

Evidence came to light showing that the shares were issued without DRD's legal authority, suggesting that the transactions were designed to benefit certain third parties. The issuance of the shares had been authorised by five DRD executive directors: Prinsloo, Vic Hoops, Dick Plaistowe, Charles Mostert and, of course, Roger Kebble. At the time, Roger was DRD's executive chairman and also a director of, inter alia, Laverton. The shares were ostensibly issued pursuant to the planned acquisition of Rawas in consideration for or in anticipation of receiving shares in and claims against various companies with ownership interests in Rawas and its mining rights.

The intention seemed to be for DRD to acquire all the Rawas assets by settling out its shareholders and creditors.

Laverton was identified as a related party because John Stratton, a director of CAM, which would become the 'new' JCI in due course, and CAM Jersey, was a corporate adviser to DRD. The special committee found that it was Stratton, acting out of DRD's office in Perth, Australia (which was later closed) who had arranged issuance of the more than eight million shares, pursuant to agreements between DRD and Laverton. DRD allotted and issued the Rawas shares at the market value of $12.4 million. While the allocation was based on each creditor's relative exposure, no proper valuation proceedings were conducted prior to issuance. According to evidence gathered during the course of the investigation, DRD's board, faced with pressure from its creditors, determined that:

- Laverton arranged the issue by DRD of ordinary shares to creditors in consideration for assets of no value, for the benefit of Laverton and its creditors and not for DRD.
- To avoid the Companies Act requirement for a special resolution, DRD issued the Rawas shares at an inflated issue price unrelated to the true value of the consideration.
- As the DRD special resolution was not obtained, the allotment and issue of DRD ordinary shares for the Rawas transaction was unlawful and invalid.

The law had been broken; criminal conduct was out in the open. Upon discovery of the illegal transactions, the DRD board decided to rescind the agreements with Laverton during 2001. At that time, DRD had received ownership of the claims against, but not the shares of, the companies in the Rawas group. As a result of this rescindment the Rawas group shares were never delivered to DRD. Rawas, in any event, had long ceased to be.

The real problem was that the money, the cash, was gone. Somebody, or some bodies, some entity or entities, or some combination of these possibilities, had made off with the loot.

For DRD, it appeared to be a dead loss.

During 2000, DRD wrote off the attributed $12.4 million value of the shares on the statement of operations as aborted acquisition costs. DRD also wrote off loans amounting to $2.9 million made to members of the Rawas group. No monies were recovered in respect of these loans.

The special committee also uncovered an unauthorised payment on 22 December 1999 by DRD's wholly owned subsidiary, DRD Australasia, of a A$5.9 million ($3.6 million) 'facilitation fee' to Noble Investments (Pty) Ltd. This was in connection with the purchase of 11 150 000 shares, representing some 11 per cent of the issued share capital of Continental Goldfields, a publicly traded company in Australia. Timothy Lebbon, an Australian citizen and businessman, owned all the entities selling the shares. Payment of the facilitation fee resulted in DRD Australasia paying A$0.70 per share for the Continental shares at a time when they were trading at a market price of A$0.10 each.

Funny stuff, this.

It was found that DRD had been substituted as the purchaser of the Continental shares; the original buyer was JCI (then CAM), controlled, of course, by Brett. The effect of the transaction was that JCI and its related companies were relieved of their contractual obligations to Noble. At the time, Roger was DRD's executive chairman, as well as being a director and shareholder of JCI and JCI Gold. On 30 June 2000, Continental owned shares in JCI that constituted some 75 per cent of its total assets.

There was more.

There was the advancement by DRD of $3.9 million to Notable Holdings (Pty) Ltd, an Australian company, for 'operational assistance'. There had been no formal agreement. The ultimate parent company of Notable was Continental Goldfields. At the time, DRD's chief financial officer, Charles Mostert, was a director of Notable. DRD wrote off $1.9 million as a bad debt in 2000, and the remainder was written off in 2002.

There was more.

There had been unauthorised advances in 2000 of $1.85 million by DRD Australasia, acting on the direction of Mostert, in connection with the purported acquisition of a bauxite mine in Venezuela. DRD Australasia had an obligation to pay a non-refundable deposit of $1.65 million for expressing serious interest in the potential deal. The amount was duly paid into a bank account nominated by T Main, the bauxite representative. Mostert, however, instructed Main to pay the money into the bank accounts of certain DRD officers, namely Roger Kebble ($298 617), Mike Prinsloo ($197 264), Vic Hoops ($117 583), Mostert himself ($542 464) and Ian Murray ($65 667). The rest was paid into the accounts of certain individuals who were not DRD employees, namely Stratton ($270 653) and Main ($157 752). More than $1.3 million of the original 'advancement' was later recovered.

Funny stuff, this.

As the facts and figures continued to unfold, Wellesley-Wood apparently discovered that even he was susceptible to the craziness and outbursts caused by an apparent genetic disorder that turns a certain breed of Brit into lager louts and soccer hooligans. For the moment, Wellesley-Wood's affliction remained dormant, but one more spark might send him on the rampage.

This was red-card territory, all right.

On 3 March 2002, a senior official in the Department of Home Affairs tele-phonically informed DRD's attorneys, Bowman Gilfillan, that Wellesley-Wood, who was overseas at the time, had been prohibited from re-entering South Africa. No reasons were given. The department's director-general, Billy Masetlha, had simply declared Wellesley-Wood a prohibited immigrant.

The next edition of *City Press*, a mass circulation Sunday newspaper, quoted Masetlha as saying that Wellesley-Wood was 'the kind of executive South Africa could do without'. DRD reminded Home Affairs that Wellesley-Wood had joined its board 'with a specific brief to improve corporate governance'.

This just wasn't bloody cricket.

A day after the travel ban was imposed on Wellesley-Wood, DRD announced that Roger Kebble had been suspended as executive deputy chairman with immediate effect, though he remained a non-executive board member. The letter informing Roger of the decision had been signed on behalf of Wellesley-Wood, who remained in London, frozen out of South Africa.

The letter referred to DRD's internal investigation of the Rawas transaction, which was nearing completion, and noted that the company had suffered 'substantial losses' as a result of Roger's role.

Kebble senior was instructed to discontinue 'with immediate effect' all executive functions on behalf of the company. The ultimate humiliation was an order banning him from DRD's premises. He was also barred from contacting any DRD employees and/or contractors, with the sole exception of the company secretary, in relation to his duties as a non-executive director.

According to Brett Kebble, Wellesley-Wood arranged for the playing of 'Another One Bites the Dust' by rock group Queen when Roger's fate was announced. Some of the popular anthem's lyrics did not augur well for Kebble cronies who remained at troubled DRD:

> *Another one bites the dust*
> *Another one bites the dust*
> *And another one gone, and another one gone*
> *Another one bites the dust*
> *Hey, I'm gonna get you too*
> *Another one bites the dust*
>
> *There are plenty of ways you can hurt a man*
> *And bring him to the ground*
> *You can beat him*
> *You can cheat him*
> *You can treat him bad and leave him*
> *When he's down*

But I'm ready, yes I'm ready for you
I'm standing on my own two feet ...

On 6 March, after a special meeting of the DRD board, it was announced that the directors unanimously supported Wellesley-Wood's continued tenure as chairman and CEO. Home Affairs minister Mangosuthu Buthelezi overruled Masetlha, and Wellesley-Wood was allowed to return to South Africa. His promise to 'take the K Factor out of DRD' was widely quoted, the 'K' standing unequivocally for Kebble. Now it was the lawyers' turn.

DRD filed two key claims in South Africa against Roger, Mike Prinsloo, John Stratton, Hennie Buitendag and JCI Ltd:

- R69.6 million (about $11.2 million at the time) for 7 644 944 DRD 'Rawas shares' issued on 9 July 1999 at a price of R9.10 each; and
- R7.6 million ($1.2 million) for 637 062 DRD 'Rawas shares' issued on 8 October 1999 at a price of R11.90 each.

DRD also instituted a claim in the Australian courts for A$6.1 million ($4.1 million) for loans and advances made to and on behalf of PT Barisan Tropical Mining, which operated the Rawas mine.

A separate action was launched in Australia on 12 December 2003 against Charles Mostert, John Stratton, Continental Goldfields, CAM Australia, Weston Investments, CAM Jersey and JCI (Isle of Man) for:

- R67 942 ($10 827), the cost of issuing the DRD 'Rawas shares';
- R77 million ($12.3 million), being profits made by third parties who were issued with the DRD 'Rawas shares' at the time; and
- R4.7 million ($0.8 million), being costs incurred to validate the shares that had been issued invalidly.

All the defendants gave notice that they intended to fight the legal action, but no counterclaims were ever filed.

According to Wellesley-Wood, DRD shareholders' funds were applied for a financial rescue of Laverton, from which DRD saw no benefit and for which the gain lay with companies in the CAM group. The result was a write-off of R122 million in DRD's 2000 accounts. Wellesley-Wood claimed that the Rawas transaction was hidden from the company, the DRD board and shareholders.

---

*   'Another One Bites the Dust' was first performed in 1980 by British rock group Queen, comprising Farrokh Bulsara (better known as Freddie Mercury), Roger Taylor, Brian May and John Deacon. The track was composed by Deacon and appeared on the album *The Game*.

'This concealment, together with obfuscation by the parties involved, has unfortunately involved me, my special committee, and the new directors of the company in a lengthy and costly investigation. I estimate that the costs involved in rectifying this dishonest transaction have amounted to R5 million, monies which could have been far better spent,' said Wellesley-Wood.

The finger was pointing straight at Brett and Roger Kebble.

The R122 million write-off by DRD required examination. If the company had lost that amount of cash, what 'third parties' had pocketed the loot?

Wellesley-Wood's allegations, supported by exhaustive forensic evidence, showed that a number of parties had conspired to acquire the Rawas assets, but Rawas was worthless. What had happened was that a number of related intermediaries, or agents, had 'sold' the apparent rights to Rawas to DRD for a massively inflated price. It was these agents who had received much of the missing R122 million, and they were by and large entities controlled by or cronies of the Kebble family.

The scenario was sickeningly familiar. In 1997, institutional investors on the London stock market paid for Randgold Resources shares at massively inflated prices. Ahead of the London listing of Randgold Resources in July 1997, then executive chairman Peter Flack was quoted in the *Financial Times* as saying the stock would be worth $30 a share. In the end, the shares were placed at $15.50 each. In November 1998, in a fresh placement by Randgold Resources, stock was placed at $1 a share.

In the Randgold Resources case, Syama had been the rotting gold mine dangled as bait to hook big cash investors. Now Rawas, another gold mine in decay, was being used in an even more sophisticated scheme, via DRD.* There was even a question mark over whether or not Rawas had ever been a gold mine of any kind.

As to the transactions associated with Lebbon, DRD sued Mostert, Stratton, Noble Investments, Leadenhall Australia, Advent Investors and Lebbon. DRD had 'agreed' to acquire the Continental Goldfields shares for A$1 115 000, and to pay the sum of A$5 910 000 to Noble for 'facilitating the acquisition'. The market value of the Continental Goldfields shares was about A$0.10, so the total price payable in terms of the agreement was A$7 025 000 – more than six times the market value.

'It appears,' bellowed Wellesley-Wood, 'that the interests of DRD shareholders have been abused as DRD was substituted for an earlier purchase contract on which JCI (CAM) failed to perform. Any strategic value in the Continental Goldfields assets could only have related to its 13 per cent shareholding in CAM to support the

---

* Apparently the so-called DRD Rawas shares experienced quite a journey. The DRD stock, issued in Perth by a Johannesburg-domiciled company, went inter alia to Mauritius and later Belgium, and was finally sold into the US market. Who needs James Bond?

Kebble-controlled structure of that company. Conflicts of interest have ... resulted in a loss for DRD shareholders ... of R35 million.'

Substitution of DRD for JCI enabled the conspirators to 'raise' cash from DRD at a massively inflated price, relative to what DRD was buying. This time hard cash, rather than DRD shares, was used. DRD shares were near-cash, to the extent that the stock could be sold with relative ease. In the Lebbon case, the collateral benefit for the Kebbles was to create artificial demand for stock in Continental Goldfields, supporting both it and the wider Kebble family of stocks.

Excluding Rawas, the total amount of irregular transactions uncovered by DRD's special committee came to $9.4 million. Settlement agreements were reached with several parties and more than $4 million was recovered. At a DRD audit committee meeting on 22 July 2002, a decision was made to dissolve the special committee, as it had fulfilled its mandate and achieved its objectives.

Wellesley-Wood's intrinsically British penchant for understatement had been sorely eroded and, in DRD's annual report for the 12 months to 30 June 2002, he disposed of Roger as follows:

> Roger Kebble retired this year. He has had a long and somewhat controversial relationship conflict between his 'passion' for DRD, which he always saw as his 'baby' and his other commercial interests. Well, the baby has grown up now and can stand on its own two feet, but we must thank Roger for playing the role of midwife.

On 11 November 2002, Roger was arrested, very publicly, at Johannesburg International Airport and charged with 38 counts of fraud and contravention of the Companies Act. It was alleged that he had fraudulently obtained more than R6 million from DRD by acting as a third party in transactions between the company and security consultant Ronnie Watson's Global Economic Research (GER). According to Brett, who by now was employing a number of professional services, including security and intelligence, Warren Goldblatt, the head of Associated Intelligence Networks (AIN), which had been appointed to assist the DRD probe, was present when Roger was taken into custody.

Roger spent the night in jail. The next day, he appeared in the Johannesburg Regional Court* and was granted bail of R250 000. The case was postponed to 24 January 2003.

---

* The Specialised Commercial Crime Court acted against Roger Kebble for an alleged contravention of Section 234 of the Companies Act and/or fraud, arising out of his failure as a DRD director to declare his interest in Skilled Labour Brokers cc. It was alleged that DRD paid invoices submitted by this entity during the period of non-disclosure.

A few days earlier, attorney Lourens van Staden of Tabacks, retained by the Kebbles, had called the police officer who was known to be sniffing around the GER case. The Kebbles had heard rumours of police involvement and wanted to offer assurances that Roger was willing to answer questions. The investigating officer told Van Staden that arrangements could be made to set up a meeting on Roger's return from abroad, but instead the police were waiting for him at the airport.

Within hours of being released on bail, Roger presented 'very strong' quarterly results for Randgold & Exploration. The dollar-gold bullion price was showing signs of confirming a protracted bull trend, but the rand price of gold had increased spectacularly on the back of a weaker domestic currency. Prices for South African gold mining stocks were soaring.

Two days later, police raided the home of Ronnie Watson, accompanied, according to Brett Kebble, by Mark Pinnington – who had served on DRD's special committee – and Kerrie Velosa from Deloitte & Touche auditors. The search warrant was later overturned due to a lack of a proper foundation in the application and apparent irregularities during the search. The return of seized documents was ordered.

Suddenly, the Kebbles were under siege. On 6 December, they were charged, along with Buitendag, with fraud related to the proposed acquisition by Western Areas of various stocks, including Randfontein.

The GER story took on a life of its own. On 20 February 2003, the Kebbles obtained an Anton Pillar* order against DRD and various other parties. Execution took place later in the day at the premises of DRD and Deloitte & Touche, Wellesley-Wood's home and the premises and/or homes of other respondents. According to Brett Kebble, the Anton Pillar order was subsequently overturned 'on an execution technicality'. The facts indicate otherwise.

On 17 April, DRD, Wellesley-Wood and Deloitte & Touche succeeded in having the Anton Pillar order set aside. The Kebbles and others were ordered to pay the legal costs incurred by DRD and Wellesley-Wood.

Afterwards, Wellesley-Wood explained: 'In the application for the Anton Pillar order, it was not disclosed that the applicants [the Kebbles] were being sued by DRD both in South Africa and Australia. Anton Pillar orders are granted for the search and confiscation of certain specified documents; in this instance, bank records and cellphone statements belonging to Roger Kebble that DRD was alleged to have obtained illegally. No such documents were found during the execution of the

---

* A special order obtained in secret, without the respondents being heard. It authorises the search and seizure of certain specified documents.

order, but others relating to DRD's litigation against the applicants, as well as my personal documents, were seized.'

All seized documents changed hands yet again.

On 20 May, the Kebbles issued summons against DRD, Wellesley-Wood and AIN for R1 million each in damages. The claim was based on allegations that AIN was hired to invade the Kebbles' privacy by obtaining personal information about them and to cause them embarrassment and commercial harm. The Kebbles were also seeking R10 million in punitive damages from DRD and AIN.

On 16 June, DRD confirmed a break-in at its corporate offices in Johannesburg the night before. In an official statement, DRD said two security officers on duty had been held up at gunpoint and pistol-whipped and had to be admitted to hospital. The intruders used angle grinders and jackhammers to gain access to the company's strong room and removed various company documents, 'but nothing of monetary value'.

On 24 June, former judge Willem Heath, one of the specialists on the Kebble payroll, completed an investigation into the circumstances surrounding Roger's arrest. According to Brett, Heath found 'conclusive and irrefutable evidence of bribery and corruption of SAPS officers' and that AIN had gained access to information by illegal means, then resorted to bribery in order to have a police docket opened against Roger.

It was stinky stuff.

AIN's Goldblatt, who dismissed Brett as 'living in cloud-cuckoo-land', laughed off these and similar allegations on numerous occasions. As was to be expected, DRD also scoffed at the accusations.

On 30 June, Gobodo Investigative and Forensic Auditing, commissioned by the Kebbles to probe Skilled Labour Brokers cc, the third party involved in transactions between DRD and GER, and of which Roger was the sole member, found 'no evidence of fraudulent practices'.

On 9 September, DRD announced that KPMG, the company's auditors, had rejected claims by Gobodo that DRD was 'in all likelihood commercially insolvent'. In a letter to Wellesley-Wood, KPMG director Ian Kramer wrote:

> We have had an opportunity to examine the … [Gobodo] affidavit and the assertions therein regarding the ability of Durban Roodepoort Deep … to meet its obligations to its creditors and we respectfully disagree with its conclusions. In our view as auditors of DRD who have recently concluded its annual review, DRD was a going concern as at 30 June 2003, and was in a position to discharge its obligations to its current creditors at that date, hence we had no difficulty in issuing an unqualified audit opinion on its financial statements for the year ended 30 June 2003.

According to Wellesley-Wood, the Gobodo affidavit was commissioned by the Kebble family and publicised in order to raise questions about DRD's ability to fund legal action for the recovery from various parties of misappropriated funds.

'While we have been in no doubt about the soundness of DRD's financial position,' said Wellesley-Wood, 'it is pleasing to have independent, third party confirmation of this even before Investec's rapid placement of 18 million DRD shares, from which we have successfully raised $43 million. The Gobodo affidavit, contrary to impressions created in the public domain, was in no way a forensic exercise; it contains assumptions, based on published information, with which we strongly disagree and goes on to make further erroneous assumptions about the implications for the company's future solvency of current and pending litigation. Yet another attempt to derail the DRD board's efforts to recover shareholders' funds through the courts has failed, and we will press on.'

Roger, who naturally enough protested total innocence, wanted his day in court. As it turned out, he had several.

- On 13 November, his application for amendment of bail conditions was postponed to 3 March 2003.
- On 24 January 2003, he appeared again in the Johannesburg Magistrate's Court and the case was postponed to 3 March.
- On 3 March, the matter was postponed to 12 May.
- On 17 March, Roger sought a further amendment to his bail conditions regarding his passport. The matter was postponed to 22 July.
- On 12 May, the case was postponed to 22 July.
- On 22 July, Roger applied to have his case struck off the roll on the grounds of unreasonable delay. The matter was postponed to 25 July.
- On 25 July, the State assured the court that its investigation against Roger was complete, but requested time to discuss certain aspects with the forensic auditors. The case was postponed to 28 July.
- On 28 July, the regional magistrate warned the prosecutor that failure to produce a charge sheet against the accused within 30 days could see the case being struck from the roll. The matter was postponed to 28 August.
- On 28 August, the State duly produced a charge sheet, and 2 February 2004 was provisionally set as the date for the trial to start.
- On 20 January 2004, Roger again sought an amendment of bail conditions and the State countered by applying for his bail to be withdrawn. The case was postponed to 4 March so that the relevant affidavits could be filed, and Roger's bail was extended.
- On 4 March, Roger again asked the court to strike the case from the roll due to

unreasonable delay. On 31 October, the State had disclosed its intention to consult with further witnesses and possibly amend the charge sheet to include the period July 1996 to June 1998. The case was postponed to 30 June.

- On 30 June, Roger's bail conditions were again extended and the matter was set down for trial on 10 January 2005.
- On 10 January, the case was postponed to 19 January so that the State could consider the merits.
- On 19 January, the magistrate refused the State's application for a further postponement and the case against Roger Kebble was struck from the roll.

The GER case was all over. It came as a shock to opponents of the Kebbles who were familiar with the case and had regarded it as open and shut. The failure of South Africa's law enforcement authorities to put together a viable case over a period of more than two years on a relatively simple matter such as GER goes a long way to explaining why the complex, sophisticated and multi-tiered Rawas affair never even got as far as a criminal indictment.

By the end of 2005, the civil cases involving Rawas in both South Africa and Australia had not yet gone to court.

At corporate level, Wellesley-Wood had stood up to the Kebbles and their hired help and emerged victorious, but Brett's untimely death put paid to any chance that he would be brought to justice. As 2006 dawned, Roger's fate lay in the hands of his lawyers and the notoriously slow turning of judicial wheels in South Africa's overburdened courts.

PART VI

The slush funds

17

Scam of the century

F OR ALL HIS apparent loyalty to gold, Brett Kebble was a man of paper, a man dragged by his paper creations into a vortex of debt. How differently things might have turned out had he stuck to gold, a quiet life in the suburbs and a modicum of recognition.

The creation of Kebble's huge and fragile pits of vapour started as early as 30 June 1997, when a JSE-listed entity, New Kleinfontein Properties (NK Props), issued 244 million shares to Consolidated Mining Corporation (CMC).* This transaction, with its dramatic provenance, was the toxic fountainhead that would taint every moment of Kebble's business career.

The shares were issued at 600 cents each, computing to a value of R1.5 billion. For one brief shining moment, due to a single transaction that rates as the biggest South African confidence trick of the twentieth century, Brett Kebble was a paper billionaire.

This was a defining deal for Kebble for other reasons as well. NK Props would soon change its name to Consolidated African Mines (CAM) and later morph into JCI Ltd, to be listed under the JSE code of 'JCD', as opposed to the original JCI, which carried the eponymous 'JCI' code. The 1997 transaction not only allowed Kebble to hijack the original JCI, but also marked the start of his full-time and flagrant abuse of investor cash through slush funds.

There is no easy definition for a slush fund, but it may be seen as the financial equivalent of guerrilla warfare waged by an entire army division.

There was already huge mischief behind the 1997 transaction. During 1996, Kebble had added many millions of rand to his personal wealth as a member of the cabal of directors at Randgold & Exploration who had talked up the company's stock price. This phenomenon, in turn, surfed on the bubbles whipped up around Randgold & Exploration subsidiary Randgold Resources, which for its part had surged on the rising tide of the Bre-X apocalypse. In March 1997, global markets had the first hint of what would eventually crystallise into the incontrovertible truth that Bre-X's Busang deposit in Indonesia was an utter fraud. Gold stocks, and especially so-called juniors and exploration stocks, tanked. Randgold Resources was battered after its listing in London, dragging Randgold & Exploration's stock

---

*   See Appendix H, item 7.

price down by around 90 per cent from its 1997 high. By this time, of course, Kebble had taken his money and run. Riding solo and in total control so as to avoid sharing his ill-gotten gains with anyone, he was conducting the series of transactions that allowed him to hijack JCI.

Kebble had sold his Randgold & Exploration shares to CMC, a company also listed on the JSE and one that he already secretly controlled. In this manner, Kebble listed his own little fortune, which he had made within months. The technique, known as a reverse listing, is hardly rare and is referred to by some investors as the materialisation of an asset. Essentially, a listed vehicle is used to execute the business model that its originators had in mind. In Kebble's case, instead of holding stock in Randgold & Exploration, he held stock in CMC, which in turn held stock in Kebble's original Randgold & Exploration holding.

These early career moves graphically illustrate Kebble's obsession with control. He didn't control Randgold & Exploration, but he secretly controlled CMC and NK Props. When NK Props issued shares to CMC, Kebble was simply issuing shares to himself.

Showing utter contempt for rules of corporate governance, and even greater disdain for the fiduciary duty of directors, with flagrant disregard for conflict of interest, NK Props bought CMC from Kebble for R1.5 billion. It was a paper transaction from start to finish. Nothing was done about Kebble issuing shares to himself, and it is likely that nothing ever will be. There is no evidence that anyone else had the vaguest idea of what was going on at the time, and given the chaos generated by the collapse of the original JCI in the midst of a slumping gold price, this is hardly surprising. There were keen, if not desperate, sellers of the original JCI, and in the early stage of Kebble's Roman candle career, he carried the highest tag of credibility he was ever to enjoy. Some sellers might even have regarded him as a momentary paragon of business beauty.

Kebble's strategy was premised on the simple sales pitch of rescuing the original backers of the sale by Anglo American and De Beers of a controlling stake in the old JCI to the African Mining Group (AMG). It had been marketed as one of the biggest BEE deals during a period when chaos allowed Kebble to deploy his talents as a scam artist to a degree that he would never exceed or even equal. To confuse the issue just a little more, there was yet another unlisted entity involved – BNC Investments, which supposedly controlled the Kebble 'family fortune', though in reality it appears to have been of no consequence.

Ownership of 244 million shares in the new JCI gave Kebble close to 50 per cent control. Furthermore, in the space of about 12 months, Kebble's apparent value had grown from little more than zero to R1.5 billion, at least on paper. Apart from the early use of slush funds, the June 1997 deal was classic Kebble in that it involved the vending of totally overvalued shares – in this case in NK Props – with Kebble as the beneficiary. The deal was rare to the extent that buyers of the overvalued shares would normally have been found among the broad investment fraternity, as was the case when Randgold Resources listed in London around the same time. In the NK Props deal, however, Kebble was on both sides and no cash changed hands. In other deals involving outside parties, Kebble would look to mop up cash, not paper. In his truly amazing Walter Mitty world, Kebble owed nobody, and the rest of the world owed him cash.

The general financial climate at the time unquestionably contributed to Kebble being able to successfully stage such a monumental con. Apart from exploiting the market chaos as the gold price tanked, Kebble leveraged every possible detail to his advantage. He networked to maximum effect. He fronted the suspect transaction by enticing a number of important names to the board of what would become the new JCI. The chairman was no less than Mzi Khumalo, head of AMG and boss of the newly acquired old JCI, the very entity that Kebble was hijacking.

Directors of NK Props included John WG Mackenzie, Alan Bruce McKerron (from the Anglo American stable), Ronald Kort Netolitzky and Jens Eskelund Hansen (both Canadian). Kebble was the CEO, of course, flanked by his faithful second fiddles: Hennie Buitendag, Roger Kebble and Paul Ferguson. Within a year of securing control of the new JCI, Kebble had booted out all the unsuspecting front men he had used for his successful corporate coup, leaving the field clear for even more of his cronies to take their seats in the boardroom.

John Stratton became a director in 1998, and Charles Cornwall replaced Ferguson in 2001. From then on, JCI's board members and Kebble's inner circle were one and the same. His father, Buitendag, Stratton and Cornwall allowed Kebble to do exactly what he wanted, when he wanted and how he wanted. As long as he was not caught out, Kebble could run the new JCI as if it were his personal *salon privé*, and Buitendag's creative financial engineering ensured that the books would always balance. It was he who kept the auditors happy.

A major consequence of Kebble issuing JCI shares worth R1.5 billion to himself was that the new JCI acquired CMC, which would be used as one of his prime slush funds. CMC was delisted shortly after acquisition, and its accounts effectively disappeared from the public domain. They could be accessed only after considerable effort by the relevant authorities in Pretoria.

As the meagre cash flows available to Kebble deteriorated, he increasingly expanded his slush fund franchise. During 1999, he acquired Consolidated Mining Management Services (CMMS), the second big slush fund under the JCI umbrella.

The third one was acquired early in 2002, when Kebble used JCI to buy out the minorities in JCI Gold.* The company's rate of debt growth had been completely unsustainable, and by assuming control Kebble could again effectively conceal the accounts from public scrutiny. JCI Gold was the remaining relic from the disembowelled old JCI and, like CMC, was delisted from the JSE.

CMMS, a 98 per cent JCI subsidiary, was never listed and would become the single most important Kebble slush fund, but both CMC and JCI Gold played useful roles in concealing what was really going on. The key directors of the slush funds were the trusted triumvirate of Kebble's father, Buitendag and Stratton.

Among those who knew Kebble, some say that if he ever had a real friend, it was Stratton. The wily British-born Australian, an indefatigable worker, was a major generator of ideas for Kebble and was often at the very core of convoluted schemes such as Rawas. No longer a young man when Kebble met him in the mid-1990s, Stratton was a retired military intelligence operative, bright but not brilliant. While a number of people would rather not do business with Stratton, he is known to have introduced Kebble to various individuals who were not only shadowy, but quite likely on the wrong side of the law. Those who gather information for a living take it from whence it comes, and secrets are not always shared in the rarified surrounds of gentlemen's clubs.

Kebble used CMMS, in particular, to buy properties, mostly ultra-luxurious, including what appears to be an orchid farm. However, CMMS was also the vehicle for a number of other activities that had little, if anything, to do with mining, such as share trading. The 2003 accounts reflect a profit of R14 million for 'jobbing', an activity synonymous with chancing, risking, hazarding, adventuring and gambling. As part of jobbing the stock market, Kebble indulged in one of his favourite bad habits, scrip borrowing, a tactic specifically designed to confuse friend and foe alike. The CMMS accounts show that the entity borrowed Western Areas shares worth R115 million under the heading 'contingent liabilities'. Kebble also borrowed stock in JCI, JCI Gold, Randgold & Exploration and CMC.

By the end of 2004, CMMS controlled 85 companies† with widely differing interests, ranging from diamond concessions in Angola to luxury properties in Cape Town's Clifton, and from trading and investment entities (such as Quick Leap Investments 137) to numerous BEE vehicles, including JSE-listed Matodzi. Old and familiar names such as Transvaal Gold Mining Estates, first registered in 1895, appeared alongside Simmer and Jack Mines, Sabie Mines, Stilfontein Gold Mining, DAB Securities, Tavlands, Samada Diamonds, Continental Base Metal

---

*   See Appendix H, item 26.

†   See Appendix A.

Mining, Lindum Reefs Gold, Palfinger SA, First Westgold Mining and Randgold & Exploration. From 1999, when Kebble took control of CMMS, the weird stuff started rolling in: New Adventure Shelf 114, Onshelf Property 74, Defacto Investments 33, Castle Ultra Trading 295, Rapitrade 306, Clifton Dunes Investments 67 and Little Swift Investments 133.

In the months following his murder in September 2005, various attempts were made to compile a comprehensive list of properties connected with Kebble. Some estimates put the number at 30 or more, with several being put on the market in the period immediately before his death.

Whatever the final analysis of Kebble's property portfolio, no one would dispute that in his guise as land baron, he honoured the realtor's mantra: location, location, location. In Johannesburg, suburbs such as Melrose, Bryanston, Illovo and Inanda got the nod, while Cape Town's 'old money' enclave of Bishopscourt was favoured. In addition to Monterey, Kebble's corporate seat in the south, there were properties in Canterbury Drive, Primrose Terrace, Rhodes Drive and Klaassens Road. In addition, Kebble had bought more than a dozen vacant plots at Stonehurst, a gated estate near the exclusive Steenberg golf estate in Tokai.

As proof that Kebble used slush funds for every kind of deal imaginable, however, Kirstenberry Lodge is a good example. This super-prime property – in Bishopscourt, again – comprises a package of adjoining erven overlooking Kirstenbosch Botanical Gardens, with the manor house a magnificent centrepiece. Andrew Golding, CEO of Pam Golding Properties, a prominent real estate agency, confirmed that Kirstenberry – acquired via funding from CMMS – was 'a Kebble property'. It was placed on the market in late 2005, and according to Golding, if sold as a package in a single transaction, would fetch up to R30 million.

CMMS allowed Kebble to hold sway over companies in ways that did not necessarily require a shareholding at all, a technique known as 'statutory control'. This saw CMMS act as secretary and/or administrator and/or manager of a captured entity. Once a company fell under the CMMS umbrella, all material ingoing and outgoing transactions would be subject to Kebble's authority. The structure allowed him access to intimate knowledge of companies sheltered by CMMS. Thus, in 2004, CMMS registered and bought under its control an entity named Sello Mashao Rasethaba Associates, for reasons that can only arouse suspicion. When it came to his BEE connections, Kebble had no intellectual, mental or emotional investment in the men and women he used as fronts.

Rasethaba was CEO of Matodzi, Kebble's 'leading' BEE company, where, of course, the finance director was Buitendag. Though he boasted that JCI held no shares in Matodzi and that Matodzi was black-controlled, Kebble in fact controlled it in just about every possible sense. CMMS had also controlled Matodzi Management Advisory since 1996.

Among many other entities under CMMS control were Koketso Capital (which apparently had a 24 per cent interest in the Luxinge alluvial diamond mining concession in Angola's Lunda Norte province); Masupatsela Angola Mining Ventures (which held a 20 per cent interest in the Dando Kwanza alluvial diamond prospecting concession in Angola's Bie province); Tlotlisa Financial Services, and Orlyfunt Financial Enterprises and Orlyfunt Strategic Investments.

In a number of cases, Kebble did in fact control shareholdings of various sizes in companies falling under CMMS, as in the case of Randgold & Exploration.

In November 2004, CMMS was officially pushed into a deregistration process by the companies office in Pretoria after Kebble failed to sign its accounts for the year to 31 March. During the latter accounting period in particular, he had been dumping controlled entities into CMMS at an unprecedented rate. When Kebble was ousted as CEO of JCI on 31 August 2005, JCI's new directors pulled CMMS back from deregistration and lodged the 2004 accounts, signed by Buitendag. Kebble had been toting them around in his briefcase for months, but never signed off on them.

The fundamental problem with CMMS was that control and complexity do not automatically produce cash, just as money does not grow on trees, no matter who owns them. Beyond CMMS, CMC and JCI Gold, the uneasy truth of the overall matter is that, under Kebble, JCI itself was a gigantic slush fund.

A thorough forensic examination and analysis of the JCI group accounts from 1997, including deconsolidation and reconstruction of the accounts, revealed that JCI had posted total losses of R792 million* from 1997 to 2004. This is simply staggering, given that at no time during this entire period did JCI have any form of normalised income. Its two biggest investments, in listed stocks Western Areas and Randgold & Exploration, controlled by either Kebble or his father from 1997, never paid dividends in the normal sense.

Just how did Kebble survive for so long with nothing in the way of normalised income? Quite simply, he forced companies under family control into various cash-raising transactions. JCI was the natural centre of gravity, given that it represented Kebble's single biggest equity interest in the 244 million shares he acquired in 1997, but Western Areas and Randgold & Exploration were tapped as well. In November 1998, Western Areas sold half of South Deep for $235 million in cash, allowing payment of a special dividend of which more than 30 per cent went to JCI. In July 2000, the Kebbles forced Randgold Resources to sell half of Morila for $132 million in cash. The bulk of this money found its way back into Kebble hands through a

---

* See Appendix C, item 13.

Randgold Resources share buy-back that generated a significant cash flow to its technical parent, Randgold & Exploration.[*]

In February 2002, Kebble sold the South Deep derivatives or hedge book for $104 million in cash. It proved to be one of the most toxic hedge books in the history of mining, given Kebble's forlornly incorrect guesses as to forward movements in the gold price. The hedge book showed Kebble to be a clear bear of the gold price, when in fact it was in the early stages of a robust bull market that would last for years. For one whose career, cash flows and future depended so heavily on the price of gold, in this deal at least, Kebble appeared to have little (if any) faith in the notion that the gold price would ever recover. While JCI possessed no normalised income, it managed to stagger along on the basis of ad hoc receipts from transactions that Kebble forced through the market. But after the sale of the South Deep hedge book, he ran out of options.

Sweltering under his own flawed delusions, Kebble was forced to fritter about, blowing his off-key clarion, moving from one rats-and-mice deal to the next, concocting one irregular transaction after another. The virtuoso moved into a *jejune* phase of his business career, seemingly determined to prove that when measured as a conventional businessman, he was a complete and utter disaster. He remained the control freak of old as CEO of the three JSE-listed stocks at the core of his falling empire: Western Areas, Randgold & Exploration and JCI. Western Areas continued to gobble cash; the sinking of the deep level twin sub-vertical shaft system at South Deep, started in 1995, was years away from completion, and would indeed remain unfinished when Kebble was ejected from all three companies on 31 August 2005.

After selling the South Deep hedge book, Kebble and his spin machine soldiered on, trampling the detritus that spread in every direction wherever he appeared. On 31 March 2003, when JCI held 35 per cent of Western Areas and 28 per cent of Randgold & Exploration, he boasted that the company was 'widely recognised as owning two of the world's premier gold assets'. Not to split hairs, but JCI 'owned' neither Western Areas nor Randgold & Exploration. Apart from the fact that it actually held less than 50 per cent of either of these entities, JCI had been nothing more or less than a slush fund for years, with nothing in the way of operations or in-house staff doing real jobs. The company had relinquished its day-to-day managerial role in Western Areas when half of South Deep was sold to Placer Dome in 1998. The biggest single element of value in Randgold & Exploration had been Randgold Resources, which had nominally enjoyed managerial independence since 1995 under CEO Mark Bristow. However, though Morila was making money,

---

[*]   See Appendix M, item 12.

AngloGold was managing it, and when Bristow was not reconstructing the history of Randgold Resources, he, like Kebble, had time to spare.

In 2003, as part of Kebble's never-ending hunt for cash, Randgold & Exploration sold a further 2.5 million shares in Randgold Resources, reducing its stake in the London and Nasdaq-listed company from 48 per cent to 43 per cent. The proceeds were used to 'fund new projects' for Randgold & Exploration and, inevitably, to 'repay indebtedness'. In June, Randgold & Exploration sold one million Randgold Resources shares for $16 million. Part of the cash was used to repay a loan from Absa Bank, while an outstanding $3.7 million loan from CMMS and a loan of $1 million from Western Areas were also settled. At least these stock sales were filed with the Securities Exchange Commission in Washington DC, though in hindsight they appear to have been dry runs made by Kebble in preparation for the truly stinky stuff that lay ahead.

By the time Kebble sold the South Deep hedge book, he had been reduced to an isolated figure in the corporate community. No longer could he call on the top names in town, be they investment bankers, bankers, stockbrokers, lawyers, auditors or other professionals. The Kebble name had been tainted beyond repair, and the shift boss's son spent most of his time and energy attacking law enforcement agents or attempting to structure BEE transactions. He had little choice regarding the latter, given legal requirements that portions of mining companies had to be sold to qualified BEE entities within specific time frames.

Ironically, the metal and commodities price environment had been favourable for some time. South African resource stocks had benefited from a weak rand in 2001, and while the currency strengthened from an all-time low to the dollar in December of that year, dollar metal and commodity prices then turned positive. By 2003, the country's mining and resource fortunes were well on the mend. The cocktail served up by global investment markets was dominated by a dollar that entered a protracted bear market early in 2002. In addition, there was increasing information of a more fundamental nature in the shape of fabulously performing emerging economies, led by China, with its voracious appetite for raw materials of all kinds.

Investors were drawn once again to South African stocks. As the US Geological Survey noted, after more than 30 years of a progressive decline in gold production, from the historical peak of 989 tons in 1970 to 395 tons in 2001, the situation in South Africa started turning around when production increased to 398 tons in 2002. With a combined capital investment of more than $1.6 billion, three large projects – Target (Avgold), South Deep (Western Areas and Placer Dome) and Moab Khotsong (AngloGold) – came on stream in 2002 and 2003, adding about 30 tons to production capacity by 2003 and another 25 tons by 2007.

SCAM OF THE CENTURY

Mines were becoming popular again, and Harmony CEO Bernard Swanepoel, a mining engineer with a dry sense of humour, was pumping out the kind of action that shareholders wanted. During 2003, Harmony merged with Patrice Motsepe's African Rainbow Minerals Gold, and subsequently acquired Avgold and its Target Mine from Anglovaal Mining. AngloGold continued to develop Moab Khotsong, and was involved in deepening the Mponeng shaft, the TauTona sub-120 metre level project, the TauTona extension project and developing the TauTona Ventersdorp Contact Reef. The company also announced a proposed merger with Ashanti Goldfields of Ghana, prompting a bizarre hint from Kebble that he might mount a counter-bid for Ashanti. Bristow launched an equally unlikely initiative, which somehow developed into a more formal process. Having apparently suffered permanent amnesia about Syama, Bristow seemed oblivious to the delicate fact that AngloGold was managing Morila, the only operating mine in the Randgold Resources stable. So there was Randgold Resources, a non-operator of gold mines, making a bid for Ashanti, including its prize asset, Obuasi, the most complicated gold mine in the world from both a technical and a social viewpoint.

Beyond the Ashanti lark, 2003 saw Kebble wandering around aimlessly. He could do nothing that remained standing. His pack of cards – CAM paper that had been turned into JCI paper – was faded and dog-eared. He bore the look of a battered, feral pool player in a run-down bar at Hotazel. What transactions he could structure and conclude were inevitably small and, upon close examination, emitted a bad odour.

As he sank steadily into deeper sloughs of despondency, Kebble maintained a public devotion to gold, but privately nurtured his ambition of becoming a serious player in African diamonds. On 30 December 2003, Randgold & Exploration entered into a loan agreement with Masupatsela Investment Holdings (MIH). As security for a loan of $11.9 million, MIH pledged 104 million ordinary shares of – surprise, surprise – JCI Ltd. The loan enabled Randgold & Exploration 'to continue to strengthen our relationships with black empowerment companies'. Right.

When the loan had not been settled by 30 June 2004, the final date for repayment was 'verbally' extended to 31 December. Who knows what happened next?

These deals were doubtless related to an agreement between Randgold & Exploration and Masupatsela Angola Mining Ventures (Pty) Ltd. In exchange for 1 492 000 of its ordinary shares,* Randgold & Exploration acquired – or so it was claimed – a 20 per cent interest in the Dando Kwanza alluvial prospecting concession in central Angola's Bie province. It was paper, again.

---

*   See Appendix K, item 11.

On 23 December 2003, Randgold & Exploration entered into an agreement with Kemonshey Holdings, in terms of which a scrip loan dating back to 28 March 2002 was settled through the transfer of 3.3 million ordinary shares in Western Areas. On 6 June 2003, Randgold & Exploration had sold 952 481 Randgold Resources shares to Kemonshey, a company incorporated and carrying on business in accordance with the company laws of Gibraltar.

Kemonshey was no doubt one hell of a thing.

The year also brought pathetic news about Syama, the junk gold mine that formed the rotten substratum of Kebble's house of cards. On 16 April, Randgold Resources and Resolute Mining Ltd, of Australia, agreed that Resolute would be given a 12-month option to buy Randgold Resources' entire interest in Somisy for $6 million. Somisy, of course, owned 80 per cent of the Syama mine in Mali, which had been on care and maintenance since December 2001. Yes, this was the same Syama that Kebble and his cronies had used to bloat the Randgold & Exploration stock price to all-time records in early 1997; the very Syama that Peter Flack and his merry band of geniuses had 'paid' more than $80 million for in October 1996; the refulgent Syama that the cabal had burked of all criticism.

The 'new' JCI had finally been formed on 16 July 2002 with the merger of JCI Gold Ltd and CAM. According to Kebble: 'An important consequence of the restructuring process has been to broaden the group's status as a prime holding company and establish itself as a prominent, specialised resource finance house, focused on developing relationships with emerging companies and investing in opportunities in South Africa and the African continent.

'Key to the process has been, and will continue to be, the company's major strategic drivers: to build on existing partnerships, focus on cost efficiencies and increased profitability, effect appropriate exit strategies and consolidate and enhance the company's role as the capital partner of choice in black empowerment initiatives, thereby contributing materially to the economic and social development of the country and continent.'

Right.

JCI, Kebble crowed in rhetoric riposte to growing numbers of cynical investors, owned 'a portfolio of quality, wealth-creating investments'. During 2003, in a further clean-up of Kebble wreckage, Barnato Exploration (Barnex) became a wholly owned JCI subsidiary and, after a scheme of arrangement, was delisted from the JSE on 30 September. Barnex's major asset consisted of shares in Golden Star Resources Ltd.

Amid the myriad woes that marked 2003, the cash-desperate Kebble was forced to hint that a rights issue would be required to continue the funding of Western Areas' interests in South Deep, where development was running behind schedule.

On 5 February 2004, Western Areas announced a rights offer to raise around R400 million.* JCI, which held 35.6 per cent of Western Areas, said it would follow its rights, as would Randgold & Exploration, with its stake of 3.8 per cent. Cape Town money manager Allan Gray, 'acting on behalf of their clients' holding in the company of 24.5 per cent', elected to do the same. Among the serious money men there are those who observe wryly that Allan Gray, generally characterised as a 'value' investor, focuses a little too heavily on value *per se*. Be that as it may, the money manager had seen the ultra-long-term value in Western Areas, and had decided to invest, period.

In a further mopping-up move, Rand Leases Properties became a subsidiary of JCI when shareholders approved a scheme of arrangement. Delisting from the JSE† followed on 17 February 2004.

Beyond these forced transactions, designed to clean up a rotting corporate structure that was sinking into a fetid morass, JCI announced that Matodzi, 'a BEE company listed on the JSE' (but controlled, of course, by Kebble) 'acquired an additional 126 million JCI shares from Anglo South Africa Capital (Pty) Ltd on 29 August 2003, increasing Matodzi's effective holding to 10 per cent of the issued share capital of JCI'.

Like just about any other Kebble deal that required cash, this one was disastrous. Matodzi announced that ownership of the JCI shares 'would pass on payment of the full purchase price. Anglo [American] has granted the company an indulgence, and an amount of R15.5 million was paid on 4 July 2003. The balance of the purchase price, together with interest, is due by 29 August 2003.'

Two years later, in August 2005, Matodzi announced that 'a loan agreement was concluded between Investec Bank, JCI Ltd and Letšeng Investment Holdings South Africa, whereby Letšeng lent an amount of R75 million to Matodzi'. These funds, Matodzi explained, would be used to settle a R68.7 million liability 'relating to the acquisition of 126 million JCI shares'.

At least part of Letšeng, Matodzi's only visible operating asset, was cast into the dungeon for debtors. In the civilised world, such mercantile manoeuvres are known as cannibalisation. Kebble was forcing one company that he controlled (Matodzi) to acquire shares in another company under his control – JCI, the mother ship of his alien antics. But JCI's stock price, which had been in decline since inception in 1997, continued to tumble. Matodzi was being used as a cannibal, but the prey was getting smaller and smaller. Kebble, on the other hand, a lavish R5 million-a-month spending habit already firmly entrenched, was getting bigger and bigger,

---

*   See Appendix L, items 5–12.

†   See Appendix H, item 33.

as if overindulgence would somehow bring relief from the multiple business crises he faced.

Like a goose stuffed silly for a harvest of liver pâté, tumescent debt remained the defining characteristic of a heavily dilated Kebble. When he staged his last big bid to raise cash, the sale of the Western Areas hedge book in 2002, he had already started hiding debt off JCI's balance sheet. Try as he might to conjure up mighty illusions with his underlying slush funds – CMMS, CMC and JCI Gold – Kebble was required by law to consolidate accounts into JCI, the tip of the pyramid. It was the horrifying and rising levels of group debt that forced him to secrete it; measures such as taking out and delisting JCI Gold were simply no longer adequate.

In the beginning, the amount that Kebble stashed off the JCI books was a fairly modest R135 million. Over the next two years, it increased to a still manageable R163 million in 2003, but then it veritably exploded, to an incredible R1.3 billion in 2004.*

Naturally enough, if JCI was hiding debt from the investing public, it was also reflecting some debt on the balance sheet. That figure was R1.6 billion in 2004.

Add the 'official' debt to the latent amount, and the once venerable mining house of JCI, which had started out as a 'new' entity in 1997 owing not a *sou* or a *centime*, was in the red to the tune of a cool R2.9 billion when Kebble awakened on the morning of 31 March 2004 – the last day of JCI's financial year.

Accumulated losses ran to R792 million. It was an impossible situation, but for the while, at least, Kebble successfully kept investors utterly confused and, far more importantly, apparently managed to keep JCI's bankers at bay. When Kebble was criticised over the lack of cash flows or levels of debt in his so-called empire, he would harangue the critic. In later years, Dominic Ntsele, Kebble's front-line quietus lobbyist, would react with celerity and tell critics that their negativity was damaging some of the country's most imaginative and important BEE deals.

Right.

It is hardly possible to fully dramatise just how fragile Kebble's kingdom was, whether in 1997 or any other year. Scrutiny of the CMMS accounts shows that it was irredeemably bankrupt from the moment that Kebble acquired it in 1999. From day one, CMMS had negative equity, something that is simply unheard of, either standing still or going forward, for any normal going concern. On 31 March 2004, CMMS had negative equity of R584 million.† It enjoyed a R468 million loan from its ultimate holding company, JCI, that was 'unsecured and interest free' and had no fixed terms of repayment. There are probably few people who would not jump

---

*   See Appendix E, item 19.

†   See Appendix J, item 15.

at the chance of loans worth hundreds of millions of rand that require no security, bear no interest and can apparently be repaid at the borrower's convenience, if indeed at all.

Such financial shenanigans were a common thread running through all the alchemy of Kebble's witchcraft, but a freeloading loan like this could conceivably have pushed demons and wizards to levels never known before or since. JCI's auditors throughout the relevant period, Charles Orbach & Company, could well argue that the accounts of JCI and its subsidiaries complied with all the technical rules that auditors are expected to apply, but there can be no question that the economic substance of JCI's accounts was unmitigated trash. Had they been presented on a see-through basis, as in the various appendixes to this book, JCI would have been stampeded by entire kennels of fiduciary watchdogs, including the SA Institute of Chartered Accountants, the Public Accountants' and Auditors' Board, the JSE (which, ironically, has a special committee to monitor accounts), the Financial Services Board and the full gamut of law enforcement agencies. The overweening naivety of these various oversight entities will remain both unthinkable and unpalatable, since history already shows that CMMS passed all apparent tests of approval.

For years, the CMMS accounts contained various 'warnings' from its auditors. The most significant among a number of factors regarding the ability of CMMS to continue as a 'going concern', said the auditors, was that 'the members continue to procure funding for the ongoing operations' of the entity. In traditional corporate finance parlance, CMMS can best be described as a special purpose vehicle (SPV), a generic entity that became world famous when Enron, once a Houston-based energy conglomerate, imploded in December 2001. The business and related objectives of CMMS were far from clear; its accounts stated that it 'operates in the fields of management and finance and also holds investments in management and finance companies and a farming enterprise'. Mining is not mentioned. According to the accounts, the CMMS holding company was CMC, with JCI as the ultimate holding company. These are all hallmarks of a slush fund, from the inexcusable complexity to the stretching of truth in every direction.

One might well ask what happened to JCI's declared accumulated losses of R792 million. Well, R459 million went the way of 'finance costs', indicating both the lengths to which Kebble was prepared to go in order to fund his fantasies and the extent to which he created cash flow pressures from the outset. It was one thing to seize control of assets in a clandestine manner, as he did in 1997, but generating free cash was another matter entirely. There was always going to be a problem when the chickens – millions of them – came home to roost.

Even after paying finance costs of R459 million between 1997 and 2004, JCI showed a 'loss' of R333 million. In the latter phase of his so-called business career, Kebble needed vast sums of money to 'stand still'. He plundered the companies he controlled to finance egregious personal spending habits, including those of his cronies. In the 2004 financial year, JCI's 'staff costs, consulting and directors' fees' were a massive R116 million, almost double the R60 million paid the year before.

A good deal of the new JCI's original debt was raised by Kebble to finance his personal acquisition of 244 million shares in the company, but it was the shareholders of a listed entity that carried the burden. If Kebble's landmark 1997 deal, which saw him effectively issue shares worth R1.5 billion to himself, was tainted, then both the debt created in the process and the interest paid on it, must be equally toxic. To label this as *JCI's* debt is nonsense; it was *Kebble's debt.*

Immediately after the 1997 deal, the debt stood at R466 million. Seven years later, it had ballooned to R1.6 billion, with another R1.3 billion tucked away in Kebble's version of Pandora's Box. When he swapped his shares in CMC for shares in NK Props, the new JCI acquired 100 per cent of CMC, and all its debt, allowing Kebble to walk away with 244 million shares and a controlling stake in a listed company, leaving JCI with debt of R2.9 billion in 2004.*

The scam of the century was a *fait accompli.*

From the date of inception, the 'new' JCI was never an operating company in the normal sense. It held just the two key investments that Kebble so fondly referred to as 'ownership'. Someone definitely needed to teach Kebble a thing or two about ownership, especially ownership of cash. Ironically, such lessons would come from the very man he ripped off royally in 1997.

---

* See Appendix E, items 16 and 17.

18

The laughing Zulu

ACCORDING TO YEARS of accounts for Brett Kebble's most important slush fund, Mzi Khumalo Enterprises 'owed' Consolidated Mining Management Services (CMMS), a 98 per cent subsidiary of JCI Ltd, R30 million. It wasn't enough that Kebble had hijacked the new JCI in mid-1997, he also raised a debt against Khumalo, the very man chosen as the BEE executive of choice to run the old JCI. In one of South Africa's earliest and biggest BEE transactions, Khumalo had led the African Mining Group (AMG) in its successful bid for the company at the end of November 1996, becoming the first black to gain control of a legendary South African mining house.

Kebble inveigled his way into the transaction by offering to fund Khumalo's personal stake, but, in fact, he used Khumalo as a front by appointing him chairman of NK Properties, which would, in due course, become the new Kebble-controlled JCI. Once Kebble had what he wanted, Khumalo got both the boot and a chit for R30 million. Khumalo *owed* Kebble, who would have no compunction about suing to recover the 'debt'.

However, the injury and insult appeared to energise Khumalo to get even. The extent of his revenge was unimaginable, but Khumalo had learnt from the master, and he would apply with stunning effect the costly lessons he had both witnessed and experienced at first hand.

While Kebble headed slowly and steadily toward the bottomless pit of debt, Khumalo banked a billion, with hundreds of millions in change. It was the first billion-rand fortune made in BEE and it was clean money, with no debt attached.

It had taken just six months. It was a world-class performance. It was *cash*.

Though their backgrounds were totally different, Khumalo, like Kebble, was a street fighter. Mzilikazi Godfrey Khumalo was named after one of the great Zulu warriors. History records that in 1795, Mashobane, chief of the small northern Khumalo clan, sired a son who would conquer more than a million square kilometres of southern Africa. The name Mzilikazi means the Great Road.

The modern-day Mzi Khumalo was born in the township of KwaMashu outside Durban in 1956. His father was a policeman, his mother a domestic worker, and Mzi was the youngest of 11 children. His mother died before he reached his teens and, like so many other young blacks at the time, economic hardship forced him to abandon his education and find a job.

While working as a petrol attendant, he became involved in the tinplating of recycled oil cans and learnt the rudiments of motor vehicle repair. He also joined the ANC's underground military wing, Umkhonto we Sizwe, and was trained in urban guerrilla warfare. Arrested in 1978 and jailed on Robben Island, he had a degree in economics to his credit when he was released in 1990. He joined the McCarthy Retail group and set up a management consultancy, MK, on the side. He was also an executive at Thebe, an ANC investment company, and served in the organisation's department of economic planning and its political structures in KwaZulu-Natal.

But Khumalo had scant interest in politics. What he wanted was to become filthy rich, and business was the route he chose. Some of his first ventures were controversial, such as Malaysian company Renong's involvement with Durban's Hilton Hotel and the sale of Transnet land in the city's Point area.

One day, long after the debacle at JCI, fortune beckoned. In April 2001, a three-way deal between the state-owned Industrial Development Corporation (IDC), Harmony Gold,* a listed stock, and Komanani Mining set the scene for catapulting Khumalo into the big league. Harmony, led by Bernard Swanepoel, one of the most attractive and investor-focused of all mining executives, was alive to the possibilities of early BEE deals and was keen to be seen as an innovative promoter of such transactions. Financing remained the biggest, and apparently insurmountable, problem. Few, if any, companies were going to simply donate chunks of equity to BEE groups. If equity was to be offered, the best that could be offered was a discount. There was consensus within the business community that BEE was necessary, given the wretched hangover of apartheid, and shareholders were likely to accept that a discount offered to a BEE grouping would be acceptable, if perceived as fair.

In one of the biggest BEE deals on record at the time, Harmony agreed to sell 10.7 million of its ordinary shares to Komanani at R36 each, a discount of 6 per cent on the 30-day average ahead of the transaction's announcement. Harmony would also make available 11 million preference shares at nominal cost, effectively

---

* Harmony Gold Mining Company Ltd was first incorporated as a public company in South Africa on 25 August 1950. Towards the end of 1994, Randgold & Exploration cancelled Harmony's management agreement and entered into a service agreement to supply executive and administrative services at market rates. In 1997, Harmony and Randgold & Exploration terminated this agreement and Harmony began operating as a completely independent gold mining company. Starting in 1995, Harmony expanded from a lease-bound operation to a world-class gold producer, increasing sales from 650 312 ounces in its 1995 financial year to 2 388 458 ounces in the 2002 financial year.

options that could be converted to ordinary shares. If conversion took place within five years, however, Harmony would have to be paid R41.50 per share.

Harmony was generously offering a 'wild-card' method of financing the deal. The IDC stumped up R400 million in cash, paying the full price of R36 each for 10.7 million shares in Harmony, plus a nominal price for the options.

The IDC would 'warehouse' the shares and options until Komanani's debt was settled. The 'break-even' point was R78 per Harmony share. At that price, the IDC could exercise its options, sell the resultant Harmony shares in the market, pay Harmony R41.50 a share and end up with R400 million in cash to retire the Komanani debt. Komanani would then walk away with an unencumbered 10.7 million shares and become Harmony's biggest single shareholder, with a stake of about 10 per cent.

The IDC normally required outside parties to chip in with 10 per cent of a deal's value, or R40 million in this case. However, the IDC agreed that Komanani would put up just R10 million or less, and even then it appeared that the IDC might be prepared to assist.

But, for reasons that were never made clear, Mashudu Romano, chairman of black-controlled media group Johnnic Communications and of Komanani, let the deal go. It was cancelled on 17 August.

Eleven days later, a new tripartite agreement was signed between Simane Investments, the IDC and Harmony. In effect, Simane was simply substituted for Komanani. Simane was presented as a broad-based BEE company with four main shareholders. At the time, the company had a total of 100 issued shares, but at a secret meeting on 31 August, Khumalo became the proud owner of 200 newly issued shares, putting him instantly in control of 67 per cent of Simane. He was elected a director and given greater signing powers than any other board member, including chairman Audrey Mokhobo. There was no evidence that Khumalo had paid a cent for the shares.

On 7 September, Harmony, ignorant of Khumalo's involvement, ratified the deal with Simane and the IDC, and the games began. Harmony's stock price reached the break-even point within months, less on a firm dollar-gold price than on a weak rand. In December 2001, the rand reached its record low to the dollar. A weak rand spelt good financial news for South African mining stocks, which pay costs in rand but receive revenues in dollar-derived rand.

No one could have known that the value of Harmony's stock would increase by just under 160 per cent, from R37.30 a share on 3 April, when the original deal was structured, to R96.50 a share on 4 February 2002. On this date the IDC converted its options into shares and sold them, making Simane the owner of 10.7 million shares in Harmony.* The acquisition was unencumbered, and Simane was debt-free. The IDC itself earned a handsome profit from the deal.

The bottom line was that Simane had become worth more than R1 billion within six months. On 24 May 2002, when Harmony's stock hit a record price of R186.80 per share, Simane's value was a stupendous debt-free R2 billion.† But there were still minorities of 33 per cent in Simane in various hands, and Khumalo wanted every sliver of this treasure trove for himself. In Simane, Khumalo had his very own slush fund, which was bleeding millions upon millions of rand in cash in every direction. There had never been anything like it.

One way or another, Khumalo bullied, cajoled, charmed and pestered Simane's minority partners into selling him their shares for a pittance. Vaya Fleet Management, trading as Vaya Investments and represented on Simane's board by Mavuso Msimang,‡ was said to have sold its 20 shares for R2 million. When Harmony's stock price peaked, a bundle of 20 Simane shares was worth R134 million.

Another minority shareholder, E-Goda Telecomms (trading as Khoetsa Holdings),

---

*   Various accounts of the Simane transaction are available. The preferred sequence of events and figures is that filed by Harmony with the Securities and Exchange Commission in Washington in 2003. On 20 June 2001, the IDC completed subscriptions for 10 736 682 Harmony ordinary shares and 10 958 904 Harmony convertible preference shares (essentially options). These subscriptions were carried out in fulfilment of an agreement dated 3 April 2001 (when the Harmony stock price closed at R37.30 a share), signed by Harmony, Komanani and the IDC, pursuant to which, subject to the fulfilment of certain specified conditions, Komanani and the IDC agreed to subscribe for 222 222 Harmony ordinary shares and 10 736 682 Harmony ordinary shares respectively, and Harmony undertook to issue those shares at a price of R36.00 each. The IDC also subscribed for, and Harmony issued, 10 958 904 convertible preference shares at a price equal to their par value of R0.50 each. If the preference shares were converted to ordinary shares within five years, the price to be paid was set in effect at R41.50 each. The Komanani transaction was cancelled as of 17 August 2001. On 7 September 2001, Harmony entered into an agreement with Simane and the IDC, where Simane subscribed for 222 300 Harmony ordinary shares 'on substantially the same terms as the Komanani subscription'. The Simane subscription was completed on 25 September. The aggregate consideration for the ordinary shares and preference shares issued to the IDC and Simane was about R400 million. During January and February 2002, the IDC converted all of its preference shares into 10 958 904 ordinary shares, transferred 10 736 682 ordinary shares to Simane and sold 10 958 904 ordinary shares to third parties in a series of transactions. The 10 958 904 Harmony shares were issued on 4 February, after the Harmony options were exercised by the IDC, at a conversion price of R41.50 each. On that date, Harmony closed at R96.50 a share. The average price for Harmony stock during January and February 2002 was R94.36 a share.

†   See Appendix N, item 19.

‡   Msimang, listed as deputy chairman of Simane, was a well-known businessman who around this time resigned as CEO of the SA National Parks Board to head up Sita, the State Information Technology Agency. He had previously served as an executive director of Satour and as CEO of Tourism KwaZulu-Natal. Holder of a Bachelor of Science degree in entomology and biology, as well as an MBA, Msimang was also listed as a director of various JSE-listed companies, including Massmart and Grintek.

was represented by Mokhobo and allegedly sold its 30 shares for R8 million. At Harmony's peak, they were worth R200 million. Khoetsa was described as 'a women's investment grouping focused on identifying opportunities where its members can leverage their skills in technology, transformation and business'. Mokhobo, holder of a master's degree in political science, was listed as a director of Capital Alliance Holdings, Barnard Jacobs Mellet, Women's Development Bank Investment Holdings, Rotek Industries and M-Net Phuthuma Trust, and was a full-time general manager at Eskom. She previously held senior positions at the Development Bank of South Africa and as special adviser in the Ministry of Public Enterprises.

Themba Langa and Jomo Ntombela represented another Simane minority shareholder, E-Sim Holdings, trading as Mageba Mining. Mageba described itself as 'an investment holding company aiming to leverage its legal and financial skills through emerging black entrepreneurs', and was associated with the ANC Youth Trust.

Langa, a Johannesburg attorney, was the tough guy on the Simane board. He held out for a market-related price from Khumalo, but settled for R10 million. The 30 Simane shares could, again, have fetched R200 million at Harmony's peak. Langa later claimed that Khumalo had threatened to force a rights issue and dilute Mageba's 10 per cent stake in Simane to almost zero. The last 20 outstanding shares were in the hands of broad-based BEE company Sifikile, and would become a major problem for Khumalo.

Part of the original agreement with Harmony and the IDC was that Simane would not dispose of or transfer any Harmony shares for a period of 18 months from the effective date of the agreement, 7 September 2001. But Khumalo could not resist temptation and started selling millions of Harmony shares almost immediately.

During June 2002, Ya Rona, one of the original Simane shareholders, became aware of the sales and went to court to stop Khumalo. By 15 July, when an order was granted to halt Khumalo's selling spree, more than 8 million of the 10.7 million Harmony shares had been disposed of. He was forced to go back to the market to reconstitute the original shares held by Simane.

Harmony had been trying for months to get information from Mokhobo about Simane's corporate structure, shareholders and agreements between the stakeholders that would enable them to participate in the empowerment initiative that formed the foundation of the original deal. She ignored all Harmony's requests, and it was not until the middle of 2003 that this author exposed the fact that Khumalo had been in control of Simane since 31 August 2001. His hijacking of the company had been a close secret.

But the Sifikile shares had continued to elude Khumalo, and he had also become involved in a dispute with Ya Rona, a genuine BEE entity,* over a claim that it had been promised but never received 10 Simane shares. When Harmony's stock price hit its peak, this 3 per cent share of Simane would have been worth R67 million.

Court papers filed by Ya Rona in its bid to halt Khumalo's sale of Harmony shares showed a relationship between Ya Rona and Harmony, based on an unsuccessful bid by the latter for the Free State assets of what was then AngloGold. In August 2001, Harmony executive director Ferdi Dippenaar suggested that if Simane really wanted to empower Ya Rona, it should offer 10 rather than 3 per cent of its shares. Ya Rona boss Tebogo Koetle accepted the offer, but as soon as Khumalo took control of Simane on 31 August, the board reneged on the deal and voted instead to transfer 20 Simane shares from Fukama to Sifikile.

September 2002 found Khumalo negotiating a R760 million loan to his asset management company, Mawenzi, from Deutsche Bank London (DBL) to finance the reacquisition of the Harmony stock he had sold too soon. One of the many preconditions for the loan was that all the Harmony shares held by Simane were pledged to the bank.

Langa, now representing Sifikile, refused to pledge the company's 20 shares in Simane unless Khumalo bought them at a market-related price in the region of R100 million. When DBL granted Mawenzi the loan, it emerged for the first time that Mawenzi was a Simane shareholder. There were several onerous preconditions for the loan:

- Harmony had to confirm that it had no objection to the agreement.
- The South African Ministry of Mineral and Energy Affairs had to confirm that it had no objection to the arrangement.
- DBL had to conclude a scrip-borrowing agreement in respect of approximately 6.4 million Harmony shares.
- DBL had to receive documentation relating to and conduct a due diligence in respect of Simane and its shareholders that rendered results acceptable to DBL.
- The relevant parties had to be in agreement regarding the loan, swap and security arrangements, and legal requirements.
- Opinions from external lawyers (acceptable to DBL) had to confirm that the arrangement did not breach any law or previous agreement relevant to the matter.
- The exchange control department of the SA Reserve Bank had to approve the relevant elements of the arrangement.

---

* The original shareholders (all located in the Free State) were listed as the Disabled Children Action Group, the Virginia Unemployment Association, the Ema Sizame Women's Development Project, Tebogo Koetle, Johanna Macotsi, Kelebogile Tauyane and Mosoeunyane Shadrack Ramathe. Earlier shareholders had included MK veterans and community HIV/AIDS groupings.

- DBL's credit department had to approve the arrangement, something only possible upon completion of all the other conditions.

The loan was granted on 13 September, implying that all the preconditions had been met. Khumalo finally paid Sifikile R62 million for its shares in February 2003. In total, he paid R82 million for the 100 minority shares in Simane, an average discount of 88 per cent on their market value.* By 2003, Simane's original profile of a broad-based BEE company had become the alter ego of a single and immensely wealthy man. If this was BEE at work, the future appeared bleak for the overwhelming majority of previously disadvantaged South Africans.

Within weeks of the author exposing Khumalo's hijacking of Simane, Mokhobo resigned as the company's representative on the Harmony board of directors. By then, Khumalo had sold most of the Harmony shares, and in due course they would all be gone. Khumalo had no interest in paper. He had no interest in BEE. He wanted cash.

Simane was to prove a slush fund of dimensions that Kebble could only have dreamt of. In effect, Khumalo not only banked more than a billion in cash, he also placed the lion's share of booty from Simane offshore. Taken at face value, the apparent granting of permission by the SA Reserve Bank to do so via DBL would constitute a contravention of South Africa's stringent exchange control laws. In addition, it would seem out of kilter with the intention behind *not* externalising substantial funds generated from a BEE transaction.† Yet Khumalo made no attempt to hide the existence of his offshore investments. Apart from high living – hiring billionaire's yachts for parties on the Mediterranean and flaunting his wealth

---

* For 80 of the minority shares, Khumalo had paid just R20 million at discounts of 95 per cent and higher. Khumalo acquired the final 20 shares in Simane for R62 million by February 2003. See Appendix N, item 15.

† Among the countless interventions the democratic South African government has made in the private sector, perhaps none are as aggressive as the assaults launched on the mining sub-sector. As early as December 2002, Marian Tupy of the Washington-based Cato Institute argued that racial quotas established by the government 'will likely result in economic harm to the country, and to black South Africans'. He observed that one of the mining companies' 'most important business decisions – the hiring of workers – will be dependent upon non-business-related criteria'. As to the agreement that mining companies would raise $10 billion over the next five years for the purchase and transfer of company stock to non-whites, Tupy argued that 'this will drive down the profit margins in the industry and the mining companies will be forced to cut their costs by hiring fewer employees than they normally would, or by letting some of their employees go. As a result, unemployment will grow. That outcome, of course, is the direct opposite of what South Africa currently needs and what the government aspires to do.' As an observer for a foreign-based entity, Tupy was fearless in noting that 'South Africa's top mining executives publicly express support' for BEE; however, 'in private they are said to be gravely concerned about the cost associated with it. That is a bad sign, for it means that the businesses will now likely resort to political manoeuvring to escape charter requirements.'

around the French Riviera – he made substantial (and public) investments abroad in foreign currency.

Khumalo had owned an offshore vehicle, Efferton Investments, since at least August 2001. On 31 August, when Simane had issued 200 new shares to Khumalo, in detail, Simane issued 170 new shares to Efferton and 30 to Nest Life, another Khumalo concern. Efferton, seen alone, was the effective controlling entity of Simane, with a 57 per cent stake. More than half of Simane had been externalised from South Africa.

Asked about Efferton and related matters, Reserve Bank executive Alick Bruce-Brand offered a terse response: 'We are not in a position to comment.'

Equally significant was Khumalo's investment in Cluff Plc, a company listed in London, but with certain operating assets in South Africa. Algy Cluff, an Englishman who could pontificate with the best of them, was an interesting mix of merchant adventurer and opportunist. Something of an anachronism, he always left the lingering impression that he walked deep in the shadows of Lonrho's Tiny Rowland. Cluff had started out in oil, bidding for North Sea licences in 1972, then had moved on to mineral exploration in Africa, making several significant discoveries before his Cluff Resources was taken over by Ashanti Goldfields in 1996. After that, he remained focused on gold.

Cluff Plc elected Khumalo to its board on 1 August 2002. Earlier, Cluff had announced that, via Khumalo's interest in Rosario International Investments and Gibbs International (both offshore companies), Khumalo was interested in 3.5 million ordinary shares in Cluff Plc. Usually, a South African company must be an operating (as opposed to investment) entity before it is allowed to invest offshore. There was no evidence that any of Khumalo's companies were operating at the time.

His interest in Cluff Plc increased to some 17 per cent following a capital issue. The cost of Khumalo's stake in Cluff Plc was around £9 million (about R112 million at the time). When Khumalo joined the Cluff board, he was a director of Mawenzi Financial Services, Mintek, African Pioneer Mining, Simane, Metallon, Efferton Investments, Nest Life, Rosario International and Gibbs International. Between 1995 and 2002, he also served on the boards of the old JCI, Anglo American, Capital Alliance, Western Areas, Telkom SA, McCarthy Retail, Momentum Life and Southern Mining Corporation.

Apart from serious questions about Khumalo's export of cash from South Africa, there was unfinished business at the IDC. On 17 February 2003, Gerrie Nel of the Scorpions contacted IDC chief executive Khaya Ngqula in connection with 'alleged irregularities pertaining to the sale of Harmony Gold Mining shares to Simane Security Investments'. Two of the most senior mining executives at the IDC conceded receiving a R6 million 'loan' from Khumalo. One of them, Andile Reve, left the IDC in 2002 to run the Khumalo-owned Metallon group.

There was another grave issue. In August 2001, Mawenzi Asset Management signed surety for R10 million in Khumalo's name. It was allegedly in support of a commercial bank loan used to meet the IDC requirement for a 'deposit' as part of Simane's R400 million deal with Harmony. The arrangement was in direct contravention of laws regulating asset management companies and gave Khumalo 100 per cent advantage in the BEE deal, without any of the risk. The surety was the equivalent of pension fund trustees guaranteeing a loan to the company CEO to play the stock market for his own benefit.

The surety was signed and countersigned by the two most senior executives at Mawenzi, Norbet Engel and Charles Graham. Between them, the two men had almost 40 years of experience in the investment industry, and had worked for household names such as Old Mutual and Norwich Life before joining Mawenzi. By signing the surety, they might well have breached Mawenzi Asset Management's publicly stated policy, which offered the following assurances:

> As an asset protection and risk control measure, Mawenzi does not have access to clients' assets. These are held in safe custody by the chosen custodian (most of the major banks are used). All assets, other than bearer securities and cash, are registered in the name of an appropriate client-approved nominee. The client directly appoints the custodian to hold the client's assets in safe custody and Mawenzi is granted a power of attorney to administer the assets.

A personal surety signed by an asset manager is simply illegal. Asset managers are subject to strict and precise legislation, mainly because their livelihood comprises the management of other people's money. Cape Town fund managers, a notoriously close-knit community, speculated that Engel and Graham subsequently received 'bonuses' of around R10 million each. Ordinarily, an allegedly illegal surety would warrant investigation by the Financial Services Board, but queries in this regard elicited a terse response: 'Mr Khumalo is the chairman of Mawenzi [Asset Management] and any release or explanation must come from him.'

Someone was stonewalling.

When the IDC was asked about the bizarre circumstances surrounding Simane, it commented as follows on 14 July 2003: 'Our records indicate that [Mzi] Khumalo was not in the [Simane] deal, did not and could not have arranged for the IDC to arrange or confirm a loan. The BEE partner is Simane Security and not Mzi Khumalo. The deal between the two parties, however it exists, is not recorded anywhere in our books.'

On 15 August, the *Financial Mail* carried a two-article whitewash of the Simane affair, stating: 'Khumalo has for the first time spoken out about the 2001 Simane deal ... Both the IDC and Harmony were aware of Khumalo's financial backing of Simane.'

Somebody was lying.

The Scorpions dropped their investigation into Khumalo's 'loan' to the two IDC executives.

Kebble always suspected that the minutes of Simane's August 2001 board meeting, at which Khumalo was issued the fresh 200 shares in the company, had been back-dated. The price at which the Harmony deal broke even, leaving Simane debt-free and in possession of 10.7 million shares, was around R78 per share. Harmony's stock entered that territory in December 2001.

Kebble also alleged, with heated insistence and in splenetic tone, that Khaya Ngqula, the chief executive of the IDC, had tipped off Khumalo to the Simane deal. But then Kebble *would* say that, wouldn't he?

The IDC's annual report to 30 June 2002 contained no mention of the Simane deal, despite its size and sensational financial success. However, bonuses paid to the nine members of the IDC's executive committee had increased by 200 per cent, from a total of R5 million in the 2001 financial year to R15 million in the next financial year.

Within three months of Khumalo's hijacking of Simane being exposed by the author in July 2003, news leaked to the effect that Ngqula would quit the IDC when his contract expired in September 2004. He did.

In seven years at the IDC, Ngqula had overseen some of the greatest value destruction in democratic South Africa. In its financial year to 30 June 2004, the IDC posted its first operating loss since being founded in 1940, yet the 12-member executive committee took home R30 million in remuneration and bonuses. Ngqula's share was R6.9 million, including a R2 million bonus.

The majority of the IDC's cash income derives from investments made up to more than half a century before, such as Sasol (1950) and Sappi (1951). In the first nine months of its 2005 financial year, the IDC was shown to be selling the family silver in order to remain afloat. Carefully tucked away between the lines was the sale some time after June 2004 of 0.8 per cent (worth about $800 million) of BHP Billiton, the world's biggest diversified resources stock.

In 2001, the IDC, which had become accustomed to 'ordinary' impairment losses under Ngqula, wrote off R1.9 billion of 'exceptional' impairment losses. A further R2.7 billion of such losses were written off in 2002.

Impairments fell to R843 million in 2003, R803 million in 2004 and were trimmed to R256 million in the first nine months of the 2005 financial year. The IDC had an operating loss of R803 million in 2004.

Ngqula, holder of a bachelor of administration degree, followed Alec Erwin's move from Minister of Trade and Industry ('head office' for the IDC) until the April 2004 elections, to Minister of Public Enterprises. The latter is 'HO' for Transnet, the notional parent company of South African Airways (SAA), where Ngqula was installed as CEO in October 2004. Ten months later, he did not endear himself to employees, passengers or the media by abandoning his post on the first full day of a countrywide strike by ground staff over a wage dispute that crippled SAA's domestic service for more than a week.

As travellers camped out in airports where chaos reigned, Ngqula was attending an 'important' social function at a luxury resort adjacent to the Kruger National Park. Embattled SAA staff often slammed his use of private helicopters and penchant for five-star luxury hotels while on airline business.

Two months later, Ngqula hit the headlines again, drawing harsh criticism when it was shown that taxpayers in the Eastern Cape, one of South Africa's most indigent provinces, had forked out thousands of rand for upgrading a road leading to Ngqula's traditional village, Rhode. The work had been carried out in preparation for the 48-year-old high-flyer's traditional Xhosa wedding to beauty queen Mbali Gasa, attended by more than a thousand guests. After the Simane deal, Ngqula had divorced Patricia Nonhlanhla, his long-standing wife, and disowned her and their three daughters.

Kebble repeatedly mentioned Ngqula and Khumalo as two of the leading so-called 'untouchables' within South Africa's new black elite. He complained bitterly that despite *prima facie* evidence of wrongdoing in their behaviour, the two men seemed immune to investigation, let alone prosecution. Following the Simane deal, Kebble claimed, Ngqula and Khumalo entered into a number of irregular transactions, both in South Africa and abroad, notably in France.

Kebble would practically froth at the mouth when accusing Khumalo of 'stealing' more than a billion rand in cash from 'his own poor brethren'. He was utterly convinced that Ngqula and Khumalo belonged to an elite cabal, allegedly led by Saki Macozoma. Why, Kebble would roar amid profanities, had Khumalo's 'loan' to the two IDC executives never been properly investigated? How had Khumalo been allowed to trample on foreign exchange laws? Why had the legal position of the surety been allowed to go unchallenged? In Kebble's mind, there was no doubt about who was protecting whom, and even less doubt about why such protection was forthcoming.

What appeared to escape Kebble was that he had 'invented' the hijacking of

BEE structures. Not only had he hijacked the new JCI in 1997, he had humiliated Khumalo in the process. It could be argued that while Kebble's actions were spawned by a precocious and massive confidence trick, if laws had indeed been broken, he had not been caught. But it could also be argued that Khumalo was inadvertently tutored by the best.

Speculation aside, Ngqula and his friend Khumalo enjoy spending time on the fashionable French Riviera, where Ngqula owns a villa at Port Grimaud, over-looking the bay of Saint Tropez. Khumalo has acknowledged that at least once he had hired the *Christina O*, one of the biggest luxury yachts available for private rental on the Mediterranean. The original owner, Greek shipping magnate Aristotle Onassis, delighted in telling guests that the barstools in the on-board Ari's Bar were upholstered in whale foreskin. Khumalo also finds this entertaining.

'It's nice,' he once told a journalist, 'when you find a lady sitting there, prim and proper, sipping champagne, and you say: You do realise that you are sitting on the biggest dick in the world? and you see how she flushes and says: Excuse me?'

On 13 September 2004, Kebble quietly announced that JCI and Khumalo had reached an out-of-court settlement in an amount of R30 million. The terse official statement said no details of the settlement would be revealed and no further public comment would be made. Apparently, JCI had taken the legal route to recoup at least R30 million relating to the issue of certain preference shares when the business relationship between CAM and Khumalo was dissolved in 1998.

The amount tallied with the debt ascribed to Khumalo in the CMMS accounts, and apparently excluded interest. In a number of utterances over the year preceding the settlement, Kebble had claimed that Khumalo owed JCI 'at least' R50 million. During the same period, Kebble publicly attacked a number of his real or imagined enemies, chief among them Bulelani Ngcuka, director of the National Prosecuting Authority at the time. Kebble alleged that the NPA was being used to settle old scores and operate according to private political agendas.

'Khumalo,' Kebble bellowed, 'a close friend of Ngcuka, has declared himself my enemy in part because I am taking legal action against him seeking repayment of moneys owed by him to me. Khumalo has sworn he will bring about my downfall, and he told me to my face that he would use his friendship with Ngcuka to that end.'

While neither Ngcuka nor Khumalo made any secret of their friendship and the bonds they shared as old struggle comrades, Kebble failed to produce any tangible evidence of the vendetta he believed they were waging against him.

But Khumalo never forgave Kebble for booting him out of JCI, and after Kebble's murder he admitted that they had been 'bitter enemies'.

19

Play it again, Brett

Having taken a leaf from his mentor Brett Kebble's book, Mzi Khumalo kept his role in Simane secret for almost two years. From July 2003, however, this author exposed the gory truth in a series of *Moneyweb*[*] reports.

The Simane revelations made Kebble livid, and he used the information to mount an attack on Khumalo, aimed at cash extraction. The R30 million settlement eventually reached by the two men indicates that Kebble's strategy had worked, though it is likely that Khumalo paid more to settle a nuisance suit than to admit any kind of liability. He was anything but short of cash, and although Kebble's case was circumstantial and patchy, at best, he might well have threatened that if the matter went to trial, the evidence would not be in Khumalo's interest. Subsequent media reports suggested that 'the laughing Zulu', as friends and associates knew Khumalo, did end up in some kind of trouble with the SA Reserve Bank.

Kebble had plenty of spare time to spend on such battles. From the moment he burst onto the investment scene in 1996, he never had a real job, and, as time passed, it became increasingly clear that he was inherently inept when it came to making money from conventional business deals.

Sensing real cash flow danger, Kebble decided to go for broke with his announcement on 9 December 2004 about the Orlyfunt BEE deal. Investors were told that Orlyfunt would acquire 'an extensive portfolio of BEE entities and various mineral right interests' for the sum of R1.4 billion from JCI.[†]

What investors were not told was that, in a classic example of Kebble alchemy, he and four BEE associates – Mafika Mkwanazi, Sello Rasethaba, Andrew Mlangeni and the ANC Youth League's Lunga Ncwana – would end up owning 42 per cent of Orlyfunt without laying out a cent.

---

[*] See www.moneyweb.co.za

[†] Real or imagined entities to be folded into Orlyfunt included JCI Telecommunications, JCI Pharmaceuticals, JCI Property, JCI Engineering, JCI Finance and Equity Holdings, JCI Mining, Cueincident, Startrack Communications, DVI Telecoms, SA Bioclones, Advanced Medical Technologies, Nutrx Trading, Mvelaphanda Properties, Boschendal, Rand Leases, Palfinger SA, OD Engineering, African Maritime Logistics, Tlotlisa Financial Services, Ikamva Holdings, Sekunjalo Group, Itsuseng Investments, and 'ordinary and preference shares in Matodzi and Witnigel Investments'. Randgold & Exploration would chip in with its 74 per cent interest in the share capital of Minrico Ltd, and its 55.1 per cent interest in the share capital of Free State Development and Investment Corporation, known as Freddev.

Orlyfunt died as natural a death as Kebble's was not, but there can be no doubt that the intention was to list Orlyfunt and raise hundreds of millions of rand from big financial institutions. How could they refuse when offered such a brilliant line-up of BEE names and entities? How could they dare say 'no' to BEE?

Almost immediately after announcing Orlyfunt, Kebble hit the biggest pothole on his rocky road through the corporate realm. His troubles began with Randgold Resources making noises about its notional parent company, Randgold & Exploration, selling down its holding in the London-listed company. Early in 2005, Randgold Resources released the results of a global shareholder identification exercise conducted by research group Ilios in December 2004. Merrill Lynch UK, a money manager, was named as the company's single largest shareholder, with 6.89 per cent of its issued stock. Randgold & Exploration's holding had evidently been reduced to 6.74 per cent, or four million shares.

On 30 June 2005, the murmurings became official and entered legal history when Randgold Resources filed its so-called 20-F annual report with the Securities Exchange Commission in Washington. Footnote 2 on page 65 referred to 14.4 million Randgold Resources shares that could not be attributed to Randgold & Exploration, despite that company's claim of ownership. Arcane as it may have sounded, the question was of vital importance to investors in Randgold & Exploration, which for many months had stated in writing that it held 18.4 million shares in Randgold Resources, worth nearly $300 million in mid-year. The SEC filing reiterated that Randgold & Exploration held a mere four million shares in Randgold Resources. Both companies were listed on the Nasdaq in the US, but Randgold & Exploration's primary listing continued to be in Johannesburg.

In 1995, Randgold Resources had been an all but irrelevant incubated backroom entity within Randgold & Exploration. From about the middle of 1996, however, the latter's stake in Randgold Resources comprised the majority of Randgold & Exploration's underlying tangible value. There was no small irony in the suspicion that Kebble had secretly been selling down the Randgold Resources stake. At the time of the SEC filing about what would become the infamously 'missing' 14.4 million shares, Randgold Resources was valued at $832 million, and Randgold & Exploration at a comparatively paltry $127 million. Of course, the shares were not missing at all – unsuspecting buyers on open markets had bought them in good faith. It was the cash that had disappeared – close on $300 million, measured by replacement value.

A clutch of additional regulatory filings concerning Randgold & Exploration spattered more fat on the fire. The JSE announced that Randgold & Exploration had failed to submit its annual report for the 2004 financial year, and annotated the stock with an 'RE', pending suspension on 29 July 2005 if compliance was not forthcoming. On 30 June, Randgold & Exploration had filed an NT 20-F form with the SEC, stating that it was unable to file its annual report because it was awaiting the 20-F from Randgold Resources (which was, in fact, filed on the same day), and had experienced delays in obtaining information necessary to prepare accounts according to US accounting standards.

Randgold & Exploration had filed a similar delaying document the year before, but then it complained only about accounting challenges, not the tardiness of Randgold Resources. In 2005, however, Randgold Resources was adamant that Randgold & Exploration only held four million of its shares, via Randgold Resources Holdings (RRH).

Randgold Resources reiterated that the four million shares claim was based on analysis of its shareholder base and other information. Under Kebble's hand, RRH filed a Schedule 13G/A with the SEC on 14 February 2005, once again reporting beneficial ownership of 18.4 million Randgold Resources shares, or 31 per cent of the company's total outstanding ordinary shares. Randgold Resources categorically informed the SEC that 'we have asked [RRH] for documentation supporting its claimed holdings, which to date has not been provided'.

Randgold Resources CEO Mark Bristow was adamant that the company had exhaustively investigated its shareholders, including nominees, often used when investors are unwilling to be identified. Bristow insisted that Randgold & Exploration could not possibly hold 18.4 million shares in Randgold Resources. He was not spoiling for a fight, he said, but was legally bound to 'discover' the identity of shareholders in Randgold Resources, whomever they were.

At the start of the 2004 calendar year, Randgold & Exploration stated that it held 21.5 million (36.9 per cent of the total) shares in Randgold Resources. Of these, 3.2 million (6.0 per cent) were sold during the year, leaving 18.4 million shares (30.9 per cent) by year's end. Of these, 9.9 million (16.7 per cent) were apparently lent to Inkwenkwezi, a BEE entity, primarily for the purchase of Anglo American's 19 million shares in Western Areas.

On 7 July 2005, Randgold & Exploration said it intended appealing to Nasdaq regarding notice of possible delisting. The company expected 'to make a timely request for a hearing with the Nasdaq Listing Qualifications Panel to review the Nasdaq staff's determination, which will stay the delisting pending the hearing and a determination'. Randgold & Exploration insisted that it had experienced delays in obtaining information needed to finalise and analyse its audited financial statements. The company was 'working diligently ... and will file its Form 20-F as soon as practicable'.

On 1 August, both Randgold & Exploration and JCI were suspended from the JSE for failing to file documents on time.

In an official notice published via the JSE on 8 August, Randgold & Exploration said it anticipated that its South African audited annual report would be posted 'on or about 15 September 2005', at which time the company would ask the JSE to lift the suspension of its shares. Kebble was believed to have made representations to Nasdaq officials following the threats that Randgold & Exploration would be delisted, but no more was heard in this regard, and on 27 September, he was killed.

On 15 August, Randgold & Exploration crashed 15 per cent on the Nasdaq to multi-year lows of $1 a share as specialist investors freely speculated that the company's 20-F annual report would not materialise, or, if it did, would be akin to some or other hideous swamp creature. Randgold & Exploration's market value at the time was just $75 million, nearly $800 million less than that of Randgold Resources.

On 21 September, just six days before Kebble was shot in an apparent professional 'hit', Randgold & Exploration was delisted from the Nasdaq for 'regulatory/ non-compliance reasons'. In a brief official notice under the heading 'security deletions', the stock was branded 'delinquent'. This was a far bolder move than the JSE suspension, though Nasdaq's action downgraded the stock to 'pink sheet' status, meaning it could still trade in the informal over-the-counter (OTC) market. However, the delisting stripped Randgold & Exploration of the vast majority of privileges that a Nasdaq listing carries. The Nasdaq is the largest electronic screen-based equity securities market in the US, with about 3 300 listed companies, more than any competitor.

Kebble's plunder of Randgold & Exploration had been carefully planned and timed to coincide with his realisation that the sale of the Western Areas hedge book was the end of one thing and the beginning of something else.

He had quit as a director of Randgold & Exploration in 1997, leaving it under control of his father, who had exerted his ultimate authority in 1998 when he booted CEO Peter Flack right out of sight. Brett moved back to Randgold & Exploration in 2003. Of course he became the CEO; of course his father remained in the chair; of course Hennie Buitendag remained the financial director, as he had been since 1999. Gordon Miller was listed as the third executive director.

The record shows that Randgold & Exploration had long used Randgold Resources as a cash cow. However, the source of the money was not normalised income, it was the proceeds of selling down shares. There was a minor sale in 1996,* but the real bonanza began with the listing of Randgold Resources on the London Stock Exchange in 1997.

---

* See Appendix M, item 2.

In 2003, Randgold & Exploration applied to the South African Reserve Bank to reduce its 'required ownership' in Randgold Resources to less than 36 per cent. With Kebble firmly in the seat, the application clearly signalled a plan to raise cash. While approval was pending, Randgold & Exploration sold more Randgold Resources shares, cutting its stake to 31 per cent.

Kebble also used Randgold & Exploration for inter-group deals. On 1 July 2003, Randgold & Exploration lent $4 million to JCI. On 31 December, the balance of the loan account stood at $4.7 million, and was miraculously repaid in full on 15 April 2004. Cash was simply being taken out of one pocket and shuffled to another.

On 10 July 2003, Randgold & Exploration converted to shares a debt of $1.8 million it was owed by Continental Goldfields Ltd (Australia) for the sale of Transvaal Gold Mining Estates Ltd in 2000. This was the same Continental Goldfields that featured in the Rawas scam, but yet another fantastically convoluted Kebble transaction involving the inter-group swapping of debt for paper gave Randgold & Exploration 40 million shares in Simmer and Jack Mines Ltd – about 18 per cent of the issued stock.

In his new role as CEO, Kebble was a busy man. On 20 June 2003, Randgold & Exploration entered an agreement with Platgold Pacific Ltd and Hazcare to buy the mining rights for the Rotifunk mineral sands project to mine for rutile, ilmenite and zircon in the Bradfield area of Sierra Leone. *Sierra Leone*? Remarkably, the purchase price of $5.2 million was apparently paid in cash. For Kebble, it seemed that few things were as attractive as buying half-baked obscure assets in dangerous countries. What kind of business model was he following?

Given Kebble's history when dealing with offshore assets, the sudden appearance of such transactions in Randgold & Exploration's books looked suspicious. In terms of an agreement dated 22 July 2003, another Australian entity, Notable Holdings (Pty) Ltd, settled its scrip-lending agreement with Randgold & Exploration through a cash payment of $3.6 million, to be made no later than 31 December 2004, together with all accrued interest and the transfer of 660 000 Western Areas shares to Randgold & Exploration. Like Continental, Notable was pivotal to the Rawas scandal.

During 1999 and 2000, DRD had 'advanced' $3.9 million to Notable for 'operational assistance'. There was no formal agreement, and in 2000, DRD wrote off $1.9 million of the amount as bad debt. The balance was written off in 2002. DRD's chief financial officer, Charles Mostert, was a director of Notable when the original amount was 'advanced'.

Kebble also leveraged Randgold & Exploration off BEE.* On 28 July 2003, Randgold & Exploration entered into a 'partnership' with Phikoloso Mining (Pty)

---

* See Appendix K, items 9–13.

Ltd to enhance Randgold & Exploration's 'strategic empowerment partnership'.
According to the company's SEC filing:

We issued 8.8 million new ordinary shares, representing 16.4 per cent of our
issued ordinary share capital, to Phikoloso in exchange for the total issued share
capital of and all the shareholder claims on loan accounts, which amounted to
$33.5 million, against Viking Pony Properties 359 (Pty) Ltd. Viking Pony held
235 000 Anglo Platinum shares, 315 000 Harmony shares and 7.3 million shares
of The Afrikander Lease Ltd, or Aflease. It also owns 75 per cent of Kabusha
Mining and Finance (Pty) Ltd, which in turn holds 23 million shares in Aflease.

At the Randgold & Exploration stock price of R29.50 a share on the day of the deal,
it was worth R260 million to Phikoloso. Kebble was issuing paper again.*

He said the deal 'brought on board several new and talented participants' in
the form of Chris Nissen (a former senior ANC official in the Western Cape),
Brenda Madumise and ANCYL's Lunga Ncwana, all of whom became Randgold &
Exploration directors. Based on the face value of the transactions, Phikoloso may
have been overpaid to the tune of around R50 million. For Kebble, the deal sealed
off another board of crony directors who would allow him to do as he wished. He
now had in place all the elements that he required, à la JCI, to rip cash wholesale
out of Randgold & Exploration.

Nothing in the company's underlying business changed between 2002 and 2003,
but from just four directors, it ended up with eight in the space of a year: the two
Kebbles (with Roger as chairman), Buitendag, Miller, David Ashworth, Madumise,
Ncwana and Nissen.

Just as Kebble had been forced to absorb the likes of JCI Gold into JCI, so he
remained under pressure to mop up other parts of the debris he had created. On
22 December 2003, Randgold & Exploration acquired a 55.1 per cent interest in
Free State Development and Investment Corporation Ltd, or Freddev, which held
mineral and mining participation rights, in exchange for 1 531 030 Randgold &
Exploration ordinary shares. The paper tiger had roared once more.

While the selling of shares in Randgold Resources had never really stopped, the
sales, aimed exclusively at raising cash, had been regular and orderly for years. That
changed after Kebble moved in as CEO of Randgold & Exploration, and during
2004 the apparent sales were both unauthorised and on a massive scale. According
to investors closest to the action, the bulk of the disputed shares, first officially
spotted by Randgold Resources itself, was sold during the third quarter of 2004.

Initial indications were that cash proceeds from the sale of the stock had

---

* See Appendix K, item 5.

disappeared into a BEE entity named Bookmark and Inkwenkwezi. But what had they done with the cash? Had either entity in fact received any cash? No one was saying. As was to be expected, although a private rather than a listed company, Bookmark was in many ways a Kebble clone. Two of the directors – Mafika Mkwanazi and Thabo Mosololi – were also directors of Matodzi. Other Bookmark directors were Eric Molefe, who had a history of involvement with Kebble's companies, and Muthanyi Robinson Ramaite, a former director-general in public service and administration. Bookmark Investment Holdings (Pty) Ltd, described as 'formerly Matodzi Investment Holdings (Pty) Ltd', was listed in Matodzi's 2005 annual report as that company's single biggest shareholder, with 24.3 per cent.

JCI's 2004 annual report (to 31 March) came into sharp relief in finding clues about the meltdown. According to this document, on 9 June 2004, JCI and Randgold & Exploration undertook to lend Inkwenkwezi 'sufficient Western Areas shares' to raise the necessary funding for acquisition of 13.7 million Western Areas shares (11.6 per cent of the total) from Anglo American. Inkwenkwezi, it was said, had to pay Anglo by 1 November. Just a few paragraphs later, JCI stated with excruciating amphibology that 'Inkwenkwezi has a twelve-month call option on the Randgold shares', yet nowhere else in the annual report were the 'Randgold shares' explained. Was the reference to Randgold & Exploration or Randgold Resources?

According to Anglo American's annual report for 2004 (to 31 December), the group had disposed of an 8.5 per cent holding of Western Areas for $48 million in December. The buyer's name was not disclosed.

Yet the 2004 Western Areas annual report stated categorically that Inkwenkwezi had 'acquired an effective 11.6 per cent of the equity of Western Areas'. This did not match the 8.5 per cent figure published by Anglo American.

The Western Areas report postulated: 'Inkwenkwezi empowerment transaction successfully restructured and required financing imminent' and 'Discussions with an institution to finance Inkwenkwezi's obligation are progressing, and should be satisfactorily concluded shortly'.

On 29 April 2005, Randgold & Exploration's preliminary results for the year to 31 December 2004 claimed that 9.9 million Randgold Resources shares had been 'lent' to Inkwenkwezi. On the same day, investors were told that Inkwenkwezi's intended purchase of 19 million Western Areas shares from Anglo American was 'currently' in its final stages. This contradicted the earlier statement that Inkwenkwezi had to pay Anglo American by 1 November 2004.

Randgold & Exploration's preliminary results reiterated that the company owned 18.4 million shares in Randgold Resources. Kebble and Buitendag signed the results, and Randgold & Exploration stated that its auditors, Charles Orbach &

Company, had reviewed them and that 'a copy of their unmodified review report on the financial statements' was available.

During our last face-to-face meeting on 7 July 2005, Kebble assured this author that Randgold & Exploration's 18.4 million shares in Randgold Resources were 'safe'. He insisted that Randgold & Exploration was the beneficial owner of the shares. Kebble conceded that 9.9 million 'lent' Randgold Resources shares had in fact been sold, but said that they would be returned to Randgold & Exploration in mid-2006. Beyond the 9.9 million shares tied up with Bookmark or Inkwenkwezi or both, two million Randgold Resources shares (3.3 per cent of the total) were being held in escrow, under Randgold & Exploration direction, by a potential Angolan diamond concession vendor. This left Randgold & Exploration holding 6.5 million Randgold Resources shares (10.9 per cent) directly and indirectly at the end of 2004.

Kebble said he had instructed the custodians of millions of Randgold Resources shares under Randgold & Exploration's name to correct the Randgold Resources register. Odiously, he also said that Inkwenkwezi boasted a R400 million NAV, which included its stake in listed Matodzi, along with 'valuable' platinum and diamond concessions.

Details of the financing arrangements and legal agreements between Randgold & Exploration, Bookmark, Inkwenkwezi and other third parties remained unavailable in the public domain. The opacity over the financing of the 9.9 million Randgold Resources on-lent shares had a significant impact on the valuation of Randgold & Exploration's stock price.

In apparent recognition that investors had more questions than answers, Kebble vowed that within weeks Randgold & Exploration would appoint two non-executive independent directors. This undertaking was first given on 29 April, and in May, Randgold & Exploration had announced that Stephen Tainton and Gordon Miller had resigned as directors.

From an asset-quality viewpoint, the nucleus of the imploding Kebble empire remained Western Areas, with its 50 per cent interest in South Deep, west of Johannesburg. By 2005, development of the South Deep twin-shaft complex had been in progress for ten years at a cost of R4 billion ($580 million), leaving Western Areas deeply in debt, and was yet to be completed. When the gold bullion price hit $500 an ounce in 2005, the total value of the option premiums payable, plus projected losses on outstanding derivative positions, left the Western Areas hedge book $500 million under water.

Western Areas was technically bankrupt, but such is the quality and life of its ore body that it simply could not be allowed to go down. Given that there was no way cash-strapped Western Areas could finance its own BEE transaction,

Kebble had been forced to mount cash raids; Randgold & Exploration had been the hapless victim via its valued holdings in Randgold Resources. Kebble's clear motive was to first attempt to protect Western Areas, and, secondly, hopefully protect his stockholding in JCI.

On 7 July 2004, JCI had coughed up R288 million in cash following a Western Areas rights issue that raised R402 million in total. But where had the cash come from?

On 30 August 2005, an avalanche of news hit the market:

- Kebble had stepped down as CEO of JCI, Randgold & Exploration and Western Areas. He was to stay on as a non-executive director of JCI, no doubt in recognition of his shareholding in the entity.
- The boards of JCI and Randgold & Exploration were dissolved and reconfigured to house members mostly connected directly or indirectly with Investec, the niche financial services outfit that had agreed to provide JCI with a R460 million standby loan facility. The financing was conditional on Kebble stepping down, and its main purpose was to enable JCI to follow its rights in terms of a new Western Areas offer. Investec also agreed that should other shareholders not take up their rights, JCI could take up additional Western Areas shares to a maximum of R250 million.
- Peter Gray, former head of Société Générale SA and Tlotlisa Securities, or T-Sec, became CEO of JCI and Randgold & Exploration, while Chris Lamprecht was appointed chief financial officer at both companies.
- Charles Cornwall, Roger Kebble, John Stratton and Hennie Buitendag stepped down as JCI directors, while Roger, Buitendag and Lunga Ncwana relinquished their board seats at Randgold & Exploration.
- At Western Areas, Sello Rasethaba (previously non-executive director) resigned; Mafika Mkwanazi quit as non-executive chairman, but remained on the board as a non-executive director. Western Areas cast around for a new independent non-executive chairman and directors, as well as a CEO.

Kebble argued that the financial demands on JCI came at a time when some companies in the group were involved in various 'bold empowerment initiatives'. He claimed that, in addition to the proposed R640 million rights issue for Western Areas, 'it became clear to me that JCI would have to be recapitalised. I have thus been involved in recapitalisation discussions with a number of financial institutions over the past several months'.

If there was any sentimentality about the dismissals, it would have been limited to Buitendag, financial director of a number of Kebble companies, including CMMS.

Curiously, while Kebble had not acquired CMMS until 1999, Buitendag had been a director of what was previously known as MIMIC* since 1988, when Kebble was but a callow youth. Kebble was neither qualified nor experienced in accounting and came to rely heavily on Buitendag, who seemed to regard Kebble as an overgrown schoolboy who often teetered out of control. Buitendag may yet be required to answer numerous questions about the various sets of accounts, but he would be the first to point out that independent auditors had signed off on those that were published. In fairness, there was no real evidence of malice in Buitendag's behaviour, though there was an old-world arrogance about his attitude.

The August 2005 shake-up deprived certain individuals, who were forced out of some major lifelines. Kebble had long been in the habit of rewarding his cronies with excessive compensation. Even at the detectable level, scavenging individuals had been paid millions. JCI's directors had received R12 million in the year to 31 March 2004. This was not only an obscene amount for board members in a passive investment company, it was also double the figure paid in 2003. Consulting and management fees, the nature of which was not explained, exited JCI to the tune of R54 million in 2004, against R23 million in the previous year. Kebble was grotesquely milking the public company coffers, let alone those hidden from prying eyes in CMMS.

Senior executives from the Investec stable moved into the companies that had been removed from Kebble control. David Nurek became independent non-executive chairman at both JCI and Randgold & Exploration; Donn Jowell was appointed independent non-executive director at both, while Peter Thomas assumed the same position at JCI, and Sam Abrahams did likewise at Randgold & Exploration. It was proposed that Abrahams and Nurek be appointed independent non-executive directors of Western Areas.

Between them, Nurek, Abrahams, Thomas and Jowell assumed some eight board positions at the three companies. Sandy McGregor, an executive at Allan Gray, would watch over the money manager's 25 per cent stake in each of the three ex-Kebble listed entities, and stayed on as an independent non-executive director at Western Areas.

On the question of possible conflict of interest, Investec CEO Stephen Koseff said the two individuals short-listed as CEO and chairman of Western Areas were 'absolutely' independent of the finance house.

Even so, problems arose. Aflease Gold and Uranium Resources (later renamed SXR Uranium One), a 12 per cent shareholder in Randgold & Exploration,† raised

---

*   See Appendix A.

†   See Appendix K, item 16.

concerns over Peter Gray becoming CEO of both JCI and Randgold & Exploration, as well as Lamprecht's position at these companies and Western Areas.

Aflease wanted to realise its investment in Randgold & Exploration at optimal price, and while it had 'no issue with the individuals', it was adamant, with reference to Gray and Lamprecht, that it was 'inappropriate to purposely place individuals in a position of conflict when there are related party transactions between these companies'. Aflease complained that Gray and Lamprecht had 'strong historical ties' to Kebble and had been associated with some of the transactions that Aflease raised in a requisition to the board to call an extraordinary general meeting of Randgold & Exploration. Aflease said it was not satisfied that Gray and Lamprecht were 'the appropriate people to provide us with an independent assessment of the recent dealings of Randgold & Exploration. We would prefer independent new appointees who would act independently and in the interests of all Randgold & Exploration shareholders.'

Koseff's take on providing a cash lifeline for JCI was simple: 'We are an investment bank,' he told the author, 'and we are in this to try and make money.' Flagging Investec's entrepreneurial spirit, Koseff said the transactions announced as part of the rescue package aligned Investec's interests with those of shareholders in each of the three target entities. Proposals for the composite transactions had hit his desk seven weeks prior to the announcement on 30 August, he said.

In the grand traditions of investment banking, Investec would take a raising fee for the R460 million facility. This would be the greater of R50 million or the aggregate of 30 per cent of the increase in value of 'the assets', and 10 per cent of the gain in the market value of JCI between 16 August and the due date for repayment, which Investec could extend for up to 18 months. If all went well, Investec stood to make more than R100 million, but, at the very least, it would be R50 million to the good. Crucially, the R460 million facility appeared to be secure. The assets referred to were those that JCI had agreed to push into an SPV, to be constituted as a wholly owned subsidiary.

These assets, which were ceded and pledged to Investec, included JCI's interests in the Letšeng diamond mine and Matodzi, 15 million Western Areas shares (which were already pledged to another financial institution), rights in the Boschendal wine estate and Jaganda (representing indirect exposure to shares in listed Simmer and Jack Mines), a further 6.5 million Western Areas shares that had been pledged to the Industrial Development Corporation, and the property portfolio of JCI and its subsidiaries.

In a nutshell, Investec had been placed in the position of preferential creditor, a development that increased the risk attached to other lenders' exposure to JCI.

Koseff contended that the value of the assets in the SPV was more than three times the R460 million facility, giving Investec gloriously comfortable cover in extending the facility in the first place.

The Western Areas rights issue proved fully successful,* not least because JCI agreed to underwrite up to R250 million of the R639 million issue; Allan Gray gave an irrevocable undertaking to follow its rights. The issue was pitched at R18 per share, almost half the 12-month high of R35. Koseff brimmed with confidence over prospects for the stock prices, insisting 'we want proper governance'.

Investec had an established association with Western Areas. In mid-2001 (at the nadir of the gold price cycle), it had been among a consortium of international banks that had set up *that* hedge book for the company. For Koseff, however, the risk was immaterial, given the 'wonderful quality and sheer size' of the South Deep ore body. He maintained that Investec's exposure was 'smaller than generally believed', and pointed out that the exposure was not to Western Areas shares as such. 'The hedge book,' Koseff explained, 'is secured by the mining asset itself – lots of gold.'

Elsewhere, the cleaning up of Kebble's mess continued on a pervasive scale.

Following requests by the author, JCI released the previously unseen accounts for CMMS in mid-October 2005. Covering the year to 31 March 2004, they showed that CMMS remained hopelessly insolvent. Accumulated losses had increased from R530 million in 2003 to R676 million in 2004, while liabilities exceeded assets by R640 million (R493 million in 2003).† This parlous situation was of little concern to either CMMS or its auditors, however, given JCI's history of propping up the slush fund.

One of the biggest *assets* at CMMS was the 'holding company loan'. This was classified as an asset because it was *interest-free*, had *no fixed terms of repayment* and was *fully unsecured*. This amount had decreased from R543 million in 2003 to R468 million in 2004. These two figures were the only two that appeared under the name of CMMS in the entire published JCI annual report for 2004. Everything else was hidden, including R68 million from CMMS that Kebble had splashed out on 'investment properties'. CMMS had paid R37 million in 'consulting and management fees' in 2004, compared to a relatively paltry R7 million the year before. Nowhere were the consultants named or details given of the services provided. However, CMMS apparently became of some concern to its auditors, Charles Orbach & Company, during 2004. The audit fee rose 275 per cent over the previous year to R1.4 million, despite the lack of evidence of substantial extra work. However, it is

---

*   See Appendix L, items 13–19.

†   See Appendix J, line 16.

not unheard of for auditors to charge a premium when extra work is required due to a perceived increase in risk in the entity under audit.

In the six financial years to 31 March 2004, CMMS losses had totalled R566 million.[*]

When JCI's new management released the CMMS accounts, which had not been signed by Kebble, it said they would not be changed and would be filed in due course. Eventually, they were.

Roger Kebble and the little-known Lieben Hendrik Swanevelder had been directors of CMMS since 1999. Swanevelder resigned in November 2004, when the registrar triggered the process for deregistration of CMMS for failure to file accounts. Stratton and Lamprecht were elected to the board, but the latter quit on 5 July 2005, only to be reappointed on 30 August, when Brett and Roger Kebble, as well as Stratton, were forced off the CMMS board. After reconfiguration, the board comprised Peter Gray, Lamprecht and Benita Morton, a lawyer.

There was no sign or suggestion that any of the various regulatory or law enforcement authorities were going to take action in respect of the Kebble debacle. Rob Barrow, CEO of the Financial Services Board, would neither confirm nor deny an investigation into the billion-rand scandal. In February 2005, the FSB had added the Securities Services Act (SSA), a particularly powerful piece of legislation with huge, sharp teeth, to its arsenal. Solid chunks of Kebble's most questionable behaviour had occurred after the new law came into force, and from June 2005, details that emerged about his conduct pointed toward the investigative side of Section 76 of the SSA, which deals with 'false, misleading or deceptive statements, promises and forecasts'.[†]

On 22 September, just five days before Kebble died, Randgold & Exploration's new management said in a statement that it did not 'currently believe that significant influence over Randgold Resources Ltd can be demonstrated'. The company withdrew the entire results announcement of 29 April with a warning that it should not be relied upon by investors. On the same day, Charles Orbach & Company resigned as Randgold & Exploration's auditors, and there was a flood of notices from other companies cancelling their connections with CMMS.

It was simply not possible to count the number of times that Kebble had lied.

---

[*]   See Appendix J, item 39.

[†]   Section 76 of the SSA states: 'No person may, directly or indirectly, make or publish in respect of listed securities, or in respect of the past or future performance of a public company any statement, promise or forecast which is, at the time and in the light of the circumstances in which it is made, false or misleading or deceptive in respect of any material fact and which the person knows, or ought reasonably to know, is false, misleading or deceptive.' A person who commits such an offence is liable on conviction to a fine not exceeding R50 million or to imprisonment for a period not exceeding ten years, or both.

He had carefully concealed the vital fact that if Anglo American was not paid by 1 November 2004 in terms of the Inkwenkwezi deal, a penalty of R70 million was payable by Randgold & Exploration.* Throughout the final chapter of his life, Kebble had recklessly and wantonly used Randgold & Exploration as yet another slush fund.

On 14 December, JCI's new management announced that forensic auditors appointed on 11 October to assess various transactions and any other issues identified during the audit and/or by the directors had made 'substantial progress'. JCI further advised that the scope of the investigation had been revisited to address issues not originally identified. It came as no surprise when JCI confirmed that the ongoing investigation had 'revealed *prima facie* evidence that there has been misappropriation of company assets, including during prior financial periods'. This indicated that accounts published for prior periods were in line to be declared not just misleading, but plain fraudulent. Work was in progress to determine the exact extent of the misappropriation, 'which could be substantial, as well as to initiate, if necessary, the relevant legal processes, including the necessary actions for the recovery of misappropriated assets', the JCI statement said.

The abysmal truth about Brett Kebble's business career was only starting to surface.

---

* In its filing with the SEC for the financial year to 31 December 2003, Randgold & Exploration referred to a 'Consortium Sale Agreement amongst Tawny Eagle Holdings (Pty) Ltd and Anglo South Africa Capital (Pty) Ltd and Chestnut Hill Investments 60 (Pty) Ltd and Randgold & Exploration Company Ltd'. Under the terms of this agreement, Anglo South Africa sold to Chestnut Hill 13 738 507 ordinary shares of WAL [Western Areas] at a price of R37.50 each for a total consideration of R515 194 012.50. This amount was payable by 1 November 2004, and bore interest at the prime rate charged by the Standard Bank of South Africa plus 1.5%. If Chestnut failed to fulfil its obligations, Anglo South Africa would be entitled to repurchase 5 268 800 Western Areas shares purchased by Randgold & Exploration at a discount of R70 million, or claim a penalty in that amount from Randgold & Exploration. Chestnut subsequently changed its name to Inkwenkwezi Gold Mining Consortium.

20

The final straw

THE STRAW THAT broke the proverbial camel's back might well have been a judgment handed down by the Johannesburg High Court on 21 October 2004. Durban Roodepoort Deep (DRD) scored a stunning R35.7 million victory against JCI Ltd and its predecessor, Consolidated African Mines (CAM). Indicating the court's irritation that the case had ever gone so far, JCI was also ordered to pay interest and costs, including those of two counsel.

The case was rooted in an undertaking Brett Kebble had given to pay DRD an option fee for warehousing shares that DRD had acquired as part of Project Eagle, JCI Gold's unsuccessful endeavour to incorporate Randfontein Estates Gold Mine into Western Areas. The case was one of many bits and pieces of collateral damage spat out after the showdown at Randfontein. DRD had instituted proceedings after JCI/CAM had paid a small portion of the fee, but refused to come up with the balance.

JCI/CAM's counterclaim for recovery of the part-payment was also dismissed with costs. The court called JCI/CAM's evidence on the accounting treatment of DRD's claim, which accrued over some 14 months, 'nonsense' and a 'deliberate lie'. It dismissed as 'manifestly false' JCI/CAM's contention that the earlier payment had been made under the mistaken belief that it was due.

Hennie Buitendag, omnipresent financial director of the core Kebble companies, was singled out by the judge as a 'dishonest witness, who in an arrogant manner made statements, which were manifestly mendacious, and an insult to the intelligence of this court'. The judgment appeared to give Kebble a severe case of aboulia.

On 15 March 2005, Ilja Graulich, a DRD executive, recalled some dramatic moments following attempts to execute the court order. He told Alec Hogg, host of the *Moneyweb Power Hour* radio show, that 'we made it quite clear over the last couple of days and weeks, when the court ordered [JCI] to pay money, that we would like to be paid that R38 million. [Kebble] did make promises, yes, that he was going to pay us yesterday and that never happened, so this morning we sent the sheriff [of the High Court] to start attaching assets. Unfortunately, we didn't find much and our next step now is to seek an application for liquidation of the CAM/JCI group of companies in order to recover the R38 million that they owe us.'

Amid the forfending, some of the money had been paid by a dyspeptic Kebble, who had nobody but himself to blame for the contretemps. Graulich told Hogg: 'Yes, this afternoon a cheque did arrive in our bank account after we threatened with the liquidation, and R12 million did arrive, but the order is for R38 million, so we are still R26 million short.'

Hogg asked when Kebble was supposed to pay the balance.

GRAULICH: Well, the first court order was issued in October and then the Appeal Court also turned him down, and then the Supreme Court of Appeal. So about two weeks ago that's what happened. Then we gave him 48 hours to pay. He asked for postponement as he believed there was a constitutional issue in all of this. He then made a statement last week, saying that he wasn't going to pursue this and he was going to pay us by midday yesterday – but no money by midday yesterday.

HOGG: But R12 million today?

GRAULICH: R12 million this afternoon, yes, so we're waiting for the R26 million. But let me make it quite clear, we are continuing with our application to liquidate the companies until all the money is in there. You would have seen in all his statements, in the waffle, that he believes he could help the company, and hopes for the better good of the company and all these things. You know, if that was so true, where's the money that we need to assist these mines that he so dearly loves?

Graulich appeared to have great difficulty with the half-baked explanation about how the balance would materialise. Kebble had claimed that a hold-up with a BEE transaction was the main reason for the delay, and, as far as Graulich could ascertain, that was the only reason given. In his attempts to stave off liquidation, Kebble had offered 'surety' to DRD in respect of the outstanding balance.

GRAULICH: He gave us, or the company gave us this morning when the sheriff arrived, about 50 million shares in Matodzi Resources, ordinary shares in Matodzi Resources. But the share certificates were made out in companies' names that we didn't know about, nor do we know whether JCI is allowed to deal on behalf of these shareholders in those shares, so obviously we couldn't accept those shares.

If anyone knew Kebble at his most splenetic, it was DRD and, in particular, its executive chairman, Mark Wellesley-Wood. He was the supreme non-simpatico, and he was not about to entertain Kebble's temporisations.

A number of those familiar with Kebble's foray into business say that his single biggest mistake was Randfontein. It was a debacle that was easily avoidable, but it spawned not only a criminal indictment against both Brett and Roger Kebble, but also against Buitendag. It also irredeemably tainted Kebble's reputation. Had he successfully executed Project Eagle, JCI's board of directors would have been formidable and palatable for even the most cynical investor: Henry 'Hank' Slack, Wiseman Nkuhlu, Roger Kebble, David Kovarsky, John Fox Brownrigg, Vaughan Bray, Mark Bristow, John Hick, Frank McKenna, Bill Nairn, Rupert Pennant-Rea, Royden Richardson, Tokyo Sexwale and, of all people, Mark Wellesley-Wood. It goes without saying that Kebble would have been the CEO.

Instead, he ended up with a new JCI that boasted himself as CEO and, as directors, Buitendag, Roger Kebble and Paul Ferguson, and later John Stratton and Charles Cornwall.

Kebble would never recover from the DRD-inspired near-liquidation of JCI. From the day Graulich practically set up camp outside the JCI head office, Kebble launched his final but futile joust against cash starvation.

When JCI's stock was suspended from trading on the JSE on 1 August at 16 cents a share, it was 98 per cent down on its lifetime high of 680 cents a share in 1997. Over the years, the wider body of investors knew nothing even approaching the full details, but had sufficient sense of depravity to quit investing in JCI.

After Kebble was forced out as CEO of Western Areas, JCI and Randgold & Exploration on 31 August, he had no way of cashing in the 244 million shares (down to 235 million, according to JCI's 2004 annual report) that he had illicitly acquired in 1997. Even if JCI had still been trading, there was no way so many shares could have been sold in the market, and once the stock was suspended, no one would have touched them.

Kebble's meltdown had commenced; there was nothing left to feed the wolf;* there was no styptic agent that would staunch the haemorrhage. He had suffered his final reversal of fortune, whatever 'fortune' was by his definition. No longer could he pay his network of obsequious spongers.

Late in February 2006, Wellesley-Wood recalled some of the dramatic events that had marked his titanic struggles with the Kebbles. When the DRD special audit committee met to dissolve on 22 July 2002, he recalled, no fewer than 21 cases had been outlined against the Kebble rubric. It was just too many; in some cases, successful settlements were arrived at. For various reasons, some cases were disregarded or abandoned. Some of the bigger cases remained unresolved, yet others could still go to trial.

---

* In Cherokee folklore, an old man tells his grandson about the eternal inner human battle. 'My son, the battle is between two wolves inside all of us. One is Evil. It is anger, envy, jealousy, sorrow, regret, greed, arrogance, self-pity, guilt, resentment, inferiority, lies, false pride, superiority and ego. The other is Good. It is joy, peace, love, hope, serenity, humility, kindness, benevolence, empathy, generosity, truth, compassion and faith.' The grandson considers this for a moment, then asks his grandfather: 'Which wolf wins?' The old Cherokee replies simply: 'The one you feed.'

'The Kebbles had a sausage machine going at DRD,' Wellesley-Wood muttered. He paused to reflect. Then, with a slight grimace, Wellesley-Wood acknowledged that he was one of the few people who had ever stood up to the Kebbles, and won. 'I still bear the scars,' he said wistfully.

PART VII

Desperado

21

By the Cathédrale
Notre Dame de la Paix

HOW DO I CALL YOU?'
'Duke Grace in the Confusion,' the man answered, giving one of the code names of a great and experienced smuggler. He had chosen the location for the meeting. It was he who had the information on Brett Kebble, so it was his call.

This was The Duke.

The meeting was at the Alimentation Mon Jardin, just off Avenue President Lumumba. It was on a hill behind the Cathédrale Notre Dame de la Paix, bounded by Avenue de Mahenge to the west, Avenue de Saio to the east and Corniche de Dendere to the north. The lake was calm and flat. It was a beautiful day with a marbled blue sky.

The cathedral stood, like a big caring lighthouse, at the base of a peninsula, one of five that pushes out into Lake Kivu. Local legend has it that God placed five green fingers in the lake at this, its most southern extension. Avenue President Lumumba swings due north before heading into the first and most important peninsula to the west. This is the peninsula that looks like a dogleg from the air.

After more than two kilometres, the avenue eventually merges, at some indeterminate point, with the Avenue des Sports. At the furthest tip of the peninsula lies the sports club, featuring the Cercle Sportif, well maintained and smart, a truly lovely hangover from the colonial era that fans out like a bouffant veil for the closest building, the Cabinet du Gouverneur.

Moving south towards the mainland, and practically in a straight line, there are various government and international organisations: provincial headquarters of the judiciary, police, education, mining and geology, the Assemblée Provinciale, International Red Cross, a major bank, the Metropole Hotel, a maternity clinic. Where the peninsula melds with the mainland, there is the Hotel Residence and its neighbour, one of many buildings in Bukavu occupied by United Nations personnel. They are everywhere, peacekeepers and professionals from every sphere of society, battling the forces that turned this corner of Central Africa into the biggest killing fields since the Second World War.

The lake is about 100 kilometres long and lies about 1 500 metres above sea level. Bukavu is just west of Cyangugu in Rwanda, and is separated from it by the outlet to the Ruzizi River. The Ruzizi carries the Lake Kivu overspill south, and is infamous for having borne many thousands of bodies down river to Lake Tanganyika during the genocide. It is said that some of the largest crocodiles in Africa live on the lower reaches of the Ruzizi. Some of them crocodiles have a highly developed taste for human flesh.

About half a million people live in Bukavu, which was established as Costermansville by Belgian colonialists in 1901. To some, Bukavu is the African Riviera, and there are certainly a number of fine villas on the lake shore. The common people live up in the hills, which rise to 2 000 metres and more above sea level, in a district known as Kadutu.

Local residents swear that it was in Bukavu that Humphrey Bogart and Katharine Hepburn filmed the classic film *The African Queen*. Anyone who has been to Bukavu and has also seen the motion picture would know for sure. More recently, Bukavu has become the staging point for jungle treks to the habitat of the magnificent silver-backed mountain gorillas.

Bukavu is one fine place, but it also happens to be the epicentre of the most volatile region in Africa.

The Duke and I had met about three hours before sunset. He was a youngish 60-something, of above-average height without being lanky, tanned and muscular, with short-cropped hair and a face peppered with stubble. He had pale blue eyes and his accent was impossible to place, laced as it was with clues from Canada and perhaps Ireland, possibly even Sweden. Certainly there were touches of a French influence, no doubt from living for an unknown number of years in what had once been colonies when French was the official language of the intelligentsia. It still was, at least in much of Africa. Perhaps the Duke was an American.

'Well, Duke, I am very happy to make your acquaintance.'

'The pleasure is all mine. You need to understand that the only reason I agreed to meet you was due to my retirement. I am leaving this continent and thought it only right that some kind of record about this man should be left.'

'Where did you first see him?'

'In Luanda. You may have heard that I met him here in Bukavu, at the Orchids Safari Club, where you are staying. That is untrue. He was never here in Bukavu, for reasons that will become apparent.'

'Of course.'

'His agents came here first, starting in about 2001. It is true that somebody who looked like him stayed at the Orchids – where else? – under a *nom d'emprunt*.

But it was not he. Why would a man who likes to be on the front pages, to be seen with the rich and famous, stay in such a dangerous country under an assumed name?'

'The hell I would know.'

'He was scared,' said the Duke. 'He was always scared, with that chicken heart of his. There was nothing he could do about it. He was born like that and there was nothing he could ever do about it. Brett Kebble and his little chicken heart …'

The Duke paused. He had driven to our meeting in a well-equipped vehicle that had been deliberately engineered down so that, superficially, it looked plain and beaten and even old. However, careful inspection showed that it was a world-class vehicle that few could afford. It was excellently maintained, if you knew what to look for. This was the vehicle of a great and experienced smuggler who knew how to stay out of trouble.

The Duke had chosen the public recreation area for a serious picnic, a barbecue. There were three large cooler boxes, a fold-up wooden safari table, two canvas seats and a wooden trunk that held all the small necessities for fine drinking and eating. There were also lighting facilities, and a weatherproof briefcase that might well have been bombproof, too.

He went over to the red cooler box and extracted a bottle of Johnny Walker, the blue label variety.

'What would you like?'

'Mützig, should you have.'

'Ah, yes,' the Duke declared. He went to the big green cooler box and extracted a bottle of very cold-looking Mützig, with its distinctive capital 'M' in white on a red oval background, the name 'Mützig' running through the 'M' in dark and ancient letters.

'An excellent choice,' the Duke said. 'From Brasseries du Congo in Pointe-Noire. Primus is also good.'

The Duke drew himself erect, a Primus in one hand and a Mützig in the other. He was one fine sight, and it was time to drink.

Mützig is an excellent beer made by Heineken, available in the Congo, Cameroon and other central African states. Primus is also made by Heineken, but is not so fine a beer, though it is said to be more popular.

The Duke gestured towards the imposing cathedral that formed the backdrop to our rendezvous.

'Brett Kebble was a Catholic,' he said, apropos of nothing, really.

A helicopter came into view from the direction of the mountains. The Duke looked up and followed its progress as it descended rapidly and turned over the Baie de Bukavu to land at the helipad just west of the port. The helicopter was mainly beige in colour, branded with a large 'UN' on each side of the fuselage, and, down each side of the tail assembly, in capital letters and dirty white paint, the words UNITED NATIONS.

'MI-17,' the Duke said, raising his voice above the hum of the rotor blades. 'Wonderful piece of Russian engineering, the most-made chopper in Russian aviation history. You can recognise it by the tail rotor sitting on the starboard side. If you like numbers, that baby has two shaft-turbine engines each delivering 2 000 shaft horsepower.'

The Duke sat down, holding his glass of whisky as if he were fondling a woman's breast. He sucked at the drink, rather than drinking it, as if he wanted the liquor to vaporise above the ice before it went up his nostrils and simultaneously hit his palate.

'So there he was, Brett Kebble in Luanda, sipping, sipping, sipping cognac. Do you know that for all his aspirations to become Mr Big in Angola, to become bigger than Lev Leviev, he only went to Luanda twice in his life? He was so terrified that he did not even stay overnight. He flew back to Johannesburg the same day, both times, on "his" Gulfstream. Do you know what an effort that is? A day trip to Luanda from Johannesburg? Four hours to fly one way, another four back, and so on. What kind of a human being does that, I ask?'

'He was there for diamonds, of course.'

'Diamonds. Only diamonds. But he did not want any deal. He did not want anything formal.'

'He did announce some diamond deals in Angola, formal ones. At least they appeared to be formal, even normal.'

'Ah,' said the Duke, as if he had just discovered something, 'he did need to have some formal diamond deals in place. You will see why. Be patient.'

It was going to be a beautiful evening. East of the Alimentation Mon Jardin, at the juncture of the Rue Irambo, Grande Corniche and Avenue President Lumumba, a mosque squatted under the peaceful skies. To the west were several buildings occupied by the UN, including its headquarters for Bukavu, situated between the headquarters of Radio Télévision Nationale du Congo and Banque Commerciale.

Maribou storks circled over the port, and crows. There are often Maribou storks, and always crows, in this part of Africa, the storks with their meat-cleaver beaks, and the crows, leaders of the *corvus* family, with the biggest brains in the feathered world. The crows could be found in the high country, right up in the mountains. They needed those big brains to survive up there.

'So, you want to know about the diamonds,' the Duke said quietly.

'That would be a good thing to know.'

'Then allow me a short introduction. Being a smuggler, I have ample time to study many things. I will tell you something about the people. You need to know a little about the people before you know about the diamonds. Today, Congo, République Démocratique du Congo, the Congo, until recently Zaire, but always *the* Congo, a country roughly the size of Western Europe, has, of course, its capital, Kinshasa. There are ten provinces: Bandundu; Bas-Congo; Équateur; Katanga (which used to be Shaba); Kinshasa; Maniema; Orientale (once known as Haut-Zaire), and then, in the east, the two Kivus, North and South, and the two Kasais, Occidental and Orientale. Some of these provinces are big, very big. Katanga, for one, is about the size of France. Orientale is probably bigger.

'Let us have a moment of deep history. From about 2000 BC to AD 500, the Bantu migrated into this country, a troublesome thing for the original peoples, the Pygmies. People moved in from Darfur and Kordofan, in today's Sudan, and then from East Africa as well. Around the fifth century, a powerful society started along about 200 kilometres of the Lualaba River in what we know as Katanga. The Lualaba is the headstream of the Congo, running from about Lubumbashi – the capital of Africa's copper and cobalt mines – to Kisangani, where the Congo River officially starts.'

The Duke went over to his vehicle and retrieved some papers.

'Here are the Lualaba tributaries.'

He pointed and spoke with rapid coordination, striking on a big map each river with his right forefinger: 'The Lowa, Ulindi, Luama, Lukuga, Lufira, Lubudi and Luvua rivers.'

'Back in time, the super-culture, the *Upemba*, would grow into the Luba kingdom. The transition was slow and not without complication, and was intertwined with mining, especially of iron ore and copper. The Luba established a far-flung sphere of influence with their metal products and ivory. A thousand years after the seeds of the *Upemba* had been sown, Luba had a powerful government structure, funded by taxes, along with an established system of chieftainship.

'The Congo, as it is now known, was formally acquired by King Leopold II of Belgium at the Conference of Berlin in 1885. He made the country his backyard, and called it the Congo Free State. After a reign of unprecedented pillaging, looting and destruction, the Belgian parliament in 1908 forcibly adopted from the mad king the Congo Free State as a colony, renaming it the Belgian Congo. Little changed. The looting and pillaging, the chaos continued, and then finally colonialism was going out of fashion. In 1959, Patrice Lumumba and his Mouvement National Congolais won the first free elections, just ahead of independence from Belgium.

Joseph Kasavubu became the president, with Lumumba as prime minister. Late in 1960, Kasavubu dismissed Lumumba, who was arrested in December and murdered a few months into 1961. The cynics will tell you that the CIA was in the background.

'Following five years of extreme instability and civil unrest, Mobutu emerged. He was born Joseph-Désiré Mobutu, but later became Mobutu Sese Seko Koko Ngbendu wa za Banga. That apparently means – and one has to memorise this, but here goes – *the all-powerful warrior who, because of his endurance and inflexible will to win, will go from conquest to conquest, leaving fire in his wake.* How was that?

'Well, Mobutu seized control in a coup d'état. A one-party system was established, and he declared himself head of state. He would occasionally hold "elections", but he was the only candidate. The evening news on television was preceded by an image of him descending through clouds from the heavens; portraits of him adorned many public places; government officials wore lapel badges bearing his portrait; and he held such titles as "Father of the Nation", "Saviour of the People" and "Supreme Combatant". Mobutu was reputedly anti-communist, and was, it was said, supported by the CIA. I do not care about the CIA stuff. In any event, Mobutu was around forever. In 1971 he renamed Congo *Zaire.* That was also when he renamed himself.

'And then the Cold War was over. On 9 November 1989, the Berlin Wall fell. Who can forget that date? In 1990, Mobutu ended Zaire's one-party system and promised to hold elections, but the next year there were riots in Kinshasa. The soldiers were not being paid. Mobutu agreed under pressure to a coalition government. But the dictator had already collapsed the state system. He had weakened each of the provinces, not only through never-ending looting and pillaging, but also by ensuring that the country had no integrated transport network. Today, Équateur, which would take up more than half of France, has less than 100 kilometres of paved road.'

Mobutu had just about killed off mining, and had ensured that what business remained was conducted by his cronies, or mostly for their benefit, according to the Duke, who had retrieved a sheaf of papers from what appeared to be a mobile library. Copper production by Gécamines, the state-owned miner working on some of the world's biggest and richest copper and cobalt reserves, peaked at more than 500 000 tons in 1975, before starting its precipitous fall to 200 000 tons at the beginning of the 1990s, and less than 40 000 tons a year by the end of Mobutu's reign. Mobutu also isolated his strongmen, applying a divide-and-rule strategy. General Kpama Baramoto, for one, ran the 10 000-strong Guarde Civile, along with gold mines in the Kivu provinces and diamond mines in the Kasai provinces, while playing a major role in military support for União Nacional para a Independência Total de Angola (Unita) in Angola, as part of a barter deal for diamonds. Mobutu and his cronies had moved increasingly into money laundering, drug trafficking and especially diamonds.

'Now, as every good criminal knows,' said the Duke, warming to his theme, 'money laundering, drugs and diamonds are a perfect match.'

Diamond mining in the Congo had not been killed off for a number of reasons. For the longest time, the state-owned La Société Minière de Bakwang, known as Miba, had a concession of more than 60 000 square kilometres, about the size of a small country such as Togo. After Mobutu 'legalised' artisanal mining in 1983 and the informal sector was allowed to mine diamonds, stones were found all over. Mobutu and his cronies wanted a permanent piece of *this* action. Diamonds had become the country's single biggest export earner, and that meant foreign currency.

'Talking about Miba, by the way, you will find that the Congo story is filled with acronyms, mostly for political entities,' said the Duke, handing over a long list of printed names before continuing.

'In 1991, the International Monetary Fund announced that Zaire would not receive new loans, and it expelled the country in 1994. This mirrored growing impatience by Zaire's former Cold War patrons, Belgium, France and the United States. Mobutu was now a financial and political liability. His grand theft of what was left of the Congo only increased, but he was also being forced to give out the right signals. He sought new private investment in mining enterprises in the mid-1990s. By then, many thousands of people in Kinshasa, Bandundu, Kasai-Occidental and Kasai-Oriental, along with areas around Kisangani in Orientale province, depended primarily on diamonds.'

The time to which the Duke referred coincided with an increase in junior mining companies on the world's alternative stock markets. The mid-1990s were the heyday of Bre-X, the great Canadian gold mining ruse in Indonesia, which saw junior miners barrelling headlong into remote tracts of Africa and Asia in pursuit of promised riches. In 1997 alone, Mobutu's regime issued more than a hundred preliminary prospecting agreements, while his Congolese schemes sought joint venture redevelopment of the formal mining sector through the infusion of capital into parastatals such as Gécamines, Miba, Société Minière et Industrielle du Kivu (Sominki) and Office des Mines d'Or de Kilo-Moto (Okimo).

On 11 January 1994, according to the Duke, Major General Roméo Dallaire sent a cable from Rwanda to UN headquarters in New York, urgently appealing for the protection of an informant who had detailed an elaborate plan by the Hutu to exterminate the Tutsi by means of nothing less than genocide. There were also plans to provoke and kill Belgian troops so as to guarantee Belgium's withdrawal from Rwanda. Dallaire's information included the location of arms caches held by the *Interahamwe*, a vicious and deadly Hutu militia. He received a reply the same day, from the desk of Kofi Annan, then the UN head of peacekeeping and later secretary-general. Not only did the organisation veto Dallaire's plan to raid the arms caches, he was also instructed to relay all the information he had to the Rwandan president, Juvénal Habyarimana, despite the fact that members of Habyarimana's inner circle were planning the slaughter.

'Habyarimana swallowed smoke soon enough,' the Duke recounted. 'On 6 April, he and the president of Burundi, Cyprien Ntaryamira, died when their jet was torched in the sky near Rwanda's capital, Kigali, not so very far from here. Both men were Hutu, but Hutu extremists, suspecting that the Rwandan president was finally about to implement the Arusha Peace Accords, were believed to have orchestrated the deadly attack. Mass killings started that night, and the Rwandan genocide was on. By 21 April, the Red Cross estimated that the death toll already ran into hundreds of thousands. In the months ahead, the total would be put at a minimum of 500 000. Some say the final number was 800 000, others say a million. The Ruzizi crocodiles were very happy,' he said, motioning in the direction of the river, south of Bukavu.

'The *Interahamwe*, which means "those who fight together" in Kinyarwanda, the language of Rwanda, was the deadliest of the militias, formed by the Hutu majority. Along with the smaller *Impuzamugambi*, they carried out the genocide. But they didn't kill enough Tutsi. In July, Kigali was liberated by the Rwandese Patriotic Front, who were Tutsi. Many *Interahamwe* fled, especially to the Congo, where they joined up with Hutu ex-soldiers from Rwanda and called themselves the Rassemblement Démocratique pour le Rwanda, which roughly translates as the Democratic Rally for Rwanda.'

The Duke stared out over the lake, in the direction of Rwanda, before picking up his lesson on the region's troubled recent past.

'After signing up big numbers of Congolese Hutu, the Armée pour de Libération du Rwanda emerged. The growing Hutu presence in eastern Congo brought Mobutu into close contact again with France, former backer of the Hutu regime. He fancied the Rwandan Hutu paramilitary units, which, for all anyone knows, might have been planning to wipe out the Banyamulenge in the Kivu provinces. They are mainly Tutsi.

'The Tutsi. Nobody is sure about their origin, but they are tall, sometimes more than two metres, and they have sharp features. It makes no difference to me, but the colonials regarded them as a Hamitic* people. Some said the Tutsi came from East Africa, maybe Sudan, Uganda or Ethiopia, around 1400, to settle around Lake Kivu. That was the beginning of the native kingdoms of Rwanda and Burundi, under a Tutsi *mwami*, or king. The Tutsi were herders, with diets of meat and milk, but they showed a readiness to be traders and businessmen. The Hutu were pasturalists.

'Both the German and Belgian colonialists exploited the existing hierarchical and aristocratic structure of Tutsi rule and Hutu submission. But everything changed in the 1960s, when the Belgians switched support to the Hutu majority in Rwanda. Resentment that had built up over centuries started bubbling to the surface. There was violence, and the Tutsi started fleeing to Uganda, Tanzania, Burundi and Zaire.

'The colonial powers settled Banyarwandans, mainly Tutsi, on vacant lands in eastern Congo, land that had traditionally belonged to indigenous customary Hunde chiefs. After independence, the chiefs extorted high taxes and fines and sold land deeds at exorbitant prices. The Banyarwandans went crazy. Zaire granted nationality to all Banyarwanda in 1971, but ten years later this was amended so that only those who could prove that their ancestors had lived in Zaire since 1885, qualified. That was the year when Leopold formally took control of the Congo.'

The day had mellowed into dusk as the Duke shared his prodigious knowledge of his adopted country's history, but he clearly still had much to impart.

In October 1996, Banyamulenge and Tutsi rebel forces, supported by Uganda and Rwanda, invaded the Kivu region in order to reclaim their revoked citizenship and escape the *Interahamwe* and Hutu threat. Following the earlier genocide, the Rwandan government had hurled abuse at Mobutu, but with the *Interahamwe* crawling all over eastern Congo in various guises, the fun was just getting started.

Towards the end of 1996, the deputy governor of South Kivu, Lwasi Ngabo Lwabanji, suddenly decreed that the more than 200 000 Banyamulenge – and these were specifically Tutsis – had one week to leave the country. Meanwhile, four local anti-Mobutu groups had formed a coalition, the Alliance des Forces Démocratiques pour la Libération du Congo-Zaire (AFDL), headed by the relatively unknown rebel leader, Laurent-Désiré Kabila. After an astonishingly rapid advance across the country, starting at Uvira, and during which Mobutu's army put up little fight, the AFDL swept into Kinshasa. Mobutu's underpaid and demoralised army offered little resistance. When Kabila entered the capital in May 1997, Mobutu and his

---

* Said to have descended from Ham, a son of Noah. According to the Bible, the sons of Ham were traditional enemies of the Jews, Egyptians and Canaanites. Ham's son Canaan was said to have fathered the Canaanites, Mizraim the Egyptians, Cush the Cushites and Phut the Phutites. A pejorative theory was that a Hamitic race identified in Africa was more 'advanced' than other tribes on the continent. The 'Hamitic Myth' was cited as justifying European colonial policy in Africa in the nineteenth and twentieth centuries, as well as the trade in slaves.

extremely large extended family had escaped by any means they could, some of his sons literally commandeering boats to cross the broad river and seek asylum in Congo-Brazzaville as the first rebels marched down the city streets.

Once installed as the new president, Kabila cancelled – or redistributed – many of the mining and prospecting agreements that Mobutu had dished out. Any number of Western mining companies flocked to the newly named Democratic Republic of Congo to secure contracts they had failed to negotiate in the final years of Mobutu's dictatorship.

Less than a year after being forced into exile, Mobutu died in Rabat, Morocco. But neither a change of regime nor their country's name brought peace or relief to ordinary Congolese.

'Kabila was a drunk and an idiot,' the Duke said bluntly. This was the same Kabila who had driven Cuban revolutionary hero Che Guevara – Ernesto Rafael Guevara de la Serna – half crazy more than three decades earlier.

The Duke paused to reflect while he replenished the drinks.

'Guevara and nearly a hundred Cuban officers spent no less than six months in the Congo in 1965, trying to help Kabila with an earlier armed rebellion. Guevara would say in later years that Kabila had a habit of issuing orders that were impossible to execute. Guevara left the Congo thoroughly disillusioned with the quality of leadership displayed by Kabila and his comrades. Kabila never once fought shoulder to shoulder with Guevara.

'In fact, he was usually nowhere near the front lines. His revolution then consisted of attending parties, raising money and collecting more supplies than his forces could use.'

When Kabila finally seized power in the late 1990s, Banyamulenge and Rwandan military officers dominated his government and security forces for the first year. But the Congo had simply exchanged one corrupt dictator for another. Kabila increasingly ignored the Banyamulenge, and towards the end of July 1998, he ordered the expulsion of all foreign soldiers from Congolese territory. Within the month he faced a multipronged rebellion, backed by Rwanda and Uganda.

Before long, the bloody conflict would become multinational, with troops from Zimbabwe, Angola, Namibia, Chad and Sudan supporting the Kinshasa regime against what were nothing less than the surrogate armies of Rwanda (RCD-Goma) and Uganda (MLC), which had occupied the eastern half of the Congo.

On 23 July, the *Washington Post* reported that American soldiers had been sighted with Rwandan troops. The US had trained, armed and funded the armies of both Rwanda and Uganda, and was silent on their invasion of territory formerly controlled by Mobutu, the CIA puppet who had been propped up by Washington for decades.

Brandishing a copy of the newspaper report, the Duke warmed to his subject. 'Kabila only accepted the Lusaka Accord* because of the implicit American threat that refusal would see even more help for the rebels. They could have destroyed the whole country. That message became clear to everyone when Kabila was assassinated in 2001. It was on 17 January, by the way – the same day that Lumumba was bulleted 40 years before.

'But let us focus on the diamonds. Those little pieces of carbon that Kebble could not resist have played a big role in African conflict. They have paid for some of the longest and bloodiest civil wars on this continent, in Angola, in Sierra Leone ... blood diamonds, we call them now, but it was different when the world looked the other way.'

Kabila took an early interest in diamonds. Long before he claimed the presidential palace – indeed, while his rebel army was still fighting its way across the vast country on the way to Kinshasa – he was making deals with adventurers who were lining up to profit from the gemstones and other resources that made the Congo a veritable natural treasure trove. In 1996, Kabila entered an agreement with America Mineral Fields to mine the gigantic Kolwezi cobalt tailings in the southern province of Katanga, along the copper belt that runs into Zambia. In March 1997, Mauritian-born Jean-Raymond Boule, founder of AMF and one-time employee of De Beers, the world's leading diamond producer, signed a $1 billion agreement with Kabila to develop a zinc mine at Kipushi and a cobalt venture at Kolwezi. According to the Duke, Boule was also given the thumbs-up to deal diamonds in Katanga and set up America Diamond Buyers in rebel-controlled Kisangani, on the Congo River in the province of Orientale. As part of the deal, Boule lent Kabila a leased jet.

'Welcome to Africa!' shouted the Duke, his grin acknowledging that the continent never fails to deliver something new, however dark.

'The robber barons, the merchant adventurers, they understood the situation. Kisangani is one of the three most important names in Congolese diamonds. Mbuji-Mayi, far to the south in Kasai-Oriental, is the headquarters of Miba's operations. Then there is Tshikapa, to the west of Mbuji-Mayi, in Kasai-Occidental.'

Another helicopter could be heard in the distance, coming in from the mountains.

'Ah,' said the Duke, 'a Halo.'

---

* A ceasefire agreement signed by combatants in the seven-nation war in July 1999. The pact was signed in the Zambian capital after a year of negotiations by regional power brokers seeking to put an end to hostilities in the DRC and implement a new political dispensation. It had not been implemented at the time of Kabila's death.

He stepped back and looked towards the source of the swish made by very heavy rotor blades, eight of them.

'I love the sound of a Halo!' the Duke shouted at the sky.

'Biggest helicopter in the world. If the MI-17 is something, the MI-26 is the mother of them all. The MI-17 has two 2 000 shaft horsepower turbine engines. The Halo pumps out more than 11 000 shaft horsepower from each of its turbines.'

The huge helicopter, decked in the same livery as its smaller cousin that we had seen earlier, was moving at tremendous speed. The monster seemed to freeze human life on the ground, where people stood and watched as its rotor blades tilted carefully to take the craft down to the heliport across the bay.

The diversion over, the Duke took up his story once again.

'The Congo has many sources of diamonds. Where kimberlite pipes have been eroded by riverine action over countless years, stones are freed and washed downstream. Only the flawless gems survive, so alluvial diamonds are the most valuable. But alluvial deposits are erratic, and the miner relies as much on luck as anything else. At Mbuji-Mayi, the diamonds come from kimberlite pipes that have low quality. All the Congo's diamonds, kimberlite and alluvials, are found in a broad but disjointed band that runs diagonally across the country from southwest to northeast. The main areas are in the southern Kasai provinces and Bandundu, on the Angolan border. There are also deposits in Équateur and Orientale. After 1983, *creuseurs*, the artisanal miners, found new deposits in Kasai and in Orientale, around Kisangani. The diggings in Équateur have produced some pretty sensational gems.'

The structure of the DRC's diamond sector is such that the stones move from *creuseurs* and Miba to middlemen – *négociants* – and then to foreign exporters or *comptoirs*. And in this, said the Duke, the role of Angola, one of the biggest diamond producers in the world, should not be underestimated.

Angola's diamond fields are scattered throughout the country, from north to south, but the highest concentration is in the Lunda provinces, with Lunda Norte bordering the DRC's province of Kasai-Occidental. High-quality stones have been distributed along the rivers that flow from northern Angola to southern Congo, and the diamonds around Tshikapa, for example, are alluvial deposits from kimberlite pipes in Angola.

For many years, said the Duke, British Diamond, or Britmond, a De Beers affiliate, held a monopoly on Miba's production, and was represented by Sediza (Société d'évaluation de diamant au Zaire). When Kabila declared that Zaire would henceforth be known as the DRC, the company changed its name to Sedico (Société d'évaluation de diamant au Congo). De Beers remained the main buyer of Miba's stones until late 1997, after which Belgian companies began offering higher bids at tender. De Beers pulled the last of its buyers out of Mbuji-Mayi in October 1998, two months after fighting erupted anew. Sedico's withdrawal from the DRC towards the end of 1999 coincided with the decision by De Beers to halt purchasing operations in Angola and, indeed, to stop buying any stones it did not mine itself or in direct partnership with other firms.

From the moment he set foot in Kinshasa, Laurent Kabila milked the diamond trade for all that he could. In February 1998, a minimum target was set for the commercialisation of diamonds, requiring *comptoirs* to pay a bond of $25 000 and to pay taxes in advance. Further fees were required depending on the number of foreign buyers operating under a *comptoir*'s licence. During the 18 months or so after Kabila took power, Congolese diamond purchases were valued at $600 million. Then the *comptoirs* had their licences revoked, and official exports for the next 18 months fell to below $300 million. Artisanal production was less than a million carats a year before 1982, increasing to nearly 6 million carats in 1983 and reaching 20 million carats in 1998, before halving – officially – in the next few years. Miba's output of 18 million carats in 1961 dropped to 12 million in 1970, to eight million in 1980 and to less than five million carats in 2000.

The story behind the dramatic decline, said the Duke, was to be found in the UN's special report on illegal exploitation of the DRC's natural resources. Investigators would uncover documentary evidence that three clans of Lebanese origin, operating as legitimate diamond dealers in the Belgian port of Antwerp, had bought stones to the value of $150 million from the Congo in 2001, either directly through Kinshasa or through *comptoirs*. All three groups, headed by men named Ahmad, Nassour and Khanafer, were 'distinct criminal organisations that operate internationally', according to the UN. Their activities, known to intelligence services and police, included money laundering, counterfeiting and diamond smuggling. Several credible sources had reported that the clans had links with Hezbollah, the Palestinian extremist group, and were supplying a group of pro-Mobutu generals with counterfeit US dollars to overthrow Kabila's government.

'That is what the UN found, for better or for worse,' said the Duke. 'It was clear to some people that the Congo was in the final stages of disintegration. The wars …' he sighed, shaking his head.

Early in 1999, rebel groups launched major offensives on at least three fronts. In July, a ceasefire was signed in Lusaka, and early in 2000, the UN Security Council authorised troop deployment in the Congo to oversee the peace agreement. In June, Rwanda and Uganda clashed for the third time in Kisangani, and more than 750 civilians were killed. Seven months later, Kabila was gunned down by one of his own bodyguards.

'There was malice in it,' said the Duke. 'The assassin, an Angolan, shot Kabila once in the throat and twice in the guts before being killed himself, almost immediately. Afterwards, there were reports that Yousef Bakri was one of 11 Lebanese, all diamond dealers, executed for involvement in the assassination. No one has ever denied those reports. It was even rumoured that Hezbollah, the "Party of God", which many governments regard as terrorists, put pressure on Kabila's son, Joseph, to return their bodies to Lebanon.

'Now this is where the story gets really interesting. Yousef Bakri's brother, Imad, had had close ties with Mobutu, and had worked hand in hand with Unita. From 1995 until the fall of Unita's stronghold at Andulo in October 1999, Bakri had served as the Angolan rebels' primary broker for arms and military equipment. Apparently he had joined Unita's diamond-trading network when he arrived in Luzamba as a buyer in the middle of 1995. By the end of the next year, he was supplying arms to Unita through Kinshasa.

'This is the world that Brett Kebble wanted. This is the world that a man with a chicken heart wanted to muscle into.'

According to the Duke, it was Bakri who had introduced notorious Russian-arms dealer Victor Bout – a wanted man in several countries – to the arms-trafficking operation he was involved in. After the fall of Mobutu in May 1997, Unita's arms were routed via Togo, with Bakri acting as the middleman.

'From 1992 to 2002, Unita ran the world's biggest and best organised arms- and diamond-smuggling operation,' said the Duke. Despite UN sanctions, Unita's illegal diamond trading continued relatively unhindered, allowing Jonas Malheiro Savimbi to continuously rearm and re-equip his forces, thus prolonging Angola's already protracted civil war. Until Kabila seized power from Mobutu, the Congo had been the main route for both Unita's diamonds and weapons. The two-way trafficking had the full backing and cooperation of Mobutu, whose son Mobutu Kongulo (head of the presidential guard) and most trusted generals, Honore N'Gbanda (head of the special presidential division) and Kpama Baramoto (head of the special council on security matters), worked closely with Savimbi. Unita had financed a large part of its war effort for more than a decade with diamonds, generating $3.7 billion between 1992 and 1999 alone.

'Cynics have noted that Kabila's mausoleum in Kinshasa depicts him in bronze, clutching a book,' the Duke observed. 'Yet this is the man who halted bookkeeping at the Congolese finance ministry. Kabila was as much of a despot as Mobutu, but far less competent. He scared off investors by jailing foreign businessmen and demanding million-dollar ransoms. He banished aid by insulting foreign diplomats. By printing money while enforcing price controls, he caused Soviet-style shortages.

By the end, petrol was so scarce that the state oil firm resorted to flushing its main pipeline with river water to force out the dregs.

'As for Savimbi, he survived more than a dozen, or perhaps 20, assassination attempts. He was killed in February 2002, after a battle with Angolan government troops on the bank of a river in Moxico province, his birthplace. It is said that he had 17 machine-gun bullets in his head, upper body and legs. There was malice.

'Meanwhile, the new privateers prospered, but Kebble still hadn't found a way to join the cabal.'

Since the first war in 1996, members of the elite network had transferred ownership of assets worth at least $5 billion from the Congolese state to private companies under their control, without paying any compensation to the Treasury. In August 2002, Zimbabwe's political–military elite signed six major trade and service agreements with the government of the DRC.

'It sounds so formal, so proper, when really, it was savagery,' said the Duke. A series of holding companies had been set up to hide the extensive commercial operations of the Zimbabwe Defence Force in the Congo, and especially the fact that President Robert Mugabe had deployed troops in the DRC to guard the assets that he and his cronies now controlled.

'They got a piece of everything – diamonds, cobalt, copper, germanium. And coltan, of course, the stuff that makes mobile telephone batteries tick. A member of the elite network, George Forrest – apparently a Belgian citizen, despite his very English name – pioneered the exploitative joint venture agreements between private companies and Gécamines.

'He was appointed chairman of Gécamines from November 1999 to August 2001, while his private companies negotiated new contracts with the explicit intention of using the Gécamines assets for personal gain. Forrest built up the widest-ranging private mining portfolio in the Congo. He had strong backing from certain political quarters in Belgium, where some of his companies were based.'

The Duke's tale had become so detailed that he constantly referred to his wad of notes and documents.

'The stakes were huge, the competition fierce. Zimbabwe-backed entrepreneurs John Arnold Bredenkamp and Thamer Bin Said Ahmed Al-Shanfari got involved. The Al-Shanfari character had gained privileged access to the Congolese government and its diamond concessions in exchange for raising capital from some powerful people in the Persian Gulf, like Issa Al Kawari, manager of the deposed Emir of Qatar's fortune.

'Bredenkamp, said to have a personal nett worth of more than $500 million, was experienced at setting up clandestine companies and sanctions-busting operations.

Also working with the ZDF was Nico Shefer, a notorious South African fraudster. The UN found that his company, Tandan Holdings, had a 50 per cent stake in Thorntree Industries, a diamond-trading joint venture with the ZDF.

'Another Zimbabwean, Billy Rautenbach – wanted in South Africa for massive fraud – headed a joint venture cobalt-mining company, and was chief executive of Gécamines from November 1998 to March 2000.

'Such levels of mineral exploitation would be impossible without the collusion of highly placed government officials, who issued mining licences and export permits in return for personal gain. A Canadian-based company that wanted to buy rights to the Kolwezi tailings offered the state a down payment of $100 million, plus cash payments, plus shares held in trust for government officials. According to documents in the UN's possession, the payments would be made to the national security minister, the director of national intelligence, the director-general of Gécamines and a former minister in the presidency. The share offer to the officials was apparently premised on a sharp rise in the company's stock price when it announced having secured some of the most valuable mineral concessions in the DRC.'

The Duke took a break and replenished our drinks.

'But I burden you. Let me tell you some more about Bukavu. There was a time, many years ago, when it truly was the African Riviera. Down there, on the prettiest peninsula, you would have found the Hôtel Lantana House, the Hôtel Léopold II, the Métropole and the Hôtel Résidence, both of which are still there. Elsewhere in the city there were the Hôtel Crémaillère, the Hôtel Touriste and the Hôtel Rotonde.

'There were elegant restaurants and places to be merry: La Taverne Royale, Au Gourmet, the Restaurant L'Ecu de France, La Bonbonnière, Le Panaché, Le Caveau.

'And the cars! All the latest models, and a thriving garage for each of the big names from both Europe and America: Dodge, Volvo, Fiat, Ford, Sedec, Volkswagen, Peugeot, Mercedes, Nash-Hudson, Studebaker, Citroën and Renault. Then there were the cinemas – the Paguidas, Cinéma Roxy, the Palace. All the pretty things, the *pensionnat*, the hippodrome, La Flamme, and the famous Avenue de Royale along the lake.

'Over there, in Baie de Bukavu, next to the port, was the Hopital des Congolais, and further up the shoreline, at a higher altitude, the Hopital des Européens. The colonial era was a time of great enjoyment and good living. But that all ended in 1960, and that was when the animosity between the Tutsis and the Hutus was rekindled.'

For all his nostalgia, there was nothing sentimental about the Duke's analysis of what happened next.

'Central Africa's collapse into poverty, social upheaval and war is rooted in colonial exploitation and abuse, and in the enduring corruption and state predation that followed independence. The rapacity of the slave trade, colonialism and post-independence governance scarred the region with a legacy of manipulation. Diamonds are one of the most easily obtained, most easily transported forms of hard currency. Poor controls and oversight in transit countries such as Rwanda, Burundi, Uganda, Zambia, Zimbabwe and Tanzania, even South Africa, and in trading countries like Belgium, Israel and India, along with secrecy within the industry, make diamonds – legal or not – easy to sell. Diamonds dollarise informal economies, linking African middlemen to international dealers, who pay big prices. Diamonds benefit artisanal miners, middlemen, exporters and state coffers, but they are often redirected through illicit channels, financing government strongmen, criminal networks and rebel groups.

'The diamond economy is based on the dream of immediate wealth – the "casino economy". Diamonds require little investment, they are portable and the trade is – or seems to be – virtually uncontrollable. Sniffer dogs can't smell them, and X-ray machines don't see them.'

By this time the Duke had his barbecue fired up, but said he was awaiting fresh fish from the lake. Down on the water, commercial fishermen were preparing for a standard night's labour. They worked neatly and impressively in pairs of longboats lashed together, each with long poles hung with pressurised kerosene lamps projecting skywards. The lights served to attract the fish.

'There are just 26 species of fish in Lake Kivu, of which the Lake Tanganyika sardine is the most important. This is the famous *Limnothrissa miodon*. You know, there is a fish down there, the stargazer mountain catfish, *Amphilius uranoscopus*. Can you imagine a fish that lives in a mountain lake and looks at the stars! I can tell you this because I am a smuggler, and I have time to learn about such things. But today, we eat Nile tilapia, my favourite,' the Duke remarked, while freshening our drinks yet again.

Returning to the main theme of his discourse, he mused: 'Brett Kebble and his diamond fantasies.'

The record shows that on 1 July 1999, Kebble put a 100 per cent holding in an entity called Ekuseni into New Mining, later renamed Matodzi and listed on the Johannesburg Stock Exchange. Ekuseni held 29 per cent of DiamondWorks, a stock listed on the Toronto exchange. At the same time, Kebble dumped Newlands Minerals and IEN Investments into Matodzi as well.

Though he invariably touted Matodzi as the flagship of his black economic empowerment empire, insiders regarded the company as Kebble's rubbish bin.

When DiamondWorks was dumped into Matodzi, it had suffered a catastrophic fall in its stock price as the result of involvement in regional conflict, ill-advised associations with mercenary outfits like Executive Outcomes, and the death or disappearance of several expatriate employees during an armed attack on an Angolan mine.

'Newlands and IEN each held 25 per cent of the so-called Letšeng-la-Terae diamond mine in Lesotho,' said the Duke.

'Now known as Letšeng?'

'The same,' he replied.

'Is Letšeng all right?'

'Letšeng is fine. It was not salted. Everyone has asked that question. Kebble was trading in diamonds, but he never tried anything funny with Letšeng. He was trading blood diamonds out of Central Africa with his network of liberation struggle veterans. You know who they are. But Kebble was a very poor smuggler. He was a brilliant con man, given the right time and the right place, but he was a useless entrepreneur. He was even more useless as a smuggler. He did not have the heart for smuggling. It was very close to his heart, but you cannot be much of a smuggler if you have a chicken heart.'

The Nile tilapia had arrived, and the Duke was beaming.

'I cut my smuggling teeth in Guajira, the badlands of Colombia,' he said, as he watched the fisherman scaling and gutting the two fish he had selected.

'First cannabis and then cocaine. Santa Marta, Barranquilla, Cartagena. You have been there?'

'Cartagena? Yes. It's a beautiful little city.'

'Those were the days, the very dangerous and very profitable days. If you survived those days, you could smuggle anything.'

The Duke sat down and was silent for a while, gazing far into the distance. The fishermen were gone. Potatoes and other side dishes were cooking in cast-iron pots over the ground fire and the barbecue was blazing.

'These days, I smuggle only gold,' the Duke continued. 'There are three, four, five Antonovs a day that fly out of here down to Lugushwa and Kamituga. They pick up the gold concentrate and bring it back here. I smuggle it into Rwanda. It's a good, clean business and nobody gets hurt. But now the Canadians, like Banro, have moved back to reclaim their concessions. These are some of the best in the world, running about 200 kilometres southwest from Bukavu. The artisanal miners at Lugushwa and Kamituga are mining illegally, and they know it, and soon the order of things will change. It will be orderly, but things will change.

'You know, Africa is a tricky place for flying. Not so long ago, an Ilyushin, a big one, the Il-76, was on the way to Croatia via Sudan. It took off late at night from Mwanza, carrying 50 tons of fish fillets, beautiful ones from Lake Victoria. It crashed about two minutes after take-off. No survivors were found. It reminded me of the days in Colombia. There were air crashes there, plenty of air crashes, but the entire business was illegal. In Africa, aircraft crash on legal flights. This one just fell out of the sky into the biggest lake on the continent and that was it. What must the fish have thought? Their brothers and sisters had just been netted, gutted and filleted, and then there they were, dumped back into the lake.

'Welcome to Africa!'

The Duke filled our glasses once more. It was turning into one hell of a night.

'You know,' he said, 'diamonds were the only thing that might have saved that Kebble person. Or maybe not. He never understood the true value of Saxendrift, and he never developed Letšeng of his own initiative. One of his big creditors in London forced that on him. In 2002, JCI bought 40 per cent of the mine from the London man.

'The London creditor still holds 10 per cent of Letšeng Investment Holdings. JCI has 40 per cent, and the rest belongs to Matodzi, so Kebble couldn't even claim Letšeng's successes as his own, not by a long way.

'And how many of those deals in 2003 were real? Koketso Angola with its interest in the Luxinge alluvials in Luande Norte? Masupatsela Angola with its interest in the Dando Kwanza alluvials in Bie province? Quantum African Mining with its interest in Somba Sul alluvials? Trans Benguela Logistics? Were those real deals? I'll tell you what was real. Apart from making a rotten business of trying to trade dirty diamonds, Brett Kebble was running contraband. It started in about 2003, when the real crush for cash hit him. He bought into a Johannesburg syndicate that was smuggling cigarettes from Southeast Asia to the UK via Belfast. That was not enough, so he bought into a cannabis-smuggling ring that also routed product from South Africa to the UK through Belfast.'

By now the Nile tilapia were sizzling on the grill and the Duke was really cheering up.

'Do you know that Kivu is an exploding lake? Every thousand years there is a massive biological extinction. The lake explodes and overflows and everything drowns. Today there are about two million people living around the lake. This inland tsunami is an unfortunate result of volcanic activity north of Goma, interacting with other geological factors. When the methane and the carbon dioxide are ready, the lake erupts.'

Just then the fire on the barbecue flared up and the Duke removed the two fish from the grill. He took a Mützig out of the big green cooler box, shot me a quick glance and exchanged it for a Primus. In a flash the bottle was open and the Duke was dousing the fire with cold beer, his reflexes still as quick as a cat's.

'In the end,' he said, almost wistfully, 'it was a diamond deal that lured Brett Kebble to his death. That night, when he went down that lonely road, he was going to pick up a parcel of dirty diamonds.'

22

Ways and means of a Robber Baron

ON 2 NOVEMBER 2005, the Johannesburg High Court unlocked the first of many doors to the Byzantine mystery of how Brett Kebble had misappropriated hundreds of millions of rand in cash from Randgold & Exploration. Just five weeks earlier, Kebble had bled to death in his luxury German sedan after being shot seven times by unidentified assailants. Four weeks before that, he had been sacked as chief executive of not only Randgold & Exploration, but also of JCI Ltd and Western Areas.

The first of several liquidation requests filed with the court by Randgold & Exploration was dealt with quickly and quietly, belying the dramatic revelations couched in legal terms.

The key lay in a name that Kebble had kept well hidden while he lived: Tuscan Mood 1224 (Pty) Ltd. Set up as a close corporation in 2003 and transformed into a private company the following year, Tuscan owed Randgold & Exploration both a large amount of money and an explanation, according to Peter Gray, who had replaced Kebble as the company's CEO and was trying to sort out the almighty mess he had inherited. Simultaneously, Randgold & Exploration sought the liquidation of Paradigm Shift cc, described in Gray's affidavit as Tuscan's 'alter ego'.

A forensic audit had shown that these two unknown entities shared a bank account, into which R34.5 million had been paid from November 2003 to October 2004 in 14 tranches, ranging from R1 million to R5.3 million each. The money had been identified as part of the proceeds of Kebble's unauthorised sale of shares in Randgold Resources, the biggest single asset owned by Randgold & Exploration.

Why Tuscan Mood, allegedly in the real estate business, and Paradigm Shift, purveyor of 'community, social and personal services', should have received these funds, and what had happened to them, were crucial questions that would require answers via a draconian inquiry in terms of the South African Companies Act.[*]

---

[*]   Section 417 makes provision, in the event of a company under liquidation being unable to pay its debts, for the Master of the High Court, or a relevant court, to subpoena any director or officer of the company, 'or person known or suspected to have in his possession any property of the company or believed to be indebted to the company, or any person whom the Master or the Court deems capable of giving information concerning the trade, dealings, affairs or property of the company'. Such person may be required to answer any question, even if the answer might tend to incriminate him or her. Normally, any examination or inquiry under Section 417 is private and confidential.

But Tuscan Mood and Paradigm were only the beginning. Early in March 2006, Randgold & Exploration sought the liquidation of a slew of other entities that had been involved, via Kebble and his cronies on the company's sacked board of directors, in 'irregular and fraudulent transactions ... related directly to misappropriation of assets'.

Customarily, a Section 417 inquiry takes place behind closed doors, but in the event of one following Randgold & Exploration's application, those called would likely range from a former apartheid-state hit squad member to the husband of a minister in South African president Thabo Mbeki's cabinet, with a parade of ANC Youth League luminaries in between.

Court papers showed that instructions for the electronic transfer of certain funds realised by Kebble's illegal sale of shares were issued to stockbrokers by Barry Bawden, whose sister, Patricia Beale, was the ubiquitous secretary in Kebble's convoluted corporate web. Bawden had served 11 of 25 years in a Zimbabwe prison for his role in a fatal car bombing at an ANC facility in Harare in 1988. He was a member of the sinister SADF hit squad, the Civil Cooperation Bureau, at the time.

Six months after Kebble's death, it became apparent that he had purloined and sold up to 18.4 million of Randgold & Exploration's shares in Randgold Resources, which was listed on both the London Stock Exchange and the Nasdaq in New York.

In his affidavit, Gray explained that Randgold & Exploration owned the entire issued share capital of African Strategic Investment (Holdings) Ltd, formerly known as Randgold Resources (Holdings) Ltd,* and registered in Jersey. On 31 December 2003, Holdings owned some 37 per cent, or 21 570 000 shares, of Randgold Resources' total issued share capital. At the foreign exchange rate on that date, the investment was worth R1 986 970 000 to Randgold & Exploration.

Two billion rand.

A 'very substantial' portion of this asset had been 'dissipated without authority', said Gray, with Paradigm and Tuscan Mood playing 'a pivotal role' in the disposal and receiving 'a large proportion of the funds generated'. Both entities had subsequently failed to account to Randgold & Exploration for these proceeds.

Tuscan Mood was first registered in 2004 to an address in Boskruin Business Park, Randpark Ridge. Gray told the court he doubted that it 'ever had any employees'. The same could be said of Paradigm Shift, registered in 2003 to Fussell House in Melrose, the upmarket northern Johannesburg suburb from which Kebble had previously conducted business out of a historic residence, Melrose House. Coincidentally, it was also the suburb in which he met his death.

Randgold & Exploration's investigation had shown that Paradigm and Tuscan

---

* See Appendix M.

Mood shared the same account at a branch of Standard Bank in Alberton, east of Johannesburg, where Tuscan also had a second account. The business dealings of the two entities were intermingled in the bank accounts and, according to Gray, they were 'really just alter egos of each other'.

Composite transactions are never simple, but trying to unravel those bearing Kebble's hallmark was more challenging than negotiating a maze, blindfolded and at night. Randgold & Exploration's stock had been suspended from trading on the JSE and Nasdaq when the company failed to produce audited statements for the financial year ended 31 December 2004. The principle reason for the failure, Gray told the court, was Randgold & Exploration's inability 'properly to account for the dissipated Randgold Resources shares'.

When the scale of investigation that would be needed to determine the fate of the missing shares became evident to the company's new management, an independent forensic accounting firm, Umbono Financial Advisory Services, was assigned to the arduous task on 7 October 2005.

Under the direction of John Louw, the financial sleuths dug particularly deep into the business of Tlotlisa Securities (Pty) Ltd, trading as T-Sec, which had brokered the disposal of the Randgold Resources shares and distributed the proceeds in terms of instructions from Bawden, acting for either Tuscan Mood or Paradigm.

Louw confirmed in his affidavit that, from November 2003 to October 2004, share certificates held by Randgold & Exploration were delivered to T-Sec at its Johannesburg offices with instructions to sell. The stock was converted into American Depository Receipts (ADRs) by the London office of Bank of New York before transfer to the New York office of Barnard Jacobs Mellet, a stockbroker, for sale into the American equity investing market. The proceeds, amounting to R34.5 million, were duly returned to T-Sec and deposited as instructed by Bawden, either telephonically or via e-mail.

Not only had the sale been unauthorised, but Tuscan Mood was unable to pay the debt arising from Kebble's fraud. The only avenue open to Randgold & Exploration's new management was to place Tuscan and Paradigm in liquidation and initiate a full investigation in terms of the bankruptcy laws. This would allow the company to compile 'the bigger picture' regarding the dissipation of all the Randgold Resources shares and, at the same time, enable Randgold & Exploration to complete its 2004 financial statements and thus comply with conditions for the readmission of its shares to the various stock exchanges for public trading.

'A substantial number of investors are now incapable of trading in the shares they acquired on the open market and Randgold & Exploration, in turn, is prevented from accessing new capital if it should be required and is severely prejudiced in its day-to-day business operations,' Gray told the court.

The next round of liquidation applications filed by Randgold & Exploration in March 2006 baldly described the share sale as fraud. New company secretary Roger Pearcey provided the court with details of how it had been perpetrated, how it had come to the new management's attention and who had been involved.

While the official announcement that Kebble and his cronies had been ousted as directors of Randgold & Exploration, JCI Ltd and Western Areas was made on 30 August 2005, the court papers showed that their expulsion from Randgold & Exploration had actually taken place on 24 August. Those axed were Brett Kebble (CEO from 24 July 2003), his father Roger (non-executive chairman from 5 March 1998), Hennie Buitendag (financial director from 1 March 2000) and Lunga Ncwana (non-executive director from 24 July 2003). Three board members had resigned earlier of their own accord. They were David Ashworth (non-executive director from 29 September 1992 to 20 August 2004), Gordon Miller (executive director from 18 November 2003 to 6 May 2005) and Stephen Tainton (executive director from 20 August 2004 to 6 April 2005).

Only two of the serving board members were not sacked in August 2005: Chris Nissen and Brenda Madumise, both appointed as non-executive directors on 24 July 2003. Gray and Chris Lamprecht were appointed as CEO and financial director respectively, and on 7 October, David Nurek joined the board as independent non-executive chairman.

According to Pearcey, the new board, 'suspecting that certain of the former directors ... had managed the affairs of [Randgold & Exploration] in a reckless and fraudulent manner', set a forensic audit in motion in October. What they uncovered was that three BEE entities – Phikoloso Mining, Viking Pony and Equitant – had been fronts, used by Kebble to steal money from Randgold & Exploration. Big names had been sucked into the scam. South African education minister Naledi Pandor's husband Sharif was listed as head of one of several BEE companies linked to Phikoloso, which was set up by ANC Youth League executives Lunga Ncwana and Songezo Mjongile.

Umbono's findings included the purported acquisition by Randgold & Exploration of Equitant Trading's shareholding in something called Viking Pony Properties 359 (Pty) Ltd for 'a purchase consideration of 8 800 000 of Randgold & Exploration's ordinary shares', then valued at about R268 million. According to Pearcey, Viking was 'registered and incorporated to serve as a vehicle or conduit in a substantial fraud perpetrated on [Randgold & Exploration] and its shareholders'.

Viking, he explained, had no assets at the date of the transaction. In terms of South Africa's new Mining Charter and the Mineral and Petroleum Resources Development Act, Randgold & Exploration was required to enter into a BEE deal that would see 20 per cent of its shareholding transferred to historically disadvantaged persons. Randgold & Exploration also wanted to raise cash for its operations.

At the beginning of 2003, Kebble and Buitendag, representing Randgold & Exploration, entered into an arrangement with Ncwana and Mjongile in terms of which:

- On or about 9 April, Ncwana and Mjongile acquired the shareholding in Equitant, a shelf company, on behalf of Phikoloso Mining (Pty) Ltd. The two were appointed directors of Phikoloso on the same date.
- On or about 2 July, Ncwana and Mjongile acquired the shareholding in Viking Pony, also a shelf company, incorporated on the same date. The two men were appointed as its directors the following day.
- Viking Pony became a wholly owned subsidiary of Equitant.
- On or about 25 July, Ncwana and Mjongile were appointed directors of Phikoloso.

Almost immediately, Phikoloso's shareholding was restructured and purportedly parcelled out among a string of BEE players. In March 2006, official records at the Companies and Intellectual Property Office (Cipro) in Pretoria* divulged the following about the entities involved:

- **Phikoloso Mining:** The directors were Ncwana, Mjongile and Lesego Thelma Mathamelo. Not surprisingly, given the storm that had erupted around Randgold & Exploration, two other directors, Madumise and Nissen, had resigned.
- **Viking Pony:** The directors were Madumise and Buitendag. Past directors were the now deceased Kebble, and Ncwana and Mjongile, who had resigned. However, given its status as a wholly owned subsidiary of Equitant, the directors of this entity were irrelevant.
- **Equitant Trading:** Two active directors, namely Ncwana and Mjongile.
- **Itsuseng Mining:** According to media statements by Randgold & Exploration during 2003, Ncwana headed what was described as 'a fully fledged BEE investment vehicle with substantial property, mineral and financial services interests'.

---

*   This office came under attack in March 2006 after auditor-general Shauket Fakie found that more than 50000 public servants in 142 government departments had failed to declare their business interests. Opposition parties said 14 cabinet members had violated the Parliamentary Code of Conduct by failing to declare directorships in private companies and close corporations. Ethics committee chairman Llewellyn Landers requested further details, and Parliament's joint committee on ethics and members' interests shot down Fakie's claims, saying he had relied on 'flawed data'. Landers said 'we know that he logged onto the Cipro website and obtained this information'. In the experience of this author, Cipro is a reliable source, though there is no harm in further verification of information provided. In some cases, there may be difficulty establishing details on a company that is one of many with a similar name.

Official records show that in early March 2006, the directors of Itsuseng Strategic Investments (as opposed to Itsuseng Mining) were Luvuyo Bekwa, Amanda Zoliso Cuba, France Lulama and Lulamile Herbert Mntumni.

- **Lembede Mining:** Purportedly headed by Mjongile, and described as a diversified investment company formed by the SA Youth Development Trust. According to official records, Lembede Mining had just one director, well-known Johannesburg attorney and businessman Themba Langa, who had successfully held out against Mzi Khumalo in the Simane saga.
- **New Line Investments:** Headed by Chris Nissen, described as chairman of the Cape Chamber of Commerce. Official records show no trace of New Line Investments, also described as Newline Investments in some media releases.
- **Marothodi Resources:** Headed by Thelma Mathamelo, and branded as an empowerment mining group with an existing 26 per cent stake in Randgold & Exploration's mineral rights business, Minrico. Official records show two directors: Mathamelo and Mogwailane Kenneth Mohlala.
- **Ikamva:** Branded as an empowerment company, headed by Sharif Pandor, with interests in platinum and holding mineral rights. Official records show no ready trace of Ikamva.
- **Leswikeng:** Branded as a BEE company with diversified interests and said to be headed by Herman Mashaba, something of a legend in business circles. At the age of 26, he borrowed R30 000 and, along with his wife Connie and two friends, started the hugely successful beauty product company, Black Like Me. Official records show no ready trace of Leswikeng.
- **Innovage:** A BEE company with 'diversified interests', said to be headed by Dennis Mashabela. Official records show no ready trace of this entity.
- **Qaqambile Capital Holdings:** Said to be headed by Khanyisa Magwensthu (sole director), and described as 'a group of black mining professionals'.
- **Khomelela:** Apparently formed by a group of professional women 'with skills in information technology, project finance, law, management consulting and corporate finance', and headed by Madumise. Official records show no ready trace of this entity.
- **Dyambu:** Labelled as a broad-based women's empowerment company, headed by Hilda Ndude, with investments in telecommunications, property and construction. Official records show no ready trace of this entity.

On 28 July 2003, Randgold & Exploration entered into a written agreement with Phikoloso and its subsidiary, Equitant, whereby Randgold & Exploration would purchase Equitant's shares and claims in Viking Pony. By this stage, Phikoloso,

Viking Pony and Equitant were one and the same, but in any event, Viking Pony purportedly owned shares valued at some R127 million* in three public companies listed on the JSE.

Viking Pony also purported to own shares in Kabusha Mining and Finance, which, in turn, supposedly held shares valued at R92 million in a public company listed on the JSE. According to official records, Kabusha's directors were Peter George, Quinton George, Lindiwe Leketi, Lethibela Mokela and Sandile Swana.

The rub was that Randgold & Exploration was to pay Equitant the 'aggregate closing price of the consideration shares on the closing date'. These were 8.8 million ordinary shares of R0.01 each in the issued share capital of Randgold & Exploration, with a market value of some R268 million.

The effect of the contract was that in allotting and issuing the Randgold & Exploration shares to Equitant, Randgold & Exploration was to receive the two lots of shares as a quid pro quo. The transaction was carried out at the end of July 2003, with Equitant acknowledging receipt of the shares on 11 August.

On 27 August, Patricia Beale addressed a letter on behalf of Equitant to stockbrokers Tradek Balderson (Pty) Ltd, subsequently known as Tlotlisa Securities (Pty) Ltd, or T-Sec. It read:

Dematerialisation† of 8 800 000 RNG [Randgold & Exploration] Shares
Please will you urgently complete the attached CM42 and send the RNG share certificate for 8 800 000 RNG shares registered in the name of Equitant Trading (Pty) Ltd to Computershare Ltd for demat, attention Mrs Connie Morkel. We

---

* In its 2003 filing with the Securities Exchange Commission in Washington, Randgold & Exploration stated that on 28 July 2003, it had entered into a partnership with Phikoloso that would 'enhance our strategic empowerment partnership. We issued 8.8 million new ordinary shares, representing 16.4 per cent of our issued ordinary share capital, to Phikoloso in exchange for the total issued share capital of and all the shareholder claims on loan accounts, which amounted to $33.5 million, against Viking Pony. Viking Pony held 235 000 Anglo Platinum shares, 315 000 Harmony shares and 7.3 million shares of The Afrikander Lease Ltd, or Aflease. It also owns 75 per cent of Kabusha Mining and Finance which in turn holds 23 million shares in Aflease.' Aflease was subsequently consolidated 0.18 to one into SXR Uranium One.

† Dematerialisation played a significant role in changing Kebble's *modus operandi*. Defined simply as the process that sees paper share certificates replaced with electronic records of ownership, dematerialisation started on the JSE in 1999, with the transfer of pilot company Harmony Gold from paper to cyberspace. The 'smooth transition', as described by dematerialisation agent STRATE, prompted market players to agree to further counters moving out of paper. The official programme began in March 2001 and was completed at the end of that year. Prior to this, Kebble would send copies of share certificates to one party, which is the legal limit in order to procure a loan, for example. He would then copy the same share certificates to another party, and a third, and so on. This kind of abuse is not possible with electronic-only records of stock ownership.

will be opening an account at Tradek for Equitant Trading, and will send the necessary Mandate and statutory documents to you tomorrow.

On 28 August, Equitant, purportedly represented by George William Poole, then employed by Consolidated Mining Management Services (CMMS, Kebble's biggest slush fund) as manager of investor relations, signed a Tradek mandate form to open an account for Equitant. Beale, it should be noted, was listed as joint company secretary to Randgold & Exploration in 2003, along with CMMS. In accordance with Poole's instructions to Tradek, the path taken by the Randgold & Exploration shares was as follows:

- On 3 and 5 September 2003, 3 088 000 shares (worth about R94 million at the time) were transferred to an account in the books of Tradek called Paradigm Shift cc.
- Between September 2003 and January 2004, 3 300 300 shares (worth R101 million) were transferred to an account in the books of Tradek called the Consolidated Investment account, operated by CMMS.
- On 16 September 2003, 142 000 shares were transferred to an account in the books of Tradek called Trans Benguela Logistics. In March 2006, the only active director of this entity was one General Deacon Sedikent Mathe.

It appeared that almost R200 million destined for BEE deals had gone somewhere else entirely. During September 2003, a further 2 270 000 shares were sold for R74 million:

- R46 million was used to purchase 56 million JCI shares. In early 2006, they were still held by Tradek on behalf of Equitant in that company's trading account.
- R20 million was transferred to an account of Itsuseng Strategic Investments in the books of Tradek.
- R7 million was transferred to Société Générale, Johannesburg.
- R742 893, together with interest, giving a total of R886 770 as at 13 February 2006, was still held in the Tradek account for the credit of Equitant.

The purchase of 56 million JCI shares was classic Kebble cannibalisation. He was using cash raised by selling stock out of Randgold & Exploration to effectively buy shares in JCI – impoverishing Randgold & Exploration to prop up demand for stock in JCI. The direction of the flow of funds was also familiar, since Kebble's equity interest was represented by a *direct* shareholding in JCI and not Randgold & Exploration (or Western Areas).

Although both the agreement and the announcement claimed that Equitant had received the full value of the 8 800 000 million shares (R268 million), it had actually received only 2 270 000 million shares that realised R74 million. According to Pearcey, the rest of the shares had been 'misappropriated and/or utilised for Randgold & Exploration's funding requirements'. The Umbono investigation showed that Randgold & Exploration had received no value from Viking Pony, which did not own shares worth R127 million as claimed, either at the time of the agreement or at any other juncture. Nor did Viking Pony ever own shares in Kabusha with a value of R92 million.

In fact, when Viking Pony entered into the agreement, it owned no assets at all. Randgold & Exploration was accordingly impoverished, and Equitant unjustly enriched at Randgold & Exploration's expense in the sum of R74 million.

Equitant was found to still own 56 million JCI shares and R886 770, described by Pearcey as 'the fruits of the shares that Equitant unlawfully and fraudulently obtained from Randgold & Exploration'.

There was also evidence that R20 million had been transferred to Itsuseng, and Randgold & Exploration duly sought that entity's liquidation as well. On 9 and 12 September 2003, Tradek had transferred R2.5 million and R17.5 million from the Equitant account to Itsuseng. Itsuseng had used the money pretty smartly:

- R2.5 million was used to pay for 56 million shares purchased on 1 September 2003 in Lyons Financial Solutions Holdings Ltd,* at that stage a public company listed on the JSE. After delisting, Lyons continued to trade as a public company, but on 14 February 2006, the 56 million shares were still held by Tradek on behalf of Itsuseng.
- R17.5 million was used on 9 October 2003 to buy nine million shares in then-JSE-listed Barnato Exploration (Barnex), a member of the JCI stable. The shares were credited to Itsuseng's trading account by Tradek. The following day, the Barnex shares were converted into nine million JCI shares and nine million JCI debentures. On 17 January 2006, Itsuseng redeemed the debentures for R11 million, credited to its account in Tradek's books. The next day, Tradek transferred R11 million as 'trust funds' to an account held by Johannesburg attorneys Kwinana Nyapotse Inc at Nedbank, Diamond Exchange Branch. Randgold & Exploration could not tell the court if KNI still held the funds, but Pearcey said redemption of the debentures and the transfer of the funds were

---

* According to official company records, active directors of Lyons in March 2006 were Glenn Eccles, Garry Fromentin, Peter Gray, David Jones (company secretary), Lunga Ncwana and Leonard Steenkamp. Past (resigned) directors included Peter Adendorff, Robert Brons, Dennis Cuzen, Peter Gain, Wynand Goosen, Paul Gray, Ian Hewett, Michael Judin, Deenadayalen Konar, Max Kretzmer, Sean Lederman, Glen Mackie, Desmond Magua, Richard Moerman, Eric Molefe, Robert Mortimer, Moltin Ncholo, Jill Parratt, Ian Pierce, David Samuels, Christopher Seabrooke, Desmond Seaton, Victor Sibiya and Casper Steenkamp.

effected on the written instructions of Andile Nkuhlu, chairman of Itsuseng Investments (yet another 'Itsuseng' and yet another leading light in the ANC Youth League). As at 14 February 2006, Itsuseng still held in its Tradek trading account 26 million JCI shares and the 56 million Lyons shares.

In seeking Itsuseng's provisional liquidation, Pearcey stated that the JCI shares, Lyons shares, trust funds and cash referred to were acquired with the 'proceeds' of funds that Equitant, and ultimately Itsuseng, had 'unlawfully and fraudulently received' from Randgold & Exploration. The company also claimed that Itsuseng had been party to the fraud perpetrated by Equitant and certain members of the 'old' Randgold & Exploration board, and that the entire transaction was tainted and should be set aside. The court granted the application for provisional liquidation.

According to Viking Pony's balance sheet as at 31 December 2003, the entity had assets worth R101 million, comprising investments of R26 million and loans receivable of R75 million. Both related to Kabusha, and a note on the statements claimed that a loan to Kabusha was secured by 23 million Aflease shares. However, there was nothing to show that Viking owned any of the shares claimed, or was in possession of the Aflease shares allegedly pledged as security. In fact, Randgold & Exploration alleged that Viking was not in possession of any Aflease shares at all, nor any in Kabusha.

Kabusha's audited balance sheet showed that it was insolvent to the tune of more than R66 million. At best, Viking would be unable to repay more than R35 million in respect of an existing shareholder's loan of some R120 million.

This chaos was part of a far bigger nightmare. The inability of Randgold & Exploration and its independent auditors* to establish the company's true financial position was the result of a large number of transactions that appeared, in Pearcey's words, 'to be at least unorthodox if not worse'. The acquisition of Viking and its financial position was just one example.

By 24 March 2006, Randgold & Exploration had been granted provisional liquidation orders in respect of Equitant (where R74 million in cash went walkabout), Viking Pony (a front company), Itsuseng (R20 million in cash missing), and Tuscan Mood/Paradigm Shift (R35 million in cash missing).

However, on that date, the company confirmed that a settlement for the full amount of R20 million had been reached with Itsuseng, whose chairman, Nkhulu,

---

* Listed as PricewaterhouseCoopers from 1998 to 2003. On 22 September 2005, Charles Orbach & Company resigned as auditors of Randgold & Exploration's financial statements for the year ended 31 December 2004.

said his company had participated in the Phikoloso transaction in good faith and 'was itself the victim of allegedly fraudulent activities'.

An agreement was also reached with Equitant, the primary vehicle for the Viking Pony transaction, to cooperate in the recovery of the proceeds.

In respect of Tuscan Mood and Paradigm Shift, Barry Bawden yelled foul, claiming to be a victim of identity theft.

The story about Investage 170 was in a league of its own. Court papers identified the directors as Charles Cornwall* and George Poole,† and illustrated a dramatic variation on the tried and trusted Kebble theme.

Randgold & Exploration alleged that, during February 2002, through an entity called Goudstad Nominees, it had owned some three million shares in JSE-listed Durban Roodepoort Deep (DRD). At the time, the stock was valued at some R90 million. After the 2005 shake-up in directors, it came to Randgold & Exploration's attention that the DRD shares had somehow been sold without the company's knowledge or consent. Randgold & Exploration had received no value for the sale.

It is crucial to note that during the 2000, 2001 and 2002 financial years, Randgold & Exploration's directors were listed as Roger Kebble (executive chairman), Hennie Buitendag, David Ashworth and Grant Fischer. Having quit the board in 1997, Brett Kebble did not rejoin until mid-2003.

Umbono's forensic investigation found that, around February 2002, Patricia Beale had opened a share-trading account in the books of Tradek Balderson in the name of PB Bawden. The account was credited with the DRD shares, and Beale then instructed Tradek to transfer and credit a portion of the shares to the following standing accounts:

- 540 624 to a company called New Heights (Pty) Ltd, of which Poole was sole director;
- 100 000 shares to a company called Hothouse Investments Ltd, of which Beale's brother, Bawden, was the sole director.

The balance of the shares remained in 'the Bawden' account opened by Patricia. With the transfers completed, and on the instructions of Beale and Poole, Tradek began trading with the DRD shares in the Bawden, New Heights and Hothouse

---

*   Cornwall was listed as a director of JCI from 2001 through 2005.

†   Poole was listed as joint company secretary (along with CMMS) to JCI from 1997 through 2001. He was also listed as company secretary to Western Areas in 1999 and 2000, as an alternate director of Western Areas in 2002 and a member of its executive committee, and as an alternate director of Western Areas in 2003.

accounts on 12 February. The proceeds – about R90 million in cash – were credited to the same accounts and then channelled through various other accounts, until R15 million was eventually deposited in the Investage account at Corpcapital Bank Ltd on 17 April, followed by another R35 million. On or about 15 July, the Investage account was drained of R50 million.

The Johannesburg High Court ordered the provisional liquidation of Investage in March 2006.

The Investage application paved the way for Randgold & Exploration to go after Kebble's mother ship, BNC Investments. Once again, the source transaction was the three million DRD shares held by Randgold & Exploration via Goudstad Nominees.

Court papers showed that Beale, employed as company secretary at Western Areas from 2001, was asked by Brett Kebble and Poole if they could use the Bawden account at Tradek for 'trading purposes'. It was her understanding that the beneficial owner of the three million DRD shares was Roger Kebble, whose tenure as a director of DRD was nearing its end, thanks to Mark Wellesley-Wood.

During February 2002, R70 million in cash was raised from the sale of DRD shares out of the Bawden account. The money, along with R17 million raised via New Heights from the sale of the same batch of shares, was moved through various private banking accounts, stockbroking accounts and an attorney's trust account.

In March 2002, Poole, purporting to represent BNC, opened a call deposit account in the company's name at Corpcapital. Some R61 million of the R87 million was deposited in the account, followed by a further deposit of R3.8 million. On 16 April, in accordance with written instructions from Poole, R64 million was withdrawn from the BNC account, R49 million being credited to a BNC term account and R15 million to an Investage term account, both at Corpcapital.

On 15 July, Poole instructed the bank to withdraw the funds from the BNC account and transfer them to 'an account of a third party', which, according to court papers, was known as the JCI Gold Ltd Scheme account at First National Bank, Carlton Centre, Johannesburg.

But the forensic audit showed that, acting on e-mailed instructions, Corpcapital had transferred some R157 million to the JCI Gold Ltd Scheme account from various accounts held by BNC and Investage. One clue to the origin of this amount could lie in an innocuous sliver of information in JCI Ltd's annual report to 31 March 2003:

> BNC Investments (Pty) Ltd and Investage 170 (Pty) Ltd, companies controlled by directors of this Company, underwrote the rights offer in terms of which an amount of R155 000 000 was raised and utilised to acquire the shares in JCI Gold which the Company did not already own.

Underwriting, a common mechanism used during rights offers, is designed to ensure an orderly placement of fresh shares. Underwriters normally agree to buy an agreed proportion of the new stock in the event that it is not taken up by existing shareholders. This is aimed at preventing sharp declines in share prices on the day when the new stock is officially listed on the exchange. Underwriters traditionally charge hefty fees.

On 2 September 2002, JCI issued 345 million new ordinary shares at 45 cents each in terms of its rights offer, underwritten by BNC (of which the directors were Brett and Roger Kebble) and Investage (of which the directors were Cornwall and Poole). At that price, 345 million new shares would raise R155 million. However, JCI's annual report showed that 80 million of the shares were bought by Cornwall and just under 100 million by Brett Kebble.

Between the two of them, the shares would have cost roughly R80 million. It was classic cannibalisation, yet again, but the real concern was that tens of millions of rand in cash had been raised by illegally alienating DRD stock owned by Randgold & Exploration to partially fund a JCI rights issue. The main beneficiaries were two individuals.

In December 2002, Brett and Roger Kebble, along with Hennie Buitendag, were indicted on various counts of fraud, conspiracy, incitement and insider trading in respect of the Randfontein debacle. Buitendag had been financial director of JCI from 1997, and financial director of Randgold & Exploration from 1999. It would be incomprehensible if he was unaware of the process behind the JCI rights issue.

From a strategic viewpoint, the liquidation of BNC Investments in March 2006 was the most significant of all the applications brought by Randgold & Exploration, given that BNC housed some 230 million JCI shares that Kebble had infamously first effectively issued to himself in 1997. For years he had used those shares to effectively control JCI, Randgold & Exploration and Western Areas.

The applications brought by Randgold & Exploration isolated three areas of focus:

• The illegal sale by Kebble of around R2 billion worth of stock in London-listed Randgold Resources once held by Randgold & Exploration. Until March 2006, only the R35 million in cash that had disappeared via Tuscan Mood and Paradigm Shift had been identified.*

---

* On 31 March 2006, Randgold & Exploration announced provisional and unaudited results for the two years ended 31 December 2004 and 2005. The report stated *inter alia* that between 2002 and 2005, Randgold & Exploration had misappropriated cash proceeds from irregularly selling the balance of its shareholding in Randgold Resources. Of the R1.8 billion cash raised, however, R1 billion was 'recycled' into JCI and R491 million went back into Randgold & Exploration. Some R367 million went to 'other parties'.

- The issue in 2003 of 8.8 million fresh Randgold & Exploration shares, worth R268 million when sold on the JSE at the time, to front BEE companies in and around the Phikoloso scheme. Most of this cash had been misappropriated by Kebble to fund his personal and other interests, while hefty chunks of cash had also gone missing after being channelled to Equitant and Itsuseng, which had apparently been duped.
- The illegal alienation of R90 million worth of stock held in DRD* by Randgold & Exploration in a conspiracy involving at least Brett and Roger Kebble and Buitendag. Much of the cash stolen appeared to have gone into the financing of a JCI rights issue.

By all accounts, Beale and Poole were patsies, but interestingly enough, while Beale's lifestyle remained fairly modest, in keeping with her status in the Kebble empire, Poole embraced the high life, complete with a mansion at the exclusive Fancourt golf estate near George, Lamborghinis and a fleet of commercial helicopters.

As for Brett Kebble, the evidence of corporate malfeasance that flooded South Africa's courts and media six months after his murder was both overwhelming and sad. In his days of thunder, riding the Syama stallion in 1996 and 1997, he had been a grifter of note. But after the Randfontein debacle, he and his accomplices descended into the murky realm of the bottom-feeder. The half nerd, half wolf was reduced to grubbing for carrion.

---

*   In its 2003 filing with the Securities Exchange Commission in Washington, Randgold & Exploration stated that a certain loan was partially repaid 'by the sale of 1.5 million shares in Durban Roodepoort Deep Ltd'. In its 2002 annual report, Randgold & Exploration claimed ownership of 3 521 513 DRD shares on 31 December 2002. The 2003 annual report claimed ownership of 500 000 DRD shares on 31 December 2003.

23

His soul of darkness

THERE ARE MANY Catholic churches in the metropolis of Johannesburg, not least among them the Church of the Resurrection, St Martin de Porres, Our Lady of the Lebanon, St Francis Xavier, our Lady of Lourdes, Immaculate Conception and St Charles.

But the one that held special meaning for Brett Kebble was Maryvale or, more correctly, Our Lady of the Wayside. When he was a schoolboy, he was often sent for holidays to his maternal grandmother, who lived in the far northern Johannesburg suburb of Wynberg and attended mass regularly. More often than not, they would walk south along Louis Botha Avenue and turn left into St Marys to enter the church. It is a solid building, with a choir section and organ upstairs, and room for more than a thousand congregants below.

After mass, Kebble and his grandmother would take a short walk, especially on hot days, along Hathorn Avenue, which marked the eastern perimeter of the church grounds. There, sitting awkwardly in the middle of suburbia, was a soft-drink bottling plant. The boy Kebble, whose youthful looks far more closely revealed his Italian blood than did his adult appearance, would relish a cooldrink. Then the pair would set off again for grandmother's house, which was a peaceful and unmistakeable example of Italian influence. It was also a house of music. Family members ate well and played lots of music in the Frittelli tradition. It seemed fitting that Kebble shared his birthday, 19 February, with Luigi Boccherini, the Italian composer and cellist.

Memories of the childhood walks and siestas with his grandmother, and especially their visits to Our Lady of the Wayside, would be among the most enduring and stabilising of Kebble's life. These remembrances would sustain him well into adulthood.

The peace and happiness he found with his grandmother were in sharp contrast to the instability and ongoing enmity from his father that Kebble faced at home. For one thing, it seemed that Roger was never home. The life of a shift boss is synonymous with long and erratic hours, and when Roger Kebble was led, through every choice of his own, into contract mining, his presence was even less reliable. When he was not working, he was whooping it up with friends and associates, hoping to be kept in mind for the next contract.

But while he neglected his family, Roger clung desperately to the prospect of a better life as a distinct possibility. Wearied by years of traipsing around the gold fields, the father somehow managed to scrape together the money required to give his children the best possible education. He married Julienne Frittelli in April 1963, and within a year, Brett was born, followed two years later by Guy and, two years after that, by Alison. All three children had their earliest taste of religion at the Catholic church in Springs, but it was mass at Our Lady of the Wayside that Brett grew to love.

To his mother and grandmother, he was a perfect little Michelangelo.

As the children grew, Brett adopted shyness as a shield. He was absorbed by interests that a swaggering braggart like Roger could not stand. From an early age, Brett and Guy were entirely different. It was patently clear that the younger Kebble son was going to be a very large man, in the physical sense. He was Roger's boy: Guy loved sport and hated anything to do with the nerdy stuff that attracted Brett. In due course, Roger started calling Brett his 'second daughter', and that, more or less, was where all the trouble really began.

In 2004, in the JCI corporate suite at Newlands in Cape Town, watching a big rugby match, Guy Kebble was well fed and, like his companions, more than a little tipsy. He was spoiling for a fight, hurling insults in all directions. Then he turned his attention on the JCI directors. He ignored Hennie Buitendag and fixed his drunken gaze on Brett.

'You faggot!' Guy yelled.

Brett swallowed, but ignored his brother.

Guy Kebble had nicknamed senior citizen John Stratton 'Turtle'. Now he roared loudly: 'Turtle!'

All the weasel-like quasi-Australian could do was ignore the biggest member of the Kebble clan.

Guy turned to Brett again and faced him head on.

'You faggot!' he roared.

On 19 February 2006, responding to news reports that his brother had frequented a gay escort agency and cultivated an intimate three-year relationship with a young male prostitute known as Vaughn, paying him up to R1 000 for each 'sex session' and showering him with gifts, including a rakish BMW M3, Guy told the media he was shocked by what he called 'these pathetic rumours'. This, he said, was 'the first I've heard' of Brett's taste for pretty toy boys.

And as for the likeness of their faces: there was the face of a man and the face of a lion on the right side of all the four: and the face of an ox on the left side of all the four: and the face of an eagle over all the four.*

While the Kebble boys and their sister were growing up, their mother Julie

---

* Ezekiel 1:10.

maintained her strong interest in the arts, especially dancing and, most of all, ballet. But the reality was that only rarely was there low-hanging fruit in the house. Succulent roasts were not standard Sunday fare.

Despite his sensitivity and artistic bent, fostered by a doting mother and grandmother, Brett was aware from an early age of the important role that money and connections could play. At school, he volunteered to run the tennis club. It wasn't that he played a good game, but he wanted to belong, to be part of a team, to have a network. At home, he was a misfit. At school, he at least had choices, and in a strangely logical way, his affinity for tennis was as understandable as his utter loathing of rugby.

From an early age, too, there were clear signs of latent entrepreneurship. When the father of one tennis player donated soft drinks to the club, Brett unilaterally decided to sell them and pocket the proceeds. This was conceivably the seminal act of his signature nostrum in the corporate world: turning the good fortune of others into personal gain.

Brett was a beautiful child and a good-looking youth. It was only in late adolescence that he began to show the coarser physical features inherited from his father's side of the family. The change carried a strange and unexpected bonus. His schoolmates seemed to regard him with more respect and adults started taking him seriously. One weekend, the Kebbles attended an auction of household goods and vehicles at a farm. A few days later, the owner telephoned Roger to arrange payment for the Mercedes that Brett had bought. The car was a wreck and would cost a fortune to restore to running order, but young Brett had recognised it as a model of particular rarity. Roger paid up and Brett became the owner of his first Mercedes.

Though father and son could not have been more different, this was the first of many occasions when Roger would bail Brett out of a difficult situation. In later years, when the two men went into the mining business together, there was a natural assumption among outsiders that they shared a close and special relationship. The truth, however, was that beyond their blood, Brett and Roger Kebble had just about nothing in common and could barely stand one another.

Roger's favourite reading was newspaper and magazine articles on financial, technical and motoring matters. He liked to watch TV sitcoms and enjoyed nothing so much as Italian food (fortunately, given his wife's provenance), washed down with Sauvignon Blanc. His taste in music ran to Eric Clapton, Elton John and Della Reese, his sporting preferences were, well, rugby, cricket and golf.

By contrast, Brett was almost obsessed with classical music. He favoured Schumann and Liszt, dismissing Mozart as a 'vanilla composer'. In food and drink, his tastes were eclectic, but always the finest he could afford. In London, his benchmark for wine with a meal was said to be anything that cost upwards of £1 000 a bottle. He was widely read, especially in the fields of the arts, and devoured anything about gold.

By the Cathédrale Notre Dame de la Paix in Bukavu, Duke Grace had read aloud from his moth-eaten copy of *Heart of Darkness*, Joseph Conrad's classic indictment of the savagery and insanity of Georges-Antoine Kurtz, an ivory trader sent by a dodgy Belgian company deep into the rainforests of the colonial Congo:

> The original Kurtz had been educated partly in England, and – as he was good enough to say himself – his sympathies were in the right place. His mother was half-English, his father was half-French. All Europe contributed to the making of Kurtz; and by and by I learned that, most appropriately, the International Society for the Suppression of Savage Customs had entrusted him with the making of a report, for its future guidance. And he had written it, too. I've seen it. I've read it.

For all his bourgeois banality, there were some surprising elements in Roger's make-up. For one thing, he often said his favourite company in the world was Eidos Plc. Based in Wimbledon, South London, this entity was part of SCi Entertainment Group, one of the leading developers of entertainment software, which, by 2006, offered three leading computer games with lurid sales blurbs:

- **Tomb Raider: Legend.** *Gaming's most famous heroine makes her triumphant return in her latest adventure.*
- **Rogue Trooper.** *He is the ultimate soldier, the last survivor of the massacred Genetic Infantrymen.*
- **Hitman: Blood Money.** *The return of the world's deadliest assassin takes killing to a whole new level.*

Eidos Plc was a great favourite in Kebbledom, though Coopers & Lybrand, auditors with a global reach, were less enamoured of the company. In August 1997, the auditing firm issued a statement saying it would not seek re-election to Eidos in the following year, due to 'lapses in corporate governance regulations'. The Eidos link to the Kebble kingdom was Charles Cornwall, who had been appointed CEO of the company in October 1995, when Eidos was 'a London- and Nasdaq-listed interactive software and technology company'. On 10 June 1999, Eidos founder Stephen Streater quit the company he had created nine years before, and in January 2000, Eidos issued a profits warning; in September, finance director Jeremy Lewis, who had originally been appointed by Cornwall, quit.

On 2 November 2000, the *New York Times* provided the story's ending:

Charles Cornwall quit as chief executive of Eidos Plc, Britain's biggest maker of video games like 'Tomb Raider' and was replaced by Michael McGarvey, the chief operating officer. Mr Cornwall, 37, postponed his resignation earlier this year as the company's earnings and stock price fell. Eidos said he quit to devote more time to technology and mining interests, including South African gold mines. Eidos's American depository receipts, which traded at $21 last December, rose 3 per cent yesterday to $4.25 on the Nasdaq stock exchange in New York.

The Eidos stock price had fallen out of bed, but Cornwall had long since made his money. While working at an investment bank in the City of London, two young geeks had given him a presentation. Cornwall was so impressed that he not only found funding for the proposed entity, but quit investment banking entirely and, quite naturally, made a fortune that should have set him up for life, by normal standards. The problem was, however, that he then signed on for a wild adventure in Kebbledom.

Cornwall was appointed a director of JCI in 2001 and remained so – despite a falling-out with Brett in early 2004 – until being forced out at the end of August 2005, along with Brett and Roger, John Stratton, Hennie Buitendag and Lunga Ncwana.

Cornwall also served as a director of Western Areas in 2000, 2001 and 2003.

Close to the loveliest of Bukavu's five peninsulas, the Duke found a passage from Conrad that sliced like a guillotine into the Kebble story:

> The young man looked at me with surprise. I suppose it did not occur to him that Mr Kurtz was no idol of mine. He forgot I hadn't heard any of these splendid monologues on, what was it? on love, justice, conduct of life – or what not. If it had come to crawling before Mr Kurtz, he crawled as much as the veriest savage of them all. I had no idea of the conditions, he said: these heads were the heads of rebels. I shocked him excessively by laughing. Rebels! What would be the next definition I was to hear? There had been enemies, criminals, workers – and these were rebels. Those rebellious heads looked very subdued to me on their sticks.

Ever since they had been students together at the University of Cape Town, Cornwall had really liked Brett, as he showed in no uncertain terms during a showdown in April 2002. During the latter part of 2001, JCI's bid to buy the so-called FreeGold assets from AngloGold had been trounced by Bernard Swanepoel at Harmony.* Roger, then chairman of JCI, had poached Neal Froneman from Harmony in October 2001 and mandated him to formulate a restructuring of JCI. Froneman

---

* On 21 November 2001, Harmony and African Rainbow Minerals Gold Ltd (ARMgold) agreed with AngloGold to purchase the so-called FreeGold assets, so named due to their location in the Free State. The two buyers jointly formed the FreeGold Company and bought the assets for R2.2 billion.

had made a good name at Harmony doing exactly that. Roger knew that the rot had set in at JCI and that something had to be done – something serious.

The meeting to present the results of Froneman's investigation took place in April 2002. He had invited Marais Steyn, a highly respected consultant, who was seated to his right. Buitendag was on Froneman's left. Sitting directly opposite Froneman at the far side of the table was Cornwall, with Brett on his left.

'I will not be telling you what you want to hear,' Froneman began.

Kebble was silent.

'We cannot pay salaries,' Froneman continued solemnly.

Nobody said anything.

Buitendag, the ubiquitous Kebble financial director, cleared his throat but uttered not a word.

'We need to execute an action plan to sell artworks, to sell Monterey, to sell Melrose House,' Froneman announced.

There it was. The Irma Sterns and Gerald Sekotos were on the endangered list. Melrose House was the elegant estate that Brett had bought from erstwhile Anglo American strongman Gavin Relly's widow. Cornwall's connections at Anglo and Kebble's most active slush fund, Consolidated Mining Management Services (CMMS), had made the purchase possible. Monterey was the classic Bishopscourt estate that served as Kebble's corporate headquarters in the Cape.

Froneman looked across the table and directly into Kebble's eyes.

'The company will go forward, but not with you as CEO.'

Kebble said nothing.

Nobody said anything, but a flush spread over Cornwall's face.

Froneman went over the facts – and there were many – about how JCI had been unable to raise finance to buy FreeGold because Brett was in the CEO seat.

'Brett,' Froneman said matter-of-factly, 'you need to step down and let somebody else do the job.'

Cornwall leapt to his feet and hurled a fair degree of verbal abuse at Froneman. He was weaving around like a prizefighter who needed a lot more training.

I think he wants to hit me, Froneman realised.

Cornwall left the room.

Brett Kebble had said not a single word since the meeting began.

Froneman looked across the table at him again.

'Step down, Brett, and we can make ten times more money for investors than you can.'

Kebble remained mute as a flustered but calmer Cornwall returned to the room.

Afterwards, out of earshot of Kebble and Cornwall, Buitendag finally spoke.

'You should have told me before, and I would have supported you.'

Like hell, Froneman thought to himself.

Of course, Brett was already way ahead of Froneman. A few months earlier, he had arranged the theft of R90 million in cash, raised from the sale of three million shares in Durban Roodepoort Deep (DRD), owned by Randgold & Exploration. Most of the cash was destined to finance the upcoming JCI rights issue. On 2 September, JCI would issue 345 million new ordinary shares at 45 cents each in terms of its rights offer.

The issue was underwritten by BNC (of which the directors were Brett and Roger Kebble) and Investage (of which the directors were Cornwall and George Poole). At that price, 345 million new shares would raise R155 million. JCI's next annual report showed that 80 million of the shares were bought by Cornwall and just under 100 million by Brett Kebble.

The lion in the stained glass window represents St Mark; he introduces his gospel with an account of St John the Baptist whom he describes as 'A voice of one crying in the desert'. The desert is the home of the lion.

On the opposite window, there is an eagle, symbol of St John. The raptor soars far into the heavens, representing St John, who carries us in introduction of his gospel to heaven itself: 'In the beginning was the Word, and the Word was with God, and the Word was God'.

The man in the next stained glass window represents St Matthew, who starts his gospel with the human ancestry of Our Lord.

The ox opposite represents St Luke, because it was the animal of sacrifice. St Luke stresses the atonement made by the sufferings and death of Christ. He goes further, in mentioning the priestly functions of Zachary.

Brett Kebble had many God-given gifts. Like the owner of a well in the desert, he could drop the bucket deep and work several kinds of magic.

One afternoon, a prominent Johannesburg businessman arrived early for lunch at a fine restaurant. He sat down and checked his voicemail, then settled down to wait for his guest. After a while, he heard a distinctive voice behind him. It was Johann Rupert, heir to the massive fortune created by his father, Anton, one of South Africa's wealthiest men.

'You know,' said Rupert, 'there's an enormous amount of goodwill towards Africa. President George W Bush – in fact, when you looked for me a week ago I was at the DaimlerChrysler meeting with President Bush Senior, and he confirmed how his son had enjoyed the meeting with President Mbeki, and with President Mandela prior to that – there's an enormous amount of goodwill.'

---

*   Adapted from unattributed writings published in October 1960, entitled *Souvenir of the Solemn Dedication and Opening of the Cathedral of Christ the King.*

The businessman listened intently as the voice continued.

'And Gordon Brown and Mr Blair as well. But we've also got to keep our house in order, and it doesn't help when the primary concern of investing countries, being rule of law, is neglected just to our north, and we do nothing about it. And we have a litmus test facing us today. So there's great goodwill, and I suspect that there will be debt write-offs. But as a proud South African who lives in South Africa, I – we – need to remind ourselves that the world has changed. Do you know that 20 years ago, there were 25, 30 countries that had democracies one wished to invest in? Today there are more than 200.'

The speaker paused. The businessman was fascinated, wishing he could record this crystalline vision.

'The world has changed dramatically,' the unseen man continued. 'There are far more opportunities for people to invest in – and we shouldn't live on handouts, we should grow our productivity.'

By this time, the eavesdropper was brimming with amazement, bristling with curiosity. He had wanted to turn around several times and, finally, he did.

Johann Rupert was nowhere in sight. The perfect rendition of his voice, his intonation, his very words, was courtesy of Brett Kebble, holding his audience in thrall.

'We've made great strides in the last decade,' Kebble/Rupert continued. 'Minister Manuel and President Mbeki ought to be applauded for their monetary and fiscal discipline. But it doesn't stop there. We've also got to make sure that the Constitution is sacrosanct, and that we abide by rule of law. So, if you look at the G8 meeting, there is goodwill, but I am perhaps too proud an Afrikaner – maybe I would like to suggest that we need foreign direct investment because the people trust us, and they wish to do business with us. There are signs of this, but we've got to be cautious all the time.'

Kebble the mimic was a hard act to beat. He was a talented imitator who could parody and satirise with the best of them, picking his targets carefully and memorising carefully selected passages of their real speech.

Julian Ogilvie Thompson, former head of De Beers, Anglo American and Minorco, was a favourite subject: 'Anglo American never lost its faith in South Africa, even in the country's darkest hours of the 1980s, when it was crippled by civil instability, international sanctions and disinvestments. We dismissed the possibility of complete social breakdown and pointed to a "managed revolution" as the only viable alternative for the future of the country. Our belief in this was confirmed when Gavin Relly, then chairman of Anglo, paved the way to civilised negotiation when he went to Lusaka in 1985 to meet the leadership of the outlawed and exiled African National Congress.'

Harry Oppenheimer, son of Anglo American's founder, was also in the Kebble repertoire: 'Disagreeable though it may be, we must admit that the racial policy which has been pursued here over the last 40 years has made South Africa stink in the nostrils of decent, humane people around the world.'

Nelson Mandela was mandatory: 'During my lifetime, I have dedicated myself to this struggle of the African people. I have fought against white domination and I have fought against black domination. I have cherished the ideal of a democratic and free society in which all persons live together in harmony and with equal opportunities. It is an ideal which I hope to live for and to achieve. But if needs be, it is an ideal for which I am prepared to die.'

Kebble, who could sing after a fashion, also loved to 'do' Louis Armstrong's gravelly version of the jazz standard, 'Mack the Knife'.

Oh, the shark has pretty teeth, dear … and he shows them pearly white
Just a jack-knife has MacHeath, babe … and he keeps it, out of sight
When that shark bites with his teeth, dear … scarlet billows start to spread
Just a gloved hand, has MacHeath, babe … and he never shows a single drop
    of red
On the sidewalk … Sunday mornin' comin' down … lies a body oozin' life
Someone's sneakin' round the corner … could that someone be Mack the Knife?

Some of Kebble's imitations were sinister and malignant, as with Martin Kingston, executive chairman of Deutsche Bank (South Africa) since July 2003. He didn't like Kingston, whom he openly accused of being 'married to the ANC'. His opinion was based on the fact that Kingston had wed not one, but two princesses of the political struggle. His first wife was Tembi Tambo, whose father Oliver was one of the most important figures in the ruling party's history. Following his death in 1993, Kingston divorced Tembi and married Pulane, daughter of Manto Tshabalala-Msimang, Thabo Mbeki's health minister and one of South Africa's most controversial politicians.

It wasn't so much Kingston's choice of partners that Kebble despised, however, as his habit of 'strutting round like a peacock, advertising his unparalleled contacts' in the ANC and other spheres of influence. It took little prompting for Kebble to launch into 'his' Kingston with lusty inflection: 'I know the president. I know Mbeki. I know Mandela. I know Bill Clinton, and I know blah, blah, blah. Pleased to meet you, how can I help you, do you know my name?'

Then he would segue into the lyrics of a Rolling Stones song, 'Sympathy for the Devil': *Pleased to meet you, hope you guessed my name, oh yeah …*

Kebble had a special vocabulary for people he did not like, and there were a good number of them, including Richard Stuart, a stockbroker who was once a partner in Fleming Martin & Company. Kebble said Stuart made Machiavelli look one-dimensional. He was especially derisive of Stuart's pronunciation, ridiculing him for referring at lunches and cocktail parties to the '*Runt*-gold people'.

But as entertaining as Kebble's mimicry could be, no one was ever really sure that he wasn't imitating himself. On the business front, he gave every indication of being the puppeteer. By 2002, Roger Kebble was a director of nearly 100 companies in the anfractuous empire Brett had created. All the world believed that the relationship between father and son was among the very best. Brett's public utterances did nothing to dispel this notion:

> What I know about mining you could write on the head of a pin with a Koki [fibre-tip] pen. But Roger's the one who has spent all of his working life doing these things, and he wants to roll up his sleeves and do it. He is the person who is prepared to go there and do it, build the relationships.

But the childhood memories recurred again and again, and when Brett related details of his visits to Our Lady of the Wayside, he always remembered the soft drinks, especially on the really hot days. In private conversations, he would disparage the father who had been either absent or aloof during his formative years.

Soft drinks have a special place in the recent history of investment. When he was just six years old, Warren Buffett, the world's richest investor for decades, would buy six-packs of Coca-Cola from his grandfather's grocery store in Omaha, Nebraska. Each pack cost 25 cents, but Buffett would sell each bottle for a nickel, pocketing a five-cent profit. Five years later, at age 11, Buffett committed the first of his money to serious investing.

During the second half of the 1990s, Brett Kebble represented himself as a very wealthy businessman, or investor, or both, loosely based in London and equipped with a small fortune made out of Eidos Plc.

On the right of the High Altar is the window of Christ the King, illustrating also the triumph of Christ by His Resurrection from the dead.

Over the window is the monogram of Christ and a crown, signs of sovereignty and victory. After His Resurrection Christ gave St Peter supreme authority over His Church.

'Simon, son of John, lovest thou Me more than these?' Christ asked.

This question was repeated thrice and the third time, Peter replied.

'Lord Thou knowest all things. Thou knowest that I love Thee.'

'Feed my sheep,' Christ said to him.

Kebble had sheep to feed, but food is seldom free.

---

*   Adapted from unattributed writings published in October 1960, entitled *Souvenir of the Solemn Dedication and Opening of the Cathedral of Christ the King.*

In addition to Cornwall, Kebble had a major British connection in Montague 'Monty' Koppel, trader extraordinaire, merchant adventurer, a peddler with one of the sharpest business noses ever. Born one month after an armistice ended the First World War in 1918, Koppel once practised as an attorney in South Africa. For many years, however, he had lived in a strange kind of exile in some of London's most expensive real estate. On visits to South Africa, where his interests were extensive in companies few had ever heard of,* he stayed in hotels under an assumed name. If one listened closely and paid careful attention, it might become evident that Kebble was somehow involved with both Cornwall and Koppel, but he never said much about either man to anyone.

The key to the Koppel legend lay in the highlands of landlocked Lesotho, home to the Letšeng diamond mine, in which Letšeng Investment Holdings South Africa (Pty) Ltd (LIH) held a 76 per cent stake. The remaining 24 per cent was in the hands of the Lesotho government.

In March 2006, official records identified the active directors of LIH as Peter Gray, Pieter Hendrik Henning, Chris Lamprecht, Mafika Mkwanazi, Sello Rasethaba and Thabo Mosololi. Gray, Henning and Lamprecht represented the post-Kebble executive administration at JCI Ltd and Randgold & Exploration. Mkwanazi, the one-time Transnet tsar, became a director of Western Areas in 2003. Rasethaba was CEO of JSE-listed Matodzi, Kebble's much vaunted black economic empowerment 'flagship'. Mosololi was the executive director of Tsogo Sun, one of South Africa's dominant hotel and gaming groups.

All three black directors of LIH also served on the board of another Kebble creation, Bookmark Holdings, until Mkwanazi resigned, along with Eric Molefe and Muthanyi Robinson Ramaite. When Kebble died, Bookmark was evidently putting together a BEE deal for Inkwenkwezi, which seemed to exist for the sole purpose of buying up stock in Western Areas. Forensic audits showed that a good chunk of the missing proceeds from Randgold & Exploration's illegal sale of Randgold Resources shares was used to buy around 5 per cent of the stock in Western Areas. This stock remained the property of Randgold & Exploration, however, and thus yet another Kebble-made BEE deal was scuttled.†

According to its 2005 annual report, Matodzi's single biggest shareholder was

---

* Inter-Freight Novelties, Eight-Seven-Nine Standerton, Pearlbrook Share Blocks Company, Patent Investment and Trust Company, Craighall Investments, Turfcom and Jacodan Investments.

† On 29 April 2005, Randgold & Exploration announced in its preliminary 2004 results that during the year, it had lent 9.9 million shares in Randgold Resources to Bookmark Holdings, 'an empowerment entity'. The transaction was structured to finance the purchase by Inkwenkwezi Gold (Pty) Ltd of 19 million shares in Western Areas Ltd from Anglo American Plc. The 2004 preliminary results were later withdrawn by Randgold & Exploration's new management.

Bookmark – previously known as Matodzi Investment Holdings (Pty) Ltd – with 24 per cent.

Far more enlightening than the new LIH board was the long list of directors who had resigned: Patricia Beale (Kebble company secretary); Hennie Buitendag (ubiquitous Kebble finance director); George Poole (a Kebble patsy with a taste for Lamborghinis and helicopters); Lieben Hendrik Swanevelder (long-standing director of CMMS); John Stratton (naturally); Kennedy Joseph Josiah Modise (a nominal BEE appointee); Lunga Ncwana (the mandatory ANC Youth League connection); Graham Wanblad (a director of Western Areas until 1997 and latterly an executive director at Simmer and Jack, Kebble's swansong redux); Stephen Tainton (executive director at Randgold & Exploration from August 2004 to April 2005); Robert Gordon Rainey (once a director at Simmer and Jack); George Henry Traub (whose only known connection to Kebble was via Bioclones, an offshoot of Traub's Lithie Investments) and Keith Whitelock, who ran Letšeng for De Beers until the mine was shut down – some say abandoned – in 1982.

Tellingly, though he had been placed on the board of nearly 100 companies, Roger Kebble was never a director of LIH. Letšeng was the brainchild of Koppel, the man who was Brett's 'other' father in many ways.

There was one more name on the list of LIH resignations: Christopher Paul Macdonald Main, address given as 32 Grosvenor Gardens, London. In March 2006, Paul Main was listed as an active director of a number of South African companies,[*] including Bateleur Polo.

Bateleur Polo. Main was in the polo set.

He was also Monty Koppel's runner in South Africa. In 1999, when Koppel flipped Saxendrift into Gem Diamonds, which was later taken over by Trans Hex, Main was on hand to collect his cheque. He walked off with R5 million in commission. It was an extraordinary way to make a living, given that it was John Bristow who had effectively bought Saxendrift to the market.

In March 2006, Cornwall was listed as having interests in various South African entities,[†] including Kurland Park Polo Club.

Kurland Park Polo Club. Cornwall, too, was a member of the chukka fraternity. The *Tomb Raider* man had come of age.

On 1 July 1999, Kebble had dumped a number of diamond interests into Matodzi (then New Mining), which was already seen by insiders as his 'BEE dustbin'. In

---

[*] Dormell Properties 366, Rowmoor Investments 451, Paulchard, Ensemble Trading 415, Dayspring Management Services, More 2000 Investments and Hancock Holdings.

[†] 8 Kurland Park Investments, Rosevean Investments 0034, Willoughby Investments, Kurland Park Polo Club, Ribotech, Bioclones (resigned), Dewberry Trading, Tanin Trading 141, Rzt Zelphy 4353.

another transaction displaying his shocking lack of business sense, Kebble dumped a 100 per cent interest in Newlands Minerals (Pty) Ltd.* This comprised, among other assets, '25 per cent of Letšeng-La-Terae in Lesotho, which is a well known Kimberlite property'. Similarly, Kebble dumped a 100 per cent interest in IEN Investments (Pty) Ltd,† which held another 25 per cent of the Letšeng-La-Terae project.

In a nutshell, Matodzi owned 50 per cent of LIH. In 2002, Koppel pushed Kebble into buying another 40 per cent of LIH from … Montague Koppel. On 31 March, Kebble coughed up R90 million in the form of 220 million fresh shares in JCI, issued at 45 cents each and $6.5 million in hard cash. Koppel was a hard man to please.

Kebble had no choice but to reopen the mine, but, as always, he was out of cash. It was at such times that he realised BEE actually *could* be of some use; that alliances formed in expediency could offer value in exigency. On 3 October 2003, Andrew Mlangeni, chairman of Matodzi, told shareholders that all was going well with Letšeng:

Matodzi holds a substantial stake in the Letšeng diamond mine in Lesotho. During the period under review, Matodzi was successful in securing funding from the IDC [Industrial Development Corporation] to complete the project. Operations are expected to commence early next year, with the mine having a projected lifespan of approximately 18 years.

In typical Kebble fashion, cash arrived late, if at all. It was not until December that LIH secured a R160 million commercial loan from the IDC to fund completion of the Letšeng diamond mine. The loan was repayable over five years.

In March 2006, Koppel still held 10 per cent of LIH. The rest – Matodzi's half share and JCI's 40 per cent – had effectively been ring-fenced within the assets secured in favour of Investec's bail-out package for JCI. Certain investors were expressing an interest in buying Letšeng, among them Clifford Elphick.

Elphick, yet another polo wallah and erstwhile CEO of EH Oppenheimer & Sons, the investment arm of South Africa's wealthiest family, had spent tens of millions of rand on his polo estate at Plettenberg Bay, as had Cornwall and as had Main. Main liked being surrounded by bodyguards and whisked from one point to the next by helicopter, for all the world as if he were on a life-threatening mission in hostile territory.

Main was among those in the private suite at Newlands who had witnessed Brett's

---

* In March 2006, the active directors of Newlands Minerals were listed as Gray, Lamprecht and Rasethaba. Past directors and officers were listed as Beale, Buitendag, Harry George Clare, Brett Kebble, Poole, Rainey, Swanevelder and Tainton.

† In March 2006, the active directors of IEN Investments were listed as Mosololi and Rasethaba. Directors who had resigned were listed as Buitendag and Brett Kebble.

mortification when his brother yelled out 'Faggot!' Koppel was in London, wondering what was to become of the 177 million shares he still held in JCI.

For three men who bore an uncanny physical resemblance to one another, the Kebble sons and father had distinctly different personalities, preferences and priorities. Brett shared his birthday, the first day that the moon was in Pisces, with Polish astronomer Nicolaus Copernicus. As the twelfth house of the zodiac, Pisces rules over drugs and secrets and large institutions such as prisons, hospitals, corporations and governments.

Brett constantly battled the bulge, starting and aborting one attempt after another to shrink his gut. He spent thousands having designer suits specially tailored to create an illusion of sartorial elegance, but never quite managed to hide his girth. He invested thousands more in footwear he'd been assured would make him seem more lithe, less chunky, though he hated the shoes and kicked them off at every opportunity.

Brett's gastronomic excesses defied every diet and slimming stratagem he ever tried. Like his father, he drove his Mercedes S-600 fast, very fast, and heavily, mainly at night when he went to restaurants or events that it was good to be seen at. One evening, as he and two associates talked business, the hands on the clocks and watches moved inexorably through the hours until, when it was fairly late, Brett said it was time to eat. He drove his companions at breakneck speed to one of his favourite restaurants in Kensington, one of Johannesburg's oldest suburbs.

It was an area favoured by the original Randlords and, more recently, had become imbued with a strong continental atmosphere, giving some of its restaurants top billing among the more affluent denizens of the northern suburbs. Brett's guests, still recovering from the terrifying cross-town journey to the restaurant, noted that the owner greeted and treated Brett like royalty, ushering him to a private area at the rear of the eatery. Their impression was that this was a table permanently reserved for Kebble's pleasure, which, that night, was a gigantic seafood platter, piled high with prawns and langoustine, crayfish and calamari, mussels and scallops.

This was going to be a big-bill meal, served with some of the finest wines in the house. Kebble ate like a demon. His associates had no idea where he put it all, but after the main course, he ordered dessert. Clearly, Kebble was no stranger to the establishment, as the 'slice' of cheesecake placed before him was the size of three normal portions. He despatched it in no time at all and still looked around as if there was more to come.

Psycho-babblers might say Kebble used food to fill the emotional hole gouged by his father's lack of affection, but to those who broke bread with Brett, it simply seemed that he loved to eat.

That said, there was no denying that Brett and Roger were locked in lifelong, if usually tacit, conflict. At some point, Roger's 'other daughter' had set out to prove just how much of a man he was. If that included being a loving, albeit often absent father, Brett's four children would be a partisan jury.

Brett and his wife, Ingrid – he always said she was 'the salt of the earth' – were married in 1989, when he was a newly qualified lawyer and she a teacher at Claremont Primary School in Cape Town. Her father sold retreaded tyres for a living, her brother had committed suicide a few years earlier. Their first home was a 1930s suburban bungalow with two bedrooms and one bath in Lelia Road, Claremont. Ingrid, who had an abiding passion for special education, walked to school across a railway bridge each day.

They sold the house, for which they had paid R163 000, after 18 months, because, Brett told a South African property magazine in 2004, 'it wasn't big enough for the family we planned'. By the time he died, 'home' for the Kebbles was Fair Seat, one of Cape Town's most magnificent residences, but Brett said of that modest first house: 'We had a wonderful time there. What's important to me is when I walk into a house and sense whether it is happy or unhappy. This was definitely a happy house.'

On an autumn day in 2003, Fair Seat was, at least temporarily, not a happy house. Ingrid was distracted and asked one of the family's domestic workers to bathe Elizabeth, the youngest and most beautiful of the Kebble children.

Someone forgot to add cold water before placing the toddler in the bath, and within seconds, the child known to most as Lily and to some as Kitty, had third-degree burns on her lower body. In a matter of days, her father had flown her to Australia to be fitted with a special hyper-barometric 'wetsuit' that would aid and speed her recovery.

Lily was little more than two years old at the time and spent many months in hospital recovering from not only the burns, but various complications, including pneumonia. If asked, Kebble would have denied that little Lily was his most beloved child – after all, who knew better than he how it felt for a parent to favour one child over another? – but after the accident, he moved the JCI head office from Johannesburg to another Bishopscourt mansion, Monterey, in order to be closer to his family. He was wracked by guilt, according to associates, and in a further drastic attempt to put his family first, he acquired the use of both a Gulfstream II and a Learjet 45 so that he would no longer be dependent on commercial flights when commuting between Cape Town and Johannesburg.

Guy Kebble was the proverbial chip off the old block, with an obnoxious arrogance to boot. Like Brett and Roger, he had gone to the parochial St Andrew's in Bloemfontein, but spent his last two years of school at prestigious Bishops in

Cape Town. Apart from a brief stint as reigning champion on a TV game show about sport and occasional sportscaster, his claim to fame was rugby. Guy had run onto the park as a prop forward for both the Western Province and KwaZulu-Natal provincial teams, as well as for the national squad.

Provisionally sequestrated in 2004 for an amount of R1 million owed to a firm of attorneys, he was the owner/chairman of the second-string Falcons rugby team in 2006.

While Brett favoured Mercedes for driving, Ferrari for bartering and Bentley for show (a Continental GT was parked in one of the four garages at his Johannesburg house on the night he died), BMW was the brand for Guy. He needed the 7 Series to accommodate his huge physical bulk, and had developed the habit of simply walking into a dealership, selecting a luxury sedan and telling the salesman to 'call Brett and sort out the finance'. But he did eventually promise to limit himself to a new car only once every four years.

Cars, and the speed at which they could be driven, were important to all three Kebble men. Rules, on the other hand, whether related to corporate governance, vehicle purchasing or the open road, were inconveniences to be flouted. The family maintained contact with St Andrew's through the Old Boys' Association, and once Roger was late setting off from Johannesburg for a meeting at the school. The road to Bloemfontein is flat and straight, and Roger drove his Mercedes like a man fleeing the devil himself.

When a traffic officer waved him down, he brought the big S-600 to a halt in a cloud of dust, but, as the lawman approached the driver's side of the car, a fistful of banknotes came flying out of the window.

'Write your ticket on that,' Roger yelled, flooring the accelerator and heading off again at breakneck speed.

Though he, like Brett, enjoyed driving a Mercedes, BMW was one of two makes Roger identified as a favourite (the other being Jaguar) in a personal profile done by *Engineering News*.

Some of his other answers were curt, yet enlightening:

What pets do you have?

'Koi fish.'

Favourite TV programme?

'Comedies.'

What was your biggest-ever opportunity?

'The Rand Mines takeover.'

Now *there* was a story. In 1991, the way Brett told it, the Kebbles bought Rand Leases from Steen Severin for one cent a share, plus the debt pile, a massive R4 million.

They promptly fired Glenn Laing, the would-be mine manager. He left the country in a hurry, and, almost simultaneously, an earth tremor broke a shaft at the miserable old mine. While working on repairs, Roger – shifting seamlessly from shift boss and contract miner to geologist – found five million tons of pay ore. That was the good news. The bad news was that the accident had broken a tribute agreement with neighbour Durban Roodepoort Deep. Brett boasted that in his first big piece of lateral thinking, he said, 'Buy DRD'.

The Kebbles duly traipsed off to see John Hall, chairman of DRD-owner Rand Mines, while the Rand Leases stock price was knocking up around 100 cents a share. Investors thought the Kebbles just had to be geniuses.

But Hall and his deputy John Turner gave them short shrift. Brett's next stroke of genius after the unsuccessful meeting was: Forget about DRD – buy *Rand Mines*, all of it. Buy the whole damn thing. Who needs money? Just buy the biggest thing in the story.

Rand Mines was in the process of unbundling, its gold assets destined to be unpacked into Randgold & Exploration. Brett again approached Hall, who noted that Rand Leases, with a market value of R4 million, could not afford Randgold & Exploration, which boasted a market value of R32 million. At this point, Brett discovered that Julian Baring of Mercury Asset Management in London was sitting on 33 per cent of Randgold & Exploration. He flew to London without delay.

Speak to Peter Flack, said the wily Baring.*

Flack – tall, bald, hawkish and magnificently arrogant – prevaricated, but finally mixed Adam Fleming into the cocktail.

Rand Leases merged with DRD.

Brett always described Flack's attitude in disparaging terms, and described Fleming as 'an egregious Pom'.

If there's a fight, Flack told Kebble, *I'll be the last one standing. I'll be the one who walks away.*

And then, in the fashion of one who has a pathological habit of rewriting history, Brett would claim that he received a fortuitous telephone call.

'We have an empowerment partner for you,' Paul Harris of Rand Merchant Bank and First National Bank allegedly told him. 'His name is Mzi Khumalo.'

'Mzi was greedy,' Brett would mumble. 'Greedy for money.'

Johannesburg, born a mining town, always a mining town, will die a mining town. In the earliest days, the city streets had three types of building: saloons, betting

---

* Baring would later tell Brett that a Kebble competitor had warned him to be wary of his new partners, lest he wake up one morning and 'find an assegai up your arse'.

shops and bordellos. There has never been enough space underground for sewers *and* mining tunnels, and the mortuary is always full.

Greed was ever the religion in this Sodom and Gomorrah.

The initial strike set off the biggest gold rush in the history of the world, and buckets of blood were spilt. In the early days, ex-hunters found that 'blackbirding' was a lucrative sideline. They would capture black people from as far afield as Mozambique and take them to Johannesburg by force. For each man handed over, the blackbirder was paid a fee equal to what the unwilling indentured labourer would earn for a year down the mines.

An outcrop of gold-bearing rock was stumbled on by chance at Langlaagte. In September 1886 President Paul Kruger declared the fields 'a public digging' and with that, the mining camp was born. Prospectors came from all parts of South Africa and then from all over the world to the 'Ridge of White Waters'. Even Mark Twain pitched up. As the numbers exploded, the Oblate Fathers from Pretoria visited and in February 1887, arrangements were made to say mass for the Catholics among the prospectors. The exact site of this first mass is unknown, but to be sure, it was in Ferreira's Camp to the west of the present City Hall. The beginnings of the new mission were rough and ready, all right. You had to search among the motley crowd of diggers for those who were Catholics and then beg them to remember their religious duties. It would be an unfinished storeroom, followed next Sunday by a stable, and on and on.

'Thing was,' Brett would continue, 'Peter Flack would not leave me alone. He wanted to be the last one standing. He wanted to take over this, merge with that. He was chairman of Randgold & Exploration, but I was owner.'

Owner? How, seemingly overnight, had Brett Kebble become the *owner* of Randgold & Exploration? It would have cost *millions*. It was at this point in the telling that Brett would never, ever mention Montague Koppel. But that was the link.

Cornwall had made money on Eidos, and Brett Kebble had made money on Eidos, but Montague Koppel had made really, really serious money on Eidos. These three were the Trinity.

'I was thinking,' Kebble would say, 'that I'm not going to cripple you, Peter Flack, but what I am going to do is fuck you, so better you get out of my life.'

'Peter Flack was not the last one standing.'

When the sea travellers eventually reached the Cape of Good Hope, from the helms of their ships, so tradition says, they gazed upon not only the great mountain, not simply a flat tabletop of stone, but a mighty stone altar. This was the altar of Africa.

Across it stretched a dazzling white altar-cloth of cloud. Like luminous candles

---

*   Adapted from writings by Reverend Father JE Brady, OMI, published in October 1960 among documents entitled *Souvenir of the Solemn Dedication and Opening of the Cathedral of Christ the King.*

the fading stars and the bejewelled cross hung suspended in the heavens. Down the sides of the altar ran silver streams of water, darkened to the colour of blood by the sandstone rock; precious streams as the saving blood of Christ.

The dawn, radiantly holy, lit up the great altar table of rock with flames of sacrifice. The clear blue sky above might have been Mary's robe as she adored before so fitting an altar; the sun arose to give more light to the glassy waters of the bay, slate-grey in colour, like the breast of a dove.*

Sometimes, when he was at Melrose House, Kebble would lead the way to a trapdoor. It led to a cellar, he would explain, where some of the Jameson raiders had taken refuge.

The Jameson Raid, planned by Cecil John Rhodes, stretched from 29 December 1895 to 2 January 1896. The raid, led by Leander Starr Jameson, was aimed at inciting an uprising by – mainly – British expatriate workers, Uitlanders, in the Transvaal. Jameson, administrator general of Matabeleland, led a force of around 600 men, equipped with rifles, six Maxim machine guns and three light artillery pieces. The Jameson Raid was a fiasco.

Kebble never lost his love for the arts. The third annual Kebble Art Awards, scheduled for February 2006, carried prize money of R600 000, ostensibly from Brett's personal coffers, though the true source of the funds will probably never be known. The inaugural competition drew 2 097 entries, of which 236 were shown in an exhibition space of more than 3 000 square metres at the four-storey Cape Town International Convention Centre.

The exhibition attracted record crowds for an event of this nature, with more than 13 000 visitors over a two-week period. Clive van den Berg, curator of the awards, and his team designed an interior with 400 running metres of wall space and 25 booths for video works and projection screens. More than 600 lights were installed to ensure optimum viewing conditions.

Hailed by critics and patrons of the arts as the most significant cultural development in South Africa's young democracy, the awards were the jewel in the crown of Kebble the philanthropist, the generous benefactor, the self-anointed emperor of aesthetics. How far he would have journeyed on this road to righteousness is a matter for speculation. The Kebble Awards were swiftly deleted from the calendar after their founder was slain on 27 September 2005.

Dear though they were to Kebble's heart, the art awards were almost certainly not uppermost in his mind that night. Four days earlier, police had arrested Peter Skeat, Tiego Moseneke and Gopolang Makokwe and charged them with defrauding

---

*   Adapted from writings by Father Desmond Murray, OP, published in October 1960 among documents entitled *Souvenir of the Solemn Dedication and Opening of the Cathedral of Christ the King.*

Jürgen Kogl, a benefactor of sacked South African deputy president Jacob Zuma, to the tune of R40 million. The three men were not only handcuffed, they were shackled in leg irons. Skeat had previously won a court case against JCI involving a complex deal and an entity known as Kabusha. The JCI management that had replaced Kebble and his cronies on 30 August paid Skeat R67 million in terms of the court order. Some time after Kebble's murder, Skeat told the *Financial Mail*:

> My arrest was manipulated by Kebble, and possibly others, because Kebble was angry that he had lost the court case in which he was obliged to pay me a lot of money. He was trying to punish me in his way. The state dropped the charges because they had clearly been trumped up.

The day before Kebble died, a splenetic David Gleason, long-standing friend of the family, had published an article attacking Aflease (now SXR Uranium One) and its CEO, *that* Neal Froneman. He alleged that Aflease had misled investors about its uranium reserves and was behind Skeat's arrest. Gleason later backed down on this claim. Meanwhile, Froneman had called a special meeting of Randgold & Exploration shareholders, including Aflease. Froneman had issues about corporate governance.

Stephen Mildenhall, chief investment officer with Allan Gray, who had been shot in front of his Cape Town house in August, had also been making noises about corporate governance.

Kebble had started stealing cash from Randgold & Exploration in 2002 through complex deals and a spider's web of front companies. The company had been looted of hundreds upon hundreds of millions of rand, and Kebble knew he was in big trouble. But the real trouble was that he was no longer of use to those who had already betrayed him.

For most of his adult life, Brett Kebble had not done an honest day's work. Nor had he salted away an emergency fund. The idiot had emerged. Kebble was not a superstitious man, but the world had turned against him and he couldn't help but wonder why.

Upstairs in the mansion at 65 Fifth Avenue, Illovo, lay videotapes that Kebble had been given by Liesl Göttert, who was producing a television documentary about the Zuma fiasco. Göttert was one of several people, including Kebble, who believed that Zuma was the victim of a carefully orchestrated smear campaign with strong political overtones. There were legal problems with her footage, mostly relating to Kebble's own accusations against prominent people he regarded as his enemies:

> These people get together on Friday evenings and drink copious quantities of Scotch and other things. They have big parties – and things happen. Because we

finance a lot of empowerment in this country, we get to hear things. We get to hear things from the inner circles.

The truth about Kebble's looting and corporate plunder would take months to reach the public domain, thanks in part to a platoon of specialists who were well paid to protect and defend the gospel according to Brett. Roger was in Paris and security supremo Clinton Nassif in Mauritius when Kebble was killed, so in the immediate aftermath, the praise-singers were led by communications consultants David Barritt and Dominic Ntsele and former judge Willem Heath, whose role in the Kebble network was vague. Their tributes were lavish, in some cases as lavish as their monthly pay cheques (Barritt reportedly got R500 000 a month to run the art awards and ensure that all other 'matters Kebble' went through the spin cycle before reaching the media). Said Barritt:

> Brett was the most incredibly generous, kind and larger-than-life personality. His contribution to the mining industry will come to be recognised as very considerable.

Ntsele was equally impressed:

> Kebble was probably the most intellectually stimulating person I've ever met. Many times he upset his friends because he acted for the common good. Most of Kebble's critics were actually beneficiaries of his generosity.

Ntsele was on record as claiming credit for Kebble's quotable quotes – *I'm Brett's communication strategist and he does not speak publicly without eliciting my view* – so it may be safe to assume that the Washington-trained lobbyist had 'approved' the statement that Kebble issued when he was booted out as CEO of three listed companies less than a month before his murder. It was so stuffed with cunning and deceit that, had it been a pig, it would have popped:

> Looking back over the past decade or so, I believe I can claim to have made some contribution to the sustainability of the South African gold mining industry. My belief – one that I share with my closest associates – in the need to create a compact between capital and labour, laid the foundation for the continued existence of at least three major mining houses that would otherwise have met their demise a decade ago.
>
> However, after a period of deep introspection, and notwithstanding the rough and ready ethos that is characteristic of our industry, I believe that some of the bruising corporate and personal battles that have taken place on my watch, while unavoidable, might have been handled in a less confrontational way. I have therefore attempted in recent months to mend some fences.

Chief among the 'closest associates' referred to was John Stratton, an erstwhile intelligence agent who had run into a spot of bother while serving at Her Majesty Queen Elizabeth's pleasure, and been shipped off to Sardinia before retiring, in a manner of speaking, to Australia. JCI's annual report for 2004 introduced Stratton, no spring chicken at the age of 70, as 'a director of various Australian companies' with 40 years of experience in the resource sector, who had 'managed a number of joint venture operations in the Persian Gulf, Papua New Guinea, the Solomon Islands, USA, Mauritius and India'.

Stratton was obsessed with the underworld and the murky figures who lurked in these sloughs of despond. He introduced Kebble to a number of them. Though he was all over the Kebble 'empire' like a plague, Stratton's precise role and purpose were undefined, but he alone had untrammelled access to Kebble. Their adjoining offices at Monterey had an interleading door and Stratton would enter Kebble's domain at will, whether there was a meeting in progress, a journalist conducting an interview or a personal visitor. No one else, not even Roger, would have dared be so intrusive.

Kebble's security detail reported directly to Stratton, though payments were made for the most part by Heath, who said of his three-year relationship with Kebble:

> We became good friends. And he was never a person who would hesitate to speak his mind, and that might have led to some unhappiness in certain quarters.

Unlike that of Heath, Stratton's name had an unfortunate habit of popping up in the wrong places. He awoke on the first day of 2006 knowing that he faced civil action in regard to Rawas in South Africa, along with Roger, Mike Prinsloo, Hennie Buitendag and JCI Ltd. He faced similar court action in Australia, along with Charles Mostert and companies that notionally fell under Brett Kebble's control: Continental Goldfields, CAM Australia, Weston Investments, CAM Jersey and JCI (Isle of Man).

Significantly, Brett was not being personally sued in either case. When he first heard about Rawas in 2001 – and the legal action that would ultimately lead to Roger being booted out of DRD – he was livid. He roared and belched fire, and almost all his rage was aimed at Stratton, whom he saw as the sole mastermind behind the Rawas scheme, though as with the Randfontein debacle, the common denominators were Roger and Buitendag.

Rawas was a thick layer of excrement that had seeped onto the even thicker layer that was Randfontein. Transactions in both had taken place over the same period, from 1999 to 2000. After Rawas, Brett was forced to mount a campaign of damage control that would cost millions and leave him burdened with sycophants until the day he died. He was putting out one fire after another; he was on a blazing treadmill.

All the available facts point to Brett Kebble having been manipulated by some of his closest allies. In Australia, Stratton was nicknamed 'Bangles' due to his propensity for gold jewellery – lots of it. During the early phase of his relationship with Kebble, Stratton was haughty, imperious even. After Rawas, it was said, he became positively obsequious. No one could explain the change.

When Kebble died, Stratton towered over everyone to organise a fitting funeral. It wasn't long, however, before he reverted to his original, bombastic self. He summoned each individual involved in the various schemes and networks that began to unravel almost as soon as Kebble's flag-draped coffin was driven through the gates of Monterey and, depending on their status, issued the appropriate warnings.

*The Cathedral of St George the Martyr in Cape Town is still incomplete. Three wars, depressions and recessions have delayed its completion. The foundation stone of the cathedral was laid on 22 August 1901 by the Duke of Cornwall and York (later to become George V).**

As Brett's coffin was wheeled down the aisle on a rainy afternoon one week after his death, some 1 000 people sang South Africa's national anthem. In simple but moving tributes, Brett's eldest son Matthew, aged 14, and daughter Hannah, aged 12, stood before the throng of politicians, tycoons, strangers they had never met, to share deeply personal memories of their father. It was all too much for Roger, though. He broke down and almost collapsed as he mounted the pulpit to deliver a eulogy, which was read by David Gleason instead:

> He was famous. His accomplishments became part of legend, and most of all, he was a kind and generous human being. It was Brett who, together with trusted colleagues, developed the strategy of a coalition of labour, capital and government.

The irony of Roger's last farewell – *I can unequivocally say: you were a man, my son* – was lost on none who knew the family secrets. The hollowness of words like 'patriot' and 'people's hero' were equally not lost on the handful of mourners who already had an inkling of the shocking corporate secrets that would emerge in months or years to come.

For all anyone knew, whoever had ordered and paid for the mafia-style hit on Kebble was in the cathedral that afternoon as well.

*   *   *   *   *

As the fishermen of Lake Kivu launched their boats for the night, Duke Grace, more than a little drunk on Johnny Walker Blue, glanced at the looming hulk of the Cathédrale Notre Dame de la Paix, and read aloud from his well-thumbed Conrad:

---

*   Adapted from unattributed materials published by the Cathedral of St George the Martyr in Cape Town.

I am not disclosing any trade secrets. In fact, the manager said afterwards that Mr Kurtz's methods had ruined the district. I have no opinion on that point, but I want you clearly to understand that there was nothing exactly profitable in these heads being there. They only showed that Mr Kurtz lacked restraint in the gratification of his various lusts, that there was something wanting in him – some small matter which, when the pressing need arose, could not be found under his magnificent eloquence. Whether he knew of this deficiency himself I can't say. I think the knowledge came to him at last – only at the very last. But the wilderness had found him out early, and had taken on him a terrible vengeance for the fantastic invasion.

Then, setting the book aside, Duke Grace in the Confusion pulled himself up to his full height, closed his eyes, threw back his head and bellowed at the dark and brooding sky:

Mistah Kurtz, he DEAD!

Epilogue

B Y APRIL 2006, the dust was only starting to settle on the wreckage that Brett Kebble had created in life and bequeathed, in death, to a small army of auditors, accountants, lawyers, tax collectors, corporate executives, shareholders, investors and family members. There were definite signals that at some point, police and prosecutors would have to get involved as well.

The media, including individuals and publications that had promoted and lauded Kebble as a modern Midas in the past, wallowed in the sensational revelations – including forensic audit reports – that showed he had been a consummate criminal and amoral man.

In a statement headed 'Massive fraud revealed at Randgold & Exploration' and issued on 31 March, Peter Gray, who had replaced Kebble as CEO in August 2005, acknowledged that there had been 'massive misappropriation and mismanagement of shareholders' assets over an extended period' during the 'Kebble era'. The 'Enron-style' transactions, uncovered when the company's new board opened 'a veritable Pandora's Box', were nothing but 'layer after layer of misrepresentation', and the relevant authorities would be furnished with all available information with a view to criminal 'or other' sanctions.

That major forces had been, were or would be linked to Kebble's monumental fraud and theft was hinted at by Gray's revelation that one of the most frustrating aspects of untangling the web had been 'the complex legal and disinformation campaigns adopted by those who were trying to get out of the firing line by spiking our guns'.

As the financial community digested details of Kebble's crooked deals, British pop star Robbie Williams was prancing around Monterey, the elegant mansion in Bishopscourt that must have been the scene of many Kebble crimes-in-embryo. On the eve of the South African leg of his world tour, part of the video for the entertainer's hit single 'Sin Sin Sin' was being filmed in the backyard – with a Rolls-Royce – and a bedroom – with smoke effects and petals – of what had been Kebble's Cape headquarters.

Meanwhile, Kebble associates, accomplices and acquaintances throughout South Africa and abroad waited anxiously for whatever would happen next. The investigation into his murder had stalled amid allegations ranging from sloppy police work to deliberate cover-up. A parallel probe initiated by the Kebble family, involving private pathologists, forensic scientists and detectives, had been halted almost as soon as it began.

In the fiscal realm, a great many people stood to lose the easy money and material benefits that had come their way until Kebble's Roman candle career was snuffed out. Randgold & Exploration had already identified claims and recoverable assets worth more than R1 billion within six months, and Gray promised 'there is more to come'.

Months, if not years, of legal wrangling lay ahead. A substantial share of the loot would most likely never be traced. But what of the main known players in the Kebble saga? How had they fared since that night in September 2005, when seven shots on a quiet suburban street destroyed their Camelot?

ROGER KEBBLE was fighting some big battles, not least against the South African Revenue Service. They wanted lots of millions from him and he was in no hurry to cough up. Roger had been forced out of his last formal job, as executive chairman of Simmer and Jack, in December 2005. He was making half-hearted attempts at putting a consortium together to buy JCI and Randgold & Exploration and restore the previous glory, whatever that meant, of the Kebble empire.

Having spent most of his career in hard-rock mining, he was spending a lot more time juggling figures. Just how much expertise in this area he had picked up from his son and how much came naturally would be hard to say. His first job, way back in 1958, had been as an articled clerk with a firm of auditors, but he found the work tedious and boring, and soon went off to do a *real man's* job, thus becoming a shift boss on a gold mine.

Along the way to becoming chairman or director of more than 100 companies, Roger joined the prestigious Rand Club in Johannesburg that had been founded by Cecil John Rhodes, the Bloemfontein Club, the Kelvin Grove Club in Cape Town, the Falcons Rugby Club and the Transvaal Automobile Club. How much time he had to frequent them in between putting out the fires that kept flaring up around his business affairs could not be determined.

MZI KHUMALO, one of the original BEE mandarins, continued to have great trouble making money from conventional business deals, much as his mentor, Brett Kebble, had struggled in this department. Both had fabulous track records of scoring big with paper-driven slush deals, but real entrepreneurial successes remained as rare as rocking horse shit.

In March 2006, the Zimbabwe High Court ordered Khumalo to cough up

$7.4 million, in US dollars of course, to businessman Lloyd Hove for breach of contract. The dispute, dating from 2002, related to Zimbabwe's number one gold producer, Khumalo's Metallon Gold. Hove sued Khumalo for reneging on an agreement to partner his company, Stanmarker, in the purchase of Independence Gold from Lonmin, listed in London and Johannesburg. Judge Yunus Omerjee found that Khumalo had acted in bad faith and set Stanmarker's damages in foreign currency. As the judge put it, gold was priced in US dollars, Independence Gold had been owned by a UK-based entity and Stanmarker's dividends would have been in greenbacks.

Elsewhere in the Khumalo empire, it was a case of stop-go, stop-go at the serial entrepreneur's 150-room hotel in the Zimbali Coastal Resort in KwaZulu-Natal. The R300 million, five-star development, of which only one-third had been completed, overlooks the sea. Neels Brink of Metallon Property said Khumalo had green-lighted the project without having all the financing in place, as he had expected to have money available after the listing of Metallon Gold. In March 2006, that potential listing was once again effectively delayed by the Zimbabwe High Court's decision.

Media reports suggested that Khumalo was keen to repatriate a large sum of offshore money to South Africa, but had been warned that this would entail a fine of about R200 million. The funds were no doubt a hangover from all that Simane stuff.

PAUL MAIN was last sighted in January 2006 at the SA Open 18-Goal Polo Tournament in Plettenberg Bay. South Africa's premier international polo competition was won by Team Bateleur, whose members were Main, Gareth Evans, David Sterling (from Spain) and Jose Donoso (from Chile).

Several people looked forward to hearing Main explain, one day, how he came to be sitting on close to R200 million worth of stock in Randgold Resources and Western Areas both before and after Kebble's death. In the event that he should be struck by amnesia on this matter, perhaps the name 'Concerto Nominees' would serve to jog his memory.

BULELANI NGCUKA, erstwhile head of the National Prosecuting Authority and of the Scorpions, perceived as Kebble's worst enemy and close friend of Mzi Khumalo, was forging ahead with BEE deals. In September 2005, Growthpoint Properties, the largest listed property company on the JSE, concluded a R1 billion deal that stood to benefit Ngcuka, his former boss and justice minister Penuell Maduna, and Lazarus Zim, erstwhile CEO of Anglo American South Africa.

JOHN STRATTON was still in South Africa, but was seldom seen at any of his usual haunts.

GUY KEBBLE had assumed the role of sleaze-fighter. Hot on the heels of his indignant responses and predictable attacks on the media when news emerged of brother Brett's penchant for toy boys in their twenties and preferably in groups of up to four at a time at the Johannesburg brothel where he was known as 'Nugget Ricky', Guy had some serious damage control to do at his Falcons Rugby Club as well.

The club, reportedly owned by Guy, was hit by allegations of after-match orgies involving players, coaches and officials. Everybody denied everything, naturally. According to anonymous sources, the action had taken place at the Bosman Stadium in Brakpan, an East Rand mining town much like Springs, from whence the Kebbles had come. One anonymous letter charged that the after-match drinks function had become an appetiser for sordid late-night parties. Guy said events had been blown out of proportion.

HENNIE BUITENDAG, one of only two people who could claim to have been in Kebble's inner circle, remained as haughty and sinewy as ever. As the numbers man, Buitendag, a chartered accountant by training and a financial wizard by nature, was in great demand among auditors trying to follow the money.

In 2004, a High Court judge had described Buitendag as a 'dishonest witness who in an arrogant manner made statements that were manifestly mendacious and an insult to the intelligence of this court', so there was much trepidation about his usefulness in cracking the metaphorical Kebble vaults.

MARK BRISTOW continued to rewrite history. On 14 November 2005, when the new Randgold Resources mine, Loulo, was opened in Mali, Bristow issued a statement of some elegance: 'Loulo is the second major gold mine Randgold Resources has discovered and developed in Mali. The first, Morila, has produced more than three million ounces since it went into production in October 2000.'

If Morila was the first, Syama must have been Mine Zero. But Bristow never mentioned Syama any more.

As for having 'discovered' Loulo, a public document* of great legal import published on 28 October 1996 included a competent person's report signed by one Dr Dennis Mark Bristow.

---

* Circular to Randgold & Exploration shareholders regarding the acquisition by Randgold Resources (Holdings) Ltd of the entire issued share capital and a portion of the loans against BHP Minerals Mali Inc. from BHP Holdings (International) Inc.

It stated, *inter alia*: 'The Loulo gold deposit was discovered in 1981 using regional and detailed geochemistry. In June 1992 BHP Mali entered into an option and share purchase agreement with BRGM [Bureau de Recherches Géologiques et Minières] and the State of Mali, referred to as the Somilo joint venture.'

In his 1996 report, Bristow stated that BHP had spent $5 million on the Loulo project. That is a lot of money for a mining company to spend on a property where someone else later discovers something.

In October 1996, BHP sold four entities: Syama, plus the rights to the Loulo, Yanfolila and Morila permits, all in Mali. The entire future of Randgold Resources had revolved around reshuffling these assets.

Speaking at the opening of Loulo, Bristow said the company believed that true value in the mining industry was created by discovery and development rather than through the reshuffling of assets.

Mark Bristow was yet to discover his first ounce of virgin gold, but shareholders should anticipate an announcement about gold being 'discovered' by Randgold Resources on one or other distant planet.

PETER FLACK was never again as confident as he had been in 1996 and 1997. He was forced out of the Randgold & Exploration structures in 1998 and took time off to spend some of his severance pay on big game hunting. This is a very expensive hobby, and Flack returned to work in due course.

He became a business undertaker via FRM Strategies with co-directors Alastair Moffat and Lindsay Robertson.

Flack had mixed successes, headed by the sweetish transformation of IST, a JSE-listed electronics group. However, the failure of MGX was seen as the second failure, after Leisurenet, by the man who wanted to be seen as South Africa's No. 1 Mr Fix-it.

In March 2006, Flack was in the headlines as chairman of Sallies, a wrecked fluorspar mining company. Results for the six months to 31 December 2005 reflected a R16.7 million loss. In words that echoed his days of thunder at Randgold & Exploration, Flack said that Sallies 'has had to contend with the rand, the Honeywell contract and delays in the approval of mining and water rights which severely prejudiced its operations. The fact that it has not only survived these adversities but now actually has a real chance of a prosperous future is little short of miraculous.'

WILLEM HEATH'S company, Heath Executive Consultants, remained 'founded on the principles of sound corporate practices' and continued to believe in 'dynamic solutions to establish long-term relationships by working towards promoting a risk free environment in which our clients can prosper'.

DOMINIC NTSELE was playing an inordinate amount of golf and hadn't put out a media statement for months.

DAVID BARRITT was suing JCI for all he could, based on the previous arrangement that had seen him rake in R500 000 a month.

THUTHUKILE SKWEYIYA, once listed as chairman of Brett Kebble's Orlyfunt fantasy, remained in the news. Early in 2006, there were howls of protest when it turned out that Deputy President Phumzile Mlambo-Ngcuka, accompanied by Zola Skweyiya (a senior cabinet minister) and his wife Thuthukile, had taken a R700 000 flight, courtesy of the South African taxpayer, to the United Arab Emirates, where, according to the deputy president, she needed to 'inspect cranes' with a view to proposed expansion of South Africa's infrastructure.

PATRICIA BEALE was living her usual mundane middle-class life in one of Johannesburg's lesser northern suburbs.

BARRY BAWDEN, Beale's brother and former CCB agent, was hunkered down on his farm at Bela Bela (formerly Warmbaths), north of Pretoria, occasionally venturing forth in his dual role as property developer in and around the capital.

GEORGE POOLE was last seen in March at Johannesburg International Airport on his way to a helicopter show, somewhere in North America.

NEAL FRONEMAN was enjoying great success as CEO of SXR Uranium One. In March 2006 the company announced the successful raising of $149 million to fund construction of the Dominion mine near Klerksdorp, west of Johannesburg. Froneman had originally planned to raise only $65 million, but was overwhelmed by heavy demand from foreign investors. It would have been difficult to raise that kind of money in South Africa, he said. SXR Uranium One was listed in Toronto and Johannesburg.

PETER SKEAT, who has a very nice wife, had taken the R67 million that JCI Ltd paid him after his successful court case against the company shortly before Kebble's murder, and dropped off the corporate radar screens.

THEMBA LANGA, a highly qualified tax lawyer, continued to live an interesting life as legal counsel for the South African Football Players' Union. There was enough trouble in South African soccer for everyone, even Langa.

DALI TAMBO was shuffling a small mountain of unpaid bills, which, he said, had been 'overlooked' by his administrative staff. From his R10 million home in the Johannesburg suburb of Saxonwold, he would have learnt that his Koketso Group was not going to make him a millionaire from diamond mining in Angola, after all. Not only had close on eight million Randgold & Exploration shares used to acquire Angolan concessions been misappropriated, the concessions themselves had been cancelled by the Angolan authorities due to gross mismanagement.

KHAYA NGQULA was still CEO of South African Airways and settling down to marital bliss with his new wife, a former beauty queen.

ESSOP PAHAD remained President Thabo Mbeki's right-hand man. The Minister in the Presidency had told people at Kebble's funeral that 'what Brett said to any of us in private should remain private'. He had also slammed the media, accusing them of 'speculation that seems to border on the obsessive' and publishing 'many articles that seem to suggest Brett is guilty'.

The diatribe by one of the men closest to South Africa's head of state flabbergasted most observers, not least because they had difficulty understanding what Pahad meant when he said 'media articles that convict Kebble do not accord him rights in a democracy where everyone is presumed to be innocent until proven guilty'. Pahad never did explain how a dead man could ever be convicted *or* acquitted, regardless of his democratic rights.

Among the matters Pahad urged should remain private might well have been the identity of a long-standing resident at Portion 1, Erf 1857, Houghton Estate, Johannesburg. The property, which has hosted a stellar parade of rich and famous visitors and pilgrims, ranging from world leaders to pop stars, Oscar winners to sporting heroes, was hidden among the assets of Consolidated Mining Management Services, Kebble's favourite slush fund. Mysteriously, records of the purchase in 2000 for R525 000 had disappeared from the Deeds Office, and an entity named Catalyst Props (Pty) Ltd had been inserted between the property and CMMS.

Registered at 28 Harrison Street, the business address of JCI Ltd, Catalyst's former directors included well-known 'struggle' attorney Ismail Mahomed Ayob, Patricia Beale, Hennie Buitendag, George Poole and – surprise, surprise – Brett Kebble. There was no indication that the iconic resident of the house in Houghton's Thirteenth Avenue knew of the Kebble link.

ADAM FLEMING had effectively retired. The former chairman of Harmony Gold was chairing a potential junior, Wits Gold, in March 2006. His days at Randgold & Exploration seemed to be a distant memory.

GORDON MILLER was involved in an internecine fight with BEE shareholders at Simmer and Jack, where he was CEO. Simmers was Brett Kebble's swansong creation, but Miller denied that in full.

Miller, a big, strapping professional mining engineer, had always been a favourite of Roger Kebble's. Miller had been a director of Western Areas in 1998 and 2003, and, more famously, a director of Randgold & Exploration from 18 November 2003 to 6 May 2005.

Ahead of the Simmers rights issue, traced back to 31 March 2005, companies under Kebble's control, including two slush funds, held 175 million of the 225 million shares in issue by Simmers.* By the time the rights issue was over, Consolidated Mining Management Services (CMMS), Consolidated Mining Corporation (CMC), Continental Goldfields (Australia) and Randgold & Exploration held but few shares in Simmers.

While Simmers had been the entity conducting the rights issue, R18 million in cash ended up in the hands of JCI. In a classic Kebble convolution, loans owed by Simmers to the Kebble entities named were converted into new Simmers shares vended into Jaganda, which then issued preference shares to JCI. In other words, Simmers was allowed to effectively kill its debt by indirectly issuing preference shares in Jaganda to JCI. It was classic Kebble alchemy.

The actual shares in Jaganda were held 51 per cent by a BEE grouping, known as Vulisango. The individual shareholders of the 51 per cent were Gibson Njenje (22 per cent), Siviwe Mapisa, Archie Mkele, Margaret Ndlovu, Baba Njenje, Nozuko Pikoli, Ayanda Sisulu, Valence Watson and Zola Yeye.

Gordon Miller, Roger Kebble, Graham Wanblad, John Berry and Ronnie Watson held the other 49 per cent of Jaganda, to the tune of 9.8 per cent each. When the squabbling broke out, Ronnie Watson crossed to the Vulisango camp, where his brother already was.

For all the rhetoric, there was no question that money played a big role in the boardroom battle. At 25 cents per Simmers share, Jaganda was worth nothing, but at 225 cents per share, where it was in early February when the author published two articles about the terrible truth, Jaganda was worth R606 million.†

It was not bad business, considering that the *entire* issued share capital in Jaganda had cost just R26.26.

The BEE component of Jaganda said, naturally, that it was 'actively involved in the struggle for the political transformation of South Africa'. In March 2006, Vulisango published an open letter to shareholders, announcing that the Simmers audit

---

*   See Appendix O.

†   See Appendix Q.

committee had appointed Umbono's John Louw, 'an eminent forensic auditor', to conduct a forensic audit of Simmers. Under the heading 'The issues of corporate governance and the Kebble legacy', issues to be raised included management's handling of the Jaganda preference share issue and management's handling of the chairman's appointment.

The latter referred to Nigel Brunette, who had been appointed chairman after Roger Kebble stepped down from the position in December 2005. Brunette had been a director of Randgold & Exploration for a number of years until 1998.

PETER GRAY was busier than ever as the new CEO of Randgold & Exploration and JCI Ltd.

CHRIS LAMPRECHT continued to find out just how interesting life could be as a financial director, serving alongside Peter Gray.

SANDY MCGREGOR remained a non-executive director of Western Areas and an executive at Allan Gray, the Cape Town money manager. In March, McGregor oversaw the sale of Allan Gray's 25 per cent stake in Western Areas to Harmony Gold. By all accounts, Allan Gray remained the single biggest shareholder in both Randgold & Exploration and JCI.

MARK WELLESLEY-WOOD was living a relatively quiet life as CEO of Durban Roodepoort Deep.

ILJA GRAULICH was doing as much as he could to re-launch DRD, with the main focus now being on its offshore operations and its new name, DRDGold.

MONTAGUE 'MONTY' KOPPEL was in London, wondering what to do with 177 million shares in JCI and his 10 per cent stake in Letšeng Investment Holdings. There were other scraps of Kebble wreckage that Koppel also found somewhat attractive.

MIKE PRINSLOO continued to await the civil trial in South Africa on the Rawas scandal. On 3 November 2000, Wellesley-Wood had announced that Prinsloo, then CEO at DRD, had taken 'indefinite leave'. Prinsloo went on to become head of South African operations at Gold Fields, a Tier 1 producer. On 1 January 2006, Prinsloo accepted the newly created position of chief executive officer of the Gold Fields Academy, which was to be renamed the Gold Fields Business and Leadership Academy.

MARTIN KINGSTON was still at Deutsche Bank in Johannesburg. His wife Pulane was doing well in BEE business.

CHARLES MOSTERT was apparently still in Australia.

BILLY MASETLHA was fired on 23 March 2006 as boss of the National Intelligence Agency (NIA). On 25 October 2005, Masetlha had been suspended from the NIA, along with deputy director-general Gibson Njenje and general manager Bob Mhlanga, following complaints that the three were spying on Sakumzi 'Saki' Macozoma.

In March 2002, Masetlha, then director-general in the Department of Home Affairs, had declared DRD's Mark Wellesley-Wood a prohibited immigrant and famously said that he was 'the kind of executive South Africa could do without'. Mangosuthu Buthelezi, then Minister of Home Affairs, overruled Masetlha.

Before being laid off from the NIA, Masetlha was also linked to an alleged hoax e-mail scandal and accused of ordering surveillance of certain individuals without court approval. Late in March, a report by Zolile Ngcakani, the Inspector-General of Intelligence, named some of those spied on as Deputy President Phumzile Mlambo-Ngcuka, finance minister Trevor Manuel, intelligence minister Ronnie Kasrils and a number of Mbeki's senior aides.

According to the *Sunday Times*, individuals who were spied on but not mentioned in the report included Joel Netshitenzhe, CEO of government communications and head of the policy unit in the presidency; Loyiso Jafta, chief director of justice, crime prevention and security in the presidency; Frank Chikane, director-general in the presidency; Bulelani Ngcuka; Leonard McCarthy, head of the Scorpions; Gerrie Nel, head of the Scorpions in Gauteng; Peter Vundla, a prominent black businessman; Izak du Plooy, a Scorpions investigator; Johan du Plooy, another Scorpions investigator; Cyril Ramaphosa, an ANC leader and businessman; Mbulelo Goniwe, ANC chief whip; Smuts Ngonyama, head of the presidency in the ANC; and Vusi Pikoli, who had replaced Ngcuka as head of the NPA.

Most of the surveillance targets were perceived as enemies by Kebble, but none more so than Macozoma. Kebble fervently believed, and said so many times, that Macozoma had orchestrated a conspiracy against Jacob Zuma with a view to becoming the next president of South Africa.

GIBSON NJENJE resigned as head of operations of the NIA in early November 2005. According to the 2005 Matodzi annual report, Njenje Investment Holdings (Pty) Ltd was the third biggest shareholder in Matodzi, with a 9.3 per cent stake. Njenje had been a director of Western Areas in 1998 and 2000. From early in 2006, he was the indirect owner of a 5 per cent stake in Simmer and Jack, via Vulisango and Jaganda.

STEVEN KOSEFF wanted to wrap up the JCI and Randgold & Exploration debacle as soon as possible. By the end of March, Investec was looking at earning fees of around R360 million for providing JCI with a R460 million bail-out facility late in August 2005. Not only would the facility be fully repaid, but the fee, which was an add-on, would rate as one of the largest in the history of South African investment banking.

CHARLES CORNWALL was last seen in a January 2006 chukka at the SA Open 18-Goal Polo Tournament in Plettenberg Bay. His team, Kurland Park, included Richard Pohl, Buster MacKenzie and JP Clarkin (New Zealand), who was replaced by Mike Todd (Australia).

The best pony award went to 'Hot and Sharp', ridden by David Sterling of Paul Main's team, while the James Twort Memorial Trophy for the best string of ponies went to Jose Donoso, another member of Main's team.

DENNIS TUCKER was working at Investec.

TOKYO SEXWALE was living the good life of an entrepreneur after his grand entry on the back of the Saxendrift/Gem Diamonds/Trans Hex deals in 1999 and 2000.

BRIAN GILBERTSON was in Moscow, working as the president of SUAL, a Russian aluminium and resources entity.

A long time ago, Gilbertson, a scientist by training, had spent two years with the American space programme at NASA and another year in Paris before joining the original JCI in 1970. In 1992, after Gilbertson was appointed to the top executive post at Gencor, formation of the world's biggest diversified resources group was under way. Just as the Kebbles burst onto the South African corporate mining scene, Gilbertson was imploding Gencor. He downsized it beyond recognition and then started building it up again, from precious little. The acquisition of offshore entity Billiton marked a first giant turning point, followed by a London listing in 1997.

On 1 July 2002, Gilbertson became the second CEO of BHP Billiton, the company he had substantially helped build, but resigned six months later.

As Roger Kebble's eulogy rang out at his son's funeral, BHP Billiton's market value was roughly $100 billion (about R600 billion). When the Kebble mother ship, the new JCI, was suspended from the JSE on 1 August 2005, its market value was R336 million. It was not worth 1 per cent of the value of BHP Billiton; it was not worth 0.1 per cent of the value of BHP Billiton. Brett Kebble and Brian Gilbertson had started out at much the same time with much the same raw material.

INGRID KEBBLE continued to approach life stoically. The four children she had with Brett were coping well enough under the circumstances. Matthew and Andrew took a degree of flak as the media continued to dramatise the sordid details of their slain father's business career. Things were somewhat easier for Hannah, and Elizabeth remained well on the mend after her horrific accident.

BERNARD SWANEPOEL stood out as the one individual who had survived the 1997 board of directors of Randgold & Exploration.

LUNGA NCWANA, former member of the ANC Youth League executive, was keeping a very low profile, more absorbed than ever in his fleet of luxury and sports cars.

CHRIS NISSEN continued to serve on the boards of Randgold & Exploration and JCI.

BRENDA MADUMISE remained on the board of Randgold & Exploration.

MAFIKA MKWANAZI relinquished his position as non-executive chairman of Western Areas on 31 August 2005, but remained on the board, and continued to be a director of Matodzi.

SELLO RASETHABA was sitting very tight, as CEO of Matodzi, on the company's 50 per cent stake in Letšeng Investment Holdings. Late in March 2006, Matodzi announced an agreement with JCI that the preference shares JCI held in Matodzi would be converted. New accounting rules deemed the preference shares to in fact be debt. JCI accepted fresh ordinary shares in Matodzi in return. The nett effect was that liabilities of R356.3 million were eliminated from Matodzi's balance sheet and the deal restored Matodzi to solvency. The number of Matodzi shares in issue increased from 149 537 000 to 363 362 000, leaving JCI in control of 59 per cent of the issued share capital of Matodzi. Kebble had always boasted that Matodzi was a '100 per cent BEE company'.

QUINTON GEORGE was lambasted by Randgold & Exploration CEO Peter Gray for applying, in March 2006, for Randgold & Exploration to be placed in provisional liquidation. Quinton's father, Peter, had baptised Kebble as a born-again Christian in his swimming pool at home just months before he was slain. Catholics, however, cannot be baptised again (here, immersed), and since Kebble had been raised Catholic but had latterly embraced one of the charismatic faiths, his funeral in an Anglican cathedral appears to have been a religious compromise.

GLYN LEWIS was loving his job as general manager of Northam platinum mine. He was less sure, however, about being the CEO. Northam is one of the toughest mines in South Africa, and Lewis was still the man you would want by your side in the trenches, if you could have only one.

BERNARD VAN ROOYEN, the 'Silver Fox', continued to serve on various boards of directors, mainly in the resources sector.

GREG HAWKINS was doing fine out of his base in Accra, Ghana. In March 2006, the affable Canadian was becoming more heavily involved as a founder and director of the African Mining Group, which holds a number of properties in Ghana. The Mankranho concession had already captured the attention of the international investment community, situated as it is on strike and contiguous with Newmont's No. 1 global development project, the $500 million-plus, 12.2 million ounce Ahafo project. African Mining Group also holds Nyankumasi, 30 kilometres south-south-west of Newmont's $500 million-plus 7 million ounce Akyem project.

JOHN BARKER was working from Johannesburg for clients he could not name, due to confidentiality contracts, consulting on various African mining projects. In March 2006, he recalled how Kebble had called him ahead of the mid-1997 listing of Randgold Resources in London.

Barker, working at the time for the Royal Bank of Canada in London, complained in a written report to clients of a number of apparent irregularities that he had identified in the prospectus published by Randgold Resources. Kebble called him and told him he was 'wrong', and then abruptly hung up.

Later, in the lobby of a hotel where a mining conference was being held, Peter Flack, then strongman at both Randgold & Exploration and Randgold Resources, confronted Barker and said he would never speak to him again. When Barker asked who Flack would speak to at RBC, Flack ignored him, choosing instead to place a mean pair of sunglasses on his face.

Flack then headed off and out the main door, cutting a lonely figure as he slipped out onto the main street.

ANDILE NKHULU was picking up the pieces after waiting in vain to meet with his benefactor on the night Kebble died. Itsuseng, of which Nkhulu was chairman, had reached a settlement with Randgold & Exploration in respect of R20 million that had gone walkabout in the infamous 2003 Phikoloso deal. A settlement of sorts had also been negotiated in respect of R74 million that had been funnelled to Equitant, headed by Lunga Ncwana.

LIEBEN HENDRIK SWANEVELDER, that mysterious ex-director of Brett Kebble's favourite slush fund, Consolidated Mining Management Services, was circulating in the western parts of the Johannesburg metropolis.

TOM DALE continued to farm happily on his lovely establishment near Parys on the Vaal River, south of Johannesburg.

In early September 1999, Dale quit Gold Fields as CEO and was replaced by Ian Cockerill, who moved across from AngloGold. In the years before he quit gold mining, Dale found himself in a number of meetings with Kebble.

'He gave me the creeps,' Dale said. Having grown up on the tough streets of Manchester, Dale saw straight through Kebble. Dale was one of the most talented mining engineers who ever set foot on South African soil, but he proved to be just too large for the industry. He may well have been the first to identify Kebble as 'a wolf in sheep's clothing'.

DUKE GRACE IN THE CONFUSION could still be found in the precincts of Bukavu in April 2006, if only you knew how to find him. He was still going to 'retire' from smuggling. Anyone who reads Robert Sabbag's book, *Smokescreen*, very carefully, might have some chance of identifying the Duke.

But it's anyone's guess as to why the Duke was so interested in the stargazer mountain catfish, *Amphilius uranoscopus*. Perhaps world-class smugglers like the Duke are always on the lookout for the next best thing to smuggle, and perhaps this fish is one of them. Whatever the answer, the Duke will go down as one of the greatest smugglers of his generation, an outlaw of taste and refinement.

BRETT KEBBLE lay at peace, as did Joseph Conrad's fictional character, Georges-Antoine Kurtz. Both had made and lost fortunes, and had he not been cheated by death and corporate governance, Kebble might have made one more. Six months after his assassination, the metals and commodities super-cycle, as subscribed to by certain bullish investors, was rampant. In early April 2006, gold touched 25-year highs around $600 an ounce, while a number of other commodities and metals were trading at or near multi-decade highs.

Resources stock prices were running, and by early April, Western Areas was trading up around 4 500 cents a share. Had Kebble not illegally sold stocks once held by Randgold & Exploration and JCI, he would have controlled assets worth more than R8 billion.

APPENDIXES

A   Directorates and administration of companies under Kebble control

B   Companies of which key players were directors on 10 June 2002

C   JCI Ltd: consolidated income statements

D   JCI Ltd: consolidated balance sheets

E   How off-balance sheet liabilities concealed the gearing of JCI Ltd

F   JCI Ltd: history

G   JCI group balance sheets, showing consolidation of slush funds
     as at 31 March 2004

H   JCI Ltd: share capital evolution

I   Assets controlled by the JCI, Randgold & Exploration and Matodzi groups,
     and assets available for pledging by JCI

J   Consolidated Mining Management Services (CMMS) financials

K   Randgold & Exploration Company Ltd: share capital evolution

L   Western Areas Ltd: share capital evolution

M   Randgold Resources Ltd: share capital evolution

N   Simplifying Simane

O   Simmer and Jack Mines Ltd: share capital evolution (I)

P   Simmer and Jack Mines Ltd: share capital evolution (II)

Q   Value of Jaganda ordinary shares

R   Glossary of names from forensics

ABBREVIATIONS

AR: annual report

cps: cents per share, referring to a stock's share price, earnings or dividends

Interims: results for a half-year period

Market cap: market capitalisation (a stock's issued shares multiplied by its prevailing price per share)

Na: not available

Ords: ordinary shares

Prelims: preliminary results for a full year

Rm: millions of rands

Cross-references within appendixes, for example E-26, denote Appendix E, line 26.

Appendix A

Directorates and administration of companies under Kebble control[1]

JCI Ltd

1996 (known as NK Properties Ltd[2])

DIRECTORS: John William George Mackenzie (acting chairman); Jonathan Lawrence Fleischer (managing); Donald Ashford Geyer; John Anderson Kirkwood Muir; Nikitas Ghikas Vontas; John Oberholzer; William Patrick P Ward; Mark Robert Dietrechsen

AUDIT COMMITTEE, REMUNERATION COMMITTEE: None due to size and nature of the company

COMPANY SECRETARY: AFC Properties (Pty) Ltd

ATTORNEYS: Not stated

AUDITORS: Coopers & Lybrand

NUMBER OF SHARES ISSUED: 17 432 393

1997 (known as Consolidated African Mines Ltd)

DIRECTORS: Mzi G Khumalo (chairman); Roger Brett Kebble (CEO); Hendrik Christoffel Buitendag; Paul Ronald Anthony Ferguson; Jens Eskelund Hansen (Canadian); Roger Ainsley Ralph Kebble; John WG Mackenzie; Alan Bruce McKerron; Ronald Kort Netolitzky (Canadian)

AUDIT COMMITTEE, REMUNERATION COMMITTEE: Not stated

---

1   Details obtained from annual reports and financial statements.

2   Consolidated Mining Corporation Ltd (CMC) delisted from the JSE on 29 August 1997, becoming a 100% subsidiary of NK Properties, which then morphed into Consolidated African Mines (CAM), which, on 8 July 2002, changed its name to (the 'new') JCI Ltd. CMMS became a 98% subsidiary of CAM/JCI in 1999. CMC and CMMS, along with parent company JCI, were the key entities in Brett Kebble's slush fund system. JCI Gold Ltd delisted on 16 July 2002 after a scheme of arrangement when it was absorbed into CAM. Barnato Exploration Ltd delisted on 14 October 2003 when it was absorbed into JCI. Free State Development and Investment Corp Ltd delisted on 23 December 2003 following a scheme of arrangement with Randgold Resources.

COMPANY SECRETARY: Consolidated Mining Management Services Ltd; George William Poole

ATTORNEYS: Brink Cohen Le Roux & Roodt

AUDITORS: Coopers & Lybrand

NUMBER OF SHARES ISSUED: 17 432 393

1998

DIRECTORS: Roger AR Kebble (chairman); R Brett Kebble; Hendrik C Buitendag; Paul RA Ferguson; John Stratton (Australian)

AUDIT COMMITTEE, REMUNERATION COMMITTEE: Not stated

COMPANY SECRETARY: Consolidated Mining Management Services Ltd; George W Poole

ATTORNEYS: Bowman Gilfillan Hayman Godfrey

AUDITORS: Charles Orbach & Company

NUMBER OF SHARES ISSUED: 527 285 706

1999

DIRECTORS: Roger AR Kebble (chairman); R Brett Kebble; Hendrik C Buitendag; Paul RA Ferguson; John Stratton

AUDIT COMMITTEE, REMUNERATION COMMITTEE: Not stated

COMPANY SECRETARY: Consolidated Mining Management Services Ltd; George W Poole

ATTORNEYS: Bowman Gilfillan Hayman Godfrey

AUDITORS: Charles Orbach & Company

NUMBER OF SHARES ISSUED: 660 610 446

2000

DIRECTORS: Roger AR Kebble (chairman); R Brett Kebble; Hendrik C Buitendag; Paul RA Ferguson; John Stratton

AUDIT COMMITTEE, REMUNERATION COMMITTEE: Not stated

COMPANY SECRETARY: Consolidated Mining Management Services Ltd; George W Poole

ATTORNEYS: Bowman Gilfillan Hayman Godfrey

AUDITORS: Charles Orbach & Company

NUMBER OF SHARES ISSUED: 665 073 403

2001

DIRECTORS: Roger AR Kebble (chairman); R Brett Kebble; Hendrik C Buitendag; Charles Henry Delacour Cornwall (British); Paul RA Ferguson; John Stratton

AUDIT COMMITTEE, REMUNERATION COMMITTEE: Not stated

COMPANY SECRETARY: Consolidated Mining Management Services Ltd; George W Poole

ATTORNEYS: Bowman Gilfillan

AUDITORS: Charles Orbach & Company

NUMBER OF SHARES ISSUED: 665 073 403

2002 (name changed to JCI Ltd on 9 July)

DIRECTORS: Roger AR Kebble (non-executive chairman); R Brett Kebble (CEO); Hendrik C Buitendag; Charles HD Cornwall; John Stratton

AUDIT COMMITTEE, REMUNERATION COMMITTEE: Not stated

COMPANY SECRETARY: Consolidated Mining Management Services Ltd; Patricia B Beale

ATTORNEYS: Taback and Associates

AUDITORS: Charles Orbach & Company

NUMBER OF SHARES ISSUED: 711 740 100

2003 (known as JCI Ltd)

DIRECTORS: Roger AR Kebble (non-executive chairman); R Brett Kebble (CEO); Hendrik C Buitendag; Charles HD Cornwall; John Stratton

AUDIT COMMITTEE: Roger AR Kebble; Hendrik C Buitendag; John Stratton

REMUNERATION COMMITTEE: Roger AR Kebble; Charles HD Cornwall; John Stratton

COMPANY SECRETARY: Consolidated Mining Management Services Ltd; Patricia B Beale

ATTORNEYS: Taback and Associates

AUDITORS: Charles Orbach & Company

NUMBER OF SHARES ISSUED: 1 750 566 255

2004

DIRECTORS: Roger AR Kebble (non-executive chairman); R Brett Kebble (CEO); Hendrik C Buitendag; Charles HD Cornwall; John Stratton

AUDIT COMMITTEE: Roger AR Kebble; Hendrik C Buitendag; John Stratton

REMUNERATION COMMITTEE: Roger AR Kebble; Charles HD Cornwall; John Stratton

COMPANY SECRETARY: Consolidated Mining Management Services Ltd; Patricia B Beale

ATTORNEYS: Taback and Associates

AUDITORS: Charles Orbach & Company

NUMBER OF SHARES ISSUED: 2 089 503 652

Randgold & Exploration

1995

EXECUTIVE DIRECTORS: Peter Hamilton Flack (chairman); Frank Abbott (financial); David Ashworth (new business and exploration, British); Dennis Mark Bristow (geology and exploration); Richard Reginald de Villiers (human resources); Lionel Hewitt; Roger AR Kebble; R Brett Kebble (commercial)

NON-EXECUTIVE DIRECTORS: Nigel RG Brunette; Jean-Antoine Cramer (Swiss); David MG Dods; Adam R Fleming (British); Thaddeus Steven Anthony Grobicki (British); Ferdinand

Lips (Swiss); David H Starling (British); Fred J Stokes

ALTERNATE DIRECTORS: Johan P Burger; JM Jephson

AUDIT COMMITTEE: Johan P Burger; Frank Abbott; Nigel RG Brunette; David Ashworth

REMUNERATION COMMITTEE: David H Starling; Nigel RG Brunette; Ferdinand Lips; R Brett Kebble

COMPANY SECRETARY: David J Haddon

ATTORNEYS: Bowman Gilfillan Hayman Godfrey

AUDITORS: Deloitte & Touche

NUMBER OF SHARES ISSUED: 38 040 700

1996
DIRECTORS: Peter H Flack (executive chairman); Frank Abbott; David Ashworth; D Mark Bristow; Nigel RG Brunette; Jean-Antoine Cramer; Richard R de Villiers; Adam R Fleming; Thaddeus SA Grobicki; Lionel Hewitt; R Brett Kebble; Roger AR Kebble; Ferdinand Lips; David H Starling

ALTERNATE DIRECTORS: Johan P Burger; Z Bernard Swanepoel

AUDIT COMMITTEE, REMUNERATION COMMITTEE, NUMBER OF SHARES ISSUED: Not stated

COMPANY SECRETARY: David J Haddon

ATTORNEYS: Bowman Gilfillan Hayman Godfrey

AUDITORS: Deloitte & Touche

1997
EXECUTIVE DIRECTORS: Peter H Flack (chairman); Frank Abbott (financial); David Ashworth (new business and exploration); D Mark Bristow (exploration); Dick Plaistowe; Richard R de Villiers (human resources); Lionel H Hewitt (engineering); Roger AR Kebble (technical); R Brett Kebble (commercial); Z Bernard Swanepoel

NON-EXECUTIVE DIRECTORS: Nigel RG Brunette; Jean-Antoine Cramer; Thaddeus SA Grobicki; Ferdinand Lips; David H Starling; Johan P Burger; Adam R Fleming

AUDIT COMMITTEE, REMUNERATION COMMITTEE: Not stated

COMPANY SECRETARY: David J Haddon

ATTORNEYS: Bowman Gilfillan Hayman Godfrey

AUDITORS: Coopers & Lybrand

NUMBER OF SHARES ISSUED: 40 918 277

1998
DIRECTORS: Roger AR Kebble (executive chairman and chief executive); Nigel RG Brunette; Johan P Burger; Adam R Fleming; Thaddeus SA Grobicki; Lionel Hewitt

AUDIT COMMITTEE, REMUNERATION COMMITTEE: Not stated

COMPANY SECRETARY: David J Haddon

ATTORNEYS: Bowman Gilfillan Hayman Godfrey

AUDITORS: PricewaterhouseCoopers

NUMBER OF SHARES ISSUED: 41 283 961

1999
DIRECTORS: Roger AR Kebble; David Ashworth; D Mark Bristow; Hendrik C Buitendag; Grant Fischer; Graham Patrick Shuttleworth

AUDIT COMMITTEE: David Ashworth; Graham P Shuttleworth; Hendrik C Buitendag; Grant Fischer

REMUNERATION COMMITTEE: David Ashworth; Hendrik C Buitendag; Grant Fischer

COMPANY SECRETARY: David J Haddon

ATTORNEYS: Bowman Gilfillan

AUDITORS: PricewaterhouseCoopers

NUMBER OF SHARES ISSUED: 41 394 134

2000
DIRECTORS: Roger AR Kebble (executive chairman); David Ashworth; Hendrik C Buitendag; Grant Fischer

AUDIT COMMITTEE: David Ashworth; Hendrik C Buitendag; Grant Fischer; Graham P Shuttleworth (resigned 29 September 2000)

REMUNERATION COMMITTEE: David Ashworth; Hendrik C Buitendag; Grant Fischer

COMPANY SECRETARY: David J Haddon

ATTORNEYS: Bowman Gilfillan

AUDITORS: PricewaterhouseCoopers

NUMBER OF SHARES ISSUED: 41 437 419

2001

DIRECTORS: Roger AR Kebble (executive chairman); David Ashworth; Hendrik C Buitendag; Grant Fischer

AUDIT COMMITTEE: David Ashworth; Hendrik C Buitendag; Grant Fischer

REMUNERATION COMMITTEE: David Ashworth; Hendrik C Buitendag; Grant Fischer

COMPANY SECRETARY: David J Haddon

ATTORNEYS: Bowman Gilfillan

AUDITORS: PricewaterhouseCoopers

NUMBER OF SHARES ISSUED: 41 701 921

2002

DIRECTORS: Roger AR Kebble; David Ashworth; Hendrik C Buitendag; Grant Fischer

AUDIT COMMITTEE: David Ashworth; Hendrik C Buitendag; Grant Fischer

REMUNERATION COMMITTEE: David Ashworth; Hendrik C Buitendag; Grant Fischer

COMPANY SECRETARY: David J Haddon

ATTORNEYS: Bowman Gilfillan

AUDITORS: PricewaterhouseCoopers

NUMBER OF SHARES ISSUED: 43 696 256

2003
EXECUTIVE DIRECTORS: R Brett Kebble (CEO); Hendrik C Buitendag (financial); Gordon Trevlyn Miller

NON-EXECUTIVE DIRECTORS: Roger AR Kebble (chairman); David Ashworth; Motsehoa Brenda Madumise (independent); Lunga Raymond Ncwana; Andrew Christoffel Nissen (independent)

LONDON COMMITTEE MEMBERS: PEC Dexter; MJ Grant

AUDIT COMMITTEE: M Brenda Madumise; David Ashworth; A Christoffel Nissen

REMUNERATION COMMITTEE: A Christoffel Nissen; David Ashworth; M Brenda Madumise; Lunga R Ncwana

COMPANY SECRETARY: Consolidated Mining Management Services; Patricia B Beale

ATTORNEYS: Taback and Associates

AUDITORS: PricewaterhouseCoopers

NUMBER OF SHARES ISSUED: 55 280 785

Western Areas Gold Mining Company Ltd[3]

1995
DIRECTORS: William Alan Nairn (chairman); John Fox Brownrigg (managing); Sydney John Maurice Caddy; WP Conn (financial); G Martin W Cross; Peter J Eustace; Dr Hugh Scott-Russell; Neil Saul Segal; Graham Peter Wanblad; Derek S Webbstock (general manager); Christopher William Popham Yates

AUDIT COMMITTEE, REMUNERATION COMMITTEE, ATTORNEYS: Not stated

COMPANY SECRETARY: JCI Ltd; Don W Sievwright

AUDITORS: KPMG Aiken & Peat

NUMBER OF SHARES ISSUED: 89 586 513

---

3   Western Areas Gold Mining Company Ltd changed its name to Western Areas Ltd on 7 September 1998.

1996

DIRECTORS: William A Nairn (chairman); JG Best; John F Brownrigg (managing); Sydney JM Caddy (consulting engineer); William P Conn (financial); G Martin W Cross; J Andre Geldenhuys; Dr Hugh Scott-Russell; Neil S Segal; Rob G Still; Christopher John Tayelor; Graham P Wanblad; Derek S Webbstock; Christopher WP Yates

AUDIT COMMITTEE: John F Brownrigg; G Martin W Cross; Christopher J Tayelor

REMUNERATION COMMITTEE: John F Brownrigg; J Andre Geldenhuys; Graham P Wanblad

COMPANY SECRETARY: JCI Ltd; Don W Sievwright

ATTORNEYS: Not stated

AUDITORS: KPMG

NUMBER OF SHARES ISSUED: 90 811 384

1997

DIRECTORS: R Brett Kebble (chairman); JG Best; John F Brownrigg (managing); Sydney JM Caddy; G Martin W Cross; J Andre Geldenhuys; Mzi G Khumalo; Rob G Still; Michael James Tavendale; Christopher J Tayelor; Graham P Wanblad; Derek S Webbstock; Christopher WP Yates (British)

AUDIT COMMITTEE: John F Brownrigg; G Martin W Cross; Christopher J Tayelor

REMUNERATION COMMITTEE: John F Brownrigg; J Andre Geldenhuys; Graham P Wanblad

COMPANY SECRETARY: JCI Ltd; Don W Sievwright

ATTORNEYS: Not stated

AUDITORS: KPMG

NUMBER OF SHARES ISSUED: 92 222 337

1998

EXECUTIVE DIRECTORS: R Brett Kebble (deputy chairman); John F Brownrigg (managing); Sydney JM Caddy (chief operating officer – offshore); David Chaim Kovarsky (finance); Gordon Miller (chief operating officer – local); Trevor Raymond (investor relations); Craig Vaughn Lawrence (human resources); Derek Webbstock (general manager)

NON-EXECUTIVE DIRECTORS: Wiseman Lumkile Nkuhlu (chairman); Vaughan Grantland Bray; Paul RA Ferguson; Marcel Jonathon Anthony Golding; Roger AR Kebble; Eric Bamoza Molefe; Tiego Moseneke; Lizo Gibson Njenje; Graham P Wanblad; Timothy Charles Aylmer Wadeson (British); Christopher WP Yates

ALTERNATE DIRECTOR: Michael J Tavendale

AUDIT COMMITTEE: Wiseman L Nkuhlu; Paul RA Ferguson; Marcel JA Golding

REMUNERATION COMMITTEE: John F Brownrigg; Craig V Lawrence; Graham P Wanblad

COMPANY SECRETARY: Don W Sievwright

ATTORNEYS: Bowman Gilfillan Hayman Godfrey; Denys Reitz

AUDITORS: Deloitte & Touche

NUMBER OF SHARES ISSUED: 92 222 337

1999

DIRECTORS: Wiseman L Nkuhlu (non-executive chairman); Vaughan G Bray (acting CEO); John F Brownrigg (managing); Paul RA Ferguson; Roger AR Kebble; David C Kovarsky; Eric B Molefe; William A Nairn; Christopher WP Yates

ALTERNATE DIRECTORS: Graham P Shuttleworth; Vincent Patrick Uren

AUDIT COMMITTEE: Wiseman L Nkuhlu; Paul RA Ferguson; Eric B Molefe

REMUNERATION COMMITTEE: Wiseman L Nkuhlu; Paul RA Ferguson; Eric B Molefe

COMPANY SECRETARY: George W Poole

ATTORNEYS: Deneys Reitz

AUDITORS: KPMG

NUMBER OF SHARES ISSUED: 105 376 337

2000

DIRECTORS: R Brett Kebble (CEO); John F Brownrigg (managing); Roger AR Kebble (chairman); Vaughan G Bray; Charles HD Cornwall; Paul RA Ferguson; William A Nairn; L Gibson Njenje; Vincent P Uren

ALTERNATE DIRECTORS: Philip George Marillier; Jacqueline Thomas

AUDIT COMMITTEE: Vaughan G Bray; Paul RA Ferguson; L Gibson Njenje

REMUNERATION COMMITTEE: Roger AR Kebble; Vaughan G Bray; Paul RA Ferguson; L Gibson Njenje

COMPANY SECRETARY: George W Poole

ATTORNEYS: Deneys Reitz

AUDITORS: KPMG

NUMBER OF SHARES ISSUED: 105 376 337

2001

DIRECTORS: R Brett Kebble (CEO); Roger AR Kebble (non-executive chairman); John F Brownrigg (managing); Vaughan G Bray; Charles HD Cornwall; William A Nairn; Sello Mashao Rasethaba; Vincent P Uren

EXECUTIVE COMMITTEE: Roger AR Kebble; R Brett Kebble; John F Brownrigg; Vaughan G Bray; Charles HD Cornwall

ALTERNATE DIRECTOR: Jacqueline Thomas

AUDIT COMMITTEE: Roger AR Kebble; Vaughan G Bray; Charles HD Cornwall

REMUNERATION COMMITTEE: Roger AR Kebble; Vaughan G Bray; Charles HD Cornwall

COMPANY SECRETARY: Patricia B Beale

ATTORNEYS: Deneys Reitz

AUDITORS: KPMG

NUMBER OF SHARES ISSUED: 105 376 337

2002

DIRECTORS: Roger AR Kebble (non-executive chairman); R Brett Kebble (CEO); Mark Angus Barnes; John F Brownrigg (managing – resigned 7 March 2003); John Chris Lamprecht (financial); Vaughan G Bray; Charles HD Cornwall; Alan Alexander McGregor; William A Nairn; Sello M Rasethaba; Vincent P Uren

EXECUTIVE COMMITTEE: Roger AR Kebble; R Brett Kebble; Mark A Barnes; J Chris Lamprecht; Vaughan G Bray; Charles HD Cornwall; Sello M Rasethaba; George W Poole

ALTERNATE DIRECTORS: David Duncan Barber; Jacqueline Thomas; George W Poole

AUDIT COMMITTEE: Roger AR Kebble; Vaughan G Bray; Charles HD Cornwall; Alan A McGregor; Sello M Rasethaba

REMUNERATION COMMITTEE: Vaughan G Bray; Charles HD Cornwall; Alan A McGregor; Sello M Rasethaba

COMPANY SECRETARY: Patricia B Beale

ATTORNEYS: Taback and Associates

AUDITORS: KPMG

NUMBER OF SHARES ISSUED: 105 376 337

2003

DIRECTORS: Mafika Edmund Mkwanazi (non-executive chairman); R Brett Kebble (CEO); J Chris Lamprecht (financial); Gordon T Miller; Mark A Barnes; Vaughan G Bray (independent); Roger AR Kebble; Alan A McGregor (independent); Sello M Rasethaba

ALTERNATE DIRECTOR: George W Poole

AUDIT COMMITTEE: Vaughan G Bray; Roger AR Kebble; Sello M Rasethaba

REMUNERATION COMMITTEE: Alan A McGregor; Vaughan G Bray; Sello M Rasethaba

COMPANY SECRETARY: Patricia B Beale

ATTORNEYS: Taback and Associates

AUDITORS: KPMG

NUMBER OF SHARES ISSUED: 105 376 337

Mining and Industrial Management Investments Corporation Ltd (MIMIC)[4]

1988

DIRECTORS: Joe MR Berardo (chairman); DM Grant-Hodge (deputy chairman); Hendrik C Buitendag; AG Netto; M van der Watt

AUDIT COMMITTEE, REMUNERATION COMMITTEE, ATTORNEYS: Not stated

COMPANY SECRETARY: Investments and Technical Management; LW Helen

AUDITORS: Theron Du Toit

HOLDING COMPANY: Johannesburg Mining and Finance Holdings Ltd

ULTIMATE HOLDING COMPANY: Johannesburg Mining and Finance Corporation

NUMBER OF SHARES ISSUED: 30 000 000

1989

DIRECTORS: Gerald Rubenstein (chairman); Hendrik C Buitendag; Norman Dror Lowenthal; Ronald Yadin Lowenthal (British); Montey Schechter

AUDIT COMMITTEE, REMUNERATION COMMITTEE, ATTORNEYS: Not stated

COMPANY SECRETARY: Investments and Technical Management; LW Helen

AUDITORS: Theron Du Toit

HOLDING COMPANY: Johannesburg Mining and Finance Holdings Ltd

ULTIMATE HOLDING COMPANY: Johannesburg Mining and Finance Corporation

NUMBER OF SHARES ISSUED: 30 000 000

1990

DIRECTORS: Gerald Rubenstein (chairman); GJS Laing (managing); Hendrik C Buitendag; Norman D Lowenthal; Montey Schechter

AUDIT COMMITTEE, REMUNERATION COMMITTEE, ATTORNEYS, ULTIMATE HOLDING COMPANY: Not stated

---

4   Forerunner of CMMS.

COMPANY SECRETARY: Investments and Technical Management; S Baker

AUDITORS: Charles Orbach & Company

HOLDING COMPANY: Consolidated Mining Corporation Ltd

NUMBER OF SHARES ISSUED: 30 000 000

Consolidated Mining Management Services Ltd[5]

1991–1994
DIRECTORS: Gerald Rubenstein (chairman); Hendrik C Buitendag; Norman D Lowenthal; Montey Schechter

AUDIT COMMITTEE, REMUNERATION COMMITTEE, ATTORNEYS, ULTIMATE HOLDING COMPANY: Not stated

COMPANY SECRETARY: Investments and Technical Management

AUDITORS: Charles Orbach & Company

HOLDING COMPANY: Consolidated Mining Corporation Ltd

NUMBER OF SHARES ISSUED: 30 000 000

1995, 1996
DIRECTORS: Norman D Lowenthal (chairman); Montey Schechter; Hendrik C Buitendag; Gerald Rubenstein

AUDIT COMMITTEE, REMUNERATION COMMITTEE, ATTORNEYS, ULTIMATE HOLDING COMPANY: Not stated

COMPANY SECRETARY: Investments and Technical Management; George William Poole

AUDITORS: Charles Orbach & Company

HOLDING COMPANY: Consolidated Mining Corporation Ltd

NUMBER OF SHARES ISSUED: 30 000 000

---

5   Previously known as Mining and Industrial Management Investments Corporation Ltd

1997, 1998
No Annual Reports

1999, 2000
DIRECTORS: Roger AR Kebble; Hendrik C Buitendag; R Brett Kebble; Lieben Hendrik Swanevelder

AUDIT COMMITTEE, REMUNERATION COMMITTEE, ATTORNEYS: Not stated

COMPANY SECRETARY: Consolidated Mining Corporation Ltd; George W Poole

AUDITORS: Charles Orbach & Company

HOLDING COMPANY: Consolidated Mining Corporation Ltd

ULTIMATE HOLDING COMPANY: Consolidated African Mines Ltd

NUMBER OF SHARES ISSUED: 30 000 000

2001, 2002
DIRECTORS: Roger AR Kebble; Hendrik C Buitendag; R Brett Kebble; Lieben H Swanevelder

AUDIT COMMITTEE, REMUNERATION COMMITTEE, ATTORNEYS: Not stated

COMPANY SECRETARY: Consolidated Mining Corporation Ltd; Patricia B Beale

AUDITORS: Charles Orbach & Company

HOLDING COMPANY: Consolidated Mining Corporation Ltd

ULTIMATE HOLDING COMPANY: Consolidated African Mines Ltd

NUMBER OF SHARES ISSUED: 30 000 000

2003
DIRECTORS: Roger AR Kebble; Hendrik C Buitendag; R Brett Kebble; Lieben H Swanevelder

AUDIT COMMITTEE, REMUNERATION COMMITTEE, ATTORNEYS: Not stated

COMPANY SECRETARY: Consolidated Mining Corporation Ltd; Patricia B Beale

AUDITORS: Charles Orbach & Company

HOLDING COMPANY: Consolidated Mining Corporation Ltd

ULTIMATE HOLDING COMPANY: JCI Ltd (formerly Consolidated African Mines Ltd)

NUMBER OF SHARES ISSUED: 30 000 000

2004

DIRECTORS: Hendrik C Buitendag; Roger AR Kebble; R Brett Kebble; J Chris Lamprecht; John Stratton; Lieben H Swanevelder

AUDIT COMMITTEE, REMUNERATION COMMITTEE, ATTORNEYS: Not stated

COMPANY SECRETARY: Patricia B Beale

AUDITORS: Charles Orbach & Company

HOLDING COMPANY: Consolidated Mining Corporation Ltd

ULTIMATE HOLDING COMPANY: JCI Ltd

NUMBER OF SHARES ISSUED: 30 000 000

The 85 companies associated with CMMS[6]

Transvaal Gold Mining Estates (first registered 1895); Pan African Exploration Syndicate (1913); Simmer and Jack Mines (1924); Sabie Mines (1937); Southern Holdings (1948); Stilfontein Gold Mining Company (1949); Sandvelt Investments (1950); Doornrivier Minerals (1950); Newlands Minerals (1958); Jubilee Prospectors (1960); DAB Securities (1965); Permus Investments (1967); Tavlands (1971); Consolidated Mining Corporation (1981); Samada Diamonds (1982); Continental Base Metal Mining (1985); Lindum Reefs Gold Mining Company (1988); Palfinger Southern Africa (1990); Catalyst Props (1992); First Wesgold Mining (1992); Randgold & Exploration Company (1992); Randgold Prospecting and Mineral Holdings (1992); JCI Technology (1995); Channelprops 16 (1996); Matodzi Management Advisory Service (1996); Brakfontein Diamante (1997); Daisy Street Investments No. 27 (1998); Northern Cape Diamond Mining and Exploration (1998); Laritza Investments No. 13 (1998); Ikamva Investment Holdings (1998); Letšeng Investment Holdings South Africa (1998); New Adventure Shelf 114 (1999); Onshelf Property 74 (1999); White Water Diamond Mining (1999); Minrico (1999); South Atlantic Fisheries (2000); Onshelf Investments 101 (2000); Bioprospect Africa (2000); Defacto Investments 33 (2001); JCI Property Development (2001); Phikoloso Mining (2002); Mvelaphanda Security Investments (2002);

---

6   CMMS was used as a device by Brett Kebble to control entities, regardless of his authority regarding shareholdings.

Mvelaphanda Services Investments (2002); Castle Ultra Trading 295 (2002); Versatex Trading 446 (2002); Proximity Properties 334 (2002); Alongshore Resources (2002); Mvelaphanda Infrastructure Development Company (2002); Miri Forestry (2003); Orlyfunt Financial Enterprises (2003); Tsafrika Food Manufacturing (2003); Tlotlisa Financial Services (2003); Nutrx (2003); Luembe Mining (2003); Viking Pony Properties 359 (2003); Matodzi Engineering (2003); Lunda Alluvial Operation (2003); Refraction Investments (2003); Rapivest 18 (2003); Orlyfunt Engineering (2003); Rapitrade 306 (2004); Kirsten-berry Lodge (2004); Ikwezi Empowerment Enterprises (2004); Dabulamanzi Resources (2004); Magnolia Ridge Properties 156 (2004); Koketso Capital (2004); Clifton Dunes Investments 57 (2004); Clifton Dunes Investments 67 (2004); Masupatsela Angola Mining Ventures (2004); Quick Leap Investments 137 (2004); C-Chest Trading (2004); Little Swift Investments 133 (2004); Urantia Capital (2004); Sello Mashao Rasethaba Associates (2004); Thari Ya Basadi (2004); Clifton Dunes Investments 173 (2004); Crowned Cormorant Investments 22 (2004); Tepona Investments (2004); Havtoohav Investments (2004); Pergola Technologies (2004); Orlyfunt Strategic Investments (2004); Telecom Mapungubwe (2004); Mogwele Trading 168 (2004); West Dunes Properties 218 (2004)

Consolidated Mining Corporation Ltd

1999
DIRECTORS: Roger AR Kebble; Hendrik C Buitendag; R Brett Kebble

AUDIT COMMITTEE, REMUNERATION COMMITTEE, ATTORNEYS: Not stated

COMPANY SECRETARY: Consolidated Mining Management Services Ltd

AUDITORS: Charles Orbach & Company

HOLDING COMPANY: Consolidated African Mines Ltd

NUMBER OF SHARES ISSUED: 1 659 066 801 (ordinary); 131 330 800 (preference)

2000–2002
DIRECTORS: Roger AR Kebble; Hendrik C Buitendag; R Brett Kebble; John Stratton

AUDIT COMMITTEE, REMUNERATION COMMITTEE, ATTORNEYS: Not stated

COMPANY SECRETARY: Consolidated Mining Management Services Ltd

AUDITORS: Charles Orbach & Company

HOLDING COMPANY: Consolidated African Mines Ltd

NUMBER OF SHARES ISSUED: 1 659 066 801 (ordinary); 131 330 800 (preference)

2003, 2004

DIRECTORS: Hendrik C Buitendag; Roger AR Kebble; R Brett Kebble; John Stratton

AUDIT COMMITTEE, REMUNERATION COMMITTEE, ATTORNEYS: Not stated

COMPANY SECRETARY: Consolidated Mining Management Services Ltd

AUDITORS: Charles Orbach & Company

HOLDING COMPANY: JCI Ltd

NUMBER OF SHARES ISSUED: 1 659 066 801 (ordinary); 131 330 800 (preference)

Appendix B

Companies of which key players were directors on 10 June 2002

ROGER BRETT KEBBLE

1. Anvil Exports cc
2. Consolidated Mining Management Services
3. Courtyard Restaurants (Pty) Ltd
4. Foston Ltd
5. Fishermans Bend 1883 Property Investment
6. Johannesburg Industrial and Commercial Industries
7. Lelia Property Holdings (Pty) Ltd
8. Lelia Property Holdings cc
9. Multonland Developments (Pty) Ltd
10. Rappfos Holdings (Pty) Ltd
11. Rand Leases Vogelstruisfontein Gold Mining Company Ltd
12. Roodepoort Gold Mine (Pty) Ltd
13. R and B Leasing cc
14. Sink Ton (Pty) Ltd
15. Tavlands (Pty) Ltd
16. Torquay Heights cc
17. The Deadbeat Club cc
18. Wood Properties (Pty) Ltd
19. Wunder Bar cc
20. Yakata cc
21. Western Areas Ltd
22. Consolidated Mining Corporation Ltd
23. Consolidated African Mines Ltd (name changed to JCI Ltd on 9 July)

ROGER AINSLEY RALPH KEBBLE

1. Pan African Exploration Syndicate (Pty) Ltd
2. Consolidated Mining Management Services Ltd
3. Rand Mines Lands Ltd
4. Doornrivier Minerals Ltd
5. The Peoples Club (Pty) Ltd
6. Corgroup Neptune Investments Ltd
7. Rand Leases Vogelstruisfontein Gold Mining Company Ltd
8. Roodepoort Gold Mine (Pty) Ltd
9. Bentonite Nominees Ltd
10. Mariner Drive cc
11. Wood Properties (Pty) Ltd
12. Torquay Heights cc
13. East Champ D'Or Gold Mine Ltd
14. Doornfontein Gold Mining Company
15. Erf 38 Melrose Estate (Pty) Ltd
16. Propwood cc
17. Portion 8 Houghton Links (Pty) Ltd (resigned)
18. West Witwatersrand Gold Holdings Ltd
19. West Witwatersrand Gold Mines Ltd
20. Crown Mines Ltd
21. Transvaal Gold Mining Estates
22. Wood Properties cc
23. Crown Gold Recoveries (Pty) Ltd
24. East Rand Pty Mines Ltd
25. Blyvooruitzicht Gold Mining Company Ltd

ROGER AINSLEY RALPH KEBBLE *(cont.)*

26. Consolidated Mining Corporation Ltd
27. Crown Consolidated Gold Recoveries Ltd
28. Simmer and Jack Mines Ltd
29. Western Areas Ltd
30. Buffelsfontein Gold Mines Ltd
31. Duff Scott Hospital (Pty) Ltd
32. Witwatersrand Refinery (Pty) Ltd
33. BNC Investments (Pty) Ltd
34. Skilled Labour Brokers cc
35. No. 7 Platinum Creswell Park cc
36. Rand Leases Pigments (Pty) Ltd
37. Blockbuster Investments (Pty) Ltd
38. Casa D'Or Homeowners Association
39. First Wesgold Mining (Pty) Ltd
40. Witwatersrand Royalties (Pty) Ltd
41. Argonaut Financial Services (Pty) Ltd
42. Randgold Prospecting and Minerals Ltd
43. Stand 752 Parktown Extension (Pty) Ltd
44. Khumalo Alliance (Pty) Ltd
45. Fences Guards (Pty) Ltd
46. Unisel Gold Mines Ltd
47. Brakfontein Diamante (Pty) Ltd
48. Tradewith 108 (Pty) Ltd
49. Falcons Rugby (Pty) Ltd
50. Erf 14 Dunkeld (Pty) Ltd
51. Erf 159 Illovo (Pty) Ltd
52. Erf 11 Dunkeld (Pty) Ltd
53. JCI Gold Ltd
54. Consolidated Main Reef Mines and Estate Ltd
55. City Deep Ltd
56. Rand Leases Properties Ltd
57. Randgold & Exploration Company
58. Chendini Investments (Pty) Ltd
59. New Mining Corporation Ltd (resigned)
60. Stilfontein Gold Mining Company
61. Luipaardsvlei Estates Ltd
62. Craftwise Investments
63. Portion 1 Erf 291 Saxonwold (Pty) Ltd
64. Catwalk Investments 208 (Pty) Ltd
65. Harmony Gold Mining Company Ltd
66. Minrico Ltd
67. Chien Hua Industry (Pty) Ltd
68. Consolidated African Mines Ltd
69. Durban Roodepoort Deep Ltd
70. Marketpro Properties 31 (Pty) Ltd
71. Mine Waste Solutions (Pty) Ltd
72. Randfontein Estates Ltd
73. Jenfin Investments No. 3 (Pty) Ltd
74. Erf 13 Dunkeld (Pty) Ltd
75. Continental Base Metal Mining
76. Consolidated African Mines Australia (Pty) Ltd
77. Consolidated African Mines Jersey Ltd
78. Consolidated Mining Jersey Ltd
79. DRD Australasia Aps
80. DRD (Isle of Man) Ltd
81. Mining Investments (Jersey) Ltd
82. Morila Ltd
83. Randgold Finance (BVI) Ltd
84. Randgold Resources Ltd
85. Randgold Resources (Holdings) Ltd
86. Randgold Resources (Côte d'Ivoire) Ltd
87. Randgold Resources (Mali) Ltd
88. Randgold Resources Mali Sari
89. Randgold Resources (Somilo) Ltd
90. Randgold Resources (Somisy) Ltd
91. Randgold Resources Tanzania (T) Ltd
92. Société des Mines de Loulo (Somilo SA)
93. Société des Mines de Syama (Somisy SA)
94. Weston Investments (Pty) Ltd
95. Big Sky Investment Holdings (Pty) Ltd
96. Moneyline 420 (Pty) Ltd
97. Capital Participations (Pty) Ltd

HENDRIK CHRISTOFFEL BUITENDAG

1. Aviation Components and Electronics Company
2. Bestmanfin cc
3. Consolidated Mining Management Services
4. Electronic and Transformer Company (Pty) Ltd (disbanded)
5. Finance Week Holdings Ltd
6. Gem Diamond Mining Corporation Ltd
7. Hadup Beleggings (Pty) Ltd (final deregistration)
8. Havelock Barberton Properties
9. Investments and Technical Management Ltd
10. Incorporated Management and Finance Ltd
11. Nugo Mining Corporation Ltd
12. Permus Investments Ltd
13. Policy Investments (Pty) Ltd
14. Samada Diamonds (Pty) Ltd
15. Sandvelt Investments (Pty) Ltd
16. Tavlands (Pty) Ltd
17. West Spaarwater Ltd
18. Watersview Participants (Pty) Ltd (final deregistration)
19. Wadup Beleggings (Pty) Ltd (final deregistration)
20. Wilderness Heights Participants (Pty) Ltd (deregistration in progress)
21. Benoni Gold Mining Company Ltd
22. Consolidated Resources and Exploration Ltd
23. Consolidated Mining Corporation Ltd
24. Duff and Fitzgerald (Pty) Ltd
25. Dalemic Investments cc
26. Energy Resources and Mining Corporation (final deregistration)
27. Galley International Trading cc
28. Gleason Publications (Pty) Ltd
29. HVL Asbestos (Swaziland) Ltd
30. JCI Gold Ltd
31. Lyntex Transport Exchange Ltd
32. Libra Assay Laboratory (Pty) Ltd
33. Minecorp Services
34. New Mining Corporation Ltd
35. Portion 1 Erf 291 Saxonwold (Pty) Ltd
36. Stand 752 Parktown Extension (Pty) Ltd
37. Tempo Engineering Works (Pty) Ltd (deregistration in progress)
38. Tinkerfri Investments (Pty) Ltd
39. West Witwatersrand Mineral and Mining Company (final deregistration)
40. West Witwatersrand Gold Mines Ltd
41. Consolidated African Mines Ltd
42. Randgold & Exploration

Appendix C

JCI Ltd: consolidated income statements

at 31 March (1997: 30 June)	1997 Rm	1998 Rm	1999 Rm	2000 Rm	2001 Rm	2002 Rm	2003 Rm	2004 Rm	Total Rm
1 Revenue					86	96	219	228	630
2 Cost of sales					-79	-42	-118	-133	-372
3 Gross profit					7	54	102	95	258
4 Other operating income					34	3	119	152	308
5 Operating costs					-80	-94	-121	-347	-642
6 Operating profit/loss					-38	-37	100	-101	-76
7 Investment income					21	3	2	6	31
8 Finance costs					-81	-134	-113	-132	-459
Nett profit/loss before exceptional items and taxation					-98	-168	-12	-226	-504
9 Exceptional items					-40	-131	165	0	-6
Nett profit/loss before taxation, minorities and associates	-8	-179	27	-262	-138	-299	153	-226	-932
10 Taxation	0	-0	-3	-2	-12	-0	-0	-13	-31
Nett profit/loss before minorities and associates	-8	-179	24	-264	-150	-299	153	-240	-963
11 Minorities	0	1	-119	-13	-57	25	0	0	-163
12 Nett profit/loss before associates	-8	-179	-95	-277	-206	-274	153	-240	-1,126
Share of earnings/loss of associate companies	0	0	106	10	12	-22	44	184	334
13 Nett profit/loss	-8	-179	11	-267	-195	-296	197	-55	-792
Staff costs, consulting and directors' fees	Na	Na	Na	Na	Na	Na	-60	-116	

Due to rounding, the figures do not necessarily add up.

These income statements are for the 'new' JCI, which started out as NK Properties in 1997, became Consolidated African Mining and finally became the 'new' JCI in 2002. The stock was listed on the JSE for the duration until it was suspended from trading on 1 August 2005.

Table shows the consolidated profits or losses of the JCI group from inception in 1997 to the end of the 2004 financial year. The figures include those of its key underlying subsidiaries, Consolidated Mining Management Services, Consolidated Mining Corporation and JCI Gold. Over the eight years shown, JCI's total losses were R792 million (see item 13).

In March 2006, JCI's new management indicated that certain previously published accounts could be withdrawn. However, this analysis is based on what was published over the years, in other words, the information that investors were expected to rely on, with the indirect blessing of parties such as the JSE.

Appendix D

JCI Ltd: consolidated balance sheets

at 31 March (1997: 30 June)	1997 Rm	1998 Rm	1999 Rm	2000 Rm	2001 Rm	2002 Rm	2003 Rm	2004 Rm
Employment of funds								
1 Investments	0	1 425	1 408	1 458	1 399	2 198	1 882	2 100
2 Listed at market value	0	1 295	1 119	1 102	1 080	1 941	1 552	1 714
3 Western Areas	0	Na	784	868	868	1 539	1 119	1 205
4 Randgold & Exploration	0	Na	Na	77	78	176	368	303
5 Other listed	0	1 295	334	157	133	227	66	206
6 Unlisted at directors' valuation	0	130	289	357	320	257	330	386
7 Letšeng Investment Holdings (40%)	0	0	0	0	0	0	166	191
8 Freddies	0	Na	14	14	19	30	22	28
9 Mvela Properties	0	0	0	0	0	0	0	8
10 Other unlisted	0	130	275	342	300	227	142	158
11 Loans	0	35	86	83	99	305	478	630
12 Associate loans (Western Areas)	0	0	0	0	21	175	192	105
13 Other	0	35	86	83	78	131	287	525
14 Property	118	87	5	6	24	71	77	204
15 Mineral rights	0	67	5	2	2	2	2	123
16 Other assets less creditors	-4	4	190	43	34	-16	-115	108
17 TOTAL (1+10+14+15+16)	114	1 618	1 694	1 592	1 557	2 561	2 325	3 165
Funds employed								
18 Borrowings		466	652	445	662	1 040	843	1 584
19 50% secured debentures							253	384
20 Western Areas				312	352	462		
21 Other		466	652	133	311	578	590	1 200
22 Equity, including minorities	114	1 152	1 042	1 147	895	1 521	1 482	1 581
23 TOTAL (18+22)	114	1 618	1 694	1 592	1 557	2 561	2 325	3 165

Due to rounding, the figures do not necessarily add up.

These balance sheets are for the 'new' JCI, which started out as NK Properties in 1997, became Consolidated African Mining and finally became the 'new' JCI in 2002. The stock was listed on the JSE for the duration until it was suspended from trading on 1 August 2005. The majority of JCI's assets were listed stocks, of which not one provided the company with a 'normalised' income. Western Areas was a nett absorber of cash from 1995; Randgold & Exploration's major investment, Randgold Resources, has not paid a single dividend since inception in 1995.

Appendix E

How off-balance sheet liabilities concealed the gearing of JCI Ltd

at 31 March (1997: 30 June)	1997 Rm	1998 Rm	1999 Rm	2000 Rm	2001 Rm	2002 Rm	2003 Rm	2004 Rm	Source
1 Off-balance sheet liabilities					135	138	163	1 315	
2 Shares borrowed and pledged as security for group loans								476	1
3 Uncovered share loan								15	
4 Randgold & Exploration lends 9 890 500 Randgold Resources shares to Inkwenkwezi to facilitate purchase of 19m Western Areas shares from Anglo American								632	2
5 Western Areas shares (19m)								-618	2
6 Other uncovered share loans								217	
7 Value of shares lent out								439	3
8 Collateral received								-222	3
9 Amounts claimed from the group						32	32	174	4
10 Security for third-party obligations					135	106	131	435	
11 Western Areas loan to DRD					135				
12 Letšeng's IDC loan								160	4
13 Banking facility associate							13	22	5
14 Other third parties						48	48	214	5
15 Loan to associate, subordinated						58	71	39	5
16 Borrowings (from D-18)	0	466	652	445	662	1 040	843	1 584	
17 Total off-balance sheet items and borrowings	0	466	652	445	797	1 178	1 006	2 899	
18 As % of equity	0.0	40.4	62.6	38.7	89.0	77.5	67.9	183.4	
19 Difference (E16 – E17)	0	0	0	0	-135	-138	-163	-1,315	

Due to rounding, the figures do not necessarily add up.

Sources – 1: JCI AR04 note 28.2; 2: Randgold & Exploration Reviewed Preliminary Results year to 31.12.04 note 1; 3: JCI AR04 notes 17 and 28.2; 4: JCI AR04 note 30; 5: JCI AR04 Annexure D

JCI's off-balance sheet activities only commenced in the financial year which ended on 31 March 2001. Table details the kind of liabilities (summarised at items 1 and 19) that JCI kept off its balance sheet. Debt shown on the balance sheet is displayed at item 16, which is referenced from App D-18.

Appendix F

JCI Ltd: history

	1997	1998	1999	2000	2001	2002	2003	2004
JCI shares in issue (m)	17	527	660	665	665	712	1 751	2 090
Shares held								
Western Areas (m)	Nil	Na	43.6	45.5	45.5	45.5	37.3	37.1
Randgold & Resources (m)	Nil	Na	Na	11.8	12.6	12.6	12.6	12.6
Year of acquisition of								
34.9% of Saflife		X						
JCI Gold control (after Saflife unbundling)			X					
JCI Gold minority (32.5%)							X	
40% of Letšeng Investment Holdings							X	
JCI Properties (100%)								X
Barnato Exploration (100%)								X

Table summarises some of the key transactions in JCI's history. JCI's key holding, in Western Areas, dates from transactions in 1997, but only became fully apparent in 1999 accounts. Shares in Randgold & Exploration were also held as early as 1997, when JCI acquired Consolidated Mining Corporation.

Appendix G

JCI group balance sheets, showing consolidation of slush funds as at 31 March 2004

CMC = Consolidated Mining Corporation (100% JCI subsidiary)
CMMS = Consolidated Mining Management Services (98% JCI subsidiary)
JCI Gold is a 100% JCI subsidiary

		CMC	CMMS	CMC con-solidated	JCI	JCI/CMC con-solidated	JCI Gold, other	JCI con-solidated
	EMPLOYMENT OF CAPITAL	Rm	Rm	Rm	Rm	Rm	Rm	Rm
1	Equities	323	178	500	347	847	1 253	2 100
2	Associate companies	200		200	294	495	1 243	1 738
	Listed at market value							
3	Western Areas 35.2%						1 205	1 205
4	Randgold & Exploration 22.9%	200		200	103	303		303
5	Unlisted at directors' value							
6	Letšeng 40%				191	191		191
7	Freddies 44.9%						28	28
8	Mvela Properties 37.5%						8	8
9	Other						2	2
10	Other equities	122	178	300	53	352	10	362
11	Listed at market value	5	42	47		47	38	85
12	Simmer and Jack	3	26	28		28	12	40
13	Stilfontein	2		2		2		2
14	Other		17	17		17	26	42
15	Unlisted at directors' value	117	15	132	53	184	-28	157
16	JCI Gold	61	15	76		76		76
17	Matodzi prefs	56		56		56		56
18	Other			0	53	53	-28	25
19	Shares held for resale	0	121	121		121		121
20	Inter-group	318	468	786	785	1 571	-1 571	
21	CMC/JCI	22		22	-22			
22	CMC/JCI	192		192	-192			
23	CMMS/JCI		468	468	-468			
24	CMC/CMMS shares							
25	CMC/Consolidated Mining Jersey (loan)	118		118		118	-118	
26	JCI/JCI Gold shares				1 634	1 634	-1 634	
27	JCI/JCI Gold loan				-9	-9	9	
28	JCI/Barnato shares				200	200	-200	
29	JCI/CAM Jersey loan				96	96	-96	
30	JCI/Weston loan				-1	-1	1	
31	Provision for losses in subsidiaries	-15		-15	-454	-468	468	

(continued)

(continued)

		CMC	CMMS	CMC con-solidated	JCI	JCI/CMC con-solidated	JCI Gold, other	JCI con-solidated
		Rm	Rm	Rm	Rm	Rm	Rm	Rm
32	Loans		623	623	15	638	-8	630
33	Associate companies						105	105
34	Other		411	411	15	426	-114	312
35	Nett short-term loans		213	213		213		213
36	Property		76	76		76	128	204
37	Fixed asset land buildings		5	5		5	31	36
38	Investment properties at fair value		3	3		3	58	61
39	Development properties		68	68		68	40	108
40	Mineral rights						123	123
41	Other non-current assets		-45	-45		-45	111	66
42	Intellectual property						10	10
43	Goodwill		-56	-56		-56	99	43
44	Other fixed assets		9	9		9	3	13
45	Deferred tax		1	1		1		1
46	Nett current assets		163	163	-80	83	11	94
	Inventories							
47	Crops		11	11		11		11
48	Merchandise						21	21
49	Raw materials & consumables							
50	Trade and other receivables		124	124		124	32	156
51	Taxation in advance							
52	Cash and cash equivalents		107	107		107	21	127
53	Deferred tax		-1	-1		-1		-1
54	Trade and other payables		-76	-76	-80	-156	-31	-186
55	Taxation		-3	-3		-3	-32	-35
56	**Total nett assets**	640	1 463	2 103	1 067	3 170	47	3 217
	CAPITAL EMPLOYED							
57	Interest-bearing borrowings		227	227	384	611	95	707
58	50% secured debentures				384	384		384
59	Collateral on loan of listed securities		222	222		222		222
60	Secured by pledge of shares						50	50
61			222	222	384	606	50	656
62	Bonds		4	4		4	45	49
63	Instalment sales		1	1		1	1	2
64	Short-term borrowings/provisions		1 871	1 871		1 871	-1 000	871
65	Freddies loan to JCI Gold						62	62
66	Randgold & Exploration loan to JCI Gold						17	17
67	Other		1 871	1 871		1 871	-1 078	793

(continued)

(continued)

		CMC	CMMS	CMC con-solidated	JCI	JCI/CMC con-solidated	JCI Gold, other	JCI con-solidated
		Rm	Rm	Rm	Rm	Rm	Rm	Rm
68	Non-interest-bearing borrowings		5	5		5	1	6
69	Borrowings		2 103	2 103	384	2 487	-903	1 584
70	Equity							
71	As published	640	-640		623	623	117	741
72	Associates at valuation				99	99	832	931
73	Loan to share incentive trust				-39	-39		-39
74	Total equity	640	-640		683	683	950	1 633
	Summary							
75	Total nett assets	640	1 463	2 103	1 067	3 170	47	3 217
76	Borrowings		-2 103	-2 103	-384	-2 487	903	-1 584
77	Equity	640	-640		683	683	950	1 633

Due to rounding, the figures do not necessarily add up.

This table is an example of the amount of elbow grease required to extract JCI's see-through accounts. The accounts were reconstructed from the bottom up by consolidating JCI's subsidiaries on the basis of individual accounts.

APPENDIX H

JCI Ltd: share capital evolution

	Issued for	Issue price (cents)	Value (Rm)	JCI (CAM) shares issued/ in issue (m)
1	**30 June 1997**			17
2	Saflife: 25 235 000 ordinaries	600	141	24
3	Saflife: 6 250 000 ordinaries	600	138	23
4	Saflife: 22 150 000 ordinaries	600	487	81
5	JCI: 3 110 750 ordinaries	600	143	24
6	Randgold: 10 000 000 ordinaries	600	39	6
7	Consolidated Mining Corporation Ltd equity	600	1 467	244
8	Witnigel Investments: 10 000 000 CRPs	600	200	33
9	JCI: 1 072 349 ordinaries	135	30	22
10	Cash	306	1	0
11	Cash	215	28	13
12	Cash	136	27	20
13	Cash	145	27	19
14	**31 March 1998**		2 728	527
15	JCI: 400 000 ordinaries	123	11	9
16	Saflife: 10 000 000 ordinaries	150	125	83
17	Simmer and Jack Mines: 9 423 000 ordinaries	120	4	3
18	Cash	70	14	20
19	Cash	75	6	9
20	Cash	120	11	9
21	**31 March 1999**		171	661
22	Western Investments: 5 331 500 ordinaries	130	6	4
23	**31 March 2000**		6	665
24	Cash	45	21	47
25	**31 March 2002**		21	712
26	JCI Gold minorities (32.5%) (also issued 202 300 024 JCI CDs and paid some cash)	45	213	474
27	Letšeng Investment Holdings SA Ltd: 40% (JCI also paid $6.5m to the vendor)	45	99	220
28	Rights offer 24.5/100	45	155	344
29	**31 March 2003**		467	1 751
30	Loan repayment	54	18	33
31	Startrack: 34%	60	79	132
32	100% of Barnato (also issued 105m JCI debentures)	65	68	105
33	Rand Leases Properties minorities	72	50	70
34	**31 March 2004**		215	2 090
35	Cash to fund empowerment	66	8	13
36	**22 October 2004**		8	2 102
37			3 617	

Due to rounding, the figures do not necessarily add up.

Notes

(a) JCI Ltd was formerly Consolidated African Mines Ltd. Name changed on 26 June 2002.

(b) Saflife's main asset, its shareholding in JCI Gold Ltd, was distributed to its shareholders subsequent to CAM's acquisition of the Saflife shares shown above.

(c) The average issue price of the 2.1 billion JCI/CAM shares, issued for a total of R3.7 billion over the period shown is 174 cents per share.

Appendix I

Assets controlled by the JCI, Randgold & Exploration and Matodzi groups, and assets available for pledging by JCI*

	Asset	As at	Note	Shares held	Controlled Valuation Cps	Date	Rm	Available for pledging by JCI Rm
1	JCI (market cap 01.08.05 @ 16 cps: R336.4m)							
2	Western Areas	15-Dec-05	1	60 627 299	4 280	27-Jan-06	2 594.8	2 594.8
3	Randgold & Exploration	31-Mar-04	3	12 635 248	890	27-Jan-06	See below	112.4
4	Letšeng Investment Holdings	30-Sep-05	6	40%	JCI directors	31-Mar-04	See below	191.4
5	Simmer and Jack Mines, through						281.1	
6	Jaganda preference shares	08-Jul-05	2	357 374 000	65	27-Jan-06	232.3	232.3
7	Simmer and Jack ords	08-Jul-05	2	21 675 083	225	27-Jan-06	48.8	48.8
8	Loans to						630.1	
9	Western Areas	31-Mar-04	3	Na	Book	31-Mar-04	105.2	105.2
10	Other parties	31-Mar-04	3	Na	Book	31-Mar-04	524.9	524.9
11	Property	31-Mar-04	3	Na	Directors	31-Mar-04	212.7	212.7
12	Portfolio of listed stock	31-Mar-04	3	Na	Market	31-Mar-04	237.8	237.8
13	Mineral rights	31-Mar-04	3	Na	Directors	31-Mar-04	122.6	122.6
14	Matodzi prefs	30-Sep-05	4	200 000 000	95	27-Jan-06	190.0	190.0
15							4 269.1	
16	Randgold & Exploration (market cap 01.08.05 @ 890 cps: R665.8m)							
17	Randgold Resources	31-Dec-04	5	18 358 000	$18/R6.145	27-Jan-06	2 030.6	
18	JCI ords	31-Dec-04	5	51 560 613	16	01-Aug-05	8.2	
19	SXR Uranium One						572.1	
20	Held through Kabusha	31-Dec-04	5	4 057 403	4 085	27-Jan-06	165.7	
21	Held directly	31-Dec-04	5	9 948 717	4 085	27-Jan-06	406.4	
22	Angolan alluvial diamonds	31-Dec-04	5	Na	Book	31-Dec-04	310.0	
23	Portfolio of listed shares	31-Dec-04	5	Na	Market	27-Jan-06	154.0	
24	Loans	31-Dec-04	5	Na	Book	31-Dec-04	118.0	
25	Mineral sands	31-Dec-04	5	Na	Book	31-Dec-04	39.9	
26	Mineral rights	31-Dec-04	5	Na	Book	31-Dec-04	35.4	
27							3 268.2	
28	Matodzi Resources (market cap 27.01 06 @ 95 cps: R148.9m)							
29	Letšeng Investment Holdings	30-Sep-05	6	Na	JCI directors	31-Mar-04	478.4	
30	Loans	30-Sep-05	6	Na	Book		113.0	
31	JCI ordinaries	30-Sep-05	6	210 255 713	16	01-Aug-05	33.6	
32							625.0	
33	Total						8 162.3	4 572.9

* JCI acquired 23.5m of the Western Areas shares shown in the Western Areas rights offers of April 2004 and December 2005 at a cost of R541.8m (see items L-5 to L-18).

SOURCES FOR NOTES

1 = Western Areas rights offer documents   4 = Matodzi 2005 interims
2 = Simmers rights offer documents   5 = Randgold & Exploration preliminary 2004 results
3 = Western Areas annual report 2004   6 = Matodzi 2006 interims

Table reflects assets **only** of JCI, Randgold & Exploration and Matodzi. In each case, it was assumed that information published by the individual companies was correct. This is the information that investors were expected to rely on and that was implicitly condoned by oversight entities such as the JSE.

Stock prices used are as of 27 January 2006. These three key companies enjoyed control of assets worth R8.2 billion (item 33). However, Brett Kebble irregularly disposed of certain assets, not least the entire remaining holding of Randgold & Exploration in Randgold Resources. This means that, in practice, R2 billion (item 17) in cash (at replacement value on 27 January 2006) is unaccounted for. Other assets were also disposed of in part or in full. It is likely that further investigation will show that Kebble was selling Western Areas shares out of JCI. There are also assets that might never have existed in the first place, such as the portfolio (item 12) apparently bought from Phikoloso for the equivalent of R260 million (see App K-5).

It is important to note that Kebble controlled assets worth an apparent R8.2 billion, yet held only minority stakes in the underlying entities. Thus, while Western Areas had 154 million shares in issue on 31 December 2005 (App L-19), JCI held only 60.6 million (item 2) or 40% of them. Yet Kebble used his shareholding in JCI (App H-7) for years to underpin his position as CEO of Western Areas and JCI. Similarly, he leveraged a JCI stake in Randgold & Exploration (item 3) to effectively control that company, which had 75 million shares in issue by the end of 2004 (App K-19). It is because of this minority or 'negative' control that the value of JCI's stake is shown as zero (item 3). The value of assets that Kebble controlled via Randgold & Exploration is shown at item 27. To attribute values to both entries would amount to double accounting.

This table does not show liabilities, but it has been estimated that those of JCI alone amounted to R1.6 billion on 31 March 2004 (App E-16). If the concealed, off-balance sheet debt of JCI is included, that figure rockets to R2.9 billion (App E-17). Thus, while JCI may have controlled assets worth some R4.3 billion in January 2005, its nett asset value would have been less than half that amount.

The broader body of investors had long been suspicious of the true state of financial affairs at the various companies. The market value of JCI, for example, was just R336 million when the stock was suspended on the JSE on 1 August 2005 (item 1). Randgold & Exploration was valued at R666 million when it was suspended on the same day, notwithstanding its apparent gross asset value of R3.3 billion (item 27).

By that time, Kebble had apparently sold R2 billion worth of stock in Randgold Resources (item 17). As negative as Kebble's control of the companies may have been, he had the power to pledge underlying assets as security for debt. There was an apparent total of some R4.6 billion of such assets available for pledging from JCI alone (item 33). Some of the resulting vastly complex details are set out in App E and App G-20 to G31.

Appendix J

Consolidated Mining Management Services Ltd (CMMS) financials

	Balance sheets 31 March	1999 Rm	2000 Rm	2001 Rm	2002 Rm	2003 Rm	2004 Rm	Change (04 on 99)
1	Plant & equipment	0.5	0.7	1.2	0.7	10.2	9.5	9.0
2	Property			8.3	8.7	14.5	76.1	76.1
3	Investments	22.8	49.1	34.9	98.9	78.0	177.6	154.8
4	Listed					14.4	42.1	42.1
5	Listed for trading	15.8	36.1	29.9	98.9	63.6	120.8	104.9
6	Unlisted	7.0	13.0	5.0			14.8	7.8
7	Loans	311.3	450.1	610.9	644.3	859.5	1 091.8	780.6
8	Holding company	283.9	398.2	503.8	477.4	543.4	468.4	184.5
9	Other	27.3	51.9	107.2	166.9	316.1	623.4	596.1
10	Other nett assets	46.9	-2.2	5.1	-3.2	-7.8	163.9	117.0
11		381.5	497.8	660.4	749.4	954.3	1 519.0	1 137.5
12	Borrowings	525.5	798.5	1 089.2	1 195.2	1 453.8	2 103.0	1 577.6
13	JCI Gold	457.2	798.2	1 065.0	Na	Na	Na	Na
14	Other	68.3	0.2	24.3	Na	Na	Na	Na
15	Equity	-144.0	-300.7	-428.8	-445.8	-499.6	-584.1	-440.1
16	Published	-145.2	-300.7	-429.5	-458.4	-493.2	-639.7	-494.5
17	Goodwill					-21.6	55.6	55.6
18	Revaluation	1.2	0.0	0.7	12.7	15.2		-1.2
19		381.5	497.8	660.4	749.4	954.3	1 519.0	1 137.5
20	Scrip borrowed						422.9	422.9

	Income statements 31 March	1999 Rm	2000 Rm	2001 Rm	2002 Rm	2003 Rm	2004 Rm	Total Rm
21								
22	Gross profit			19.8	21.1	41.3	54.1	
23	Fair value adjustments	11.5	12.0				65.7	
24	Other	0.0	0.0	19.8	21.1	41.3	-11.7	
25	Other operating income					6.9	10.9	
26	Fair value adjustments	-13.3	-57.8				7.0	
27	Profit on disposal of subsidiary					6.0		
28	Other					0.9	3.9	
29	Operating costs			-18.7	-38.8	-68.3	-169.4	
30	Consulting & management fees	-0.5	-2.4	-4.2	-1.5	-6.9	-36.8	
31	Directors' remuneration					-4.3	-4.3	
32	Staff costs					-13.3	-24.8	
33	Goodwill amortisation					-3.8	-19.6	
34	Accounts payable					0.0	-128.8	
35	Other					-40.0	44.9	
36	Investment income						0.7	
37	Finance costs	-20.1	-79.6	-130.0	-11.3	-14.8	-43.8	
38	Taxation						-0.9	
39	Nett loss	-69.9	-155.5	-128.8	-28.9	-34.8	-148.4	-566.4

CMMS, Brett Kebble's main underlying slush fund, recorded negative equity of R584 million on 31 March 2004 (item 15). After acquisition by Kebble in 1999, borrowings in the name of CMMS increased by R1.6 billion (item 12). CMMS posted total losses of R567 million in the six years from 1999 to 2004 (item 39).

Appendix K

Randgold & Exploration Company Ltd: share capital evolution

		Seller/reason for issue	Asset acquired	Shares issued		
	Issued shares			No. (m)	Cps	Value (Rm)
1	31-Dec-01	Shares in issue		41.7		
2		Options exercised	Cash	2.0	1072	21.4
3	31-Dec-02	Shares in issue		43.7		
4		Options exercised	Cash	1.3	1334	16.7
5	01-Aug-03	Phikoloso Mining (Pty) Ltd	Total issued shares of and all the shareholders' loan accounts against Viking Pony Properties 359 (Pty) Ltd, owner of 235 000 Amplats, 315 000 Harmonies and 75% of Kabusha Mining and Finance (Pty) Ltd (holder of 22 500 000 shares in Aflease)	8.8	2950	259.6
6	22-Dec-03	Freddies shareholders	55.1% of Free State Development and Investment Corporation Limited (12.5/100)	1.5	2938	45.0
7				11.6	2774	321.3
8	31-Dec-03	Shares in issue		55.3		
9	30-Mar-04	Lunda Sul Holdings (Pty) Ltd	100% of Lunda Alluvial Operations (Pty) Ltd	2.3		
10	23-Jun-04	Koketso Angola Joint Venture	24% interest in Luxinge alluvial diamond mining licence	1.3		
11	23-Jun-04	Masupatsela Angola Mining Ventures (Pty) Ltd	20% interest in Dando Kwanza alluvial diamond prospecting concession	1.5		
12	23-Jun-04	Quantum African Mining (Pty) Ltd	20% interest in Somba Sul alluvial diamond prospecting concession	1.4		
13	23-Jun-04	Trans Benguela Logistics (Pty) Ltd	Mining equipment and assets	1.5		
14				8.0		
15		Unknown (options?)		0.0		
16	09-Sep-04	The Afrikander Lease	94 000 000 Aflease shares	9.4		
17	26-Oct-04	Pan Palladium Ltd	13 000 000 Pan Palladium shares	2.2		
18				19.5	1608	314.1
19	31-Dec-04	Shares in issue		74.8		
20		Funds raised since 1 January 2002 by the issue of new shares				656.8

Cost of Angolan diamond interests, assuming issue price of 1608 cents: 7 958 000 x R16.08 = R127 965 000

Brett Kebble issued millions of shares out of Randgold & Exploration after taking over as CEO in 2003. Barring Aflease (item 16) and Pan Palladium (item 17), most of these deals are likely to have come to naught. The Phikoloso deal, however, is an example of a deal that raises questions that go beyond business competence. According to an affidavit filed in

November 2005 by Peter Gray, the new CEO of JCI and Randgold & Exploration, Viking Pony simply never owned the shares that were claimed in the transaction. It is likely that similar problems pertained to a number of other deals, such as Startrack (App H-31).

Appendix L

Western Areas Ltd: share capital evolution

	Issued to	Issued for/to	Issue price (cents)	Value (Rm)	No. of shares (m)	JCI's interest (m)	JCI's interest
1	31-Dec-99				105.4	45.5	43.13%
2	17-Oct-02	Non-JCI shareholders re distribution of JCI Gold loan from Western Areas				-7.4	
3		Sold by JCI				-0.8	
4	31-Dec-02				105.4	37.3	35.38%
5	27-Jul-04	Rights offer 12.5/100	3 050	401.7	13.2		
6		JCI as shareholder	3 050	143.0	4.7		
7		JCI as underwriter	3 050	145.0	4.8		
8				288.0	9.4	9.4	
9		Randgold & Exploration	3 050	15.4	0.5		
10		Allan Gray	3 050	96.8	3.2		
11		Other	3 050	1.5	0.0		
12	31-Dec-04				118.5	46.7	39.42%
13	15-Dec-05	Rights offer 29.95 / 100		639.1	35.5		
14		JCI as shareholder	1 800	250.8	13.9		
15		JCI as underwriter	1 800	2.9	0.2		
16				253.8	14.1	14.1	
17		Allan Gray	1 800	153.3	8.5		
18		Other	1 800	232.0	12.9		
19	31-Dec-05				154.1	60.8	39.48%

Western Areas, a South African–listed company, holds as its principal asset 50 per cent in the South Deep Joint Venture – the South Deep mine – with Canada's Placer Dome, wrecently acquired by Barrick Gold Corporation. Western Areas is the beneficiary of just under 51 per cent of the gold production for the life of South Deep, plus an additional 1.75 per cent of Placer Dome's attributable gold production, should annual production at South Deep exceed one million ounces.

South Deep is located near Johannesburg, close to the Kloof gold mine owned by Gold Fields. The joint venture covers the old Western Areas mine (south shaft) and the new South Deep twin-shaft complex. By the end of the first quarter in 2006, development of the twin-shaft complex had been in progress for ten years at an attributable cost of R4 billion ($580 million) and was still incomplete.

Appendix M

Randgold Resources Ltd: share capital evolution

Note		Date	Brief description	New shares issued (m)	Total shares (m)	Price per share ($)	Cash flow ($m)	Cumulative cash flow ($m)
1	a	August 1995	Establishment	8.00	8.00	0.63	5.00	
2	b	February 1996	Private placing	0.95	8.95	9.63	9.10	14.10
3	b(i)		*Randgold & Exploration convertible bonds*				*48.00*	
4	c	October 1996	Internal issue	3.21	12.16	25.50	0.00	14.10
5	d	July 1997	London listing	5.00	17.16	15.50	77.50	91.60
6	e		To BHP				-32.20	59.40
7	f		To Randgold & Exploration	1.09		16.50	18.00	77.40
8	g	November 1998	To Randgold & Exploration	13.25	31.50	2.50	33.20	110.60
9	h	November 1998	To IFC	1.16				
10	i	July 2000	Morila deal				132.00	242.60
11	j		Repay Barnex				-51.80	190.80
12	k	October 2001	Stock buy-back	-11.60		7.00	-81.20	109.60
13	k(i)	See note						
14	l	July 2002	US IPO	5.00	26.06	6.50	32.50	142.10
15	m	Sundry		1.54	27.60		?	
16	n	June 2004	Stock split		58.55		0.00	
17	n(i)	Sundry		0.68			?	
18	o	December 2004			59.23			
19	o(i)	Sundry		0.72			?	
20	p	November 2005	Capital issue	7.00	66.95	13.50	94.50	236.60

Randgold Resources is listed in London and on the Nasdaq in the US.
The following notes, except *m*, *n*(i) and *o*(i), are summaries of filings made by Randgold Resources with the Securities Exchange Commission in Washington.

a. Randgold & Exploration (R&E) transferred its interests in mineral activities outside of the Randblock to Randgold Resources Ltd (RR) in August 1995 for $5 million by means of eight million shares issued to R&E.

b. In February 1996, RR raised approximately $9.1 million through the issue of 945 000 shares in a private placement to fund continued exploration activities.

b(i). Non-RR. $48 million convertible bond issued in 1996 by R&E subsidiary Randgold Finance (BVI) Ltd (RF BVI).

c. In October 1996, R&E, through an intermediate holding company, Randgold Resources (Holdings) Ltd (RRH), acquired from BHP the entire issued share capital of BHP

Minerals Mali (later renamed Randgold Resources Mali Inc., or RRMI) and the benefit of $78 million in shareholder loans. RR then acquired the investment in RRMI in exchange for the issuance of 3 212 812 new shares at $25.50 each.

d. In July 1997, RR listed on the London Stock Exchange and completed its initial public offering of five million ordinary shares, resulting in nett proceeds of $77.5 million.

e. The London issue proceeds were part-used to retire the retained loan from BHP of approximately $32.2 million.

f. At the same time, RR converted an $18 million loan owed to a subsidiary of R&E into 1.09 million ordinary shares.

g. RR completed an offering of 13.2 million ordinary shares, resulting in proceeds of $13.2 million before expenses and conversion of R&E's $20 million shareholder loan into shares.

h. RR acquired a further 10% interest in Somisy (Mali) and related shareholder loans through the issue of 1.1 million ordinary shares to the International Finance Corporation.

i. In July 2000, RR sold half its stake in the Morila joint venture (40%) to AngloGold for $132 million in cash.

j. In the year to 31 December 2000, RR repaid $51.8 million cash to settle a short-term $50 million bridging finance loan in the previous financial year from Barnex.

k. In a mandatory share repurchase programme, RR bought 11.6 million ordinary shares from its shareholders at $7.00 each. RR bought 6.8 million ordinary shares from R&E for $48.1 million.

k(i). In September 2001, R&E used proceeds from RR share repurchase to redeem the $48 million convertible bond issued in 1996 by R&E subsidiary, RF (BVI).

l. RR completed an IPO of five million ordinary shares, including American Depository Shares, resulting in gross proceeds of $32.5 million.

m. Reconciliation item: after the IPO, RR stated: 'After this offer, there were outstanding 27 599 796 ordinary shares.'

n. Effective 11 June 2004, RR split its ordinary shares, increasing issued share capital from 29 273 685 to 58 547 370 ordinary shares.

n(i). Reconciliation item.

o. As of 31 December 2004, RR had outstanding 59 226 694 ordinary shares, par value $0.05 each.

o(i). Reconciliation item.

p. Capital issue of seven million new RR shares.

Randgold Resources also filed the following with the SEC:

1996 BONDS

Under the terms of the bonds issued by Randgold Finance (BVI) Ltd, a wholly owned subsidiary of Randgold & Exploration in 1996, and which were guaranteed by and convertible into shares of R&E, Randgold Resources became a party to a trust deed dated 3 October 1996 between Randgold Finance (BVI), R&E, Randgold Resources and Marine Midland

Bank as trustee. Randgold Resources Holdings also guaranteed the bonds. In September 2001, R&E repaid these bonds in full, principally with proceeds from Randgold Resources mandatory share repurchase.

LOAN FROM RANDGOLD & EXPLORATION
On 25 November 1999, Randgold Resources entered into a loan agreement with Randgold & Exploration consolidating prior amounts advanced to RR by R&E and providing for additional funding. This loan accrued interest at the prime rate as charged by Standard Bank of SA Ltd to R&E plus 1%. The largest amount outstanding under this loan since 1 January 1999 was $6.6 million. The loan was fully repaid in that amount from the proceeds of the Morila loan and RR's sale of 50% of its Morila joint venture to AngloGold.

BARNATO EXPLORATION LTD
During the nine months ending 31 December 1999, Randgold Resources obtained a short-term loan of $50 million from SA-listed company Barnex. The loan, which was Rand denominated, bore interest at the SA Reserve Bank's prime rate plus 1% and was convertible into equity of Morila at 31 March 2000 if not repaid. Subsequent to 31 December 1999, the conversion date was extended to 15 August 2000 for an additional $3 million and a daily fee of $32 787 for every day that the loan was outstanding beyond 1 July 2000. The total loan and fees were fully paid by 3 July 2000.

Appendix N

Simplifying Simane

		Harmony shares	Per share (Rand)	Cash flow (Rm)
	On 20 June 2001			
1	IDC buys	10 736 682	36.00	-387
2	IDC buys options	10 958 904	0.50	-5
	On 25 September 2001			
3	Simane buys	222 300	36.00	-8
4	**Simane debt to IDC** (excludes interest)			**-400**
	January, February 2002 **IDC exercises options**			
5	Buys Harmony shares	10 958 904	41.50	-455
6	Sells Harmony shares	10 958 904	94.36	1034
7	Nett proceeds			579
8	IDC kills Simane debt			-400
9	Profit to IDC			179
10	Transfer to Simane	10 736 682	*Gratis*	*Gratis*

Knocking out the Simane minorities at huge discounts

		Simane shares (number)	Sold for: (Rm)	Peak value (Rm)	Variance (Rm)	Variance (%)
11	Vaya Investments	20	2	134	-132	-99%
12	Khoetsa Holdings	30	8	200	-192	-96%
13	Mageba Mining	30	10	200	-190	-95%
14	Sifikile	20	62	134	-72	-54%
15		100	82	668	-586	-88%

Simane's debt-free value

	Value of Simane (2002) on:	(Rm)	Per Simane share (Rm)	
16	28 February	1 284	4.28	
17	28 March	1 368	4.56	
18	30 April	1 469	4.90	
19	**24 May**	**2 003**	6.68	

Table shows how the Industrial Development Corporation financed the Simane deal. When the Harmony options were exercised (items 5 and 6), the IDC itself made a substantial profit (item 9) after handing 10.7 million debt-free Harmony shares to Simane. The other items illustrate the 'cost' of acquiring the Simane minorities and the value of Simane at the peak of the Harmony stock price on 24 May 2002.

Appendix O

Simmer and Jack Mines Ltd: share capital evolution (I)

	05/03/31 (m)	JCI group sells shares/ Top-Gold & Newfound buy (m)	Convert JCI loan of R89.3m into 357.4m Jaganda prefs	Simmers repays balance of loan	Then	Issue further new shares ito 516.2m rights issue @ 25 cps	Adjust for p 44 of 2005 Simmers AR	Then Number (m)	Then %
1 Consolidated Mining Management Services Ltd	85.1	-85.1				17.1		17.1	2.3
2 Consolidated Mining Corporation Ltd	9.4	-9.4				4.6		4.6	0.6
3 Continental Goldfields (Pty) Ltd (Australia)	40.0	-40.0							
4 Randgold & Exploration Company Ltd	40.0	-40.0							
5 JCI subsidiaries and associates	174.5	-174.5				21.7		21.7	2.9
6 Jaganda (Pty) Ltd						378.6		378.6	51.1
7 Shares effectively obtained by converting JCI loan						357.4		357.4	48.2
8 Shares effectively bought with R5m from management						20.0		20.0	2.7
9 Shares bought with R308 364 from Roger Kebble						1.2		1.2	0.2
10 Top-Gold AG mvk/ SIS Sergainseattle		100.0			100.0	116.0	15.8	231.8	31.3
11 Newfound Capital		74.5			74.5		-37.0	37.5	5.1
12 Simmers Share Trust	21.5				21.5			21.5	2.9
13 RAR Kebble (21.25 cps)	4.0				4.0			4.0	0.5
14 GT Miller (25 cps)	3.5				3.5			3.5	0.5
15 J de V Berry (25 cps)	3.5				3.5			3.5	0.5
16 GP Wanblad (25 cps)	3.5				3.5			3.5	0.5
17 JP Schumacher (25 cps)	1.0				1.0			1.0	0.1
18 Other	6.0				6.0			6.0	0.8
19 Minorities, Orlyfunt, balancing	28.9				28.9		21.2	50.1	6.8
20 Orlyfunt	11.3				11.3		0.0	11.3	1.5
21 Other	17.6				17.6		21.2	38.7	5.2
22	224.9				224.9	516.2	0.0	741.2	100.0
23 JCI loan to Simmers	R 69.7m	R 25.0m	-R 89.3m	-R 5.4m					
24 JCI cash from the deals		R 18.5m			R 5.4m	R 23.9m	-R 5.4m	R 18.4m	
25 JCI holding of Jaganda prefs(m)			357.4		357.4			357.4	
26 Management's Jaganda prefs(m)						20		20	

338

In normal circumstances, a rights issue is a simple thing. A listed company such as Simmer & Jack issues new shares to investors, providing there is a demand; the issuer banks the cash after paying hefty fees to investment bankers and stockbrokers.

The Simmers rights issue depicted here was anything but simple. First, JCI and its subsidiaries, including some of Brett Kebble's key slush funds, sold old Simmers shares into the rights issue (items 1 to 5). In the end, JCI banked cash of R18 million from the rights issue (items 24 and App P-22).

While a rights issue is normally for hard cash, it can also include an issue of shares to a creditor. In this case, Simmers owed money to JCI and its subsidiaries and thus issued fresh shares and converted loans from those parties (item 23). These 357 million new shares were then placed into Jaganda, which in turn issued 357 million preference shares to JCI and its subsidiaries. The latter thus effectively swapped a loan owed by Simmers for preference shares in Jaganda, which in turn had a sizeable stake in Simmers.

While Simmers CEO Gordon Miller vehemently denied that Kebble had anything to do with the creation of Jaganda, preference share structures were one of his favourite financial tools. Kebble secretly controlled Matodzi through preference shares (item I-14). During 2005, following a change in accounting rules, Matodzi decided that the relevant so-called Matodzi prefs and Witnigel prefs 'should have been disclosed in the financial statements as debt and not as part of shareholders' equity'.

Simmers was no Matodzi, however. The Jaganda prefs were structured with very different objectives in mind. Analysis of Jaganda's see-through economic substance shows that JCI undermined the rights of its own shareholders. Jaganda was nothing more than a disguised stock options scheme (App Q). The beneficiaries, however, were individuals who had very little to do with JCI.

Simmers management holding 49% of Jaganda were named as Roger Kebble (who stepped down in December 2005), Gordon Miller, John Berry and Graham Wanblad, each holding 9.8%. The unnamed, apparently carefully hidden, remaining 9.8% 'management' shareholder was none other than Ronnie Watson, who, like most of the Jaganda BEE individuals, hailed originally from the Eastern Cape, which is not much of a mining province. The 51% BEE entities in Jaganda were variously described as Richtrau No. 47 and/or Vulisango and/or Msobomvu Mining.

APPENDIX P

Simmer and Jack Mines Ltd: share capital evolution (II)

		Placement 13 October 2005 @ 59 cps	Placement 27 October 2005 @ 64.5 cps	31-Dec-05	
				Number (m)	%
1	Consolidated Mining Management Services Ltd			17.1	2.0
2	Consolidated Mining Corporation Ltd			4.6	0.5
3	JCI subsidiaries and associates			21.7	2.6
4	Jaganda (Pty) Ltd			378.6	44.6
5	Shares effectively obtained by converting JCI loan			357.4	42.1
6	Shares effectively bought with R5m from management			20.0	2.4
7	Shares bought with R308 364 from Roger Kebble			1.2	0.1
8	Top-Gold AG mvk/SIS Sergainseattle			231.8	27.3
9	Newfound Capital			37.5	4.4
10	Simmers Share Trust			21.5	2.5
11	RAR Kebble (21.25 cps)			4.0	0.5
12	GT Miller (25 cps)			3.5	0.4
13	J de V Berry (25 cps)			3.5	0.4
14	GP Wanblad (25 cps)			3.5	0.4
15	JP Schumacher (25 cps)			1.0	0.1
16	Other			6.0	0.7
17	Minorities, Orlyfunt, balancing	37.0	71.0	158.0	18.6
18	Orlyfunt			11.3	1.3
19	Other	37.0	71.0	146.7	17.3
20		37.0	71.0	849.1	100.0
21	JCI loan to Simmers			0	
22	JCI cash from the deals			R18.4m	
23	JCI holding of Jaganda prefs (m)			357.37	
24	Management holding of Jaganda prefs (m)			20	

Appendix Q

Value of Jaganda ordinary shares*

	Cents per Jaganda pref (377 374 000 in issue)				Value of 378.6m Simmers (Jaganda's total holding) (Rm)	Amount payable on redemption of 377.4m Jaganda prefs (Rm)	Amount borrowed to buy an additional 1.2m Simmers (Rm)	Value of Jaganda ordinary shares (Rm)
----	Simmers stock price (cps)	Basic (cps)	20% of 25 cents per Simmers (cps)	Redemption price (cps)	----	----	----	----
1	25	25	0	25	94.65	94.34	0.31	0.00
2	50	25	5	30	189.30	113.21	0.31	75.78
3	75	25	10	35	283.96	132.08	0.31	151.57
4	100	25	15	40	378.61	150.95	0.31	227.35
5	125	25	20	45	473.26	169.82	0.31	303.13
6	150	25	25	50	567.91	188.69	0.31	378.92
7	175	25	30	55	662.56	207.56	0.31	454.70
8	200	25	35	60	757.21	226.42	0.31	530.48
9	225	25	40	65	851.87	245.29	0.31	606.27
10	250	25	45	70	946.52	264.16	0.31	682.05
11	275	25	50	75	1 041.17	283.03	0.31	757.83
12	300	25	55	80	1 135.82	301.90	0.31	833.61
13	325	25	60	85	1 230.47	320.77	0.31	909.40
14	350	25	65	90	1 325.13	339.64	0.31	985.18
15	375	25	70	95	1 419.78	358.51	0.31	1 060.96
16	400	25	75	100	1 514.43	377.37	0.31	1 136.75
17	425	25	80	105	1 609.08	396.24	0.31	1 212.53
18	450	25	85	110	1 703.73	415.11	0.31	1 288.31
19	475	25	90	115	1 798.39	433.98	0.31	1 364.10
20	500	25	95	120	1 893.04	452.85	0.31	1 439.88

The redemption price of Jaganda's preference shares is the aggregate of 25 cents per Simmers share, plus 20% of the 30-day weighted average traded JSE price as at the date of redemption, in excess of 25 cps. Thus R245 million would go to JCI (item 9) for preference shares redeemed when Simmers was trading at 225 cps. The R606 million balance available (item 9) would go to ordinary shareholders in Jaganda, who paid a total of R26.26 for all the shares issued. A relatively small number of Jaganda preference shares were owned directly by management (item O-26).

---

* Note: no provision has been made for Capital Gains Tax

Appendix R

Glossary of names from forensics

On 7 April 2006, JCI published a glossary of entities that appeared in reports prepared by KPMG Forensic after a six-month investigation commissioned by JCI. These are the names, long and short, that played various parts during the late Brett Kebble's business career. Names in italics are those published in a similar glossary on 31 March 2006 by Randgold & Exploration. The forensics there were undertaken by Umbono Financial Advisory Services.

Aconcaqua: Aconcaqua 24 Share Block Company

Aculsha: Aculsha Nominees Limited

Aflease: The Afrikander Lease Limited

Alibiprops: Alibiprops (Proprietary) Limited

Anglo: Anglo South Africa Capital (Proprietary) Limited (a subsidiary of Anglo American Corporation Limited)

Amplats: Anglo American Platinum Corporation Limited

AngloGold: AngloGold Limited

Baobab Aviation: Baobab Aviation (Proprietary) Limited

Bioprospect: Bioprospect Africa (Proprietary) Limited

BNC: BNC Investments (Proprietary) Limited

Bookmark: Bookmark Holdings (Proprietary) Limited

Boschendal: Boschendal wine estate

Cape Verde: Cape Verde (Proprietary) Limited

Catalyst: Catalyst Props (Proprietary) Limited

Citation: Citation SA

Clifton Dunes: Clifton Dunes 67 (Proprietary) Limited

CMMS or the Group Treasury: Consolidated Mining Management Services Limited (a subsidiary of the JCI Group)

Continental: Continental Goldfields NL [Australian]

DRDGold: DRDGold Limited (formerly Durban Roodepoort Deep Limited)

Freddev: Free State Development and Investment Corporation Limited

Harmony: Harmony Gold Mining Company Limited

Highland Night: Highland Night 157 (Proprietary) Limited

IDC: Industrial Development Corporation of South Africa Limited

Investage: Investage 170 (Proprietary) Limited

Investec: Investec Bank Limited

Inkwenkwezi: Inkwenkwezi Gold Consortium (Proprietary) Limited

Jaganda: Jaganda (Proprietary) Limited

JCI Debentures: Convertible Redeemable 50% Secured Debentures of R1.25 each

JCI or the Company: JCI Limited

JCIIF: JCI Investment Finance (Proprietary) Limited (a wholly owned subsidiary of JCI)

JCI Gold: JCI Gold Limited (a wholly owned subsidiary of JCI)

JCI Group: JCI Limited (JCI Group and its subsidiaries)

JCI Technology: JCI Technology (Proprietary) Limited

Kelgran: Kelgran Limited

Kirstenberry Lodge: Kirstenberry Lodge (Proprietary) Limited

KPMG Forensic: KPMG Services (Proprietary) Limited

Laverton: Laverton Gold NL [Australian]

Letšeng Diamonds: Letšeng Diamonds Limited

Letšeng: Letšeng Investments (South Africa) Proprietary Limited

Masupatsela: Masupatsela Investment Holdings Limited

Matodzi: Matodzi Resources Limited

Moregate: Moregate Investments (Proprietary) Limited

Mvela Props: Mvelaphanda Infrastructure Development Company (Proprietary) Limited

Onshelf 74: Onshelf Property Seventy Four (Proprietary) Limited

Onshelf 101: Onshelf Investments One Hundred and One (Proprietary) Limited

Orlyfunt: Orlyfunt Holdings (Proprietary) Limited

Paradigm Shift: Paradigm Shift cc

Paradise Creek: Paradise Creek Investments 83 (Proprietary)

Phikoloso: Phikoloso Mining (Pty) Limited

Pilgrims Rest: Pilgrims Rest Estates Limited

Randgold: Randgold & Exploration Company Limited Group

Rapivest: Rapivest 18 (Proprietary) Limited

RRL: Randgold Resources Limited

Safco: South African Fisheries (Proprietary) Limited

Simmers: Simmer and Jack Mines Limited

Skygistics: Skygistics (Proprietary) Limited

Slipknot: Slipknot Investments 203 (Proprietary) Limited

SocGen: Société Générale

Topgold: Topgold AG mvk

Tuscan Mood: Tuscan Mood 1224 (Proprietary) Limited

Viking Pony/Kabusha: Viking Pony Properties 359 (Pty) Limited/Kabusha Mining and Finance (Pty) Limited

Witnigel: Witnigel Investments (Proprietary) Limited

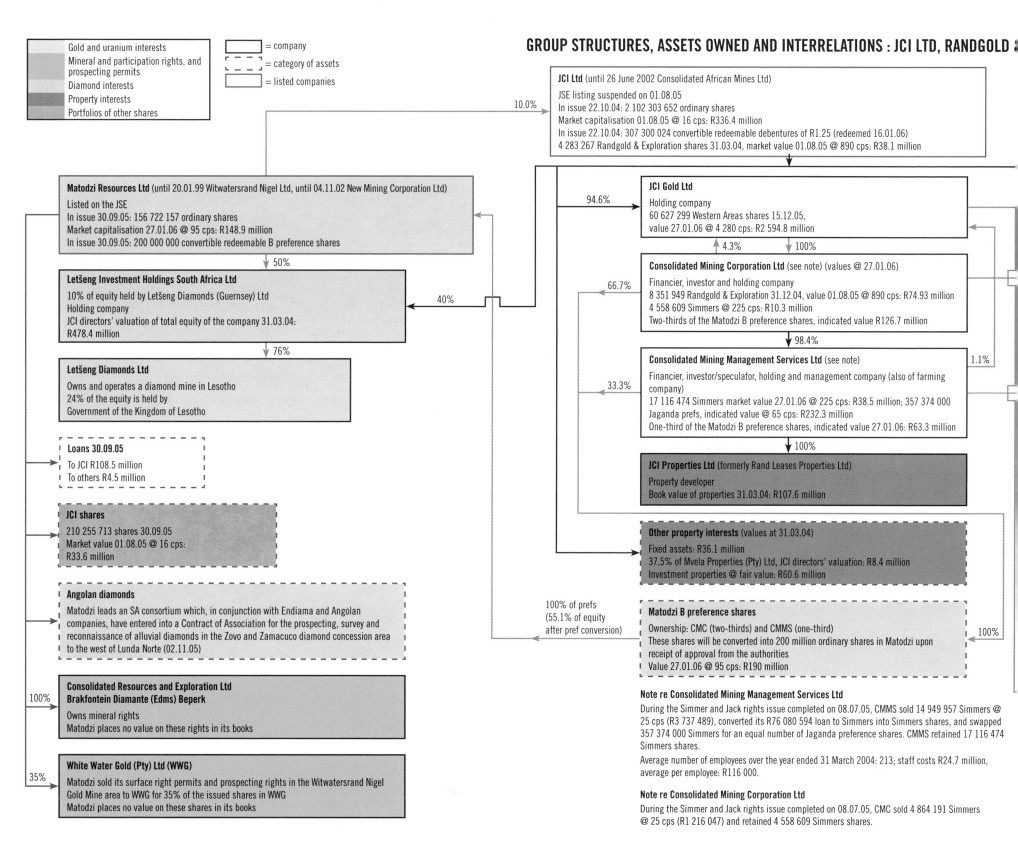

GROUP STRUCTURES, ASSETS OWNED AND INTERRELATIONS : JCI LTD, RANDGOLD

Legend:
- Gold and uranium interests
- Mineral and participation rights, and prospecting permits
- Diamond interests
- Property interests
- Portfolios of other shares

- ▢ = company
- ⊡ (dashed) = category of assets
- ▢ = listed companies

JCI Ltd (until 26 June 2002 Consolidated African Mines Ltd)
JSE listing suspended on 01.08.05
In issue 22.10.04: 2 102 303 652 ordinary shares
Market capitalisation 01.08.05 @ 16 cps: R336.4 million
In issue 22.10.04: 307 300 024 convertible redeemable debentures of R1.25 (redeemed 16.01.06)
4 283 267 Randgold & Exploration shares 31.03.04, market value 01.08.05 @ 890 cps: R38.1 million

10.0%

Matodzi Resources Ltd (until 20.01.99 Witwatersrand Nigel Ltd, until 04.11.02 New Mining Corporation Ltd)
Listed on the JSE
In issue 30.09.05: 156 722 157 ordinary shares
Market capitalisation 27.01.06 @ 95 cps: R148.9 million
In issue 30.09.05: 200 000 000 convertible redeemable B preference shares

94.6%

JCI Gold Ltd
Holding company
60 627 299 Western Areas shares 15.12.05,
value 27.01.06 @ 4 280 cps: R2 594.8 million

50%

40%

4.3%   100%

Consolidated Mining Corporation Ltd (see note) (values @ 27.01.06)
Financier, investor and holding company
8 351 949 Randgold & Exploration 31.12.04, value 01.08.05 @ 890 cps: R74.93 million
4 558 609 Simmers @ 225 cps: R10.3 million
Two-thirds of the Matodzi B preference shares, indicated value R126.7 million

66.7%

Letšeng Investment Holdings South Africa Ltd
10% of equity held by Letšeng Diamonds (Guernsey) Ltd
Holding company
JCI directors' valuation of total equity of the company 31.03.04:
R478.4 million

76%

Letšeng Diamonds Ltd
Owns and operates a diamond mine in Lesotho
24% of the equity is held by
Government of the Kingdom of Lesotho

98.4%

1.1%

Consolidated Mining Management Services Ltd (see note)
Financier, investor/speculator, holding and management company (also of farming company)
17 116 474 Simmers market value 27.01.06 @ 225 cps: R38.5 million; 357 374 000 Jaganda prefs, indicated value @ 65 cps: R232.3 million
One-third of the Matodzi B preference shares, indicated value 27.01.06: R63.3 million

33.3%

100%

Loans 30.09.05
To JCI R108.5 million
To others R4.5 million

JCI Properties Ltd (formerly Rand Leases Properties Ltd)
Property developer
Book value of properties 31.03.04: R107.6 million

JCI shares
210 255 713 shares 30.09.05
Market value 01.08.05 @ 16 cps:
R33.6 million

Other property interests (values at 31.03.04)
Fixed assets: R36.1 million
37.5% of Mvela Properties (Pty) Ltd, JCI directors' valuation: R8.4 million
Investment properties @ fair value: R60.6 million

Angolan diamonds
Matodzi leads an SA consortium which, in conjunction with Endiama and Angolan companies, have entered into a Contract of Association for the prospecting, survey and reconnaissance of alluvial diamonds in the Zovo and Zamacuco diamond concession area to the west of Lunda Norte (02.11.05)

100% of prefs
(55.1% of equity
after pref conversion)

100%

Matodzi B preference shares
Ownership: CMC (two-thirds) and CMMS (one-third)
These shares will be converted into 200 million ordinary shares in Matodzi upon receipt of approval from the authorities
Value 27.01.06 @ 95 cps: R190 million

100%

Consolidated Resources and Exploration Ltd
Brakfontein Diamante (Edms) Beperk
Owns mineral rights
Matodzi places no value on these rights in its books

35%

White Water Gold (Pty) Ltd (WWG)
Matodzi sold its surface right permits and prospecting rights in the Witwatersrand Nigel Gold Mine area to WWG for 35% of the issued shares in WWG
Matodzi places no value on these shares in its books

Note re Consolidated Mining Management Services Ltd
During the Simmer and Jack rights issue completed on 08.07.05, CMMS sold 14 949 957 Simmers @ 25 cps (R3 737 489), converted its R76 080 594 loan to Simmers into Simmers shares, and swapped 357 374 000 Simmers for an equal number of Jaganda preference shares. CMMS retained 17 116 474 Simmers shares.
Average number of employees over the year ended 31 March 2004: 213; staff costs R24.7 million, average per employee: R116 000.

Note re Consolidated Mining Corporation Ltd
During the Simmer and Jack rights issue completed on 08.07.05, CMC sold 4 864 191 Simmers @ 25 cps (R1 216 047) and retained 4 558 609 Simmers shares.

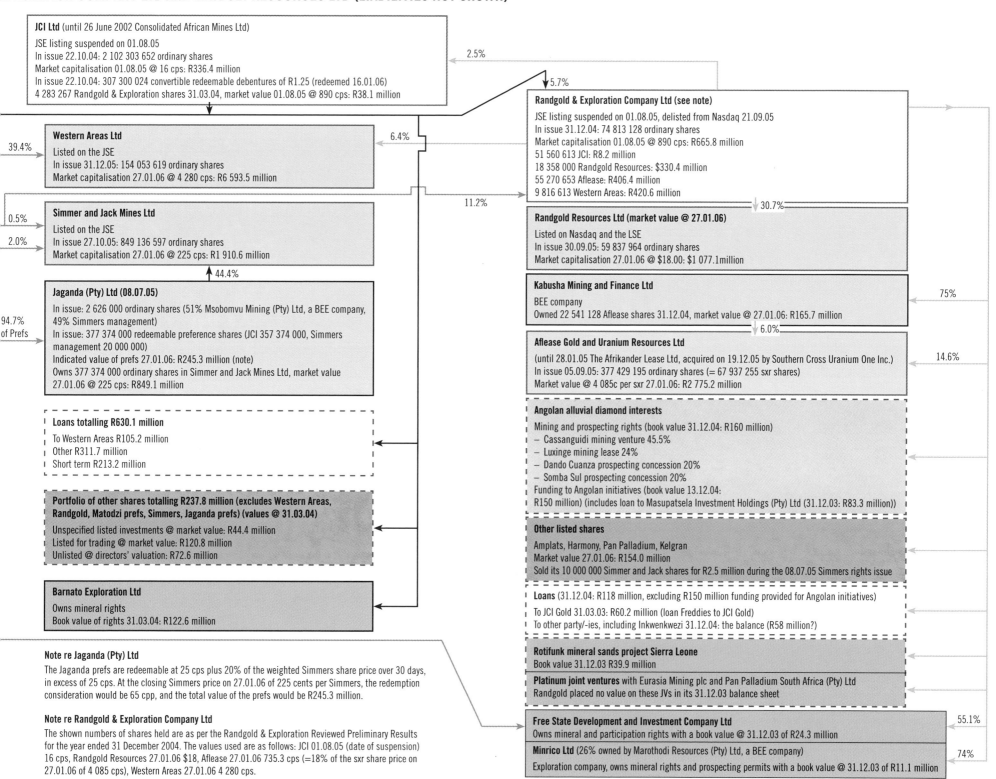

EXPLORATION COMPANY LTD AND MATDOZI RESOURCES LTD (LIABILITIES NOT SHOWN)

JCI Ltd (until 26 June 2002 Consolidated African Mines Ltd)

JSE listing suspended on 01.08.05
In issue 22.10.04: 2 102 303 652 ordinary shares
Market capitalisation 01.08.05 @ 16 cps: R336.4 million
In issue 22.10.04: 307 300 024 convertible redeemable debentures of R1.25 (redeemed 16.01.06)
4 283 267 Randgold & Exploration shares 31.03.04, market value 01.08.05 @ 890 cps: R38.1 million

2.5%

5.7%

Randgold & Exploration Company Ltd (see note)

JSE listing suspended on 01.08.05, delisted from Nasdaq 21.09.05
In issue 31.12.04: 74 813 128 ordinary shares
Market capitalisation 01.08.05 @ 890 cps: R665.8 million
51 560 613 JCI: R8.2 million
18 358 000 Randgold Resources: R330.4 million
55 270 653 Aflease: R406.4 million
9 816 613 Western Areas: R420.6 million

39.4%

6.4%

Western Areas Ltd

Listed on the JSE
In issue 31.12.05: 154 053 619 ordinary shares
Market capitalisation 27.01.06 @ 4 280 cps: R6 593.5 million

11.2%

30.7%

Randgold Resources Ltd (market value @ 27.01.06)

Listed on Nasdaq and the LSE
In issue 30.09.05: 59 837 964 ordinary shares
Market capitalisation 27.01.06 @ $18.00: $1 077.1million

0.5%

2.0%

Simmer and Jack Mines Ltd

Listed on the JSE
In issue 27.10.05: 849 136 597 ordinary shares
Market capitalisation 27.01.06 @ 225 cps: R1 910.6 million

44.4%

Kabusha Mining and Finance Ltd

BEE company
Owned 22 541 128 Aflease shares 31.12.04, market value @ 27.01.06: R165.7 million

75%

6.0%

Jaganda (Pty) Ltd (08.07.05)

In issue: 2 626 000 ordinary shares (51% Msobomvu Mining (Pty) Ltd, a BEE company, 49% Simmers management)
In issue: 377 374 000 redeemable preference shares (JCI 357 374 000, Simmers management 20 000 000)
Indicated value of prefs 27.01.06: R245.3 million (note)
Owns 377 374 000 ordinary shares in Simmer and Jack Mines Ltd, market value 27.01.06 @ 225 cps: R849.1 million

94.7% of Prefs

Aflease Gold and Uranium Resources Ltd

(until 28.01.05 The Afrikander Lease Ltd, acquired on 19.12.05 by Southern Cross Uranium One Inc.)
In issue 05.09.05: 377 429 195 ordinary shares (= 67 937 255 sxr shares)
Market value @ 4 085c per sxr 27.01.06: R2 775.2 million

14.6%

Loans totalling R630.1 million

To Western Areas R105.2 million
Other R311.7 million
Short term R213.2 million

Angolan alluvial diamond interests

Mining and prospecting rights (book value 31.12.04: R160 million)
– Cassanguidi mining venture 45.5%
– Luxinge mining lease 24%
– Dando Cuanza prospecting concession 20%
– Somba Sul prospecting concession 20%
Funding to Angolan initiatives (book value 13.12.04: R150 million) (includes loan to Masupatsela Investment Holdings (Pty) Ltd (31.12.03: R83.3 million))

Portfolio of other shares totalling R237.8 million (excludes Western Areas, Randgold, Matodzi prefs, Simmers, Jaganda prefs) (values @ 31.03.04)

Unspecified listed investments @ market value: R44.4 million
Listed for trading @ market value: R120.8 million
Unlisted @ directors' valuation: R72.6 million

Other listed shares

Amplats, Harmony, Pan Palladium, Kelgran
Market value 27.01.06: R154.0 million
Sold its 10 000 000 Simmer and Jack shares for R2.5 million during the 08.07.05 Simmers rights issue

Barnato Exploration Ltd

Owns mineral rights
Book value of rights 31.03.04: R122.6 million

Loans (31.12.04: R118 million, excluding R150 million funding provided for Angolan initiatives)

To JCI Gold 31.03.03: R60.2 million (loan Freddies to JCI Gold)
To other party/-ies, including Inkwenkwezi 31.12.04: the balance (R58 million?)

Note re Jaganda (Pty) Ltd

The Jaganda prefs are redeemable at 25 cps plus 20% of the weighted Simmers share price over 30 days, in excess of 25 cps. At the closing Simmers price on 27.01.06 of 225 cents per Simmers, the redemption consideration would be 65 cpp, and the total value of the prefs would be R245.3 million.

Rotifunk mineral sands project Sierra Leone
Book value 31.12.03 R39.9 million

Platinum joint ventures with Eurasia Mining plc and Pan Palladium South Africa (Pty) Ltd
Randgold placed no value on these JVs in its 31.12.03 balance sheet

Note re Randgold & Exploration Company Ltd

The shown numbers of shares held are as per the Randgold & Exploration Reviewed Preliminary Results for the year ended 31 December 2004. The values used are as follows: JCI 01.08.05 (date of suspension) 16 cps, Randgold Resources 27.01.06 $18, Aflease 27.01.06 735.3 cps (=18% of the sxr share price on 27.01.06 of 4 085 cps), Western Areas 27.01.06 4 280 cps.

Free State Development and Investment Company Ltd
Owns mineral and participation rights with a book value @ 31.12.03 of R24.3 million

55.1%

Minrico Ltd (26% owned by Marothodi Resources (Pty) Ltd, a BEE company)
Exploration company, owns mineral rights and prospecting permits with a book value @ 31.12.03 of R11.1 million

74%

Index